About World Wildlife Fund

World Wildlife Fund (WWF) is the largest private U.S. organization working worldwide to conserve nature. WWF works to preserve the diversity and abundance of life on Earth and the health of ecological systems by protecting natural areas and wildlife populations, promoting sustainable use of natural resources, and promoting more efficient resource and energy use and the maximum reduction of pollution. WWF is affiliated with the international WWF network, which has national organizations, associates, or representatives in nearly 40 countries. In the United States, WWF has more than one million members.

Funding for *Statewide Wetlands Strategies* was provided by The Florence and John Schumann Foundation, The David and Lucile Packard Foundation, the Richard King Mellon Foundation, the U.S. Environmental Protection Agency, the H. John Heinz III Charitable Trust, and Scott and Penny Barnes.

About Island Press

Island Press, a nonprofit organization, publishes, markets, and distributes the most advanced thinking on the conservation of our natural resources—books about soil, land, water, forests, wildlife, and hazardous and toxic wastes. These books are practical tools used by public officials, business and industry leaders, natural resource managers, and concerned citizens working to solve both local and global resource problems.

Founded in 1978, Island Press reorganized in 1984 to meet the increasing demand for substantive books on all resource-related issues. Island Press publishes and distributes under its own imprint and offers these services to other nonprofit organizations.

Support for Island Press is provided by the Geraldine R. Dodge Foundation, The Energy Foundation, The Charles Engelhard Foundation, The Ford Foundation, Glen Eagles Foundation, The George Gund Foundation, William and Flora Hewlett Foundation, The Andrew W. Mellon Foundation, The Joyce Mertz-Gilmore Foundation, The New-Land Foundation, The J.N. Pew, Jr. Charitable Trust, Alida Rockefeller, The Rockefeller Brothers Fund, The Rockefeller Foundation, The Florence and John Schumann Foundation, The Tides Foundation, and individual donors.

STATEWIDE WETLANDS STRATEGIES

STATEWIDE WETLANDS STRATEGIES

A Guide to Protecting and Managing the Resource

WWF

World Wildlife Fund

ISLAND PRESS

Washington, D.C. □ *Covelo, California*

Cover photograph is from WETLANDS OF NORTH AMERICA, by William Niering, photography by Bates Littlehales, published by Thomasson-Grant. Copyright © 1991 Thomasson-Grant. Photography copyright © 1991 Bates Littlehales. For more information, direct inquiries to Thomasson-Grant, Inc., One Morton Drive, Charlottesville, VA 22901. 1-800-999-1780.

Illustrations by Lisa Wilcox-Deyo.

Library of Congress Cataloging-in-Publication Data

Statewide wetlands strategies : a guide to protecting and managing the resource.
      p.   cm.
     Includes bibliographical references.
     ISBN 1-55963-205-4
     ISBN 1-55963-206-2 (pbk.)
     1. Wetland conservation—Government policy—United States—States. 2. Wetlands—Management—Government policy—United States—States. I. Island Press.
     QH76.S665   1992   92-3563
     353.9'382326—dc20   CIP

Printed on recycled, acid-free paper
Manufactured in the United States of America

STATEWIDE WETLANDS STRATEGIES

A Guide to Protecting and Managing the Resource

WWF

World Wildlife Fund

ISLAND PRESS

Washington, D.C. □ *Covelo, California*

Cover photograph is from WETLANDS OF NORTH AMERICA, by William Niering, photography by Bates Littlehales, published by Thomasson-Grant. Copyright © 1991 Thomasson-Grant. Photography copyright © 1991 Bates Littlehales. For more information, direct inquiries to Thomasson-Grant, Inc., One Morton Drive, Charlottesville, VA 22901. 1-800-999-1780.

Illustrations by Lisa Wilcox-Deyo.

Library of Congress Cataloging-in-Publication Data

Statewide wetlands strategies : a guide to protecting and managing the resource.
      p.   cm.
    Includes bibliographical references.
    ISBN 1-55963-205-4
    ISBN 1-55963-206-2 (pbk.)
    1. Wetland conservation—Government policy—United States—States. 2. Wetlands—Management—Government policy—United States—States. I. Island Press.
    QH76.S665   1992   92-3563
    353.9′382326—dc20   CIP

Table of Contents

PART II: ORGANIZING A STRATEGY DEVELOPMENT PROCESS   41

PART III: MECHANISMS FOR PROTECTING AND MANAGING WETLANDS   61

PART IV: WETLANDS DATA SOURCES AND COLLECTION METHODS   161

Preface

Wetlands have become one of the most controversial environmental issues of our time. Recent disagreements about the definition of wetlands and the government's authority to regulate wetlands on private property have thrust them into the forefront of environmental debate. Around the country government officials are deluged with complaints about current wetlands programs: many claim that regulatory programs are too restrictive and burdensome for landowners, while others assert that these programs are not tough enough to protect wetlands adequately. What is clear amid all the controversy is the dissatisfaction with the current situation and the urgent need for change.

This guidebook offers a new approach to wetlands conservation—comprehensive statewide wetlands strategies. We believe this approach holds enormous potential for addressing the current controversies. It is both more inclusive and more responsive to regional and local needs than current approaches. It draws on all levels of government and the private sector to focus and coordinate efforts to work toward the goal of no net loss of wetlands.

The guidance we provide on developing statewide wetlands strategies draws on World Wildlife Fund's (WWF's) work over the past five years to develop practical solutions to address the problem of wetlands loss. In 1987, The Conservation Foundation, now incorporated into WWF, convened the National Wetlands Policy Forum. This diverse group—representing industry, government, farming, ranching, and environmental concerns—reached a historic consensus on over 100 recommendations for improving wetlands protection. It was the Forum that first proposed the goal of no net loss of wetlands.

The Forum's recommendations provide the foundation for this guidebook. In searching for the best way to translate these recommendations into action, the Forum focused on states and encouraged them to take the lead in wetlands protection by developing comprehensive programs to achieve no net loss. This guidebook expands on this idea and provides general guidelines for developing such a comprehensive strategy.

In developing this idea and writing the guidebook, we worked closely with state and local wetlands program managers, federal agencies, wetlands scientists, and public policy specialists. We began our research with a workshop in September 1990 to help clarify what a statewide wetlands strategy should be, and to determine what kind of guidance states would need to undertake such a strategy. The workshop brought together 25 participants from 17 states, two municipalities, and several federal agencies. Following the workshop we convened a nine-member state advisory committee to steer our research efforts and ensure that the guidebook would best meet the needs of the states.

We believe that states can play a vital role in changing the trends of the past—in reversing the pattern of wetlands destruction to achieve no net loss and eventual net gain of the nation's wetlands resource. This guidebook was put together to help states recognize the great opportunities for improving wetlands protection and to address the challenges they will face along the way.

Acknowledgments

As with many projects, this one continued to expand throughout its life, as did the number of people involved. The stalwart guiding light throughout the project, however, was the state advisory committee. In addition to working overtime to manage wetlands programs in their states, our advisory committee showed an unflagging commitment to improving wetlands protection by constantly helping us sort through issues, focus our efforts, and provide us with "reality checks." They also had the courage and fortitude to wade through the voluminous first draft of the guidebook. Our sincere thanks to all the advisory committee members for their invaluable help.

This project was directed by Heidi Sherk. It was through her vision, perseverance, and good humor that the project came to fruition. Paul DeLong, Nancy Fishbein, Debra Prybyla, and Rebecca Skidmore also invested long hours of hard work in preparing the draft. Robert McCoy and Martha Cooley edited the manuscript, and helped see it through production. Terry Selby-Colburn assisted in producing the manuscript. Staff from RESOLVE, (an independent program of WWF), facilitated the September 1990 workshop, and Part II is based on RESOLVE's consensus-building experience over the past 15 years.

Jon Kusler, a member of the advisory group and executive director of the Association of State Wetland Managers, provided WWF staff with important guidance throughout the project. In addition, U.S. EPA's Office of Wetlands, Oceans, and Watersheds and their Environmental Research Lab helped to refine our efforts by commenting on numerous drafts of the guidebook.

This project would not have been possible without the generous support of our funders. Major funding was provided by The Florence and John Schumann Foundation, The David and Lucile Packard Foundation, the Richard King Mellon Foundation, and the U.S. Environmental Protection Agency. Additional funding was provided by the H. John Heinz III Charitable Trust, and Scott and Penny Barnes. We are grateful for their support.

James P. Leape
Senior Vice President

State Advisory Committee

Mary E. Burg, Washington State Department of Ecology

David Burke, Maryland Department of Natural Resources

David Chambers, Office of the Governor (Louisiana)

Scott Hausmann, Wisconsin Department of Natural Resources

Marvin Hubbell, Illinois Department of Conservation

Christy Foote-Smith, Massachusetts Department of Environmental Protection

Jon Kusler, Association of State Wetland Managers

Patricia Riexinger, New York State Department of Environmental Conservation

David Saveikis, Delaware Department of Natural Resources and Environmental Control

Other State, Local, and Federal Advisors

Ken Bierly, Oregon Division of State Lands

Peg Bostwick, Michigan Department of Natural Resources

Tom Calnan, Texas General Land Office

Linda Cooper, Yorktown Conservation Board (New York)

Steve Gordon, Lane Council of Governments (Oregon)

Peter Grenell, California Coastal Conservancy

Tom Talley, Tennessee State Planning Office

U.S. EPA Office of Wetlands, Oceans, and Watersheds (J. Glenn Eugster, Sherri Fields, Dianne Fish, Thomas Kelsch, Menchu Martinez, Doreen Robb, Lori Williams)

Principal Authors

Introduction
  Jon Kusler, Association of State Wetland Managers
  Heidi Sherk, WWF

WWF Research Assistants

Christina Halvorson
Leslie Harroun
Terrence Hines

WWF Reviewers

Donald Barry
Gail Bingham
James P. Leape
Michael O'Connell

Production Staff

Jean Bernard, proofreader
Martha Cooley, editor
Robert McCoy, senior editor
Allison Rogers, assistant editor
Terry Selby-Colburn, production assistant
Rings-Leighton Limited, typesetting and graphic
    design
Lisa Wilcox-Deyo, illustrator

Introduction

State officials in Michigan have spent a year disputing federal authorities and a developer about the impact of a golf course project on a wetland and adjacent river. Landowners on Maryland's Eastern Shore claim that new wetlands regulations now leave their lands undevelopable; costly, time-consuming litigation lies ahead. Farmers, developers, landowners, and highway departments across the nation feel that they bear an unfair burden for our belated recognition of the value of wetlands and the confusion about how we will protect them. Yet, no matter how the issues are finally resolved, states have the most to gain by clearing up the current disarray.

In the United States, we continue to lose 290,000 acres of wetlands each year, an area almost half the size of Rhode Island.[1] Programs to protect wetlands lack consistency, predictability, and timeliness. Local, state, and federal guidelines often conflict, and no program can be effective and fair under these circumstances. Meanwhile, we lose productive wildlife habitat, groundwater quality, and flood control, and state officials remain mired in time-consuming conflicts reconciled case by case.

This guidebook describes a process for putting wetlands programs in order through a comprehensive strategy. A statewide wetlands strategy:

- draws clear guidelines that eliminate confusion;
- brings all interested parties into the decision-making process before conflicts become intractable;
- streamlines existing state and local programs to address gaps and shortcomings;
- dovetails with federal programs where possible;
- makes better use of staff and financial resources; and
- creates a coherent plan to protect wetlands tailored to the state's particular needs.

States are uniquely positioned to take the lead on wetlands because they occupy a middle ground between local jurisdictions that are often strongly influenced by a few relatively powerful players and the federal government, which often cannot meet local needs with appropriate flexibility. States are in a position to find creative solutions and strike a balance. At present, states are also displaying the greatest initiative in wetlands policy and a conviction that wetlands are vital to their economic and ecological health.

What Is a Comprehensive Statewide Wetlands Strategy?

A comprehensive statewide wetlands strategy is an organizational tool to identify opportunities to make programs work better. It is not intended to be a land-use plan for wetlands or a new level of bureaucracy. It is simply a process for bringing together citizens, government officials, development interests, and others to help identify the state's specific wetlands problems and to develop workable and equitable solutions that achieve wetlands protection goals.

The National Wetlands Policy Forum

In 1988, a group of industry and government leaders, farmers, and environmentalists came together to brainstorm and debate measures to improve wetlands protection. In a year and a half, the National Wetlands Policy Forum agreed on over 100 policy improvements to protect wetlands while reducing unnecessary frustrations with regulatory programs. Its members found that an overall goal for wetlands protection was necessary to provide the consistency and focus missing from current wetlands protection efforts.

The Forum recommended an overall goal of "no net loss and long-term net gain"—a goal that reflects a sense of urgency yet provides flexibility to accommodate the need for economic growth. This goal was seen as a strong foundation on which to build equitable and effective wetlands policies.

Forum members agreed that comprehensive statewide wetlands strategies were the best way to implement no net loss. State strategies provide three key elements necessary to achieve the goal: a comprehensive approach, flexibility, and a regional focus.

- A *comprehensive approach* can address all threats to wetlands (not just the most conspicuous) and mobilize a broad array of programs from the government and private sector.
- A *flexible approach* recognizes the many ways to achieve no net loss. Statewide wetlands strategies do not prescribe a solution but encourage the use of a combination of programs and approaches suited to each state.
- A *regional focus* allows the most challenging issues, such as conflicts between developers and environmentalists, to be resolved where site-specific information can be gathered and where customized solutions can be reached.

Why States Should Take the Lead

States are well-positioned to implement wetlands protection and management programs. They have experience in managing environmental programs such as the Clean Water Act, the Clean Air Act, and the Coastal Zone Management Act. States are equipped to help resolve local conflicts flexibly and can identify the local economic and geographic factors that lead to wetlands losses. Working with local governments, states can integrate wetlands conservation into comprehensive land-use plans. States can also promote private stewardship of wetlands through a variety of nonregulatory measures, including property tax incentives, local land trusts, and zoning techniques such as transfer of development rights.

At present, states hold the most promise for mustering the political will necessary to achieve the comprehensive reforms that no net loss will require. Although President Bush's endorsement of the goal of no net loss has helped focus public attention on the issue, progress in implementing no net loss at the federal level has been slow.

Many states, in contrast, have been making steady progress toward no net loss. The National Governors' Association set the tone by unanimously endorsing the goal soon after the Forum issued its final report. Washington, Delaware, and South Carolina convened state-level wetlands forums to develop recommendations for state action. In April 1989, Maryland passed the first state wetlands legislation with an explicit goal of no net loss. Louisiana has initiated an aggressive coastal wetlands restoration program funded by a state trust fund. In spite of difficult opposition, these states and others have found common ground and made great strides—educating the public, balancing interests, and developing innovative programs.

Elements of a Statewide Strategy

There is no "recipe" for developing a statewide strategy, nor will any two strategies look alike. To be successful, however, statewide strategies should contain the following elements:

An overall goal. An overall goal is the glue that holds the strategy together. We encourage states to adopt the goal of no net loss and long-term net gain. This goal ensures the vigorous protection of wetlands and provides a specific benchmark for assessing the effectiveness of a strategy. It also recognizes that some wetlands will be altered but requires that these alterations be fully compensated.

Information about a state's wetlands (i.e., where they are located, what type) and the

threats that put these wetlands at risk. Clearly, the more information a state has about where wetlands are located and why they are being lost, the easier it will be to address the problem. However, years of research are unnecessary. A strategy based on existing data can call for future research where needed.

An assessment of current wetlands protection efforts. To understand a state's capability to address wetland loss, one must know the strengths and shortcomings of current programs. An assessment can help states decide how to eliminate gaps, inconsistency, and overlap and identify opportunities for coordinating programs.

An action plan. Based on a state's existing programs and specific needs, an action plan can address shortcomings identified by the assessment and draw on the help of government and the private sector. For instance, a state may choose to develop a joint permitting process if the assessment shows that multiple agencies (floodplain, storm-water sediment control, zoning) require permits for activities in wetlands. Existing federal and state subsidy programs that pay landowners to protect wetlands can be targeted to fill the gaps in coverage of existing regulatory programs. Where economic development is being derailed by wetlands protection, local governments can be encouraged to use flexible zoning techniques to increase the density of development in less environmentally sensitive areas. Government and private resources can be combined to restore wetlands as part of an effort to control nonpoint source pollution.

> **F**ocus on finding opportunities and innovative ways to improve wetlands protection (e.g., link wetlands protection with other natural resource protection efforts).

State Approaches to Wetlands Protection

- **California**'s Coastal Conservancy provides technical and financial assistance to land trusts working to protect wetlands.
- **Maryland** has a statutory no net loss goal for nontidal wetlands and has created a sophisticated Geographic Information System for mapping wetland areas.
- In **Alaska,** Juneau and Anchorage have developed local wetlands management plans.
- **Illinois** has a statutory no net loss goal that applies to public projects and activities and an extensive computerized wetlands mapping system.
- **Washington** helps local governments improve ordinances to better protect wetlands and has developed wetlands educational materials, including videotapes and curricula guides.
- **Connecticut**'s centralized data coordination, gathering, storage, and analysis capability includes wetlands as one component and provides information to all agencies and local governments.
- **Wisconsin** has digitized wetlands and floodplain maps. In southeastern Wisconsin, wetlands and associated watersheds are being protected through regional planning and ''environment corridor'' approaches that include extensive use of conservation and scenic easements.
- **Oregon** encourages local governments to develop comprehensive plans to protect wetlands.
- **New York** has detailed maps of tidal and freshwater wetlands with notice to landowners, an ''adopt a wetland'' stewardship program, and an aggressive restoration program.
- **New Jersey**'s freshwater wetlands legislation establishes wetlands buffer requirements. The state has also established special state agencies and special management areas to protect particular wetlands, including the Pinelands and Hackensack Meadowlands.
- **Ohio** uses its authority under Section 401 of the Clean Water Act to protect wetlands.
- **Minnesota** adopted a new wetlands law in 1991 that includes an easement program, education and training grants, a state regulatory program, and property-tax exemptions.
- **Massachusetts,** the first state to adopt a wetlands protection statute, is mapping its wetlands statewide and notifying all landowners with wetlands on their property.
- **Florida** uses ''critical area'' legislation to designate and protect larger wetland complexes (e.g., Big Cypress) and has an aggressive program to acquire wetlands and other sensitive lands.
- **Michigan** has assumed the federal Section 404 program and uses a combination of shoreline zoning, wetland regulation, and lake protection and management to protect wetlands.

A funding strategy. Even if an action plan does not call for new programs, a state may still need additional funds. Budget deficits and competition for use compel states to look to a wide variety of revenue-generating mechanisms and nontraditional sources of funding, including programs not specifically designed for wetlands, such as federal grants for nonpoint source pollution control.

A monitoring and evaluation plan. To protect a state's investment in wetlands protection, an accounting system must be established to measure wetlands gains and losses and monitor progress. This can help point out deficiencies in the strategy and suggest adjustments.

The Role of the Federal Government

A stronger role for states will not supplant the need for federal involvement. A strong federal regulatory program can complement and support a state strategy and provide a safety net to ensure a minimum level of wetlands protection across the country. Federal regulation as well as acquisition, incentives, and research will continue to make important contributions to wetlands protection. In addition, federal resources can help states develop strategies. Grants from the U.S. Environmental Protection Agency (EPA) are funding the development of strategies in 10 states.

A wetlands strategy should ensure that a state gets the most out of federal programs. As a state develops its strategy, it should identify what federal programs currently affect its wetlands. It may be possible to leverage federal resources to help achieve state goals. States should coordinate efforts with federal programs where possible. State wetlands strategies should also work to modify federal programs that may be at odds with wetlands protection.

Statewide Strategies and Section 404

Section 404 of the Clean Water Act is the major federal regulatory program to protect wetlands. Although strategies have a valuable role to play in increasing the effectiveness of this program—ensuring that it is implemented as part of a comprehensive strategy—linking strategies to state assumption of Section 404 suggests that the primary role of strategies lies in the regulatory program. This is not the case. Regulatory considerations should be only one component of the overall strategy, not the driving force.

Given the highly controversial nature of Section 404, an attempt to tie a state strategy to Section 404 assumption may also make this strategic process more difficult. A statewide wetlands strategy and Section 404 assumption are not, however, mutually exclusive. A state may decide that it wishes to assume responsibility for Section 404 as part of its plan for achieving its goals.

The Role of Local Governments

Local governments should play an extremely important role in developing and carrying out a statewide strategy. This level of government is closest to the local population and is often best equipped to represent its needs and concerns. Because local governments control most land-use decisions, they can also do much to promote wetlands protection. A statewide strategy should recognize and address local needs as well as encourage or require local governments to incorporate wetlands protection provisions into land-use plans and zoning ordinances (and where otherwise appropriate).

The Role of the Private Sector

Businesses, nonprofit organizations, and other representatives of the private sector should participate in the development of a wetlands strategy to ensure that their needs are incorporated into the state's wetlands protection plan. Private organizations can also contribute significantly to carrying out a strategy. Private efforts to protect wetlands are diverse, ranging from corporate funding for restoration to educational tours. A successful strategy must look to the private sector and factor its resources into the process of achieving the strategy goal.

Why Undertake a Statewide Wetlands Strategy?

Why Wetlands Should Be Protected

We are coming to understand better every day the environmental and economic values of wetlands and why saving them is crucial to a prosperous future.[2]

Flood control. Wetlands detain floodwaters, reducing their size and destructiveness.

DuPage County, Illinois, is a rapidly developing suburban community approximately 30 miles west of Chicago. The county covers 332 square miles, of which approximately two-thirds were formally wetlands. . . . The Salt Creek watershed on the eastern side of the county currently has less than one percent of its wetlands remaining. This area now experiences frequent flood damage, mostly in the headwater areas above the flowing creek. These damages are directly traceable to the loss of the shallow basin wetlands. A catastrophic flood in 1987 caused, in just a few days, an estimated $120 million in damages to a few thousand residences in the lowest-lying areas. The county is now developing engineering works, including diversion of floodwaters into quarries, to replace the flood storage lost from the destruction of wetlands. These works will cost the taxpayer an estimated $100 million (or $20,000 to $50,000 per damaged residence).

Water Quality. Wetlands absorb and filter pollutants that could otherwise degrade ground-water or the water quality of rivers, lakes, and estuaries.

Homeowners now face increased sewage-treatment costs to remove sediments and polluting nutrients whose source is increased runoff caused in part by loss of wetlands. The costs of modifying sewage treatment plants in Maryland and Virginia that discharge into the Chesapeake Bay have been estimated at more than $1 billion. For Long Island Sound, the working estimate of installing nutrient removal systems at all sewage treatment plants has been estimated to be at roughly $6 billion. Sewage treatment plants discharging into freshwater bodies face similar requirements, often with the focus on phosphorous, which is the primary nutrient of concern in freshwater.

Fisheries. Wetlands provide direct spawning and rearing habitat and food supply that support both freshwater and marine fisheries.

America's fisheries are big business in both a commercial and recreational sense. Fish landed in 1990 had a direct, dockside value of $3.6 billion, which served as the base of a fishery processing and sales industry that generated total consumer expenditures of $26.7 billion. The National Marine Fisheries Service estimates that 71 percent of the value of commercial fish consists of species that need estuaries for reproduction, as nurseries for young fish, for food, or for migration.

The estuaries and rivers of Oregon, Washington, Idaho, and northern California provide the main spawning and rearing areas for salmon in the contiguous United States. . . . The magnitude of these salmon fisheries is indicated by their dollar values. In 1985, for example, the commercial salmon catch of Washington, Oregon, and northern California yielded salmon with a wholesale value of $143 million. This catch employed more than 16,000 fishermen in Washington, Oregon, and California, at least part-time.

Waterfowl Habitat. Wetlands provide the principal habitat for virtually all waterfowl.

The Rainwater Basin encompasses 4,200 square miles of prairie, mostly corn fields, within 17 counties of south central Nebraska. Although the area once contained at least 4,000 major wetlands basins and several smaller wetlands forming more than 200,000 acres, agricultural expansion has left no more than 34,000 acres of wetlands. . . . Millions of waterfowl, however, use the basin every year. These include approximately 90 percent of the entire population of white-fronted geese, 50 percent of the breeding mallards, and 30 percent of the breeding northern pintail that use the mid-continental United States. A single wetland basin may contain more than 100,000 birds. Unfortunately, the loss of wetlands is crowding birds together in such a way as to trigger outbreaks of disease. More than 200,000 birds died of avian cholera between 1975 and 1990 alone.

Biological Diversity. Wetlands provide important habitat for an enormous diversity of plants and animals, including a large portion of federally listed threatened or endangered species.

The Louisiana black bear, which the U.S. Fish and Wildlife Service listed as threatened in early January 1992, inhabits bottomland forests in the lower Mississippi River Valley. Fewer than 100 are believed to remain. The principal reason for its endangerment has been habitat destruction; by 1980 over 80 percent of its habitat had disappeared. It suffers not just from loss of habitat, but also from a loss of contiguous habitat, so that, in general, any development that fragments portions of bottomland forests could have a highly disproportionate impact.

Groundwater Recharge. Some wetlands recharge aquifers that provide drinking water.

In many portions of North Dakota, temporary and seasonally flooded potholes tend to occur higher in the landscape, and water tends to percolate down and recharge groundwater. . . . Groundwater is the drinking source for most rural North Dakotans. In various surveys, between 11 and 13 percent of North Dakota's groundwater tested showed concentrates of nitrate above federal safe drinking water levels. The majority of all samples showed some nitrate contamination. Nationally it is estimated that 37 percent of the counties in the United States have nitrate contamination in the groundwater due to agricultural activities. . . . Potholes can absorb nitrogen by incorporating it into plant tissue and then absorbing the plant tissue into the buildup of organic soils.

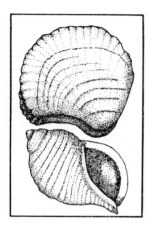

Erosion and Land Formation. Wetlands stabilize shorelines and prevent erosion by binding stream banks and by absorbing wave energy. Wetlands also play an early and fundamental role in land formation, particularly in coastal areas that regularly lose land to the ocean.

In arid areas where inputs of sediment are high, cotton-willow wetlands systems play an important role in stabilizing streambanks. . . . When this vegetation is removed, streambanks collapse, leaving wide channels of sediment-filled murky water. The potential magnitude of this impact was shown during the ''arroyo-cutting'' of a turn-of-the century period of intensive land clearing and cattle grazing. Deprived of wetlands vegetation, channel beds of many western rivers decreased by several meters. The loss of these banks flattened out the stream so much that surface flow was actually lost in some stream reaches. Remaining vegetation was soon scoured away. Nearly a century later, rivers are still recovering.

Recreation. Wetlands support a multi-billion dollar fishing, hunting, and outdoor recreation industry nationwide.

America's greatest trout fisheries occur in the northwest and northern Rocky mountain states. More than 11 million people fished for trout (outside the Great Lakes) in 1985, for an average of roughly 15 days each, spending an estimated total $1.6 billion. . . . Recreational salmon anglers in Washington, Oregon, Idaho, and California spent an estimated $109 million in 1985.

Problems in Wetlands Protection and How a Strategy Can Help

Wetlands are causing controversy in part because of their unique physical qualities. What allows them to perform their valuable functions also makes them tough to manage. They are some-

times difficult to identify because they are not wet year round; activities at other locations, such as upstream contamination or water diversions, can have a severe impact on them. In addition, our somewhat recent recognition that wetlands are valuable areas and not disease-infested swamps means that time will be required to change people's perceptions as well as public policy.

The problem of wetlands loss has not been ignored. There are an array of public and private programs to protect wetlands. However, these programs address only limited aspects of the problem and have been adopted haphazardly and incoherently. A strategy can remedy some of the major flaws of wetlands programs by addressing the following issues.[3]

Conflicts between development and wetlands protection. Many times, clashes between development interests and wetlands protection are caused by uncertainty. A strategy can make great progress in resolving many of these conflicts by anticipating problems and attempting to reconcile different needs. For example, a strategy can help to focus resources in areas of the state with high concentrations of wetlands to identify in advance where wetlands are located and areas that are suitable for development. In addition, representatives from the development community should be involved in creating a strategy, and help to ensure that it addresses their concerns and problems.

Failure to consider both land use and hydrology in wetlands protection. Wetlands are the interface between land and water, often falling under the jurisdictions of water (pollution and water supply) as well as land-use agencies. Because both land and water programs are critical to protecting wetlands, a statewide strategy can ensure that wetlands protection is considered in the management activities of a broad range of agencies.

Overreliance on regulatory programs. Although strong regulatory programs are necessary, they will never provide adequate wetlands protection. More emphasis should be given to encouraging private landowners (who own almost three-quarters of the wetlands in the lower 48 states) to protect these areas voluntarily. A statewide strategy, through good education programs and extensive use of economic incentives, can develop a complementary mix of regulatory and nonregulatory approaches to achieve no net loss.

Inadequate maps and other data. Good information is needed to help determine the location of wetlands, track trends, evaluate their functions, determine the probable impacts of various activities on wetlands, design restoration and creation efforts, and so on. A wetlands strategy can help gather this information efficiently and cost-effectively by identifying and compiling existing data from a variety of federal, state, and local sources and helping to identify areas where more information should be gathered. Moreover, a strategy can help identify the agency or agencies best equipped to gather, update, store, and analyze data and identify opportunities for multiagency funding or implementation, since managing information is an expensive and time-consuming task.

Inadequate tracking of permits and changes in wetlands. In most states, there has been little tracking of wetlands permits for compliance or of the success of restoration and creation efforts. A statewide wetlands strategy can establish such a tracking system by developing common reporting forms for wetlands, floodplain, coastal area, public water, and other agencies; by providing a centralized and geographically referenced depository for permits; and by requiring follow-up monitoring (perhaps on both a random and selected basis) utilizing the staff of each of the participating agencies.

Lack of wetlands protection policies for public lands. Most states do not have explicit wetlands policies for their public lands, such as wildlife refuges, parks, forests, recreation areas, and lands owned by public universities. A wetlands strategy could help establish general policies (e.g., buffer zones, avoidance of wetlands, mitigation) and multiagency procedures and cooperative agreements for evaluating impacts and restoring wetlands. In addition, a strategy could establish mechanisms for working with federal agencies to encourage the adoption of similar policies for federal land management.

Lack of policies for public infrastructure planning and development. In some states, public works agencies (highway, sewer and water, floodplain management) view wetlands protection as hindering projects and making them more expensive. Often, state wetlands regulatory programs do not apply to state public works projects or many federal or federally funded projects. A statewide wetlands strategy can establish a common policy for state public works agencies and projects—e.g., roads, highways, reservoirs, dredging, channelization, and pipelines—to provide greater certainty in decisionmaking and facilitate mitigation banking or joint mitigation projects.

Limited scope of regulatory programs. No wetlands statute regulates all activities in all wetlands. A strategy can draw not only on explicit wetlands regulatory statutes but on pollution control, sediment control, floodplain, solid waste disposal, incentive, and other programs to help fill the gaps in current protection efforts. In addition, most state wetlands statutes exempt existing uses, agriculture, and forestry. Networking wetlands protection with existing nonwetlands regulatory measures could help remedy these problems. For example, agricultural activities might be regulated pursuant to nonpoint source pollution control statutes, pesticide control statutes, or sediment control statutes.

Duplication and inconsistencies in permitting. One of the biggest complaints about wetlands regulation is the inefficiency and frustration involved in having to apply separately for a local, state, and federal permit. A statewide wetlands strategy can help establish mechanisms for joint permitting, including a common application form or forms and perhaps a joint permitting board.

Limited budgets, staff, and expertise. Lack of funding, budgets, and expertise limits the effectiveness of most wetlands programs. A statewide wetlands strategy can make better use of available staff and experts in all agencies by setting up mechanisms such as joint compliance surveys by the staffs of wetlands, floodplain, and public waters agencies and joint permit processing involving several agencies.

Failure to identify sites with restoration potential. Achieving no net loss and long-term net gain will require wetlands restoration and creation. At present, no state has mapped and examined in detail sites with restoration or creation potential throughout the state. A statewide wetlands strategy can establish goals, standards, and guidelines for wetlands restoration and creation and might initiate a multiagency effort to identify appropriate sites.

Lack of acquisition priorities. In recent years, many states have made some progress in establishing state wetlands acquisition priorities for all agencies through the State Conservation Out-

Approach strategy development as a "win-win" opportunity for agencies and groups that have been frustrated in achieving their goals by lack of staff, budgets, political support, or common goals.

Work to gain political support for strategy development—it will be crucial in gaining the attention and cooperation of a wide range of interests and in securing financial support.

door Recreation Planning Process and various surveys conducted independently by states or in conjunction with the U.S. Fish and Wildlife Service. Nevertheless, priorities usually have been based on a relatively narrow set of objectives. A statewide wetlands strategy involving a broad range of agencies might further define priorities and coordinate actual acquisition efforts.

How to Use This Guidebook

Developing a strategy is not a linear process with clearly defined sequential steps. Many activities that are integral to strategy development, such as gathering information, are not done once and for all but will be required repeatedly. In addition, states are at very different stages in the development of wetlands programs; they also have different political and financial constraints. Each state may begin the strategy development process in a different way. By providing some general guidelines rather than rigid steps—a resource manual rather than a cookbook—we hope to encourage states to take advantage of specific opportunities as they arise.

The guidebook is organized in four parts.

Part I explores, in its first section, the need for an overall goal and reasons why no net loss/net gain is a viable goal. This opening section also presents general guidelines for strategy development. The second section of Part I offers seven specific steps for strategy developers to follow and discusses those steps in detail.

Part II describes how to organize a sound and effective process for developing a strategy. It includes information on:

- how to launch the process of developing a statewide wetlands strategy;
- how to involve "stakeholders" in developing and implementing a wetlands strategy, and why doing so is important;
- how to select appropriate processes to build and maintain support for a viable strategy; and
- how to manage a collaborative process.

Part III provides extensive information on the wide array of programs that can be used to protect wetlands and their strengths and challenges. It includes detailed sections on current federal, state, local, and private wetlands programs. These sections can be used to find out what federal programs are available, what state programs might be used to protect wetlands, how local programs can incorporate wetlands protection, and what kinds of activities are carried out by private organizations.

Part IV is a comprehensive overview of data sources for wetlands. The introduction presents guidance on where or how to obtain information to answer basic questions, such as where wetlands are located and how rapidly they are being lost. The review of data sources and evaluation methods provides detailed information on:

- wetlands classification schemes;
- maps and national data bases;
- data sources on wetlands status and trends;
- rapid methods for evaluating, ranking, or categorizing wetlands; and
- intensive methods for evaluating individual wetlands.

The **appendixes** provide detailed information useful in developing a strategy, including excerpts from existing no net loss goals, an accounting system for measuring no net loss, and wetlands contacts at the state and federal level.

Notes

1. T.E. Dahl and C.E. Johnson, *Wetlands Status and Trends in the Coterminous United States Mid-1970's to Mid-1980's* (Washington, D.C.: U.S. Department of the Interior, Fish and Wildlife Service), p. 1.

2. This section is excerpted from *How Wet Is a Wetland?* (Washington, D.C.: Environmental Defense Fund and World Wildlife Fund, 1992).

3. The following section is based on Jon Kusler, *State Wetlands Plans: Achieving No Net Loss Through Networking and Building Upon Existing Programs* (unpublished ms., 1990).

PART I
Creating a Statewide Wetlands Strategy

Setting a Direction

One of the fundamental purposes of a wetlands strategy is to integrate often disparate efforts to protect and manage wetlands, thus ensuring that all programs affecting wetlands work toward the same end. The first and most important steps in developing a wetlands strategy are to establish an overall goal and then to consider how to achieve that goal.

THE OVERALL GOAL

For states with urgent practical decisions to make, a strong overarching goal isn't optional—it's a necessity.

Various wetlands conservation goals have been established at federal, state, and local levels. Most of these goals, however, lack clarity and depth. Typically, they apply to only one program and speak in general terms of an intent or a need to "preserve," "protect," and "maintain" the resource.

To be effective, a goal needs to serve five purposes.

What a Goal Should Do

1. A goal should promote consistency.

By focusing all efforts toward the same end, a goal helps ensure that programs are consistent— that resources are not consumed by one agency or program to the detriment of another. Consistent programs can better meet the needs of the regulated community, which deals with an often frustrating array of players and programs. Consistency also provides a strong basis for coordination among programs.

A goal can promote consistency among different levels of government and the private sector while accommodating regional needs by allowing flexibility in the means used to achieve the goal.

> Vermont's Act 200 establishes 12 statewide planning goals (goal 4 is "to identify, protect, and preserve important natural resources including . . . wetlands"). All plans prepared by regional planning commissions and state agencies must be consistent with these goals. While the goals provide a uniform standard for encouraging appropriate development in the state, they also give local and state agencies the flexibility to use mechanisms best suited to their own situations to achieve those goals.

2. A goal should provide a benchmark for assessing progress.

The effectiveness of a strategy can't be determined without an overarching goal. Similarly, the strategy's components can't be fine-tuned unless their performance is measured against a goal. (See

When programs share a consistent goal, the state sends a strong signal to both the general public and the regulated community that it is serious about protecting its wetlands resource.

3. A goal should help garner support.

Establishing and publicizing a goal for a state's wetlands strategy can be an effective way to gain support for all the activities and programs that implement the goal. A goal can help the public understand the issues. A promotional campaign focused on a goal can generate broad public awareness of the problem of wetlands loss and the strategy being developed to address the problem. For elected officials and the public, a goal can become a cause to identify with and promote.

In the early 1980s, Illinois confronted the problem of extensive and increasing soil erosion by setting a goal for addressing the problem. This goal, "Tolerable Soil Loss by the Year 2000," was established in administrative guidelines through the state's Soil and Water Conservation Districts Act. Since adopting the goal and raising awareness of the problem, the state's Department of Agriculture has been successful in securing funding from the general assembly for implementing programs needed to achieve the goal.

4. A goal should provide an underlying purpose for all activities carried out as part of a wetlands strategy.

A goal gives strategy implementors a clear, unified rationale for their work. This can help increase motivation by providing a sense of purpose and the ability to see how specific efforts contribute to meeting the goal.

5. A goal should help transcend changes in leadership.

A change in federal, state, or local leadership can drastically change program priorities and can have a profound effect on an agency's agenda. A strong goal helps ensure that the wetlands strategy endures through such inevitable political changes.

In 1989, Oregon adopted a plan to bolster economic growth. "Oregon Shines" established 160 goals for strengthening the state's economy (no net loss of wetlands is included as one of the goals). Although then-governor Neil Goldschmidt did not run for re-election in 1990, both major party candidates adopted the goals as their own, and the newly elected governor, Barbara Roberts, has requested that agency heads pursue these goals. The legislature is also drafting a bill to establish these goals as state policy.*

---

* "Lessons Offered by State and Local Governments," *National Journal*, April 20, 1991, p. 930.

No Net Loss and Long-Term Net Gain as the Goal

Despite important differences in the kinds of wetlands protection problems facing states and options available to address those problems, all states confront the same fundamental issue. The continuing loss and degradation of wetlands is unacceptable for both environmental and economic reasons. The goal of any wetlands strategy, then, must reflect the urgency and severity of this problem and present a realistic but ambitious target for wetlands protection and management efforts. The goal of no net loss and long-term net gain (NNL) serves such a purpose.

The NNL goal evolved during meetings of the National Wetlands Policy Forum, a group representing all major interests in wetlands policy, including government, agriculture, industry, and the environment. In November 1988, after examining the wetlands issue for a year, the Forum published its final report. It recommended that

> the nation establish a national wetlands protection policy to achieve no overall net loss of the nation's remaining wetlands base, as defined by acreage and function, and to restore and create wetlands, where feasible, to increase the quality and quantity of the nation's wetlands resource base.

This goal has driven the wetlands policy debate since that time. President Bush has endorsed no net loss, and several states, federal agencies, and local governments have formally adopted it. (See Appendix A for excerpts from existing statutes, rules, and policies that establish goals of no net loss/net gain.)

The broad appeal of NNL is that it is a fundamentally balanced goal. It recognizes the urgent need to stabilize and eventually increase the nation's wetlands inventory while acknowledging that some wetlands losses are inevitable because of natural events and legitimate development needs. NNL is thus a reasonable, achievable aim.

Adopting the Goal: Process Considerations

Some states have found it politically feasible to begin development of a wetlands strategy with the NNL goal as a mandate. A recently enacted Texas statute, for instance, directs the state to develop a plan for state-owned coastal wetlands that will achieve no net loss. In California, Governor Pete Wilson's two-year conservation initiative, dubbed "Resourceful California," calls for the state to develop a wetlands conservation plan by 1992 to achieve no net loss and long-term net gain. And Michigan, in developing its wetlands strategy, has moved directly to "net gain," setting a goal to increase the state's wetlands by at least 500,000 acres by the year 2000.

Even with such mandated goals, states still need to find ways to involve all the interested parties in the strategy development process. This can be done by using collaborative processes to set interim goals, objectives, and methods of implementation. (Part II offers detailed information about group processes.)

Some states may find that initiating strategy development with a preordained goal is problematic. In New York, for example, even though Governor Mario Cuomo endorsed no net loss, the strategy-building process began with public workshops to establish an overall strategy goal. New York chose this alternative because of the high level of controversy that wetlands issues had generated in the state. In such cases a state should design a process to identify a goal that involves all the stakeholders. Such a process may still result in a goal of no net loss, but because that goal is generated by the group, it is more likely to become a more readily acceptable premise for strategy development.

A goal-setting process may also generate a dif-ferent goal. Other goals may be less comprehensive than no net loss, such as a goal to increase the use and effectiveness of nonregulatory programs or to increase coordination among all programs affecting wetlands. Such goals can nonetheless provide a strong basis for improving wetlands protection and management and should not preclude future efforts to establish NNL as the ultimate goal.

Defining the Goal

Since the Forum recommended the NNL goal in 1988, the meaning of no net loss and long-term net gain has been debated at length. Although the Forum made extensive recommendations for reforms needed to achieve the goal, it didn't address the specifics of implementation. In the absence of national guidance, each state embracing the NNL goal needs to define it clearly in order to direct public and private actions and to assess progress.

What are wetlands?

To measure progress toward no net loss, a state must determine its current "wetlands base." To do this, a state needs a consistent definition of wetlands. At the federal level, the definition of wetlands

The goal of no net loss/net gain provides a balanced premise for a strategy that will succeed over the long haul. This goal combines flexibility with strong resource protection. It doesn't imply that wetlands in every instance will be untouchable, but it does require finding an equilibrium between short-term gains and losses and achieving an increase over the long term.

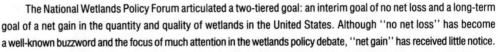

Don't Forget "Net Gain"

The National Wetlands Policy Forum articulated a two-tiered goal: an interim goal of no net loss and a long-term goal of a net gain in the quantity and quality of wetlands in the United States. Although "no net loss" has become a well-known buzzword and the focus of much attention in the wetlands policy debate, "net gain" has received little notice.

In taking steps to achieve no net loss, states shouldn't overlook the need to work toward an eventual net gain in wetlands. A net gain is necessary to make up for the 100 million acres of wetlands lost since the mid-1800s and recapture some of the valuable functions that these lost areas have performed. In addition, working toward a net gain will help make up for losses resulting from unsuccessful mitigation projects and other uncompensated losses.

To protect and improve a state's wetlands resource base, an overarching goal for the wetlands strategy should include both the interim and the long-term goals—no net loss *and* net gain.

is based on the presence of three physical characteristics: hydrology, hydrophytic vegetation, and hydric soils. The 1989 *Federal Manual for Identifying and Delineating Jurisdictional Wetlands* was developed to ensure consistency in the methods federal agencies use to identify wetlands that may be subject to federal regulation under Section 404 of the Clean Water Act or the "Swampbuster" provision of the Food Security Act. (As of this writing, revisions to the 1989 Federal Delineation Manual have been proposed and are undergoing public review and comment.)

Potential disagreements over a wetlands definition may be avoided by adopting a broad definition of the wetlands base for the overall strategy (such as the definition used by the U.S. Fish and Wildlife Service for the National Wetlands Inventory) and a more restrictive definition (consistent with the federal definition) for regulatory activities. In this way a state can encourage voluntary protection and enhancement of a wider range of ecologically valuable areas, such as riparian and deepwater habitats of particular significance to a state, while applying regulatory programs to a subset of these areas. Basing regulatory decisions on federally established criteria will also help promote consistency among all regulatory programs and encourage interstate cooperative efforts.

What is wetlands loss?

Various criteria must be considered in determining when a loss of wetlands acreage or function has occurred. The so-called footprint of fill material or a permanent structure in a wetland are easily measured; however, losses of area or function are not confined to such direct impacts. Hydrological modifications in one area, for instance, can destroy wetlands in another area; pesticide use on uplands may contaminate wetlands that are located far downstream.

States must also decide how to treat losses resulting from natural processes and unregulated activities. To achieve no net loss, states will ultimately need to offset these losses with government- or private-sponsored restoration or creation projects. In addition, technical criteria may be necessary to distinguish the causes of various losses—for example, to determine if losses of a streamside marsh are occurring naturally or induced by channelization projects upstream.

Maryland's Nontidal Wetlands Regulatory Program, which operates under a NNL goal, requires mitigation for documentable impacts—impacts that can be measured directly, such as fills and easily detectable hydrologic impacts. To compensate for less easily measured impacts that are likely to occur, the state carries out supplemental mitigation projects in addition to those required through the permitting process.

What is no net loss?

"No net loss" is a quantitative and qualitative equilibrium between losses and gains in wetlands acreage and function.

States must decide on the types, functions, and locations of wetlands restoration or creation that can be undertaken to compensate for losses. No net loss is most readily assured if compensation is:

- "in-kind" (i.e., the same wetlands types in the same hydrologic settings),
- with equivalent values, functions, and area, and
- on or very near the location (e.g., watershed) of the losses.

Compensation that is "out of kind" and at some other location in the state could also be permitted, but this requires a more complex assessment of the wetlands losses and gains.

In effect, no net loss requires the development of a master "balance sheet" to track progress toward the NNL goal. Commonly accepted procedures for accomplishing this task do not exist; therefore, states must decide how to proceed. (Part I.2 provides a framework for setting up such an accounting system.)

In some cases, resource allocation and budgetary needs may be better served by providing a date (either short- or long-term) for achieving the NNL goal. In other cases, a timeframe may not be necessary as long as continuous progress can be demonstrated.

Progressive Implementation of the Goal

As the nation's wetlands base continues to shrink daily, the urgency to adopt NNL increases. After all, NNL will be a meaningless goal if the starting point is a further diminished resource base. Because of the diversity of local situations, however, the NNL goal will be implemented in different ways and achieved at different rates by each state. Several factors will affect the rate at which a state progresses toward the goal, including political and public support, existing programs, current rate of wetlands loss, current causes of loss, and opportunities for long-term gain.

With these factors in mind, a wetlands strategy can be designed to allow for *progressive implementation*. For instance, a state may choose to "get its house in order" first by requiring no net loss in state-funded activities. As a next step, the state could require that no net loss be achieved within the state regulatory program. It could then institute new public- and private-sector incentive programs to restore and enhance wetlands. In contrast, a state

with well-developed existing wetlands programs might be able to move more quickly and aggressively toward adopting a NNL goal and legislation applying to all public and private activities.

The virtue of progressive implementation is its pragmatism. Not all wetlands protection activities can be undertaken or coordinated simultaneously; not all states can undertake a rapidly paced set of programs. As long as activities are thoughtfully planned with the overarching goal in mind, their implementation can be "staged" in line with political and economic realities.

GENERAL GUIDELINES FOR STRATEGY DEVELOPMENT

Simply put, a wetlands strategy should promote efficient and effective approaches to wetlands protection and management. To accomplish this, the strategy's components should be in harmony with the following guidelines.

1. **A strategy should reconcile environmental and economic needs and should identify opportunities to reduce conflicts between development and protection interests.**

Economic development is a basic concern of states and local governments. In creating and building support for a wetlands strategy, a state must consider the prevailing economic forces and how to work with those forces to achieve outcomes satisfactory to both development and environmental interests.

This is a tall order—but there *are* options for achieving such a balance of outcomes.

Advance planning. Several advance planning processes have been developed to ease con-

In generating and evaluating options, strategy developers must be continuously sensitive to diverse opportunities for improving wetlands protection. They must also acknowledge any constraints that might limit or hinder the effectiveness of certain options.

flicts in areas with sensitive wetlands resources that are under strong development pressure (see Part III.2, "Clean Water Act and Special Area Management Plans"). These planning processes can help channel development away from important wetlands by designating in advance where permits for development may be issued. Although such designations are typically only advisory, they do provide developers with some predictability. Advance plans also accommodate the needs of developers by identifying and designating areas suitable for development. One criticism of such planning processes, however, is that they often designate "low-value" wetlands for development as a trade-off for protecting "high-value" wetlands.

In the late 1970s and early 1980s, Anchorage, Alaska, faced intense conflicts between urban development and wetlands protection. (Nearly 30 percent of Anchorage's undeveloped land is wetlands.) To protect critical wetlands without hampering growth, the city developed a Special Area Management Plan that placed wetlands in four categories: special study, conservation, preservation, and developable. Developable wetlands are covered by a general permit issued by the Corps of Engineers and administered by the city of Anchorage that allows these areas to be filled with only minimal delays. Alterations in other categories of wetlands are subject to individual Section 404 review.

Flexible zoning. Several flexible zoning techniques can be used both to protect wetlands and to meet development needs by increasing the density of development in less environmentally sensitive areas. (Naturally, for these techniques to work,

less environmentally sensitive lands must be available for development.) *Cluster zoning* allows higher densities of development on one portion of a parcel to provide open space or protection of sensitive environmental areas elsewhere on the same parcel. *Transferable development rights* allow development rights for wetlands areas to be sold for development rights in a designated growth area. (See Part III.4, "Regulation and Zoning.")

"Wetlands-friendly" development. Development can be planned around wetlands in a way that benefits developers and homeowners. Home sites adjacent to wetlands often have more privacy and are considered prime lots. Amenities such as hiking trails and scenic views can also increase property values.

The Mission Springs housing development in West Bloomfield, Michigan, incorporated wetlands protection into its master plan. The 101-acre site includes approximately 40 acres of wetlands. Choosing a planned subdivision option, the developer was able to increase density in upland areas to avoid construction of homes on the wetlands. Thirty-five-foot buffers are maintained around the wetlands, and nature trails have been constructed throughout the subdivision. Lots adjacent to the wetlands sell for up to 25 percent more than other lots.

2. A strategy should build on the strengths of existing programs.

In developing a strategy, a state should exploit opportunities to make existing programs more effective and efficient. (See Part I.2, Steps 3 and 4.)

Working with Patterns of Development

In July 1982, after lengthy administrative proceedings, several conservation groups and the federal government legally settled on a development proposal for Marco Island in Collier County, Florida—one of the fastest-growing areas in the state. The undeveloped land in this area is predominantly freshwater wetlands or mangrove swamp.

The settlement provided for the protection of 95 percent of the wetlands on the proposed development site and the construction of the same number of housing units initially proposed by the developer. To achieve this result, the density of housing was increased; multi-family and high-rise units were built on upland areas adjoining the wetlands, thereby giving many residents spectacular vistas of the wetlands.

In this case, restriction of development was achieved only because of an alteration in the *pattern* of development. Had the result been a large decline in the potential for construction of housing in the area, the pressure to develop other nearby resources would have mounted, and the net environmental benefits to the area would have been lost. (Letter from John Tripp, Environmental Defense Fund, to Fred Bosselman, August 9, 1990.)

Coordination with Federal Initiatives

In North Carolina, the U.S. Army Corps of Engineers issued a general permit that allows for joint processing of state Coastal Area Management Act permits and Section 404 permits. Within the 20 coastal counties, permit applications for alterations falling under the jurisdiction of both the Corps and the state are accepted simultaneously by the state and the Corps. The state prepares a field report that is furnished to the Corps. The Corps then conducts a federal agency review while the state conducts its review process. The state develops a permit that incorporates both the state and federal positions, if the positions are not in conflict.

In many of Maryland's agricultural areas, development pressures are strong and land values high. As a result, payments through incentive programs for land protection are often insufficient to influence landowner decisions effectively. In an attempt to interest more farmers in joining the federal Conservation Reserve Program, from 1988 to 1990 Maryland's Department of Agriculture added a $20/acre payment to federal CRP payments in areas within the Chesapeake Bay Critical Area (1000 feet from the bay or tidal waters) or areas qualifying as vegetated filter strips (located 66 to 99 feet from a stream).

Because initiating new programs often consumes considerable time and resources, strategy developers should include new programs in their strategy only after careful deliberation. In many cases, states may find that the necessary mechanisms for wetlands protection are already in place. Strategy development is then a matter of refining and coordinating those mechanisms by expanding successful programs and eliminating overlaps and inconsistencies in others.

Coordination of programs should take place among all levels of government and the private sector.

State-federal coordination. State-federal program coordination is perhaps most needed to establish a procedure for joint wetlands permit evaluations. Many other coordination opportunities exist, however. Agencies can collaborate to help direct federal acquisition and restoration projects within a state, or they can "piggy-back" similar state efforts to increase the benefits of both state and federal activities.

Coordination among state agencies. A multitude of state agency programs affect wetlands and can be effectively coordinated to improve wetlands protection. Natural resources agencies can work with public works agencies to develop policies for siting public works projects (e.g., highways, sewer and water lines, flood-control projects) and for developing appropriate mitigation requirements. Agencies with acquisition programs can collaborate to define priorities and coordinate acquisition

efforts. All agencies with maps and other relevant data on wetlands can share information and plan for coordinated data gathering and updating.

South Carolina with financial support from the National Oceanic and Atmospheric Administration (NOAA) has launched a five-year research and demonstration project to investigate the applications of geographic information systems (GIS) as a tool for decision making and comprehensive environmental planning. The state is developing a GIS system for the Edisto River sub-basin, a 3,120-square-mile area that includes extensive swampland and bottomland hardwoods. Gathering data and updating the data base, which includes information on soils, wetlands, land use, environmental permits, water quality, threatened and endangered species, fisheries, and so on, has required the cooperation and involvement of all 13 of the state's natural resources agencies. These agencies provide relevant information to the data base and have access to information provided by others.

State-local coordination. Many important decisions regarding wetlands (notably land-use decisions) are made at the local level. Good communication and coordination between state and local governments are therefore crucial for implementing an effective wetlands strategy. A state can encourage or require that local plans contain a wetlands element to ensure consistency with the state strategy. Moreover, state-local joint permitting (e.g., permitting for wetlands, floodplains, stormwater, sediment control) can help eliminate duplication and inconsistencies.

In Oregon, individual permits issued by the Division of State Lands (DSL) are required for any direct physical alteration of the waters of the state. Through the approval of a local wetlands conservation plan with a no net loss goal, however, the state can pre-authorize permits and transfer permitting authority to local governments with the appropriate local ordinances to issue permits. DSL will also conduct an expedited review if the agency has approved the local plan but the local government lacks the necessary means to issue permits.

Coordination of government and private-sector programs. Governments can enter into joint ventures with the private sector to expand or enhance the ability of each to protect wetlands resources. For example, EPA recently awarded a $50,000 grant to an Illinois chapter of the Sierra Club to help enforce the Section 404 program. The Sierra Club's "Swamp Squad" is a group of 100 volunteers who patrol wetlands and report suspected violators to the Corps of Engineers.

Ducks Unlimited (DU), a national organization, has signed agreements with the Bureau of Land Management, the U.S. Fish and Wildlife Service, and the Office of Surface Mining (OSM) to coordinate efforts to achieve the goal of no net loss of wetlands. DU is helping OSM locate sites for the creation of wetlands on surface mines and other disturbed areas.

3. A strategy should include both regulatory and nonregulatory mechanisms.

In pursuit of an equitable approach to wetlands protection, strategy developers need to look beyond regulatory programs at a wide range of options, including: acquisition programs; planning programs; incentive programs; restoration, creation, and management programs; and education, technical assistance, and research programs. Nonregulatory programs can complement and enhance the effectiveness of regulatory programs by targeting activities or types of wetlands not covered by regulatory programs. Moreover, nonregulatory programs can help resolve regulatory conflicts by offering incentives to would-be developers to protect wetlands areas or by acquiring wetlands on potential development sites. (See Part III.)

4. A strategy should include both statewide and site-specific policies and programs.

Viable wetlands strategies operate at two levels. Statewide efforts are essential to develop overall policies, regulations, and coordination mechanisms. Such efforts might include improvements to state acquisition and regulatory programs and the development of a statewide mitigation policy. Applying policies to specific areas and local circumstances, however, may require more detailed information and site-specific planning. Site-specific plans (which require too much expertise and too many

---

Site-Specific Planning

Various state "special management units" have been created for management of areas of special importance, including floodplains, wetlands, and rivers. Some have been specifically created for wetland areas, such as Big Cypress, Florida, and Hackensack Meadowlands, New Jersey. Others aren't primarily wetlands oriented but provide opportunities for wetlands protection as part of broader resource management.

One example is Adirondack State Park in New York. In 1971 the New York legislature created Adirondack State Park—the largest park in the United States, with 6 million acres of land. It is twice the size of Yellowstone Park and larger than the states of Delaware and New Jersey combined. Of the park's total acreage, approximately 2.3 million are state owned and 3.7 million are privately owned. Approximately 30 percent of the total area is wetlands.

The 1971 statute created an Adirondack Park Agency to conduct an inventory of and plan for both private and public lands within the park. Since its inception the Park Agency has strongly emphasized wetlands protection in its assessment, planning, and regulatory efforts because of the importance of wetlands to the park as a whole and to its streams and rivers. Wetlands have been mapped, and detailed, stringent regulations have been adopted for wetlands areas. In addition, a wetlands interpretative center has been constructed.

In addition to state special management units, a variety of site-specific advanced planning efforts have been undertaken as part of the Section 404 program and the Coastal Zone Management Program. These programs identify areas that should be off limits to deposits of fills.

resources to be carried out statewide) can address issues such as the ranking of wetlands values or the establishment of mitigation banks.

5. A strategy should recognize the unique nature of wetlands as the interface of land and water, and should consider water resources as well as land use.

Too often, land-use programs fail to consider the effects of hydrologic modifications on wetlands. Interfering with either the quantity or quality of water supplying a wetland can destroy or drastically alter that wetland's functions. Water diversion upstream can deprive a wetland of necessary water flow; activities such as agriculture or forestry can cause sedimentation and chemical contamination in wetlands downstream.

Two approaches can be used to control the effects of water resources modifications on wetlands.

Water quantity reviews. Reviews of water resource development projects (through state environmental policy acts, Section 401 certification, or other state regulatory programs) can help identify and limit the negative effects of such projects on wetlands. Water rights laws in some states provide for claims for instream flow rights to ensure an adequate water supply for wetlands. In Washington, for example, the Department of Ecology can establish minimum flows for streams to protect wildlife, fish, scenic, aesthetic, and other environmental values. The state can also acquire the rights to water saved from state-funded water conservation projects (such as more efficient irrigation systems) and use those rights to maintain instream flows rather than for water diversion. (See Part III.3, "Water Rights Programs.")

Water quality reviews. In conjunction with EPA, the states administer a variety of water quality programs. By including wetlands in the definition of their waters and developing water quality standards for wetlands, states can use the Section 401 certification program (as well as other programs for controlling point and nonpoint pollution sources) to protect wetlands. (See Part III.2, "Clean Water Act: Water Pollution Control.") States can also add buffer requirements to their regulatory programs to protect wetlands from polluting activities on adjacent lands.

In August 1991, Wisconsin adopted comprehensive water quality standards for wetlands. These standards are the basis for decisions on regulatory, permitting, planning, or funding activities that affect water quality and wetlands. In particular, the standards are used in carrying out the state's responsibilities to certify (under Section 401 of the Clean Water Act) that Section 404 permits meet the state's water quality standards as explicitly outlined for wetlands. Under the new standards, no project can have a significant adverse impact on water quality-related functions and values of wetlands, including sediment and pollutant attenuation, storm and flood water retention, hydrologic cycle maintenance, shoreline protection against erosion, biological diversity and production, and human uses such as recreation.

6. A strategy should promote landscape approaches as the basis for wetlands protection and management decisions.

As the interdependence of natural systems is better understood, it has become apparent that a broader approach to wetlands protection and management is needed. To manage and safeguard this resource in a responsible fashion, states need to look beyond the boundaries of individual wetlands. This broader perspective recognizes ways in which activities on upland areas or upstream may affect a wetland and the kinds of landscape alterations that may result from a cumulative loss of wetlands.

Watershed-based approaches targeted at improving water quality are the most prevalent of current efforts to manage a resource on a landscape level. Water quality in the once-pristine Heron Lake in Minnesota, for instance, was significantly degraded by the early 1980s because of intensive agricultural practices causing soil erosion and both point and nonpoint pollution. Concerned about this problem, a consortium of public and private groups initiated a watershed-based rehabilitation program that involves acquiring and restoring wetlands to help improve water quality and decrease sedimentation. In addition, highly erodible areas are being identified and enlisted in the Conservation Reserve Program and other easement programs throughout the entire 472-square-mile watershed area.

Developing a Strategy

Developing a statewide wetlands protection strategy is a time-consuming and sometimes complex task. To a considerable degree, success depends on clear-headed observation, sound political instincts, and a keen awareness of earlier efforts that have been made—their strengths and weaknesses. Ultimately, a viable strategy is one that deals directly with specific wetlands problems and exploits any existing opportunities, large and small, for improving wetlands protection.

After identifying the extent of the wetlands problem and establishing goals and objectives, strategy developers need to be open to multiple possibilities. Capitalizing on current programs, using political and public support, taking advantage of positive and negative events, and exploring diverse funding possibilities—all these approaches should be considered. Strategy developers must also take into account any limits on a state's ability to implement a certain option while simultaneously dealing creatively with the resources at its disposal.

The process thus involves looking beyond the bounds of traditional efforts. Innovative approaches can be found across the country. They might entail linking wetlands protection to a program for nonpoint source pollution control, using volunteers to help enforce regulations, or funding an acquisition program with lottery proceeds. Whatever they

are, they're bound to require imagination as well as critical thinking.

Step 1
Identify the Extent of the Problem

When strategy developers have a sound understanding of a state's wetlands and the threats faced by them, they are in a good position to make realistic choices about specific policies and programs. The following questions are intended to help pinpoint the precise nature of the wetlands problem. Although it is unlikely that information will be available to answer every question, the more detailed the characterization of the wetlands problem, the more finely tuned the solution can be.

Part IV includes detailed guidelines on how to obtain the types of information discussed here.

How many wetlands does the state have, and where are they located?

An inventory of wetlands establishes a baseline from which to measure changes in the resource and progress toward no net loss. This information can also focus attention on certain areas of a state, such as those with high concentrations of wetlands that may warrant site-specific plans. Knowing where the wetlands are located helps a state anticipate problems that may be caused by future growth

A sledge hammer isn't the best tool to use when a little oil or a wrench would do the job. The purpose of collecting good information on the problems surrounding wetlands loss is to ensure that appropriate tools are chosen to deal with those problems.

and development in these areas. And inventories can provide other useful information, such as ownership and size, location in a watershed or landscape, and whether the area surrounding the wetlands is urban or rural—all factors that influence how the wetlands can be best protected.

What kinds of wetlands are they?

There are many different types of wetlands, including bogs, marshes, bottomland hardwoods, swamps, prairie potholes, and so on. Wetlands of the same type share similar traits and may therefore perform similar functions and react to stress in a similar fashion. Determining the types of wetlands that occur in the state provides insight into potential management and protection requirements. Protection of coastal marshes may be most effectively accomplished through a state's coastal zone management program, whereas protection of seasonally flooded freshwater wetlands in agricultural areas may require an education program to change farmers' cultivation practices.

What are the wetlands' functions?

A wetland's function can itself suggest opportunities for protection. For example, wetlands that help control flooding may be purchased by a local government as part of a floodplain management program. Wetlands that contribute to water quality improvements may be protected through water quality programs for point and nonpoint source pollution control. And wetlands that serve as endangered species habitat may be best protected through a state or federal endangered species statute. Although measuring wetlands function is an imperfect science, a variety of techniques are available (see Part IV).

What condition are the wetlands in?

Information on the physical and ecological condition of wetlands is critical in defining protection and management options. Whether a wetland is degraded or pristine will determine what management tools are needed and what priorities are appropriate.

How rapidly are wetlands disappearing, and where is most of the loss concentrated?

Information about the rate of loss and where loss is occurring helps focus efforts on those areas most threatened.

What activities are most responsible for wetlands degradation and loss?

Knowing the causes of wetlands losses will help determine appropriate management. Losses from highway construction will require different responses from losses due to agriculture. Natural losses may require an extensive restoration program; losses due to urban expansion may require land-use planning approaches or an acquisition program targeted at urban areas.

What are the consequences of loss?

Knowing how wetlands loss is affecting a state (e.g., impacts on fish and wildlife, water quality, flooding, and so on) can help strategy developers gain public support for appropriate ways of curtailing loss. If commercial fisheries are declining because of coastal wetlands degradation, for example, education campaigns may be able to mobilize support for more stringent regulations.

Analyzing in detail the problem of wetlands loss should give strategy developers a general sense

---

Gathering information can take a lot of time and resources, delaying strategy development for years. To the extent possible, a state should draw on existing data and the professional judgment of people familiar with the state's wetlands. As gaps in data are identified, objectives can be set for collecting and analyzing any missing data and information.

How Much Information Is Enough?

Information gathering is a balancing act. Enough information needs to be amassed to allow for sound policy choices, but collecting too much information can stall action. It's important to remember that decisions can be made and actions taken *before* all the needed information has been gathered.

For example, Michigan's wetlands law (the Goemaere-Anderson Wetlands Protection Act of 1979) was developed on the basis of available information on existing wetlands resources and losses. The state had determined that a statewide wetlands inventory was needed—and the law required the Department of Natural Resources to carry out this inventory. Significantly, the legislature made a conscious decision not to delay wetlands protection simply because the inventory had not been undertaken.

of the types of programs needed to address specific problems in their state. This general overview can then be compared with existing programs to help identify shortcomings, direct revisions, and initiate new programs.

Establish Strategy Goals and Objectives

Along with an overall goal (discussed in Part I.1), a wetlands strategy also needs interim goals to help ensure that progress is actually being made toward achieving the overall goal. Interim goals might include the following: no net loss of a specific type of wetlands; no net loss in a particular geographic area; no net loss as a result of state-funded activities; or no net loss of regulated wetlands.

Additionally, individual program goals should be established for both public and private efforts on behalf of wetlands conservation, taking into account the scope of particular programs. For example, a state regulatory program may adopt the NNL goal, but the state land acquisition program may have its own goal of purchasing 5,000 acres of threatened wetlands over the next two years. The state may also set a goal of restoring 8,000 acres of wetlands through private and joint-venture projects. Local governments might establish wetlands goals for their local planning and zoning programs, and private-sector organizations could be encouraged to set program goals that contribute to the state's overall goal. (These might include acquiring or restoring a specific number of acres or types of wetlands or improving public understanding of wetlands through educational programs.)

Programs with less direct effects on wetlands should also incorporate wetlands protection into their program directives. Any program that encourages development, ranging from the expansion of public facilities such as roads and sewers to government housing loans, should ensure that program implementation considers wetlands protection issues.

Certain existing program goals will probably need to be revised to promote wetlands protection. (This may be the case in programs such as highway projects and other land and water resource development projects that are not specific to wetlands but that may destroy or alter wetlands.) Moreover, conflicts among program goals need to be identified, and a plan for resolving such conflicts needs to be an integral part of strategy development. Opportunities to incorporate the NNL goal into broader natural-resource protection efforts (such as multi-objective planning programs) should also be explored.

Goals and Objectives of the Chesapeake Bay Agreement

The Chesapeake Bay Agreement, signed by the bay states and the federal government in 1987, was designed to develop comprehensive solutions to conflicting demands on the bay's resources. The Agreement included a directive to develop a regional policy for the protection of tidal and nontidal wetlands.

The Chesapeake Bay Wetlands Policy establishes an immediate goal of no net loss with a long-term goal of net gain. The policy implementation plan includes the following objectives for the first phase:

- Develop and implement a 10-year cyclic mapping program to map all tidal and nontidal wetlands in the Chesapeake Bay watershed at a scale and resolution needed to support the actions specified in the policy.
- Initiate a five-year cyclic analysis of the status and trends of bay watershed wetlands.
- Develop technical guidelines for wetlands protection for landowners, developers, and regulators to use in designing and evaluating regulated activities.
- Develop advisory criteria for the review and approval of mitigation plans.
- Formulate and begin execution of incentive programs as appropriate to achieve no net loss and net gain.
- Develop programs to provide current information to the public about wetlands values and protection needs.
- Formulate and begin execution of technical training programs for wetlands managers in the areas of wetlands identification, delineation, functional assessment, and mitigation and creation practices.
- Coordinate and expand technical assistance programs to support local governmental protection efforts.
- Establish a process to direct wetlands research funds to achieve the goals of the Chesapeake Bay Wetlands Policy.

Washington's Department of Ecology is currently working to resolve two conflicting goals within the agency. One goal is to improve water use efficiency; the other is to achieve no net loss of wetlands. In many agricultural areas of eastern Washington, wetlands have been created as a result of irrigation projects. Improving the efficiency of these projects will in many cases result in the loss of wetlands, and the department is considering how to treat such losses with respect to its NNL policy.

A state can use various methods to establish the goals and objectives of its wetlands strategy, including legislation, regulation, executive orders, and policies.

Legislation

In 1989, Maryland became the first state to adopt legislation with an explicit goal of no net loss. Several factors were important in securing passage of the legislation. First, the Maryland Department of Natural Resources had been running an education program to inform Maryland residents of the importance of wetlands. This resulted in strong public awareness, interest, and support for the bill. Second, in 1987 Maryland had signed the Chesapeake Bay Agreement, which established a goal of a net gain in wetlands acreage and function. Although this goal wasn't established statutorily, the Bay Agreement was signed by the governor and represented a strong commitment on the part of the state's leadership. Third, the governor supported the NNL bill.*

Strengths
- Legislation is binding and enforceable.
- Legislation can survive changes in administration and agency personnel.
- Legislation can apply to both public and private activities.

Challenges
- Securing passage of legislation requires strong political support.
- Passing legislation can be time consuming and resource intensive.
- The give-and-take of the political process may tend to weaken the statutory language and the provisions for enforcement.

* David Burke, "Maryland's New Nontidal Wetlands Protection Act," *National Wetlands Newsletter* (September-October, 1989), p. 2.

Key Considerations
- How much political support exists for the goal?
- Are sufficient resources available for a legislative effort?
- Will the legislative process delay strategy development?
- How important is it that the goal have legislative "teeth"?

Regulation

When Vermont's Wetlands Act was passed in 1986, the concept of no net loss had not yet been developed. Five years later, however, the state adopted freshwater wetlands rules that included the NNL goal. Using the rule-making process, Vermont was able to update its wetlands law. (The state legislature's Legislation and Rules Committee, which ensures that any new regulations meet the intent of the law, determined that the original law provided the latitude for the subsequent NNL rule.)

Strengths
- Regulations have the full force of law within the scope of an agency's authority.
- The process of establishing regulations provides opportunities for public comment.
- Regulations can be promulgated more quickly than legislation.

Challenges
- Regulations are limited by the scope and intent of the authorizing law.
- Regulations can be easily revised and amended.
- Regulations that expand existing programs can generate a negative backlash in the legislature.

Key Considerations
- Is there adequate statutory authority to adopt the goal?
- Can the regulation be written to cover a wide range of activities?

Executive Orders

Washington's Governor Booth Gardner signed an executive order in 1989 that adopted a state agency goal of no net loss of wetlands. The governor used this executive order to show his strong support for wetlands protection. After the state legislature failed to pass the 1990 Wetlands Management Act, a bill developed by Washington's state-level wetlands forum, the governor signed a second executive order that further clarified state agencies' responsibilities to protect wetlands. Without legislative backing, the governor took steps to control activities within his purview—the activities of the executive branch. Although they must operate within existing authorities, state agencies are currently pursuing better ways to use those authorities and to clarify existing regulations.

Strengths
- Executive orders can have broader scope than a regulatory action taken by a single agency.
- Executive orders are expedient (only the support of the governor is needed).
- Executive orders help agencies set priorities in carrying out existing mandates.

Challenges
- Executive orders apply only to actions of executive agencies.
- Executive orders may not survive changes in administration.
- Executive orders don't create new authorities (i.e., they can't expand state agency jurisdiction).

Key Considerations
- Does the governor support the proposed goal?
- How much can be accomplished through a goal that applies only to state agencies' activities?

Policies

In April 1990, the Massachusetts Water Resources Commission, which sets statewide water resources policy and includes representatives from five state agencies, adopted a short-term goal of no net loss and a long-term goal of net gain. Although the policy is only advisory, it sends a strong message to the public as well as to state agencies about the importance of wetlands and the Commission's strong commitment to protecting them.

Strengths
- Policy adoption is often less time consuming than legislation or regulations.

- A policy can raise public awareness of an issue and send a strong signal regarding an agency's commitment to the issue.

Challenge
- Policies are often advisory only.

Key Considerations
- Is there an appropriate agency or commission to establish a policy?
- Can a policy adequately promote the goal?

Step 3
Identify and Assess Existing Programs

Conducting an inventory of current programs is a fundamental step in strategy development and should provide an opportunity to do the following:

1. **Locate and establish contact with groups whose programs affect wetlands.**

   A program inventory can identify those parties who should participate in strategy development, including those involved in implementing wetlands-related programs (e.g., government agencies, non-profit organizations) as well as those whom the programs affect (e.g., landowners, developers, etc.).

2. **Discover successful programs that may serve as models.**

   Successful programs can be identified to serve as useful models for improving existing efforts and developing new programs.

3. **Identify areas where cooperative efforts are possible.**

   Identifying similarities in program goals, common concerns, and overlapping jurisdictions can help facilitate cooperative efforts.

4. **Identify weaknesses of programs or inconsistencies and gaps among them.**

   Some programs are ineffective in accomplishing their aims, and certain programs, though effective independently, may conflict with one another or with strategy goals. This analysis should help pinpoint weaknesses, inconsistencies, and gaps in existing programs.

5. **Locate sources of technical information and other useful resources.**

   Private groups and government agencies dealing with wetlands issues collectively possess con-

Some mechanisms for wetlands protection, such as regulatory programs, address only specific types of alterations (such as filling). Others, such as acquisition programs, can protect wetlands from most physical alterations but often can't control off-site impacts such as water pollution.

siderable technical expertise. Opportunities for sharing information, equipment, and expertise can be uncovered by conducting an inventory of existing programs. The relationship that a particular group has with a constituency (e.g., the Soil Conservation Service with farmers) can also be a useful resource. (See Appendix B for detailed information about examining existing programs.)

Step 4
Make the Best Use of Federal, State, Local, and Private Protection Mechanisms

In devising its wetlands strategy, a state can incorporate programs found at all levels of government as well as private-sector programs. This section offers guidance in making the most of existing programs and discusses means of improving various programs' effectiveness in contributing to the goals and objectives of a statewide strategy. (See Part III for detailed information on the mechanisms discussed here.)

Federal Programs

Federal programs provide direct protection of wetlands as well as much-needed technical assistance and funding. What follows are some guidelines for incorporating federal programs into a state wetlands strategy.

- Take advantage of federal programs that provide direct authority to states, such as Section 401 water quality certification, consistency under the Coastal Zone Management Act, and assumption of Section 404 permitting responsibilities.
- Work with federal agencies to influence federal restoration and acquisition programs such as the North American Waterfowl Management Plan.
- Use federal technical assistance and grant programs, such as the National Wetlands Inventory and EPA's Wetlands State Development Grants and wetlands hotline.
- Use available federal funding to support state wetlands acquisition, including fund-

---

Key Federal Mechanisms for Wetlands Protection

ACQUISITION
Land and Water Conservation Fund
North American Waterfowl Management Plan
Pittman-Robertson and Dingell-Johnson Acts

REGULATION
Section 404 of the Clean Water Act
Water Quality Certification (Section 401)
Consistency under the Coastal Zone Management Act

PLANNING
Advanced Identification (Section 404)
Special Area Management Plans
State Comprehensive Outdoor Recreation Plans (SCORPs)

RESTORATION, CREATION, AND MANAGEMENT
Farm Bill programs: Wetlands Reserve Program
North American Waterfowl Management Plan
National Coastal Wetlands Conservation Grants
Coastal Zone Management Act

INCENTIVES AND DISINCENTIVES
Farm Bill programs: Swampbuster
Coastal Barrier Resources Act
National Flood Insurance Program

TECHNICAL ASSISTANCE, EDUCATION, AND OUTREACH
National Wetlands Inventory
EPA Wetlands Program State Development Grants

ing under the Pittman-Robertson and Dingell-Johnson acts, the Land and Water Conservation Fund, and the North American Wetlands Conservation Act.

- Educate the public about federal incentive programs such as the Wetlands Reserve Program.
- Examine existing federal programs such as the Coastal Zone Management Act as models for developing a state strategy and integrating federal, state, and local regulatory and nonregulatory programs.
- Consider existing federal programs (such as Section 404 if not assumed by the state) as part of the strategy. Rather than using state resources to duplicate these efforts, complement and build on them.
- Work to direct certain federal planning processes, such as Special Area Management Planning and Advanced Identification, to areas that need intensive planning to help resolve conflicts between development and protection interests.
- Build on federally required planning efforts such as State Comprehensive Outdoor Recreation Plans (SCORPs) to ground strategy development.

State Programs

A state can incorporate and make improvements in many different state programs—not all of which have to be directly related to wetlands. To address specific wetlands problems, states should seek out and use broader programs for the protection of natural resources. The following are some guidelines for improving or enhancing state programs.

- Incorporate wetlands protection into programs for floodplain and shoreline management.
- Develop water quality standards for wetlands

Key State Mechanisms for Wetlands Protection

ACQUISITION	wildlife habitat programs
	parks and recreation programs
	natural areas acquisition programs
REGULATION	tidal/nontidal wetlands regulations
	point and nonpoint source programs
	floodplain management programs
	shoreline management programs
PLANNING	statewide land-use plans
	special area plans
RESTORATION, CREATION, AND MANAGEMENT	wildlife enhancement programs
	water quality programs
	public land management
INCENTIVES AND DISINCENTIVES	tax incentives
	registration programs
TECHNICAL ASSISTANCE, EDUCATION, AND OUTREACH	local government assistance programs
	landowner assistance programs
	environmental education curricula
RESEARCH	state universities
	scientific and policy research programs

so that Section 401 certification can be used effectively (along with other point and nonpoint source water quality programs).

- Undertake statewide land-use planning that incorporates strong wetlands protection provisions and requirements for local consistency into the statewide plan.
- Undertake special area planning to protect important wetlands areas and to address conflicts between development and wetlands protection.
- Incorporate wetlands protection into all public works activities.
- Strengthen coastal and estuarine wetlands protection by involving these areas in broader watershed management planning efforts for rivers and streams in order to protect water quality and quantity, sediment supply, and habitats for estuarine and coastal areas.
- Ensure that potential impacts on wetlands are evaluated under state environmental protection acts.
- Provide technical assistance and funding to local governments to adopt and implement wetlands protection programs.
- Develop a coordinated and prioritized program for wetlands or natural areas acquisition.
- Improve state wetlands regulations to make them more effective and efficient.

Local Programs

In most states, the law gives local governments substantial regulatory, acquisition, and taxing authority that can play an important part in a statewide wetlands strategy. Moreover, local governments offer a unique perspective on wetlands protection because of their understanding of local resources and circumstances.

The land-use framework already in existence at the local level has a direct bearing on strategy development, and a successful strategy will carefully build on that framework. The strategy should strike a politically acceptable balance between local autonomy and state control.

States can help enhance the effectiveness of local programs by following these guidelines:

- Encourage local governments to look at wetlands protection as part of a multi-objective program including public works, parks, and planning and development.

- Encourage or require local governments to include wetlands protection in local zoning ordinances.
- Promote the use of flexible zoning techniques such as cluster development and transfer of development rights to help accommodate both development and wetlands protection needs.
- Encourage the initiation of local greenway protection efforts.
- Encourage the development of local wetlands management plans.

Private Programs

At all governmental levels, lack of resources and authority limits initiatives to protect wetlands. These constraints can be overcome in part by working with and strengthening nongovernmental constituencies for protecting wetlands—including small recreational and environmental organizations, corporations, individual landowners, and concerned citizens.

As demonstrated by many success stories throughout the country, nonprofit conservation organizations can and do provide the leadership, commitment, and flexibility essential to protecting wetlands. Private nonprofit organizations have played significant roles in acquiring, restoring, and preserving wetlands and educating the public about their values.

- Research and advocacy organizations provide public education and bring scientific expertise and political impetus to wetlands protection efforts.
- Hunting, fishing, or other recreational groups may acquire, protect, and maintain wetlands and educate the public about wetlands functions and values.
- "Watchdog" groups participate in federal, state, and local regulatory decisions and litigate to promote their objectives.
- "Friends of" groups or watershed associations build public interest in and support for an area through community celebrations and so forth and may help with resource management.
- Foundations raise funds for protecting specific areas.
- Land trusts work with major landowners and benefactors to acquire and protect critical parcels.

Corporations, landowners, and concerned citizens can contribute to a statewide strategy by doing the following:

- responsibly protecting, enhancing, and possibly creating their own wetlands;

- selling, donating, or otherwise contributing wetlands to a public or private organization for conservation purposes;

- publicizing threats to wetlands values;

- developing and building public support for protecting wetlands;

- understanding the land development process and participating in land-use decisions; and

- lobbying and negotiating with elected officials and developers.

Step 5

Seek Funding from a Diversity of Sources

The mechanisms that a state can use to address wetlands issues may be determined in large part by the funding available to implement such tools. In light of the tight fiscal constraints that most states face, nontraditional sources of funding are of growing importance. Exploring these sources often involves tapping the resources of programs that aren't specifically designed for wetlands protection.

The indisputable fact that funding is often hard to obtain increases the need for strategy developers to educate themselves about a diverse range of revenue-generating mechanisms.

Key Local Mechanisms for Wetlands Protection

ACQUISITION
critical habitat programs
parks and open-space programs
water quality programs

REGULATION
zoning
floodplain and stormwater management
subdivision regulations
transfer of development rights

PLANNING
comprehensive local land-use plans
floodplain, watershed, or wetlands plans
zoning and infrastructure plans

RESTORATION, CREATION, AND MANAGEMENT
public land management
wastewater treatment programs
wildlife enhancement programs

INCENTIVES AND DISINCENTIVES
tax incentives
capital improvements programming
subsidies

TECHNICAL ASSISTANCE, EDUCATION, AND OUTREACH
environmental awareness programs
landowner assistance programs

RESEARCH
community colleges
staff biologists

Federal Funding Opportunities

Substantial funding for wetlands conservation is available through a wide variety of federal programs. Funding available to states often has caps, however, and may require state matches. The amount of funding available also varies from year to year, depending on congressional appropriations.

The following are key federal funding sources for state-level wetlands protection efforts. (See Part III.2).

Acquisition

- The Coastal Wetlands Planning, Protection and Restoration Act (National Coastal Wetlands Conservation Grants) can be used to acquire coastal wetlands.
- Coastal Zone Management Act grants can also be used to acquire coastal wetlands.
- The Land and Water Conservation Fund can be used to acquire wetlands that provide outdoor recreation opportunities.
- North American Wetlands Conservation Act grants can be used to acquire wetlands that further the North American Waterfowl Management Plan and international treaties on migratory birds. (Special funding is available for wetlands in coastal states.)
- The Federal Aid in Sport Fish Restoration Act (Dingell-Johnson) and Federal Aid in Wildlife Restoration Act (Pittman-Robertson) provide funding for fish and wildlife conservation (including wetlands acquisition).

Regulatory Programs

- Coastal Zone Management Act grants can be used to develop and implement CZM programs (which must include wetlands conservation).
- EPA Wetlands Program State Development Grants can be used to incorporate wetlands into state water quality standards, to improve Section 401 water quality certification programs to protect wetlands, for development of state wetlands regulatory programs, and to assist state Section 404 assumption efforts.

Planning

- Coastal Zone Management Act grants can be used for Special Area Management Planning.
- EPA Wetlands Program State Development Grants can be used for planning (including development of statewide wetlands strategies).
- National Park Service grants are available for the development of the wetlands portion of State Comprehensive Outdoor Recreation Plans.
- For high-priority estuaries, EPA will provide technical assistance and 75 percent of the funding for conservation plans, which most likely will include wetlands conservation.

Restoration, Creation, and Management

- Coastal Zone Management Act grants can be used for wetlands management.
- North American Wetlands Conservation Act grants can be used for restoration and/or management of wetlands that further the goals of the North American Waterfowl Conservation Plan and international treaties on migratory birds.
- The Coastal Wetlands Planning, Protection, and Restoration Act targets funding for Louisiana wetlands restoration projects.
- National Coastal Wetlands Conservation Grants can be used for coastal wetlands restoration, management, and enhancement.
- The Dingell-Johnson and Pittman-Robertson Acts provide funding for wetlands restoration and maintenance for fish and wildlife purposes.

Technical Assistance, Education, and Outreach

- Coastal Zone Management Act grants can be used for educational activities related to wetlands.
- EPA Wetlands Program State Development Grants can be used for training leading to the development of state wetlands protection programs.

Research

- Coastal Zone Management Act grants can be used for research in National Estuarine Research Reserves.
- EPA Wetlands Program State Development Grants can be used for research leading to the development of state wetlands protection programs (i.e., for monitoring of wetlands losses).

State-Level Funding Opportunities*

Most wetlands protection activities at the state level are funded by general revenues that come from a variety of funding sources, including state income taxes, corporate taxes, and sales taxes. These revenues are appropriated to various programs by the state legislature on an annual or biennial basis. The allocations normally reflect the spending priorities of the state. Although general revenues are an equitable source of funding—everyone pays, everyone benefits—revenues dedicated to wetlands programs can fluctuate according to priorities or fiscal conditions.

In view of increasing demands on general revenues, funding a wetlands strategy will probably involve looking at alternative financing mechanisms such as dedicated fees and taxes. These mechanisms are being used increasingly by states because unlike general revenues, they can be targeted directly at wetlands programs. Dedicated funds may be deposited into a special account or trust fund, which means that the money will go directly to a particular program, or they may be deposited into the state's general fund with the understanding that a certain amount will be set aside for specific activities.

Although alternative funding sources are potentially exciting opportunities, they may raise several problems. A state legislature will often allow

This section is based on Financing State Wetlands Programs, *a report prepared in 1990 for the U.S. Environmental Protection Agency by Apogee Research, Inc. (See also Part III.3).*

a dedicated funding source to be created only if a program gives up its general revenue financing. If dedicated fees and taxes are the only funding source, state programs may be limited by the varying availability of such funds from year to year. These mechanisms therefore may be better viewed as funding supplements than as independent sources.

What follows is a list of specific types of alternative financing mechanisms. Brief descriptions are given along with the advantages, disadvantages, and examples of each mechanism.

Fees

Fees are a charge for a particular public service or activity. Permit fees are the most widely used fee for supporting wetlands programs. The intent of fees is to establish a link between the demand for a particular service and the cost of providing that service. If structured correctly, fees require program beneficiaries to pay for program costs.

Fees may be set on a flat or variable schedule. A flat-rate fee is often used when an activity or service is provided by the state and its cost for each party is equal. Variable-rate fees are used when the cost of services varies for different parties. A variable-rate fee schedule may also be used to charge users on the basis of the environmental impacts of their activities.

Advantage

- Fees are a relatively common and well-accepted revenue source for wetlands programs.

Costs can and do change over time. Demonstrating the full cost of public services to those who benefit from them is necessary to increase the acceptability of any additional costs.

Fees to Support Regulatory Programs

New Jersey requires a permit for any project involving the excavation, dredging, drainage, fill, construction, or destruction of plant life in a freshwater wetland. The Division of Coastal Resources of the N.J. Department of Environmental Protection (DEP) administers the permit program. The fees are collected when an application is submitted under guidelines set by the Freshwater Wetlands Protection Act of 1987. Rates are set according to the cost of the service provided. The fee schedule may be adjusted by administrative rule to cover the cost of supporting DEP's wetlands management program.

Wisconsin's Department of Natural Resources charges a fee for projects requiring water regulation permits under Sections 30.28 and 31.39 of the Wisconsin State Statutes. The cost of the fee (from $5 to $65) is based on estimated project costs and the number of applications filed. The fees do not cover administrative costs of the permit program, and fees must be refunded if the permit is not granted. Fees are deposited in the state's general fund, and the Bureau of Water Regulation and Zoning does not have direct access to the funds.

Disadvantage

- If fees are the only revenue sources, wetlands projects may experience cash-flow problems because fee revenues are often sporadic.

As part of Maryland's wetlands protection efforts, the Tidal Wetlands Compensation Fund was created to finance acquisition of valuable wetlands areas. Compensation fees may be assessed by the state's Board of Public Works for certain projects affecting wetlands. Fee revenues are deposited in the Tidal Wetlands Compensation Fund and are dedicated to the acquisition of wetlands habitats. The fund is administered through the state's Open Spaces Program.

Taxes

Two types of taxes are important to wetlands: excise taxes and waterfowl or habitat stamps. Excise taxes, collected from the sale of certain goods or services, are compulsory and applied throughout state governments' jurisdictions. Excise taxes include property transfer taxes (often used for financing land-acquisition programs); tobacco and liquor taxes; hunting and fishing equipment taxes; taxes on automotive and marine fuels; restaurant and hotel income taxes; and severance taxes on minerals.

Waterfowl or habitat stamps are required by many states with the purchase of a hunting license. Revenues from these stamps are used to acquire or manage habitats.

Advantages

- Taxes can be levied on those who either benefit from or affect wetlands programs.
- Acquired revenues may be earmarked for specific projects.
- Dedicated revenues may be collected from a fiscal agency and credited to an appropriate account or fund.

Disadvantages

- State legislatures are reluctant to dedicate tax revenues to individual programs.
- Collecting dedicated taxes places an additional administrative burden on the agency responsible for tax collection.

Taxes to Fund Acquisition

Tennessee maintains a dedicated fund for the acquisition of wetlands and bottomland hardwood forests, supported by a portion of the state's property transfer tax revenues. The Tennessee Wildlife Resources Agency (TWRA) implements the program. As of August 1991, over 17,000 acres of land had been purchased for about $9.8 million. A property transfer tax of $0.03 per $100 (a portion of the state's tax of $0.32 per $100) provides the funding for TWRA's acquisition program. The tax supports only the appraisal, survey, and purchase of wetlands. It is levied by the counties on all transfers of property in the state. Revenues are transferred to the state's Finance and Administration Department and deposited monthly in the Wetlands Acquisition Fund, which receives approximately $340,000 per month (around $4 million each year).

Missouri citizens passed a constitutional amendment in 1976 that added one-eighth of 1 percent (0.125 percent) to the state's general sales tax and dedicated the revenues to the Missouri Department of Conservation (MDC). The goal was to acquire 300,000 acres of land for fish and wildlife habitats. To date, 270,000 acres have been acquired, most of which is wetlands acreage. The sales tax is collected by the Missouri Department of Revenue, and the dedicated percentage is credited daily to the Conservation Department Fund. MDC adopted a Missouri Wetland Management Plan in September 1989; it is supported by the sales tax. This plan, which also implements portions of the North American Waterfowl Management Plan, guides the protection, restoration, and management of wetlands in the state to the year 2000.

An important program affecting wetlands in Iowa is the Prairie Pothole Joint Venture (PPJV), a cooperative effort of the Iowa Department of Natural Resources, the U.S. Fish and Wildlife Service, county conservation boards, and nonprofit organizations. Its mission is to buy wetlands and uplands and to restore privately owned wetlands in Iowa for wildlife habitats. The PPJV is financed in part through the sale of habitat and waterfowl stamps. Habitat stamp revenues are earmarked for wildlife habitat acquisition, and waterfowl stamp revenues are earmarked for waterfowl habitat acquisition.

Fines and Penalties

Fines and penalties are usually collected for violations of state regulations. Related to either criminal or civil offenses, they may be levied judicially or administratively. The money collected usually enters a state's general fund.

The New Hampshire Wetlands Board, for example, is authorized to impose an administrative fine of up to $2,000 per offense on any person violating provisions of the state's wetlands statutes or rules. Proceeds of the fines and penalties are placed in a nonlapsing fund in the state's treasury and may be spent by the Wetlands Board for restoration, research, and enforcement relative to wetlands.

Advantages
- Fines and penalties can be effective enforcement mechanisms.
- They can be used for acquisition and restoration to compensate for wetlands losses.
- The money collected can be dedicated to special funds for wetlands protection.

Disadvantages
- Fines and penalties often are not directed toward specific wetlands programs.
- They fluctuate as a source of revenue; therefore, projects can't depend on them.
- Enforcement efforts are often weak, and in many cases fines and penalties are rarely imposed.

Bonds

Governments can borrow funds from investors by issuing debt in the form of bonds. Bonds are used to provide up-front capital for major investments such as land acquisition. The issuer receives funds and repays the bond over time through debt services.

General obligation bonds are most often used for wetlands protection programs. These bonds are paid out of general revenues, and the issuing state or local government pledges to use its revenue-raising power to repay bondholders. These bonds may require voter approval; usually, a ceiling is placed on the debt that can be issued by the governmental entity.

New York's Department of Environmental Conservation has been acquiring lands for natural resources protection and restoration for many years. Funding for the purchase of these lands has been raised primarily through bond revenues. New York issued general obligation bonds in 1960, 1962, 1972, and 1986 to finance a range of environmental programs, including land acquisition. These bonds are sold only after legislation authorizing their issue is passed by the state legislature, signed by the governor, and approved by voters. The 1986 Environmental Quality Bond Act provided $250 million for land acquisition and other environmental programs.

Advantage
- Bonds are good for programs with large initial capital costs that will have future benefits.

Disadvantages
- Because bonds must be repaid, they are not an independent source of revenue.
- Bond revenues are used to cover the initial capital costs of a program (i.e., initiation costs); thus, revenues often are not available for operating costs.

Lotteries

Lottery revenues are being used by many states as a source of funding for environmental programs. Lottery revenues fund Colorado's Conservation Trust Fund for the acquisition, development, and maintenance of conservation lands ranging from state parks and historic sites to wetlands. In Arizona, voters approved creation of the Arizona Heritage Fund with 64 percent of the vote in November 1990. Annual lottery proceeds of $20 million are being dedicated to a variety of conservation uses.

Advantage
- State lotteries are more acceptable to voters and state legislatures than less "voluntary" revenue sources.

Disadvantages
- Lottery revenues are seen as a regressive source of income; that is, lower-income groups bear a greater financial burden than higher-income groups.
- Natural resources programs must compete with other programs often funded by lotteries, such as educational and economic development programs.

Voluntary Contributions

Voluntary contributions such as income tax check-offs and matching funds for land acquisition can be used to support wetlands and other environmental projects. Thirty-two states have check-offs on their tax forms, mainly for funds for nongame wildlife protection. Matching funds for wetlands protection often are raised from hunters interested in promoting greater fishing and hunting opportunities through the acquisition and development of wildlife habitats.

Advantages
- Contributions are voluntary, so citizens are giving because of their concern for the environment.
- Contributions to matching funds are tax deductible.

Disadvantages
- Because the contributions are voluntary, citizens who are not environmentally conscious may refuse to give.
- Check-offs have become so popular that wetlands must compete with other social concerns.

Trust Funds

Trust funds are developed when funds from a particular source are earmarked for a specific program. Trust funds are an effective mechanism for managing funds and ensuring that dedicated revenues are used for their intended purpose. They are also good for accumulating monies for capital-intensive uses (e.g., land acquisition or restoration).

There are two methods of earmarking revenues for trust funds: constitutional or legislative. Most constitutionally earmarked funds require no legislative appropriation to release the deposits, which are readily available for the purpose named in the state constitution. In some cases the state legislature dedicates revenues from a funding source and develops a trust fund to manage them. The release of these statutorily dedicated funds may or may not require legislative appropriations.

As an example, in Minnesota a constitutional amendment on the November 1990 ballot dedicating 40 percent of lottery proceeds to the state's Natural Resources Trust was overwhelmingly adopted by voters (80 percent to 20 percent).

Advantages
- Trust funds are used only for specific purposes.
- Even though constitutional dedication is more difficult, it secures funds with less threat of political interference.

Disadvantages
- Establishing and maintaining an independent fund creates increased administrative burdens.
- Both legislative and administrative forces may oppose the creation of a separate fund.
- Trust funds may provide only an illusion of security for program revenues (i.e., funds may be "borrowed" if there is a higher

Potential interruptions of funds can be avoided by obtaining tax or fee revenues that are dedicated to a program, establishing a trust fund, or founding a distinct institution with its own revenue-raising and implementation powers.

Voluntary Contributions in Three States

Since 1982, New York has raised revenues from its "Return a Gift to Wildlife" check-off, totaling about $1.7 million per year. The Department of Environmental Conservation can use these funds for projects that cannot be financed through the state's annual budget. Return a Gift to Wildlife provides revenue for fish and wildlife habitat programs, public education programs, research programs, and programs to protect endangered and threatened species.

In Ohio an account was created to receive contributions from the "Ohio Natural Areas" check-off as well as direct contributions. These revenues are dedicated to supporting a program administered by the Department of Natural Resources to identify and protect unique natural areas in Ohio, including wetlands.

Minnesota operates the Critical Habitat Private Match to protect or improve critical habitats for fish, wildlife, and rare and significant plant and animal species under the state's Reinvest in Minnesota program. Wetlands are considered a critical habitat. Critical Habitat Private Match is administered by the Department of Natural Resources and uses state funds appropriated to the program's account to match contributions, dollar for dollar, from private individuals and organizations. Contributions are made in cash, land, easements, or as a pledge for a specific project. Since 1986, $4.7 million in private donations and pledges has been received through the program.

priority within the state that needs financing).

Local Funding Opportunities

Local governments have successfully used creative approaches to fund the acquisition of natural areas, including wetlands. Sales taxes, acquisition set-asides, "tourist impact" taxes, tax-free bonds, and real-estate transfer taxes are among the many mechanisms employed at the local level. (See Part III.4.)

(See Part III.4.)

Step 6
Look for Other Opportunities to Strengthen Wetlands Protection Efforts

State and local fiscal constraints and a natural resistance to change can impede the task of generating and evaluating options for wetlands protection. Strategy developers, therefore, need to be vigilant in searching for opportunities to undertake needed changes.

Taking Advantage of Positive and Negative Events

Problems that can be linked directly to the loss of wetlands can prompt the initiation or strengthening of wetlands protection activities. Such problems include flood disasters, water quality degradation, and decreases in fish and wildlife populations.

Many opportunities exist for protection or restoration and creation of wetlands to reduce existing levels of pollution and to prevent new pollution. Numerous urban areas are considering or utilizing created wetlands for tertiary treatment of sewage. Some cities are also considering the use of created wetlands to help purify stormwater to reduce pollution and to comply with EPA's new water quality initiatives for stormwater. The Soil Conservation Service is developing guidelines for created wetlands or buffer strips to reduce nutrient and other types of pollution from agriculture.

Negative events are not the only impetus for action; a positive event can also help create a strong constituency for wetlands protection. If an individual or corporation donates a wetlands area to a state or local government, for example, the event may be an opportunity to launch a public education program at the site or to initiate a broader acquisition effort. Other positive events might include favorable media coverage of the importance of wetlands or special "wetlands awareness" campaigns.

EPA, along with 50 public and private organizations, sponsored the first annual American Wetlands Month in May 1991. The goal was to increase public awareness of the importance of wetlands and to encourage action to protect, enhance, and restore

In generating and evaluating options, strategy developers must be continuously sensitive to diverse opportunities for improving wetlands protection. They must also acknowledge any constraints that might limit or hinder the effectiveness of certain options.

Local Greenway and Multi-Objective Stream/River Corridor Management

Throughout the nation an estimated 500 local greenway efforts (targeted at areas adjacent to rivers or streams, lakes, or the coast) have been completed or are underway. It is in fact unusual for medium-sized or large local governments *not* to have initiated a greenway effort for at least some portions of their waterfront. These efforts are usually community based and serve multiple objectives, such as recreation, flood loss reduction, or pollution reduction. Greenway efforts are among the most exciting community-based environmental activities occurring across the United States. They offer the potential to protect not only individual wetlands in a river or stream corridor but also the wetlands' water supplies, buffer areas, and linkages with other areas.

Boulder Creek, the major natural creek in Boulder, Colorado, flows through the center of the town. As part of a broad open-space initiative, Boulder began a program in the 1970s to create a greenway along the creek and to protect and preserve it for future generations. The greenway project has been funded through general revenues, bond issues, private contributions, and assistance from several nonprofit groups (including Colorado Open Lands and The Nature Conservancy). This greenway has involved public acquisition of land along more than 9 miles of the creek and construction of a bike and walking trail, fish viewing area, and picnic areas. A 29-acre cottonwood willow grove has been acquired on the upper creek for scientific study and for use as a University of Colorado riparian field station. Additional wetlands areas have been acquired at upstream and downstream sites.

wetlands. Activities were undertaken throughout the country, including proclamations by Governor Carroll Campbell of South Carolina and Governor Barbara Roberts of Oregon, and displays and informational flyers prepared by the city of Indianapolis. Eugene, Oregon, took advantage of the state's focus on wetlands and released its draft wetlands plan. The Corps of Engineers also announced that Eugene's Amazon Creek corridor had been selected as a demonstration site for its national wetlands research program.

Using Political and Public Support

The support of a governor can provide important opportunities to launch agency initiatives or even to secure issuance of an executive order directing state agencies to protect wetlands. Such support may also encourage the state legislature to support legislation on amending existing statutes or creating new authorities and initiatives.

Grassroots efforts to protect wetlands, such as "adopt-a-wetlands" or "wetlands watch" programs, should be considered valuable tools to include in a wetlands strategy. As an example, the Fans of Fanno Creek, located outside Portland, Oregon, reached agreement with a developer planning a subdivision along the creek. The agreement includes the following provisions:

- a 50-foot buffer along the creek,
- a $3,000 fine for violation of the buffer protection provision,
- an inventory and protection of all seeps and springs, and
- the right of Fans to inspect the property during construction.

Develop Monitoring and Evaluation Plans

Why should time and energy be spent on monitoring and evaluating a wetlands strategy? The answer is that just as wetlands strategies are not self-funding, they also are not self-implementing or self-correcting. A good monitoring and evaluation plan is vital to ensuring that all of a strategy's components are being implemented and that overall goals and objectives will indeed be met.

Monitoring and evaluation results assist program managers throughout the implementation process. Using these results, managers review policies, procedures, and outcomes and make program corrections before problems become significant. The results can also be used to update interested parties—including the media—on the status of strategy implementation.

In 1990, Florida's Department of Environmental Regulation (DER) was ordered by the legislature to conduct a study of the state's 10-year-old wetlands mitigation policy. The study was requested in response to several independent studies that identified significant problems with implementation. The DER study showed that less than one-third of the freshwater mitigation/replacement projects were successful, and only about half of the saltwater ones were successful. In addition, in 1 of 12 cases, developers were allowed to fill in and build on wetlands created as mitigation for earlier projects. Other problems were found with permit language and reporting requirements. Ultimately, only about 300 of 3,300 filled acres were replaced. Had periodic monitoring and

---

After a Flood Disaster

Extensive flooding in the Denver, Colorado, area in 1965 resulted in a proposal by the Corps of Engineers to channelize the South Platt River through the city. The city of Littleton, located upstream from Denver, lobbied the Corps and Congress to acquire land along the river as an alternative to channelization. With funds from the Corps provided by the 1974 Water Resources Development Act, a special bond issue, and monies from state and federal agencies, Littleton purchased a 625-acre natural area that runs for 2 miles along the South Platte River. The area, which has been made into a park, contains (in addition to the river) six lakes, some mature woodlands, a mixture of grasslands and wetlands, and a significant wildlife population.

In 1983 Littleton and the South Suburban Park and Recreation District entered into a management agreement and adopted a master plan for the area. A nature center has been built, as have trails. The Arapahoe Greenway trail, which runs through the area, provides visitors with opportunities to view wildlife and to fish, hike, bicycle, and horseback.

evaluation occurred, many of these problems would have been caught before thousands of acres of wetlands were lost.

For purposes of this discussion, monitoring is a day-to-day tracking of program progress and outcomes, and evaluation is a less regular and more comprehensive overview of program implementation. Appendix I contains a more detailed discussion of monitoring and evaluation plans.

Monitoring

Essentially, monitoring is the continuous tracking of measurable program results—such as the number of permits issued, attendance at public workshops, or the costs associated with an acquisition program. Monitoring gives relatively rapid feedback (weekly or monthly) on program activities. Good monitoring identifies trends as they develop, not after the fact. Although monitoring isn't compliance auditing, it can also serve as a less threatening way of reviewing compliance progress.

Monitoring relies on an information tracking system that can be easily updated and accessed. Information may be gathered from random site visits or permit reviews. The results of monitoring can be used to modify individual projects, track repeat offenders, or assess the penetration rates of specific approaches.

Evaluation

There are two types of evaluation: process and impact. A process evaluation is qualitative and addresses goals, policies, implementation procedures, and relationships. Process evaluation is useful for understanding the context (e.g., political climate, resource constraints) in which a program operates and for assessing the effectiveness of its implementation strategies. In contrast, impact evaluation is quantitative; it is used to measure program impacts (outcomes) against specific goals and targets over specific timeframes. Impacts measured can include acreage protected or restored as well as program costs. Although impact evaluation and monitoring both measure program results, impact evaluation provides a longer-term, more in-depth analysis.

Process evaluations typically involve data gathering through structured, one-on-one interviews with program staff and other related parties, focus groups, and telephone surveys of the general public and participants (such as field staff and developers). Additional data are compiled from program records. These data are then analyzed in terms of specific evaluation questions such as these:

- How well are program goals and objectives communicated?
- What are the barriers to implementation?
- Have public awareness efforts been successful?
- What is the reaction of target audiences to the program?

Impact evaluation methodologies generally involve quantifying program outcomes over a given period (typically one year) and comparing them to a standard, such as program targets or other agreed-upon measures of impact (e.g., economic benefits and costs to state or local communities).

Cleaning Up Dump Sites

Several years ago it was estimated that as many as 60 percent of all Superfund sites were located close to wetlands. In addition, other wetlands were often used in the past as private, local, or regional dump sites. Some of these wetlands could be restored as part of Superfund cleanup efforts or as part of broader efforts to reclaim dump sites.

The city of Buffalo, New York, acquired Thrift Farm, located 3 miles south of the downtown business center of Buffalo, in 1972. The farm is bordered by railroad tracks serving heavy industry and is separated from Lake Erie by Route 5, a busy highway.

The city planned to dump nearly 2 million cubic yards of refuse from Squaw Island, the city's garbage dump, on the farm. Concerned citizens lobbied the city to preserve the farm and its many wetlands. The city responded with a comprehensive management plan for the area. The garbage from Squaw Island was put on a 40-acre section of the farm, sculpted into small hills, covered with dirt, and revegetated with wildflower and grass seed. A system of trails and boardwalks was constructed through much of the remaining area, which includes many wetlands. A nature center was constructed and is now operated by the Buffalo Science Museum.

Not all impacts are readily identified; for example, it may be necessary to identify all development projects, not just those that undertake wetlands permit applications, to measure a program's impacts. Thus, impact evaluations rely on statistical analyses using relatively small samples and may also involve some form of econometric modeling to estimate net impacts by discounting events that would have occurred without a given program.

Making Use of Findings

Monitoring and evaluation are pointless if the results aren't put to good use. Lengthy final reports are typically read in detail only by the few people who are directly affected by the findings, and often too late to take advantage of opportunities for program improvement. It is therefore helpful to issue interim reports and then to have a final presentation of the findings. An executive summary can also be prepared for circulation to a broader audience.

Measuring Progress toward the NNL Goal

Measuring progress toward the goal of no net loss is the most challenging but also the most important aspect of a monitoring and evaluation plan. Such an assessment requires baseline information on the acreage and functions of existing wetlands and a system for tracking gains and losses. Activities in three principal areas should be tracked.

Authorized Alterations

Establishing a tracking system for written authorizations of wetlands alterations is an obvious first step in accounting for wetlands losses or gains. A variety of state, federal, and local institutions maintain records on losses (see Part IV.2). For example, the U.S. Fish and Wildlife Service (FWS) now provides "Status and Trends" reports on wetlands; these reports will be produced at five-year intervals, and interim estimates will be provided as necessary. Over the next three federal fiscal years, FWS will intensify the national sampling grid so that more precise information on changes in regional wetlands acreage can be developed for the Atlantic and Gulf coasts, the Great Lakes, the Lower Mississippi River Alluvial Plain, and the Prairie Pothole Region. Also, the Corps of Engineers has installed a computer software program, the Regulatory Analysis and Management System (RAMS), in 9 of 38 regulatory offices throughout the nation. RAMS can track each step in the Section 404 permit process, account for the number of wetlands acres converted to other uses, and track the location and type of required mitigation. EPA's Wetlands Research Program has also developed software for tracking permits and mitigation and is customizing and implementing the software in conjunction with several state wetlands programs.

Although these and other state or local sources of information may be useful, they are unlikely to generate all the information needed to evaluate losses of wetlands area and function. For example, RAMS would not typically generate data on losses involving drainage or other actions occurring outside the Corps' jurisdictional authority. Nevertheless, agency records do contain valuable data, and a single state agency should be charged with responsibility for comprehensively assessing these data. Once compiled, the information can serve as a basis for evaluating the effectiveness of existing regulatory and quasi-regulatory controls over wetlands alterations.

Restoration, Creation, and Enhancement Gains

In addition to losses resulting from alterations, gains in wetlands restoration, creation, and enhancement should also be tracked. State, federal, and local governments as well as private interests are involved in many types of wetlands improvements. Permitting agencies typically require wetlands mitigation; public or private wildlife organizations create or enhance wetlands for waterfowl habitats; and park and recreation authorities often create lakes or ponds with associated wetlands. Conservation trust organizations may be active in purchasing former wetlands sites that can be restored. Finally, state and federal forest managers may be involved with various wetlands improvement activities.

Formal arrangements should be made to obtain periodic reports from the most active organizations. Simple reporting forms can be completed to describe relevant programs; follow-up visits or phone calls may be needed to assess these programs' potential contributions to the NNL goal.

A sound reporting system is needed to document as many wetlands restoration, creation, and enhancement activities as possible. Such a system can ensure that programs that can legitimately be credited toward meeting the goal of the wetlands strategy aren't overlooked. An extensive reporting system will also substantially reduce the need to depend on permit programs as the primary impetus for wetlands creation, restoration, and enhancement.

A Word About Maps and No Net Loss

Maps may be useful in supporting a regulatory or nonregulatory program, although they can be extremely costly to produce and maintain. The dynamic nature of wetlands requires constant mapping updates. Natural erosion, changes in wetlands hydrology due to climatic conditions, local or regional drainage patterns, sea-level rise, or natural cyclical patterns can substantially affect acreage totals from one mapping interval to the next. And wetlands boundaries can move, making regulatory delineation impossible.

Using maps to determine no net loss may be difficult because changes in methods over time may account for changes in acreage, thus blurring the actual gain or loss due to human activities or natural alterations. For example, changes in the scale and type of photographic image, interpretation technique, or field methods used in map production can greatly influence the total acreage of wetlands. Changes in technology or the relative levels of funding may affect a mapping project. Wetland acreage in Staten Island, New York, for instance, ''doubled'' from draft to final maps because of technological advances in mapping techniques and an improved understanding of wetlands.

Resource Assessment Studies

In addition to the monitoring of "paper" transactions, acquiring a comprehensive picture of wetlands function/area gains and losses also requires periodic assessments of the actual condition of wetlands (see Part IV.2). These assessments increase wetlands managers' understanding of the effects of natural and human changes on various types of wetlands. Observing actual changes to the resource and documenting their likely causes are crucial tasks in the process of implementing the overarching goal of no net loss.

Resource assessment studies can be undertaken statewide or within selected areas to form an overall picture of changes in wetlands over a specific period. Although some indicators of wetlands function can be determined with remote-sensing techniques, direct observation is also useful. Obvious or subtle shifts in function may be indicated by changes in plant species composition; abundance of animal species; organic matter and sediment accretion; nutrient and chemical characteristics of wetlands waters; and other factors. EPA has begun implementing a nationwide Environmental Monitoring and Assessment Program (EMAP) that will monitor exactly these kinds of changes over four-year intervals in all wetlands types.

Accounting Systems

Without question, accurately measuring the implementation of a policy of no net loss of both acreage and function is beyond the scientific community's current capabilities. However, information gained from tracking efforts can help paint a useful picture of progress toward the goal of no net loss.

Appendix D presents a hierarchical classification scheme—in essence, a simplistic but useful "shell"—for recording wetlands losses and gains. Although its categories won't apply to all states, it gives an idea of how to develop a useful framework, geared to a state's unique situation, for tracking acreage/function changes over time.

Wetlands managers should consider the possibility of developing both tracking and accounting protocols on a regional basis, particularly if interstate wetlands management is ongoing or planned. Interstate coordination can set the stage for various cooperative efforts, including:

- shared data gathering,
- coordinated protection strategies, and
- interstate creation, restoration, and enhancement projects.

For example, the interstate Chesapeake Bay Agreement has provided an opportunity for Virginia, Maryland, and federal agencies to share the costs of mapping the distribution of submerged aquatic vegetation in the bay. Such cooperation adds value to the individual efforts of the separate partners.

Remote-sensing techniques can help quantify changes in wetlands acreage and type. Airphoto interpretation and satellite-based "change detection" techniques identify causes of losses and resource "shifts"— for instance, former emergent wetlands now classified as scrub-shrub wetlands.

PART II
Organizing a Strategy Development Process

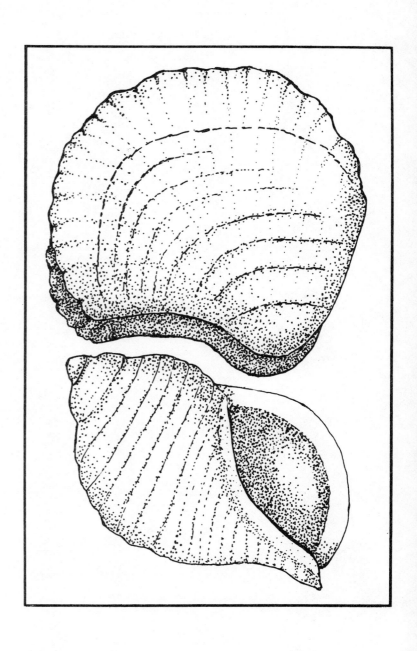

Organizing a Strategy Development Process

etlands issues are often controversial, and they affect many disparate individuals and organizations. For this reason, the process by which a comprehensive wetlands strategy is developed is particularly important. Simply put, a strategy needs broad-based support if it is to succeed.

Like other public policy issues, wetlands protection and management are complex and not conducive to quick fixes. Changes in wetlands policies affect individuals and organizations with a wide range of interests and values. As a result, building and maintaining support for a comprehensive wetlands strategy is no small task.

It is crucial that the people or groups affected by the strategy—that is, the strategy's stakeholders— be included in its development. Stakeholders not involved in strategy development are likely to influence the strategy's outcome negatively by either discrediting the process or blocking its implementation. Conflicts cannot be sidestepped; they crop up eventually and can derail even the best initiatives if they aren't acknowledged and dealt with as they emerge.

Developing a strategy for wetlands protection and management *is* a process, not a cookbook activity with guaranteed outcomes. However, thoughtfully selected processes can help produce a sound strategy and build the support necessary to ensure the strategy's implementation. Process options range from informal meetings with individual interest groups to formal mediated negotiations. The complexity of issues, number of stakeholders involved, and objectives are among the many criteria to consider in selecting the right process.

Although collaborative processes are challenging, they provide the greatest opportunities for developing a wetalnds strategy that can actually be implemented and will retain long-term support. Undeniably, devising a strategy requires considerable effort. That effort has to be made, however, if the aim is to protect and manage a state's wetlands effectively. When the right questions are addressed from the start, the rewards can be surprising.

This section of the guidebook looks at questions and considerations that surround the achievement of a basic goal: to build and maintain the support necessary to implement a statewide wetlands strategy successfully.

GETTING STARTED

Perhaps the most essential early step in any strategy development process is to identify a process

Practical proposals for change often languish because insufficient attention is paid to the process of building support for them and sustaining that support over the long haul.

The National Wetlands Policy Forum: Overcoming the Differences

At first glance, it might seem as if differences in views about wetlands protection and management can't help but stall any process of determining what to do about wetlands. Each stakeholder has significant concerns. The regulated community is concerned that the regulatory process is overly burdensome. Environmentalists are concerned that wetlands are being lost at a too-rapid rate despite regulations. Federal and state agencies point to a frustrating lack of coordination and consistency among diverse wetlands policies and regulations, which result in duplicate efforts in some areas and conflicting activities in others.

The story isn't one of inaction, however. In 1987, the National Wetlands Policy Forum—composed of three governors, a state legislator, various heads of state agencies, a town supervisor, chief executive officers of numerous environmental groups and businesses, farmers and ranchers, academic experts, and senior officials from five federal agencies—came together to address major policy questions regarding wetlands. By dealing with issues of importance to everyone involved, the Forum turned out to be a very positive example of collaboration. Participants reached agreement on over 100 recommendations that, if implemented, would result in an improvement in wetlands management from the perspective of all stakeholders.

The Forum was able to break new ground by collectively developing recommendations that addressed its members' differences. Some of those recommendations have been implemented; others are currently part of the national debate on wetlands policy; still others, such as comprehensive state wetlands planning, are the subject of this guidebook.

coordinator. The coordinator needs political support to be effective; therefore, the governor or legislature should either select or approve the coordinator to lend legitimacy and momentum to the ensuing process.

Logically, a state agency or other government entity is the best coordinator of the strategy development effort. This makes sense because the government is likely to have the requisite expertise, resources, and information and will be primarily responsible for the strategy's implementation.

Criteria for selecting an appropriate process coordinator vary, depending on the scope of the desired strategy and the structure of the state bureaucracy. The process coordinator can serve as a facilitator of the process, a substantive expert, and/or an implementor of the outcome. For example, if multiple agencies have responsibilities and jurisdiction and the strategy is to be comprehensive, the governor's policy and planning office is a good candidate to facilitate the strategy development process. Alternately, a private citizen with

Building Political Support in New York and Oregon

In 1989 the New York Freshwater Wetlands Advisory Committee recommended that New York prepare a state wetlands conservation plan. The Commissioner of the New York Department of Environmental Conservation (DEC) supported the recommendation. The DEC then sought the support of Governor Mario Cuomo's office to facilitate interagency cooperation and to heighten public interest in the plan. In response, the governor directed the DEC and the Adirondack Park Agency to prepare a state wetlands conservation plan to help achieve no net loss, a goal he had endorsed a year earlier.

In Oregon a large number of agencies are involved in wetlands issues. As a result, support for a wetlands strategy had to be generated among various agencies as well as in the governor's office. At the outset of the process, the Division of State Lands began coordinating with the governor's office and other relevant state agencies to build political support. A task force was put together, including representatives from the Division of State Lands (as coordinator) and the departments of Land Conservation and Development, Fish and Wildlife, Environmental Quality, Agriculture, and Economic Development. With the support of the governor's office, the task force developed a successful proposal to EPA to fund the planning process cooperatively.

substantive expertise (e.g., from academia) may be well-equipped to facilitate one stage of the process, particularly if it involves multiple stakeholders. If one agency has primary authority over wetlands management, that agency is likely to provide expertise and to handle implementation responsibilities.

STRATEGY DEVELOPMENT PROCESSES

Strategy development is likely to involve the use of *multiple* processes. The utility of any one process will depend on the aims of the strategy and the relevant stage of strategy development. Early on, for example, gathering information from all the stakeholders is likely to be imperative. At this juncture the process selected should be able to accommodate a large number of stakeholders—everyone with useful information about the state's wetlands. Later on, the aim may be to reach agreement on an action plan, and the process for doing so will necessarily be different from the data-gathering process. In particular, stakeholders must be willing to commit significant time to the process, and the number of stakeholders that can be accommodated will be smaller.

Although there are few rigid definitions of collaborative processes, several general types can be identified.

Informal Outreach

Using informal outreach, the process coordinator communicates with individuals or groups both to provide information and to determine the priorities and concerns of each. Informal meetings, opinion surveys, and toll-free telephone information lines might be useful. Newsletters, brochures, and other informational materials are a good means of letting the public know about wetlands and the strategy development process and for building a constituency.

Strengths

- Informational outreach is generally an inexpensive method for generating interest in and understanding of a strategy and determining the concerns of a variety of people.
- It allows for efficient assessment of stakeholders' knowledge and perceptions.
- There is no need to coordinate large groups.
- Informal outreach often can be undertaken in a short time.

Limitations

- This kind of process does not let interested stakeholders hear what is important to other stakeholders.
- It limits chances to generate options that satisfy diverse stakeholders.
- It seldom eliminates conflict, but simply delays its manifestation.

Public Meetings

Public meetings are meetings that any interested stakeholder can attend. The process coordinator can structure a public meeting for either one-way communication (with the lead agency explaining an issue and listening without comment

---

Process Coordinators: The Minnesota and Delaware Experiences

Ronald Nargang, the director of the Minnesota Department of Natural Resources Division of Water, coordinated the 18-member Minnesota Wetlands Workgroup. The director initiated the process in response to proposed legislation that affected regulations within his division. As coordinator, he brought together the stakeholders to assist the agency in developing a proposal for wetlands legislation. He also chaired the Workgroup meetings, drawing on previous dispute-resolution experience.

Andrew Manus, the chair of the 14-person Delaware Roundtable and a wetlands scientist at the University of Delaware, was selected because he was viewed as a substantive expert and was respected by all sides in the wetlands debate. The chair's role was to facilitate the Roundtable process, serve as liaison to the governor, and prepare background information to ensure that all participants had comparable knowledge of each issue.

Using Multiple Processes in Wetlands Planning

Eugene, Oregon, is developing a comprehensive wetlands plan designed to protect the most valuable wetlands resources while meeting community development needs with lower-value wetlands. The city council and planning commission contracted with the Lane Council of Governments (L-COG) to coordinate the planning process, which involved the use of several collaborative processes, including advisory committees, workshops, and informal outreach.

A technical advisory committee composed of representatives of federal and state agencies was formed to ensure that the plan was consistent with federal and state policies and to develop support for the plan at those levels. Outreach programs have included field trips, educational materials, newsletters, and citizen dialogue. In addition, an inter-departmental staff team was formed to conduct much of the technical work necessary to develop the plan. The team included representatives from L-COG and the West Eugene Department of Public Works and Department of Planning and Development.

to the public's concerns) or two-way communication (with the agency responding to comments and questions from the floor). Different formats are possible, ranging from a single large-group meeting to a large-group information session followed by small-group sessions for discussion. Public meetings may be a legal requirement in some cases.

Strengths
- These kinds of meetings allow any stakeholder to share views publicly and ask questions in some cases.
- They let stakeholders hear one another react to different issues and proposals.
- They require a relatively modest investment of resources.

Limitations
- Public meetings offer limited opportunities to discuss areas of agreement and disagreement.
- They do not promote collaboration.
- They may allow conflict to surface but don't provide a forum in which to address conflict.
- Public meetings may promote grandstanding and posturing; vocal parties may dominate meetings.

Workshops

In a workshop, representatives of various stakeholders discuss issues related to one or more stages of the strategy. Unlike public meetings, participation in workshops may be by invitation only. Workshops are usually designed to provide the opportunity for stakeholders to understand one another's concerns and develop new options. Topics for

discussion are clearly defined in advance; however, agreement on options is usually not expected.

Strengths
- Workshops let diverse stakeholders focus on specific issues of interest.
- They foster increased public understanding.
- They encourage interactive discussions and new ideas.
- They enable some disputes to be resolved or narrowed.

Limitations
- The process coordinator needs time to identify participants, plan an agenda, and ensure that workshop objectives can be achieved.
- Participation may be limited, thereby increasing chances that important perspectives will be excluded.
- All disputes are unlikely to be resolved; conflicts may emerge in other forums.

Advisory Committees

An advisory committee involves representatives of diverse stakeholders meeting to provide guidance and feedback for overall strategy development or for one or more of its components. Individual members meet periodically with the coordinator, who must carefully select members and clearly articulate the committee's responsibilities.

Strengths
- Advisory committees allow diverse stakeholders to help guide strategy development and explore difficult issues.

Building a Constituency

Effectively building a constituency—including elected officials, community leaders, stakeholders, and the general public—for a strategy development process entails a combination of awareness, education, and involvement.

Raising *awareness* is a vital first step. The public can be reached through broadcast and print media, public meetings, and outreach to civic groups and schools. The coordinator must communicate clearly with the public about the strategy development process. It is better to be candid and tell people something they don't want to hear than to be perceived later as having misled them.

An extension of awareness, *education* of the public about wetlands and the strategy development process can directly support and strengthen that process. Educational efforts often rely on the media, public meetings, and outreach; in addition, field trips, newsletters, and workshops can increase the public's understanding. As educational activities are undertaken, the coordinator should work to develop a better understanding of the public's interests and concerns about wetlands. Listening is at least as important as informing.

Finally, *involving the public directly* in the strategy development process is crucial. Direct involvement creates public "ownership" in the strategy. The coordinator must clearly articulate how stakeholders can become involved and how their involvement will benefit the process.

- They encourage interactive discussions.
- They provide opportunities for developing recommendations on some issues.

Limitations
- Committees can be time consuming and resource intensive.
- The process coordinator needs time to identify participants and ensure that an advisory committee is used appropriately.
- It may be difficult to select a good range of stakeholders but keep the committee small enough to foster interactive dialogue.
- Committee members may not adequately represent their constituents, particularly if they fail to report back.
- All issues may not be resolved; remaining conflicts will probably be waged in another forum.

Formal Negotiations

Using formal negotiations, stakeholders' representatives meet to develop agreements on the strategy or some of its stages. It is crucial that all stakeholders be represented in a negotiation process. A mediator can provide additional assistance by helping all sides determine the feasibility of negotiations, appropriate representation, and scope of the issues and by facilitating the actual negotiations.

Strengths
- Formal negotiations allow diverse stakeholders to explore ways of achieving joint gains—options that help one or more stakeholders without harming any others.
- Negotiations can be effective in breaking

Some stakeholders may incur political risks by participating in a collaborative process. Their constituencies may frown upon collaboration or may feel bound to stick with publicly stated positions. In such cases, workshops or an advisory committee may still be appropriate because they allow for discussion without necessitating formal agreement.

Using Workshops to Involve the Public

In developing the West Eugene Wetlands Plan, the Lane Council of Governments conducted a series of nine public workshops over the course of three years. The purpose of the workshops was to educate the general public about wetlands and the planning process and to allow individuals to offer feedback on the plan. Each workshop focused on a different aspect of the plan. Topics included a general discussion of wetlands, the nature of the area's wetlands, establishing goals for managing those wetlands, generating alternatives, and evaluating these alternatives. Stakeholders were able to provide valuable input and to increase their understanding of the wetlands resource and the planning process. L-COG prepared summaries of each workshop and distributed them to the county planning commission, county commissioners, city council, state and federal agencies, and the public.

Negotiating Agreements:
The Minnesota and Delaware Experiences

The Minnesota Wetlands Workgroup

In 1989 the Minnesota Department of Natural Resources established the Minnesota Wetlands Workgroup to develop legislation to improve wetlands management and protection. The Workgroup was composed of 18 members representing stakeholders from agriculture, development, forestry, hunters, local government, environmental groups, and three state agencies. The director of the DNR's Division of Waters coordinated the process, serving as chair of the Workgroup.

The Workgroup's initial meetings centered on developing a common information base. The Workgroup heard from experts on a range of issues affecting wetlands management. It then spent 14 months developing draft legislation, using a bill drafted by the DNR as a starting point. The Workgroup was able to reach consensus on all but three issues. It forwarded the draft bill to the legislature, which resolved the remaining issues. The Workgroup continued to meet, educating the public about the bill through panel discussions, newsletters, and press releases. The bill was signed into law in 1990.

The Delaware Roundtable

In May 1988, Delaware Governor Michael Castle issued Executive Order 56, establishing the Freshwater Wetlands Roundtable. He charged it with three tasks: developing a workable definition of freshwater wetlands; recommending a freshwater wetlands conservation program for privately held lands; and reporting on the budgetary ramifications of such a program and recommending a timetable for implementation. The governor also encouraged the Roundtable to establish a goal of stabilizing the freshwater wetlands acreage.

The governor appointed the Roundtable members, selecting representatives from various stakeholder groups: development interests, environmental groups, local government, academia, forestry, and agriculture. The Roundtable involved two phases, a fact-finding process and an effort to build consensus on recommendations. The Roundtable organized itself into representative working groups to address specific issues, including wetlands definition; Section 404; permissible and prohibited uses; mitigation, restoration, and creation; acquisition; and education. Each working group drafted a background paper and reported its findings to the Roundtable, which then reached consensus on recommendations generated by the reports. The Roundtable released a consensus report in June 1989, outlining recommendations and implementation guidelines for each of the categories discussed.

Joint Fact-Finding in the Delaware Roundtable

The Delaware Freshwater Wetlands Roundtable, composed of representatives of development interests, environmental groups, local government, academia, forestry, and agriculture, began its deliberations by conducting a joint fact-finding process. Recognizing the need to develop a shared information base from which to develop recommendations, the Roundtable held meetings over a four-month period to solicit input from federal and state regulatory agencies, private consultants, and the public. The Roundtable reviewed reports and conducted field trips to wetlands sites during the fact-finding process.

The Delaware Roundtable also used a second, more traditional fact-finding process. During its deliberations the Roundtable identified an information gap related to the economics of wetlands conversion for agriculture. Roundtable members developed a specific research task and jointly agreed on a person to conduct the research. After the study was completed, the Roundtable used the results of the analysis in developing its recommendations.

political stalemates and garnering broad support.

- Stakeholders will have an investment in the outcome, which will facilitate implementation.

Limitations
- Formal negotiations can be time consuming and resource intensive.
- A strong preliminary effort must be made to ensure that there are sufficient incentives to reach agreement, that the process is structured to achieve its objectives, and that the appropriate people are involved.
- Members of a committee may not adequately represent their constituents, particularly if they fail to report back.
- Use of a mediator increases the cost.

Joint Fact-Finding

This process is designed to collect and analyze data using a procedure acceptable to all stakeholders, in cases where the data either do not exist or are in dispute. Joint fact-finding can be the outgrowth of a specific recommendation that data be collected or part of a larger process, such as negotiation.

Strengths
- Stakeholders can overcome barriers to agreement related to data.
- Data-collection resources are focused on areas that everyone agrees are most critical.

- Significant resources aren't wasted on studies subsequently regarded as irrelevant or inadequate.

Limitations
- Fact-finding can be time consuming and difficult.
- Resources may not be available to undertake all data collection efforts.

ASKING THE KEY QUESTIONS

Determining the best way to involve stakeholders in developing a viable wetlands strategy is challenging because each state faces a unique situation; there's no blueprint or guaranteed formula. A certain amount of improvisation is not only necessary but desirable. Moreover, as noted earlier, strategy development is likely to benefit from the use of multiple processes, each designed to solicit an appropriate level of stakeholder involvement and support for a particular component.

To choose the right process(es), the coordinator needs to address several important questions.

What decisions have to be made?

Developing a strategy involves numerous decisions on such matters as the scope of the strategy; how much data should be collected; how the regulatory program should be applied; what role mitigation should play; how educational tools should be used; how limited funding should be allocated; and who should direct implementation. These and other decision points should be identified and then

As the technical complexity of the issues increases, the ability of some stakeholders to participate effectively decreases. Joint fact-finding or providing funds to stakeholders who cannot afford a technical expert can mitigate this problem.

The scope of the decisions made at each stage of the strategy development process will affect how subsequent questions are answered and which stakeholders should be involved.

Using Advisory Committees

In 1988 the Commissioner of the New York Department of Environmental Conservation (DEC) appointed the Freshwater Wetlands Advisory Committee, charged with developing recommendations on how to improve DEC's wetlands regulatory program. The committee, made up of eight members representing local government, development interests, environmentalists, state government, and academia, recommended that the state prepare a statewide comprehensive wetlands plan. The DEC commissioner supported the recommendation, and the governor endorsed it in 1990 when he directed the DEC to prepare a plan to help achieve no net loss.

As part of the Virginia Wetlands Roundtable, an advisory committee was formed to solicit technical guidance from stakeholders who were not members of the Roundtable. This so-called technical resource group was composed of staff from state agencies and local governments. The group provided technical assistance to Roundtable members throughout their deliberations.

linked to specific components of the strategy development process.

Decision makers will need to address several issues regarding each decision point. For example, deciding on data collection methods will probably entail asking these questions: What data currently exist? What additional data are needed? How will the data be used? What data are of highest priority? Who should collect the data? How should the effort be funded?

What's the desired outcome?

The process coordinator needs to think through the issue of what's most desirable: consensus on an entire strategy, policy ideas for a few selected issues, greater communication among stakeholders, information gathering, or something else. Also, the willingness of stakeholders to participate will naturally influence the decision-making process.

Who are the stakeholders?

A stakeholder is any agency, organization, group, or individual who will be affected by wetlands policy decisions or who has decision-making authority, relevant information, or the ability to assist or complicate the implementation of a strategy. If any stakeholders are left out of the process or choose not to participate, the outcome is almost certain to be less than positive. If, for example, agricultural interests are not included, discussions of issues related to cropped wetlands will be severely hampered. Not only will the perspectives and interests of agricultural groups be absent, but these groups may attempt, later on, to block implementation of any recommendations that they feel will affect them adversely.

Because stakeholders often are organizations, not individuals, the process coordinator needs to make sure that the people participating in a collaborative process are genuinely backed by the organizations they represent. Individuals can be authorized in advance to speak for and commit their organizations or can obtain ratification of tentative agreements by their organizations. In any case, organizational constituencies need to be kept informed throughout the process.

The formation of coalitions may further complicate decision making; nonetheless, coalitions can be very helpful when the number of stakeholders exceeds 30. As group size increases, the effectiveness of a collaborative process decreases. Coalitions allow a manageable number of stakeholders to "sit at the table." However, the challenges of maintaining good communications with constituencies increase with coalitions.

Developing a wetlands strategy is a political undertaking; nevertheless, the selection of participants needs to be evenhanded. All stakeholders must be represented, and individual representatives should be credible to their constituents and able to represent their interests effectively. An agreement is unlikely to be acceptable to constituents who believe they've been unrepresented or underrepresented by those at the table.

What are the relevant issues?

Issues of concern will vary among stakeholders. Some stakeholders may believe, for example, that current information is adequate for developing a strategy; others may think that extensive new data are needed. Still others may feel that additional data are necessary but can be gathered later. Differing views are likely on many other questions that will be encountered in strategy development.

There's no substitute for talking with people to identify the most essential issues. Asking for comments on a preliminary set of issues almost always produces useful input.

How controversial are the issues?

Answers to this question are necessarily subjective; however, the level and type of controversy clearly affects the type of process selected. Common sense and good judgment are, of course, the best guides.

As a general rule, the more controversial the issues, the more formal the process necessary to deal with them. Structured negotiation processes help stakeholders address their differences constructively. Highly controversial issues probably require the use of an outside mediator. (A less structured process, such as a workshop, will not give stakeholders the time needed to work through difficult issues; as a result, controversy will either be ignored or insufficiently addressed.)

In some cases the issues may be so controversial that even formal negotiations will not yield success; those issues will have to be resolved in an even more formal venue (e.g., the state legislature, governor's office, Congress, courts). If one or more stakeholders believe in advance that an issue is so controversial that it can't or shouldn't be resolved through dialogue, a process can be developed to concentrate on other issues while explicitly acknowledging the exclusion of the most controversial issue and outlining how it will be addressed.

Questions for Assessing the Appropriate Process

Different processes for involving stakeholders in strategy development are appropriate under different circumstances. What process is appropriate can best be assessed by conducting interviews with individuals and groups affected by or interested in wetlands management and protection. In some cases, the strategy coordinator can conduct such interviews. If the coordinator is not fully trusted by some stakeholders, however, a neutral mediator may need to be used to ensure that all stakeholders candidly answer the interview questions.

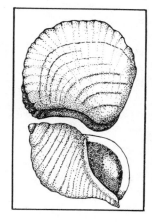

Providing Background on the Assessment Process

Every assessment interview should begin with a clear explanation of both the strategy and the assessment process. A stakeholder may not be able to answer some of the assessment questions accurately unless those questions are posed in the appropriate context. The assessment process also provides an important opportunity to increase stakeholder awareness and understanding of strategy development. For these reasons, the coordinator (or neutral mediator) should provide as well as solicit information. The proposed scope of the strategy and its overall goal, applicable time lines, and role of the coordinator should all be explained and discussed.

Eliciting Viewpoints

During the assessment interviews, the coordinator or neutral mediator should discuss the involvement and perspective of each individual or entity regarding wetlands management and protection and the strategy development process. Interview questions might address these concerns:

- the interviewee's experience with wetlands management and protection;
- major perceived strengths and weaknesses of the current approach to wetlands management and protection;
- issues and problems regarding development of an effective and comprehensive statewide wetlands strategy;
- expectations for the strategy;
- how the interviewee would like to be involved in developing the strategy (this may vary according to the stage in the strategy development process);
- whether agreement among various interests is possible and how it could be gained; and
- others who should be interviewed about the strategy (i.e., other groups or people with views or information about wetlands that should be included in the assessment process).

Sharing Information on the Mechanics of a Collaborative Process

The coordinator or neutral mediator should assess stakeholders' views on the utility of using various processes to develop a wetlands strategy. Questions asked during the assessment might thus address the interviewee's views on:

- who needs to be involved in the strategy-development process;
- who could best represent the interviewee's interests in the process (if there is a need to create a group of manageable size);
- any resource barriers to participation; and
- the logical alternatives for resolving differences over wetlands management and protection through the development of a strategy.

Following Through

At the conclusion of each assessment interview, the coordinator or neutral mediator should clearly articulate the next steps. At a minimum, each individual or entity interviewed should be informed about process-related decisions once they are made, whether or not each interviewee will be asked to participate directly.

It may be useful to prepare a brief report summarizing the assessment interviews and any conclusions reached. The report should not, however, include confidential information shared during the interviews, nor should it attribute statements to specific individuals. An assessment report will help educate stakeholders about one another's perceptions and priorities, thereby identifying specific opportunities and challenges to be dealt with during strategy development.

Ultimately, there is no substitute for judgment in selecting a collaborative strategy-building process. That said, each process type does have characteristics (both strengths and weaknesses) that suggest when it should be used. When certain factors *aren't* present, it may be appropriate either to choose a less resource-intensive type or to find ways to alter the situation or compensate for it.

What follows is a set of general guidelines for selecting an appropriate process. These "if-then" lists suggest the use of particular processes for particular situations. Further guidance can be obtained by reviewing the discussion under "Asking the Key Questions."

Informal Outreach may be appropriate when:
- the objective is providing or soliciting information
- issues are well understood
- issues are not complex
- not all stakeholders are known or actively involved in the issues
- stakeholders trust the process coordinator
- stakeholders are unlikely to block decisions seen as adverse
- level of controversy is low
- implementation does not need to be coordinated

Public Meetings may be appropriate when:
- the objective is providing or soliciting information
- issues are not complex
- stakeholders are numerous and not easily represented by coalitions
- stakeholders trust the process coordinator
- Stakeholders are unlikely to block decisions seen as adverse
- level of controversy is low
- implementation does not need to be coordinated
- law requires public meetings or hearings

Workshops may be appropriate when:
- the objective is information or guidance from stakeholders
- issues are viewed differently by stakeholders
- issues are relatively important to stakeholders
- stakeholders have relevant information
- large number of stakeholders are present
- stakeholders are unlikely to block decisions seen as adverse
- implementation does not need to be coordinated

Right Process

Advisory Committees may be appropriate when:
- the objective is guidance from stakeholders
- issues are viewed differently by stakeholders
- issues are complex
- issues are important to stakeholders
- stakeholders have relevant information
- stakeholders are numerous but have identifiable coalitions
- stakeholders are willing to participate
- implementation may require coordination

Formal Negotiations may be appropriate when:
- reaching agreement is the objective
- issues are viewed differently by stakeholders
- issues are complex
- issues are very important to stakeholders
- high level of controversy exists
- stakeholders have relevant information
- stakeholders are numerous but have identifiable coalitions
- all stakeholders can gain from change in status quo
- all stakeholders are willing to participate
- stakeholders will block decisions seen as adverse
- stakeholders do not trust the process coordinator
- resources are available to fund process and participants
- implementation requires coordination

Joint Fact-Finding may be appropriate when:
- the objective is stakeholder concurrence on data collection method
- key information is missing
- stakeholders may have relevant information
- issues are complex
- issues are very important to stakeholders
- controversy exists over validity of existing data and/or proposed methodologies for data collection
- all stakeholders are willing to participate (or accept results)
- resources are available to conduct fact-finding

Using a Facilitator/Mediator may be appropriate when:
- issues are numerous and complex
- stakeholders are numerous
- issues are contentious
- personality conflicts are present
- funds are available

Even when some topics will be resolved in another forum, informal processes are valuable tools. For example, if stakeholders are unwilling to discuss wetlands regulation, they still might be willing jointly to explore wetlands inventory needs, economic incentives for wetlands protection, or wetlands acquisition or restoration programs.

How important are the issues to stakeholders?

Each stakeholder's investment in a strategy development process will depend on the importance the stakeholder attaches to the issues and the confidence that the stakeholder has that its interests will be genuinely satisfied. If, for example, one group is interested primarily in changing a regulatory program, it may not want to participate in a dialogue focused solely on nonregulatory programs. As another example, a stakeholder concerned about the effects of wetlands loss on a localized endangered species may hesitate to commit time to a dialogue for developing a comprehensive statewide strategy, but may be willing to be represented by another group with similar but broader interests.

Can everybody gain by changing the status quo?

If affected stakeholders have nothing to gain from change, they are unlikely to be willing to engage in a process, particularly a formal one, designed to "improve" the current situation. If, however, a stakeholder satisfied with the status quo realizes that change is inevitable, this stakeholder may feel compelled to participate in order to limit the extent of change or delay its implementation. The result may be a lengthy process that frustrates everyone.

The process coordinator thus needs to consider the possibility that certain stakeholders may use a particular process to stall. If this is likely, a shorter-term, lower-investment process (such as a public meeting or workshop) may be more suitable.

What are the potential risks of dialogue?

If one or more stakeholders believe they can satisfy their interests more effectively outside the strategy development process (e.g., by lobbying the state legislature), the utility of any process will decline significantly. For example, if a state legislature appears on the verge of passing a wetlands regulatory program that one or more stakeholders support, those parties are not likely to participate in a dialogue focused on designing a regulatory program.

Who is responsible for implementation?

If a collaborative process is used, the implementing authorities should either be at the table or willing to implement the recommendations that emerge. In many states, multiple agencies have jurisdiction over wetlands. Thus, even if one agency is the process coordinator, all implementing agencies should be represented. (It often takes only one agency to bring to a halt the implementation of recommendations arrived at through a process in which that agency didn't participate.)

Legislative bodies are difficult, if not impossible, to represent in a strategy-building process. However, the legislature may provide the necessary resources for implementation or be asked to implement changes in law. The legislature also may set a deadline to prompt stakeholders to collaborate efficiently. Legislatures are therefore an important source of support for a wetlands strategy.

Although no individual can speak for the entire legislature, key members such as committee chairs may sometimes participate. Alternatively, key legislative staff can attend workshops or negotiations as observers and provide a useful perspective and communications link with legislative committees. Participants need to remember, however, that any legislative recommendations resulting from the collaboration will be subject to the political process.

The governor is likely to be another crucial implementor; therefore, obtaining his or her support at the outset of the process is vital. If an agency decides not to involve the governor's office directly, it needs to obtain that office's support and input during the strategy development.

What resources are available?

Collaborative processes can be expensive and time consuming. Public-interest groups are often given resources to allow them to participate and, when appropriate, to enable them to hire technical experts. If funds for such actions aren't available, a different process must be selected or resources raised by one or more of the other stakeholders.

Would a mediator be useful?

A facilitator or mediator can provide valuable assistance, particularly if the issues are complex or divisive or if many stakeholders are involved. A mediator may be helpful in the following areas: determining whether a negotiation process is feasible; determining how to conduct a strategy development process; ensuring that all affected stake-

---

If the effectiveness of the current regulatory program is in dispute, a joint fact-finding process to evaluate the program independently might be appropriate as options are being generated and addressed.

Even if everybody has something to gain, the coordinator needs to assess each stakeholder's incentives for participating in a given process and to think through what can be done to increase those incentives.

Using a Mediator

The Virginia Nontidal Wetlands Roundtable was established in 1989 to develop recommendations to improve nontidal wetlands management. The multi-interest group was convened and facilitated by neutral mediators from the Institute for Environmental Negotiation (IEN) who facilitated the meetings and helped establish meeting agendas. The Roundtable implemented the mediators' suggestions that:

- a technical resource group, composed of staff from state agencies and local governments, be organized to provide technical assistance and input into the process, and
- representatives of applicable federal agencies be invited to observe the meetings and provide input as necessary.

holders are represented; helping stakeholders set an agenda; helping stakeholders form coalitions when appropriate; assisting stakeholders in focusing on issues central to implementation; facilitating communications and keeping the process moving; and recording agreements.

The use of a mediator will increase the initial cost of the process, but in many cases the final cost is reduced because the process is shortened and/or the outcome strengthened.

MANAGING A COLLABORATIVE PROCESS

A collaborative process for wetlands strategy development is shaped by specific circumstances and local features. However, certain steps are relevant to most processes and need to be undertaken after a process coordinator has been selected. A dispute resolution professional can be very helpful to the coordinator as a process consultant, providing a more complete understanding of how to manage a collaborative process.

Step 1:
Lay the Groundwork

Before launching into a strategy development process, the process coordinator must be clear about the precise mandate from the governor, legislature, state agency, or other authority. Established goals as well as time and resource constraints must be acknowledged at the outset, as they affect everything else that happens.

Initially the process coordinator should:
- gather information about the mandates and interests of all stakeholders;

- develop a workplan that is responsive to any mandated constraints that cannot be removed, even if they reduce the options available to the coordinator at the outset;
- conduct outreach activities before requesting participation in more time-intensive tasks to ensure that stakeholders appreciate the intent of the strategy development process and what they can achieve by participating; and
- begin working with the media.

Step 2:
Select Participants

The selection of participants clearly depends to some degree on the choice of process: the two decision points are interconnected. In general, participants should include representatives of groups that are likely to be affected by the outcome, that bring information or resources to the process, and that have the power to block implementation or will play a role in it.

Selecting participants can entail:
- meeting directly with representatives of all stakeholders;
- using interviews and background materials to research the issues from all perspectives;
- assisting potential participants in understanding incentives and disincentives for participation; and
- helping stakeholders with similar interests form coalitions, when necessary.

In some cases incentives for participation will need to be offered. It is important, for example, to spell out clearly how a potential participant's views will be incorporated into the strategy. Resources to cover participant time and/or travel also may occasionally be required.

Firm deadlines, even artificially imposed ones, increase the likelihood that a strategy development process will be successful.

Stakeholders in wetlands planning may include representatives of the agricultural community, developers, businesses, private landowners, environmentalists, hunting and fishing groups, government agencies, local planners, and others affected by wetlands issues.

Step 3:
Develop Objectives

Although objectives may be proposed by the coordinator before the process is initiated, at a minimum stakeholders need to be aware of the objectives and their implications so they can decide, on the basis of realistic information, whether they want to participate. Ideally, the process coordinator will develop the objectives in consultation with stakeholders.

For example, a governor may mandate the preparation of a wetlands strategy with an overall goal of no net loss. The process coordinator may determine that the first step will be to establish interim goals. Next, the coordinator has to design a process to develop consensus on those interim targets.

If participants have different objectives, the process can falter. For instance, if one stakeholder assumes that the objective is to develop a joint research agenda but the process coordinator's objective is simply to air views about research needs, the stakeholder is likely to become frustrated. Clarity and agreement on objectives are essential.

To develop such agreement, the process coordinator should:

- draft an objective that encompasses as many of the interests of the various stakeholders as possible, making it worthwhile for them to participate;
- facilitate agreement by working with stakeholders to revise the objective as needed; and
- link future activities and discussions to the group's agreed-upon objective.

Step 4:
Establish Protocols

When multiple stakeholders are involved, protocols or ground rules are needed. Protocols should cover decision making, participation, and timelines. Because most of these rules will be pertinent at some point, the process leader needs to propose them at the outset. If they are discussed openly, fewer problems will arise later on.

To improve the utility of protocols, the process coordinator should encourage participants to agree to use them, refine them, and anticipate problems that may arise.

Step 5:
Delineate the Issues

Because stakeholders bring different priorities to the table, in some cases identifying the issues may itself be the objective of one stage of the strategy-building process. If so, the process leader's task is to provide a forum for all participants to present the issues they feel are important. The coordinator should make it clear how the information generated will be used.

When the objective is to develop specific recommendations, all stakeholders must be allowed to express their interests at the outset. The most successful processes usually involve consultation and agreement on the scope of the issues to be discussed.

To assist in the clear delineation of issues, the process coordinator can:

- ask each stakeholder to state his or her high-priority concerns;
- clearly articulate any issues that aren't open

Generic Protocols

Numerous issues should be included in protocols developed for any collaborative process, including:

- *Decision making*

How will the group make decisions? (If consensus, what does this mean?)

How can caucuses be utilized?

How will subcommittees make decisions?

How can the group be dissolved?

- *Participation*

Who can participate (both the full group and subcommittees)?

How can members of coalitions participate?

How can additional participants be added?

How can members withdraw?

How can resource people be utilized?

What are the safeguards for participation (e.g., confidentiality, talking to the press, attendance, preparation of meeting summaries)?

Are the meetings open to the public?

- *Schedule*

How often will the group meet?

What deadlines exist?

- *Facilitation and recordkeeping*

What is the role of the facilitator?

What information will become part of the written record?

Who will prepare meeting summaries and reports?

How will agreements be recorded?

In addition, every process will have unique characteristics that may suggest additional protocols.

---

to negotiation and allow stakeholders to identify issues that, by being included or excluded, will affect their decision to participate;

- encourage the group to discuss the list of issues and jointly consider how to address them (e.g., gathering additional data, establishing subcommittees, grouping issues); and
- provide opportunities for stakeholders to develop a common understanding of the issues through educational programs.

Step 6:
Build Effective Support

The success of any collaborative process depends on the interaction of the participants. Each stakeholder needs to emerge from a collaborative process with a better outcome than that person or organization is likely to gain in another forum. Although negotiations among diverse stakeholders are challenging, certain principles can assist stakeholders in reaching solid agreements (see "Getting to Yes" box).

The process coordinator can help build support by:

- creating an atmosphere of give-and-take among the stakeholders by helping participants understand the multiple needs that an outcome must satisfy;
- identifying high-priority actions for each stakeholder and narrowing disagreements to only the most important issues; and
- helping stakeholders meet one another's needs by fostering creativity in developing options.

Step 7:
Develop an Agreement

The types of agreements reached can vary dramatically, depending on the objectives of the process, the issues confronted, and the mode of implementation. One fact is clear, though: an agreement that can't be implemented is useless. By the same token, if agreements that solve problems for all sides are developed, successful implementation is much more likely to happen.

A consensus-building process can be successful even though agreement isn't reached on all issues. Conversely, even a written agreement doesn't ensure a successful process. The ultimate measure of success is how fully an agreement is *implemented* and the extent to which future conflicts are avoided or minimized.

In some cases an agreement that achieves the objectives of the process may not be forthcoming. If no time constraints are defined, it becomes important to identify the point at which a group has accomplished as much as it can even though the initial objective hasn't been accomplished. This is difficult because such factors as deadlines, funds, and organizational priorities may cause some stakeholders and/or the process coordinator to withdraw. Nonetheless, participants should consider the role they can play as a group in implementing the

wetlands strategy even if agreement isn't reached or isn't a goal.

When consensus isn't reached, it is also helpful if the decision makers articulate the rationale for their decisions and highlight how various views were incorporated. This enables everyone to see how necessary trade-offs occurred and reduces the sense that decisions were made behind closed doors.

The process coordinator can foster agreement by:

- developing a list of agreement points or agreements in principle to show progress and create momentum for additional agreement;
- using a mediator or other go-between to conduct private discussions with stakeholders who are unable to agree; and
- deciding to put some decisions aside to a later date or another forum if implementation of other agreements can proceed without them.

Using a Process During Implementation

Following the Delaware Freshwater Wetlands Roundtable's report on implementation guidelines for the consensus recommendations it developed in 1989, the Delaware Department of Natural Resources and Environmental Control (DNREC) drafted legislation incorporating the Roundtable's recommendations. In August 1990, DNREC established four committees to review the draft document.

- A federal committee reviewed the draft for consistency and accuracy related to assumption of the regulatory program.
- An interagency committee reviewed the draft to ensure that all state agencies charged with implementation had the authority, understanding, and commitment necessary to implement the recommendations successfully.
- A committee of stakeholders representing agriculture, forestry, development, environmental groups, and local government reviewed the draft to ensure that it was mutually acceptable.
- An agricultural advisory committee composed of farmers, farm organizations, forestry interests, and government agencies reviewed the draft to ensure that the bill's agricultural provisions addressed farmers' concerns.

In June 1991 a bill was introduced in the Delaware Senate. Roundtable members jointly issued an op-ed in the statewide newspaper reiterating their support for the legislation.

Step 8:

Implement Outcomes and Maintain Support

Implementing a broad-based strategy is undeniably difficult. It is important, therefore, to consider implementation issues all the way through—at the outset, in any negotiations, and during development of an agreement. Moreover, participants should consider who will be responsible for implementing a particular provision of an agreement; how much latitude will be left to the implementor; how funding will be obtained; how changes in information will be handled; and how implementation will be evaluated.

A number of different agencies and organizations are likely to have implementation authority or responsibility. Successful implementation becomes more likely when:

- stakeholders reconvene if disputes arise;
- all groups that can affect implementation participate from the beginning;
- constituencies are kept informed;
- decisions are based on good information and analysis; and
- regular reports are generated during the process.

A successful wetlands strategy will require support from stakeholders over the long haul. Long-term support requires ongoing participation (e.g., through advisory committees or annual meetings) and opportunities to revise plans as circumstances and information change.

PART III

Mechanisms for Protecting and Managing Wetlands

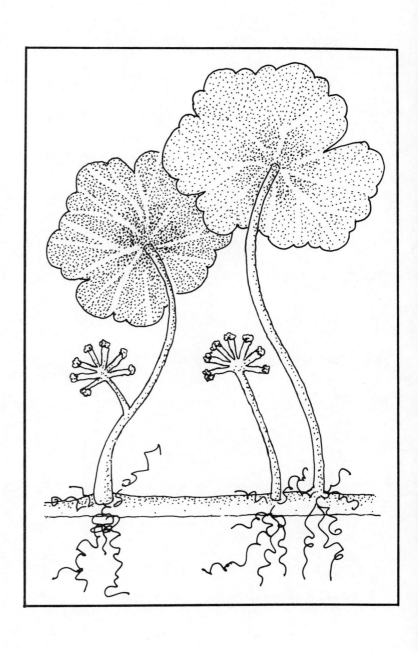

Introduction

Although the safeguarding of almost any natural resource demands considerable energy and commitment, the protection and management of wetlands pose certain unique challenges. To start with, information about the resource is often limited. Additionally, issues of both land and water use are involved. Wetlands are located predominantly on private property, and they often cross jurisdictional boundaries. Finally, very few protection mechanisms are designed specifically for wetlands.

Effective wetlands strategies take into account these particular challenges. They also make the most of any and all available resources by tapping the staff and budgets of multiple agencies and organizations concerned with wetlands, land use, and water issues. To devise sound strategies, wetlands managers must thus look beyond state-level programs and test the potential of federal, local, and private programs to further their wetlands-related goals and objectives. What most state strategies require is a creative and coordinated combination of wetlands-specific and broad natural-resources protection mechanisms.

Parts III.2 through III.5 provide more detailed information on the various mechanisms discussed in this section.

Mechanisms for protecting and managing wetlands can be grouped into eight general categories: acquisition; regulation; planning; restoration, creation, and management; incentives and disincentives; technical assistance, education, and outreach; research; and cross-cutting tools (coordination and landscape approaches).

Distinctions among these categories are not absolute; some mechanisms easily fit in more than one category. Moreover, some are better suited than others to address specific wetlands problems or losses. And, even when a mechanism is appropriate, a state's political or economic situation may preclude or limit its use. Mechanisms should be considered in relation to one another and in the context of relevant social, political, and economic factors.

ACQUISITION

Both public and private entities can protect wetlands by acquiring them. Protection can be achieved through a purchase of all or some property rights or through techniques such as donations or leases. (See the discussion of acquisition techniques in Part III.5.)

Ownership of land is often analogized to ownership of a ''bundle of rights'' including, for example, the right to control access to the land, develop property,

It is easy to associate a public or private entity with just one or two protection mechanisms— for example, the federal government with Section 404, states with planning tools, local government with zoning, and the private sector with acquisition. But don't make that mistake! The entire range of mechanisms should be considered for each group.

hunt on the land, and so forth. When one entity owns all the rights associated with a parcel, that entity owns the land ''in fee simple''; however, these rights can be owned separately, in which case the owner is said to own a ''less-than-fee'' interest.

Strengths

- can ensure permanent protection and management of the site
- can be tailored to specific needs of the acquiring organization and landowners by using complete or "fee-simple" acquisition, which involves acquiring full ownership of the land and all the rights thereof, or partial acquisition, which involves acquiring only some of the rights (as in a conservation easement)
- can offer numerous opportunities to coordinate with other organizations and mechanisms such as tax incentives, planning, and research
- can avoid "takings" claims and political controversies

Challenges

- may require extensive resources for purchasing and managing lands
- may require careful management, monitoring, and enforcement, as conditions and ownership (especially in cases of partial acquisition) may change over time
- may be difficult to acquire the area needing protection—the landowner may be unwilling to sell

- does not guarantee protection; the acquiring organization may not have the resources to manage the site properly
- cannot control activities outside the property's boundary; owning the wetland will not necessarily protect it from harmful off-site impacts such as the diversion or contamination of its water supply
- may take property from the local tax base, which could be met with resistance

Key Opportunities

Federal: Land and Water Conservation Fund
North American Wetlands Conservation Act
Pittman-Robertson and Dingell-Johnson Acts
State: natural area acquisition programs
parks and recreation programs
Local: parks and open-space programs
Private: land trusts

At the national level, the National Audubon Society has acquired approximately 500,000 acres of wetlands to preserve bird habitats. In 1983 The Nature Conservancy began a $55 million National Wetlands Conservation Project, which has protected several hundred thousand acres of wetlands around the country. Hunting and fishing groups also provide leadership in wetlands acquisition and protection as well as education of the public about wetlands values. Ducks Unlimited, for example, has acquired more than 3 million acres of wetlands in the United States and Canada and has spent major sums on

---

Local Land Trusts

A local land trust can be defined as ''a private, nonprofit organization devoted to the preservation of locally significant parcels of natural areas and open space. The trust receives its land as gifts from individual landowners (through donations and bequests) and developers, and through purchase. It uses the land for passive purposes which are educational, recreational, and/or scientific in nature. A voluntary board of directors runs the trust, and its membership is open to the general public. In addition, a land trust may provide other educational opportunities and assist its town with acquisition of open space and land use planning.'' (From Suzanne Wilkins and Roger Koontz, *Connecticut Land Trust Handbook*, Connecticut Land Trust Service Bureau, 1986.)

The number of local land trusts—one of the most dynamic, effective sectors of the conservation movement—is growing rapidly. According to the Land Trust Alliance, a national organization that provides support to land trusts, almost 900 local land trusts are located throughout the country; there is at least one in every state. These trusts have over 750,000 members nationwide and have protected over 2 million acres. Land trusts vary greatly in geographic scope, degree of professionalism, and types of resources they seek to protect. Close to half were incorporated during the last decade and almost one-third since 1984. Most land trusts are operated entirely by volunteers.

habitat restoration. Ducks Unlimited and similar groups operating locally make rental payments to wetlands owners for habitat management, hunting, and fishing. Gun clubs in southern California have donated over 25,000 acres of marshes, worth approximately $20 million, to The Nature Conservancy for subsequent transfer to the state.

REGULATION

Regulations are used to protect public health, safety, and welfare. Federal, state, and local governments all have regulatory programs that affect both publicly and privately owned wetlands. Some programs (such as New Jersey's tidal and nontidal wetlands regulatory programs) focus directly on the wetlands resource, while others focus on activities that can potentially alter the resource (such as dam construction). Wetlands protection may be only a small part of the latter programs.

Strengths

- can explicitly prohibit activities
- can be enforced—regulations have "teeth"
- can be adopted at various levels of government
- can be flexible, with levels of control commensurate with activities (e.g., regulations can allow reasonable use of the land while restricting harmful uses)
- can promote most suitable uses

Massachusetts adopted the first wetlands protection laws in the country in the early 1960s. Several years

---

Classification of Wetlands: A Growing Controversy

The idea of classifying or ranking wetlands according to their functions and values, and regulating different categories of wetlands differently, has recently generated intense controversy.

Advocates of ranking wetlands point out that all wetlands are not equally valuable and therefore are not deserving of equal protection. They argue that ranking will channel development pressures to the least valuable wetlands, away from those of high value. They also argue that using a ranking system will legitimize regulatory programs that now are subject to ridicule because some of the areas regulated have little or no ecological value. In addition, proponents note that a classification system would increase certainty in decision making.

Opponents of ranking argue that it is impossible to *value* individual wetlands, much less compare different wetlands in different regions. Too little is known about wetlands and their values to rank them in a meaningful way. Opponents also are quick to point out that a scheme to classify and rank all the wetlands in the United States would take years, and would be prohibitively expensive (even if it could be accomplished). Such a system also would increase the administrative burden on resource agencies. In addition, some opponents contend that any ranking system would be arbitrary and therefore subject to legal challenges. For example, the value of a wetland will change depending on the scale (local or regional) at which it is evaluated. Some opponents also point out that restoration has still not been proved possible, and therefore writing off low-value wetlands will invariably result in a deviation from no net loss.

Several states, including New York, Maine, and New Jersey, have classification schemes within their regulatory programs. In light of first-hand experience with the benefits and problems of classification in New York's program, Pat Riexinger, wetlands program manager for New York, makes the following recommendations for future applications of classification within a regulatory program:

- Classification should be limited to regional approaches within or between states. Do not classify at the national level, or even major regions of the country.
- There must be a clear link to a sound regulatory system containing management strategies intended to ensure resource conservation and no net loss.
- Even the lowest class of wetlands must receive protection and consideration. It cannot be a mechanism for eliminating or exempting whole classes of wetlands from protection.
- Distinctions between classes must be clear cut, with easily or realistically measurable characteristics.
- Avoid a system that classifies based on presumptions, because it probably will not accurately reflect the real functions or values of an individual wetland.

(Recommendations excerpted from an article written by Pat Riexinger which appeared in the Autumn 1991 edition of "Great Lakes Wetlands," published by the Tip of the Mitt Watershed Council.)

ago the state launched the Wetlands Conservancy Program to administer both its coastal and inlands wetlands acts. This program will map all wetlands in the state over the next 10 years, register them, and place land-use restrictions on them that allow only activities that do not harm the wetlands functions. Once wetlands are mapped, property owners and developers will know in advance where wetlands are located and what can and can't be done in these areas.

Challenges

- may be resource intensive, requiring funding and expertise to implement and enforce effectively
- depending on scope, may exclude valuable wetlands and many activities harmful to wetlands
- may be unpopular, as they impose limitations on private activities
- are primarily reactive rather than preventive
- may cause "takings" challenges

Key Opportunities

Federal: Section 404
Section 401 water quality certification
Consistency under the Coastal Zone Management Act

State: wetlands regulatory programs
floodplain management programs
shoreline management programs
coastal zone management programs

Local: zoning
floodplain regulations
stormwater regulations

PLANNING

Planning should be part of all wetlands protection efforts but can also be used as a tool itself. Comprehensive planning involves analyzing the needs of a particular area and setting goals or priorities for meeting those needs. Plans are based on the past and present situation and, most importantly, on the desired future for the planning area. Coordinated, continuous planning should lead to better-informed decision making.

Strengths

- can be adapted to fit a wide range of situations—from local land-use plans for a particular area to regional plans that encompass entire ecosystems
- can encourage coordination among programs in the planning area and can help address unique areas in an integrated fashion
- can account for cumulative impacts by showing the "big picture"
- can help reconcile or avert development-versus-preservation conflicts
- can offer predictability and consistency in government regulation and land-use decisions

---

West Eugene Wetlands Plan

In 1985 a permit to fill a pond adjacent to the Willamette River in Eugene, Oregon, near a shopping center stirred controversy among local environmental groups. The permit was never issued, but the controversy prompted the cities of Eugene and Springfield to jointly fund a new natural resources inventory for the area.

As part of the new inventory, a 765-acre concentration of wetlands was identified in West Eugene in an area designated for industrial development. Foreseeing future problems as efforts were made to develop this area, the City Council and Planning Commission launched the "West Eugene Wetlands Special Areas Study," a comprehensive wetlands plan.

The planning process began with a series of workshops for property owners, development interests, environmental groups, and others. A technical advisory committee composed of state and local agency representatives was formed to provide technical guidance and support. A detailed inventory of the area was also carried out.

The draft plan, released in March 1991, recommends protection for 1,070 acres of wetlands of the total 1,430 acres of jurisdictional wetlands (the plan recommends acquisition of the protected wetlands sites). The plan also calls for the establishment of a regional mitigation bank as the primary means of compensation for 360 acres of wetlands proposed for development.

- can involve stakeholders throughout the planning process

In 1988 Louisiana prepared a Wetlands Priority Conservation Plan as part of its State Comprehensive Outdoor Recreation Plan (SCORP) that drew attention to the value of wetlands and the high rate of wetlands loss in the state. An important element of the planning process was an advisory group composed of 11 public agencies and private-interest groups concerned about wetlands protection. This process helped build ties among interest groups and also helped coordinate the actions of various government agencies.

Challenges
- may be difficult to translate the plan into action and amend it if necessary to ensure successful implementation
- may be time consuming and resource intensive
- may be difficult to secure the interest, participation, and agreement of affected parties in a fair and efficient way
- may offer predictability but usually not the certainty some parties desire and expect from the process
- may be difficult to secure leadership that will outlast political changes

Key Opportunities
Federal: State Comprehensive Outdoor Recreation Plans
Advanced Identification
Special Area Management Plans
State: statewide land-use plans
Local: comprehensive local land-use plans
floodplain plans
wetlands plans
zoning and infrastructure plans

RESTORATION, CREATION AND MANAGEMENT

The restoration of degraded wetlands and the creation of new wetlands are often associated with mitigation requirements for regulatory programs. In addition to these efforts, however, broad nonregulatory programs for restoration and creation can often increase or enhance the wetlands base, thereby playing an important role in a statewide strategy. Effective management of existing as well as restored or created wetlands is also an important mechanism for ensuring that the quality and quantity of wetlands are sustained and improved over time.

Strengths
- can be used to help offset inevitable natural losses of some wetlands
- can offer opportunities to regain or create multiple wetlands functions (e.g., waterfowl production, water quality)
- can offer opportunities to target a particular area
- can be coordinated with other regulatory and nonregulatory programs
- can be relatively easy and inexpensive; for example, a restoration program that simply returns water to an area that was previously a wetland may require few resources
- can encourage willing landowners to become involved in management and restoration efforts

In Minnesota, local sportsmen banded together to form the Swan Lake Wildlife Association after the lake began to deteriorate as a waterfowl and wildlife refuge. Using local volunteers, they began clearing vegetation to create nesting sites. With the encouragement of the state's Department of Natural Resources, The Nature Conservancy was able to strengthen these efforts by obtaining an interest-free loan to purchase a 184-acre farm on the lake. The department pledged to purchase half the property, and local sports clubs are also helping to repay the loan. Funds for restoration are being provided by the legislature and the Reinvest in Minnesota program.

Challenges
- may require extensive technical expertise and research
- may require substantial funding and staff time to ensure successful implementation and long-term monitoring and management
- may be difficult to coordinate efforts when multiple owners and/or agencies are involved
- may disturb natural flora and fauna
- have had questionable success rates (especially with wetlands creation programs)

Key Opportunities

Federal: North American Waterfowl Management Plan

National Coastal Wetlands Conservation Grants

Coastal Zone Management Act

State: wildlife enhancement programs

water quality programs

Local: wastewater treatment projects

parks and recreation programs

Private: waterfowl enhancement programs

INCENTIVES AND DISINCENTIVES

Incentive programs encourage wetlands protection by offering landowners a financial incentive such as a lower tax rate on property preserved for wetlands. Disincentive programs discourage the destruction of wetlands by providing landowners with a financial disincentive such as loss of eligibility for governmental funds if a wetland is converted. Incentive and disincentive mechanisms are usually in the form of various tax policies and sub-

---

Mitigation Banking: The Pros and Cons

Mitigation banking involves restoring or creating wetlands in one area to compensate for wetlands losses at other sites. Mitigation banks can be set up in a number of ways. Generally, a developer makes payments to the mitigation bank to accrue "credits." These credits are debited as the developer incurs wetlands losses.

To date, mitigation banking has been used primarily by state highway departments to compensate for wetlands losses resulting from transportation projects. The success of most of these banks is uncertain. In many cases, adequate measures of success have not been established, or monitoring data are not available. The U.S. Fish and Wildlife Service's 1988 report *Mitigation Banking* found that of eight wetlands mitigation banks, one bank was successful, three showed some degree of success, three were too new to make a determination, and one lacked sufficient monitoring data.

Advantages

- increases likelihood that mitigation will succeed because sites can be carefully selected
- consolidates mitigation for small wetlands losses and can provide a larger, more environmentally valuable area that is more efficient to develop and manage than several scattered sites
- can provide mitigation in advance of wetlands impacts
- increases efficiency and economies of scale, as restoration or creation may be more cost effective on a larger scale
- makes monitoring and evaluation easier (data collection is necessary at only one site rather than many scattered sites)

Disadvantages

- results in off-site mitigation
- may cause a net loss of small, isolated wetlands (if banks are used to mitigate all small, isolated wetlands losses, the important functions performed by these areas may be lost)
- could increase alteration of wetlands by making wetlands compensation easy (if strict "sequencing" is not required)
- relies on restoration and creation projects that have an unproved success rate
- requires use of wetlands evaluation techniques that currently are inadequate for effectively quantifying a comprehensive set of wetlands values in terms of "credits"

In light of the potential difficulties presented by mitigation banks, the National Wetlands Policy Forum provided the following guidelines for establishing such banks as part of a regulatory program:

- The banks should be established consistent with statewide wetlands strategies.
- Contributions to a bank could be made only if permit review determined the contribution to be appropriate.
- The banks should include only restored or newly created wetlands.
- Restoration and creation of the banked wetlands should, to the extent possible, precede the compensated losses.
- Effective monitoring and enforcement systems should be established to ensure the success of banking efforts.

sidies. Awards and recognition programs also serve as nonfinancial incentives, acknowledging exemplary land stewardship or conservation work.

Strengths

- can encourage voluntary protection by making protection more profitable than conversion (or can at least provide some compensation for protection)
- often popular tools that elicit strong public support
- less intensive or coercive than regulatory programs

Minnesota's 1991 Wetlands Conservation Act, passed in the final 57 seconds of the legislative session, includes a property tax exemption for certain wetlands. A landowner with a wetland located in a high-priority wetland area in the local comprehensive water plan and within a high-priority area designated by the state Board of Water and Soil Resources can apply to the county for designation as a Wetland Preservation Area. These areas can be exempted from property taxes, and limits are placed on eminent domain actions and the installation of public water, sewer, and drainage systems.

Challenges

- do not guarantee protection, as actions cannot be required or prohibited
- may be costly
- sometimes misperceived as regulations (i.e., Swampbuster)

Key Opportunities

Federal: Farm Bill programs
Coastal Barrier Resources Act
National Flood Insurance Program

State: tax incentives
registration programs

Local: property tax incentives
transfer of development rights

Private: awards programs

TECHNICAL ASSISTANCE, EDUCATION, AND OUTREACH

These mechanisms encompass agency-to-agency assistance (either directly or through manuals, maps, and other aids); classroom education and hands-on exhibits; videos on the importance of wetlands protection; and many other options. The Nature Conservancy, for example, cooperates with state agencies in developing an ecological inventory of the state's natural resources and setting priorities for their protection. This national natural-heritage network covers all 50 states. Kansas' Fish and Game Department administers a Wildlife Education Service available to all state public and private schools. This program provides reading materials and teaching guides, including information on wetlands as they relate to wildlife and their habitats.

Strengths

- can target a narrow or broad audience, such as a specific landowner, government agency, or the general public, and can focus on a particular message

California Coastal Conservancy

The Coastal Conservancy was established by the California legislature in 1976. It was empowered to implement wetlands restoration and enhancement programs in California's coastal zone and San Francisco Bay. The agency has undertaken over 70 wetlands enhancement projects and is active in most of California's major bays, estuaries, lagoons, and other coastal wetlands as well as numerous watersheds.

The Conservancy undertakes wetlands restoration and enhancement activities in cooperation with local governments, nonprofit organizations, resource conservation districts, and other agencies. It also helps cities and counties implement their Local Coastal Programs as mandated by the Coastal Act of 1976. Various public agencies, private landowners, and coastal permit applicants have sought the Conservancy's assistance with mitigation efforts.

To address the continuing loss of wetlands in the San Francisco Bay, the Conservancy and the San Francisco Estuary Project are jointly funding a $1.575 million wetlands enhancement. This project will test various restoration techniques, including building levees, controlling water flow, and regrading channel bottoms, at eight different sites.

- can be tailored to match the resources available (i.e., as elaborate or as modest as budgets and resources permit)
- can elicit strong public and political support
- can offer opportunities for coordination between agencies and between the public and private sector
- can increase the effectiveness of other non-regulatory and regulatory programs for wetlands protection
- can encourage voluntary protection

Washington's Department of Ecology has issued a Model Wetlands Protection Ordinance for local governments to consider in adopting wetlands protection plans and programs. The model ordinance includes a general wetlands rating system, a mitigation policy with compensation ratios, and buffer standards. Technical staff within the Department of Ecology also provide training and site assistance to local planners with respect to wetlands plant and soil identification as well as wetlands classification and delineation.

Challenges
- may be time consuming and resource intensive, often without visible or readily measurable benefits
- often the first programs to be eliminated if budget cuts occur

Key Opportunities
Federal: National Wetlands Inventory
EPA technical assistance programs
State: local government assistance programs
environmental education curricula
Local: landowner assistance programs
environmental awareness programs
Private: education programs

RESEARCH

Sound research on wetlands values and functions, techniques for wetlands restoration, and other related topics provides important information on which to base wetlands protection policies and programs. Federal, state, and local agencies conduct wetlands research on their own and also provide support to research organizations.

Strengths
- can provide data to justify other wetlands programs and to garner public and political support for those programs
- can increase the effectiveness of other regulatory and nonregulatory programs
- can help set priorities for protection as well as for evaluation of protection programs
- can heighten public awareness

Education and research are the primary goals of the National Estuarine Research Reserve System, which currently has 18 reserves throughout the United States. The National Oceanic and Atmospheric Administration (NOAA) provides financial assistance on a 50-50 matching basis to coastal states and territories (including the Great Lakes) to acquire, develop, and operate estuarine areas at research reserves. The system protects hundreds of thousands of acres of estuarine waters, marshes, shorelines, and adjacent uplands as natural laboratories. NOAA has identified biogeographic regions around the country to facilitate the inclusion of examples of all ecosystem types in the system.

Challenges
- may be time consuming and resource intensive; immediate questions may take years to answer
- may be difficult to disseminate results
- may be difficult to ensure that action is taken on the basis of research findings
- may be difficult to obtain funding for research

Key Opportunities
Federal: Coastal Zone Management Act
EPA Wetlands Program State Development Grants
State: state universities
Local: community colleges
Private: nonprofit and corporate research programs

CROSS-CUTTING TOOLS

Of all the tools discussed in this section, two—coordination of programs and landscape approaches—probably offer the greatest possibilities for enhanced wetlands protection. As with the mechanisms just discussed, the use of coordination and landscape approaches involves capitalizing on opportunities for wetlands-specific and broad natural resources protection. These cross-cutting tools should be an integral part of every wetlands strategy.

Coordination

Many programs have a stated intent or the potential to protect wetlands; too often, however, they operate in isolation rather than complementing one another. The greatest challenge for strategy developers may thus be the ongoing process of forging and maintaining links among mechanisms to protect wetlands.

Strengths

- can help define conservation priorities and maximize efforts for everyone's benefit
- can promote better use of available resources such as staff and expertise
- can minimize duplicated efforts and inconsistencies at all levels of government

In 1986 the U.S. Army Corps of Engineers and the Pennsylvania Department of Environmental Regulation initiated a coordinated program for state and federal permits for wetlands alterations. As part of that program, a joint permit application was developed by the Corps (in conjunction with the state) that simplified the permit application and review process by requiring only one submittal. A state and federal interagency committee meets monthly to discuss, review, and coordinate wetlands permit applications.

Challenges

- may be difficult and time consuming
- may be hard to overcome turf struggles
- may be difficult to overcome contradictions among perspectives; different individuals with different training and backgrounds tend to staff particular agencies, which can result in a deep-seated lack of understanding among agencies

Landscape Approaches

Because wetlands are part of an interdependent natural system connected to surrounding landscapes in many ways, they are affected by activities on adjacent lands as well as in more remote areas. A dam many miles upstream, for example, can directly alter the amount of water flowing into a wetlands area.

Traditional approaches to wetlands protection and management generally fail to consider what might be called the *landscape context*. The most serious consequence of this failure is that the potential *cumulative* impacts of wetlands losses or alterations go unrecognized. Specific tools to measure landscape-level functions and cumulative impacts are only in the developmental stages (see Part IV.2); however, a state wetlands strategy should acknowledge the necessity of moving toward such approaches with respect to both regulatory and nonregulatory tools.

Strengths

- can control impacts that occur beyond wetlands boundaries
- can account for cumulative impacts

EPA's Wetlands Research Program is examining the environmental effects of cumulative wetlands loss. As part of this ongoing effort, a method is being developed to assemble generally available data into a scientific framework that ranks watersheds according to the relative importance of wetlands functions and loss. This method, referred to as the synoptic approach, is being developed as a rapid and inexpensive assessment technique for use in routine Section 404 permit requests. EPA has conducted pilot studies of this approach in Louisiana and Washington.

Challenges

- may be difficult to manage wetlands on the basis of landscape boundaries because landscape units extend beyond traditional political boundaries
- may be difficult to measure landscape-level wetlands functions

Federal Mechanisms

This section of the guidebook describes federal wetlands protection mechanisms that can be used in developing statewide wetlands strategies. Federal programs are often modified; several may be subject to change because of imminent legislative or administrative action. In particular, upcoming reauthorization of the Clean Water Act may result in significant changes in certain programs. The descriptions are not intended as a legal interpretation of these programs; professional legal advice should be sought for specific problems. The programs are discussed in the following order:

Clean Water Act:
1. *Section 404*
2. *Advanced Identification*
3. *General Permits*
4. *State Assumption*
5. *Water Pollution Control*
6. *Water Quality Certification*
7. Coastal Barrier Resources System
8. Coastal Wetlands Planning, Protection and Restoration Act
9. Coastal Zone Management Act
10. Emergency Wetlands Resources Act
11. Endangered Species Act

12. EPA Wetlands Program State Development Grants
    Executive Order 11988 (see *National Flood Insurance Program*)
13. Executive Order 11990: Protection of Wetlands
    Farm Programs:
14. *Conservation Reserve Program*
15. *Farmers Home Administration Wetlands-Related Programs*
16. *Swampbuster*
17. *Water Bank*
18. *Wetlands Reserve Program*
19. Federal Aid in Sport Fish Restoration Act, Federal Aid in Wildlife Restoration Act
20. Federal Wetlands Research and Technical Assistance
21. Fish and Wildlife Coordination Act
22. Fish and Wildlife Service Private Lands Restoration Initiative
23. Internal Revenue Code
24. Land and Water Conservation Fund Act
25. Migratory Bird Conservation Fund
    National Coastal Wetlands Conservation Grants (see *Coastal Wetlands Planning, Protection and Restoration Act*)

26. National Environmental Policy Act
27. National Estuary Program
28. National Flood Insurance Program
National Wetlands Inventory (see *Emergency Wetlands Resources Act*)
National Wetlands Priority Conservation Plan (see *Emergency Wetlands Resources Act*)
29. Near Coastal Waters Program
30. North American Waterfowl Management Plan
31. North American Wetlands Conservation Act
32. Ramsar Convention
33. River Conservation and Management
Small Wetland Acquisition Program (see *Migratory Bird Conservation Fund*)
34. Special Area Management Plans
35. State Comprehensive Outdoor Recreation Plans (see *Land and Water Conservation Fund Act*)
36. Surplus Federal Property Transfer
37. Water Resources Development Acts of 1986 and 1990
38. Watershed Protection and Flood Prevention Act

The programs may be useful for the following purposes (discussed in Part 1.2, Step 4, and Part III.1):

ACQUISITION

8. Coastal Wetlands Planning, Protection and Restoration Act
9. Coastal Zone Management Act
10. Emergency Wetlands Resources Act
Farm Programs:
14. Conservation Reserve Program
15. Farmers Home Administration Wetlands-Related Programs
17. Water Bank
18. Wetlands Reserve Program
24. Land and Water Conservation Fund Act
25. Migratory Bird Conservation Fund
National Coastal Wetlands Conservation Grants (see *Coastal Wetlands Planning, Protection and Restoration Act*)
30. North American Waterfowl Management Plan
31. North American Wetlands Conservation Act

Small Wetland Acquisition Program (see *Migratory Bird Conservation Fund*)
State Comprehensive Outdoor Recreation Plans (see *Land and Water Conservation Fund*)

REGULATION

Clean Water Act:
1. Section 404
2. Advanced Identification
3. General Permits
4. State Assumption
5. Water Pollution Control
6. Water Quality Certification
9. Coastal Zone Management Act
11. Endangered Species Act
21. Fish and Wildlife Coordination Act
26. National Environmental Policy Act
28. National Flood Insurance Program
33. River Conservation and Management
34. Special Area Management Plans

PLANNING

Clean Water Act:
1. Section 404
2. Advanced Identification
9. Coastal Zone Management Act
10. Emergency Wetlands Resources Act
11. Endangered Species Act
24. Land and Water Conservation Fund Act
27. National Estuary Program
National Wetlands Priority Conservation Plan (see *Emergency Wetlands Resources Act*)
30. North American Waterfowl Management Plan
33. River Conservation and Management
34. Special Area Management Plans
State Comprehensive Outdoor Recreation Plans (see *Land and Water Conservation Fund*)
37. Watershed Protection and Flood Prevention Act

FUNDING

8. Coastal Wetlands Planning, Protection and Restoration Act
9. Coastal Zone Management Act

12. EPA Wetlands Program State Development Grants
19. Federal Aid in Sport Fish Restoration Act, Federal Aid in Wildlife Restoration Act
24. Land and Water Conservation Fund Act
    National Coastal Wetlands Conservation Grants (see *Coastal Wetlands Planning, Protection and Restoration Act*)
28. National Flood Insurance Program
30. North American Waterfowl Management Plan
31. North American Wetlands Conservation Act

RESTORATION/CREATION/MANAGEMENT

8. Coastal Wetlands Planning, Protection and Restoration Act
9. Coastal Zone Management Act
    Executive Order 11988 (see *National Flood Insurance Program*)
    Farm Programs:
14. Conservation Reserve Program
15. Farmers Home Administration Wetlands-Related Programs
17. Water Bank
18. Wetlands Reserve Program
19. Federal Aid in Sport Fish Restoration Act, Federal Aid in Wildlife Restoration Act
22. Fish and Wildlife Service Private Lands Restoration Initiative
    National Coastal Wetlands Conservation Grants (see *Coastal Wetlands Planning, Protection and Restoration Act*)
28. National Flood Insurance Program
30. North American Waterfowl Management Plan
31. North American Wetlands Conservation Act
33. River Conservation and Management
36. Water Resources Development Acts of 1986 and 1990

INCENTIVES AND DISINCENTIVES

7. Coastal Barrier Resources System
    Farm Programs:
14. Conservation Reserve Program
15. Farmers Home Administration Wetlands-Related Programs

16. Swampbuster
17. Water Bank
18. Wetlands Reserve Program
19. Fish and Wildlife Service Private Lands Restoration Initiative
23. Internal Revenue Code
37. Watershed Protection and Flood Prevention Act

RESEARCH AND TECHNICAL ASSISTANCE

19. Coastal Zone Management Act
20. Federal Wetlands Research and Technical Assistance
22. Fish and Wildlife Service Private Lands Restoration Initiative

1. Clean Water Act: Section 404
(33 U.S.C. § 1344 (1986 & Supp. 1991))

States can assume responsibility for the Section 404 program, which regulates the discharge of dredged or fill material in wetlands and other waters of the United States. States may also influence the issuance of Section 404 permits through Section 401 water quality certification or coastal zone consistency. States, local government, private groups, and individuals can comment on proposed permits and can help bring violations to the attention of the Corps of Engineers and EPA. This program may be subject to change as part of the Clean Water Act reauthorization now underway in Congress.

Section 404 of the Clean Water Act is the primary federal program regulating activities in wetlands. The Section 404 program is administered by both the Corps of Engineers and the U.S. Environmental Protection Agency (EPA), while the U.S. Fish and Wildlife Service (FWS) and National Marine Fisheries Service play important advisory roles.

The Corps has primary responsibility for the permit program and is authorized, after notice and opportunity for a public hearing, to issue permits for the discharge of dredged or fill material into "waters of the United States," including wetlands, as long as the proposed activity is in compliance with environmental guidelines (the

Section 404(b)(1) guidelines). The Corps receives roughly 15,000 permit applications for Section 404 discharges each year.

EPA is responsible for reviewing and commenting on permit applications being evaluated by the Corps. In addition, EPA's responsibilities include the following:

- *Environmental guidelines:* EPA is responsible for establishing the environmental criteria used in permitting (referred to as the Section 404(b)(1) guidelines).
- *Veto power:* EPA can veto a Corps permit decision if it would have certain unacceptable adverse effects (Section 404(c)). In addition, EPA can request that individual permit applications be sent to Corps headquarters for a determination of compliance with the regulations.
- *State assumption:* EPA oversees state assumption of the permit program (Section 404(h)).
- *Exemptions:* EPA determines the applicability of exemptions specified in Section 404(f) to the permitting requirements.
- *Enforcement:* EPA takes enforcement actions against unauthorized discharges of dredged or fill material into wetlands and other waters of the United States (Section 309). EPA shares this enforcement authority with the Corps.

The environmental guidelines used to evaluate Section 404 permits generally prohibit discharges of dredged or fill material into U.S. waters unless the following conditions apply:

- There is no available, practicable alternative with fewer effects on the aquatic ecosystem.
- Dischargers will neither violate other applicable regulations or laws (e.g., state water quality standards, toxic effluent standards, Endangered Species Act) nor significantly degrade the waters into which they discharge.
- All appropriate and practicable steps have been taken to minimize and otherwise mitigate impacts on the aquatic ecosystem.

A February 6, 1990, Memorandum of Agreement between EPA and the Corps clarified that mitigation should occur in the following sequence: (1) avoidance of impacts through evaluation of practicable alternatives; (2) minimization; and (3) compensation for unavoidable impacts through restoration or creation.

In evaluating individual Section 404 permit applications, the Corps evaluates compliance with Section 404(b)(1) guidelines and carries out a public-interest review. This review involves balancing such public-interest factors as conservation, economics, aesthetics, wetlands protection, cultural values, navigation, fish and wildlife values, water supply, and water quality.

Under the "veto" authority of Section 404(c), EPA may prohibit, withdraw, or restrict disposal of dredged or fill material into waters of the United States if the discharge would have unacceptable effects on municipal water supplies, shellfish beds and fishery areas (including spawning and breeding areas), wildlife, or recreational areas.

Under Section 404(e), the Corps is authorized to issue general permits on a nationwide, state, or regional basis for categories of activities that will have minimal individual and cumulative impacts. General permits allow certain activities to occur without individual permit approval as long as the discharger complies with standard conditions issued by the Corps. (See *Clean Water Act: Section 404 General Permits.*)

Section 230.80 of the Section 404(b)(1) guidelines provides for a planning process whereby EPA and the Corps, in conjunction with the affected state, can identify wetlands that are generally suitable or unsuitable for discharge permits in advance of any specific permit applications. (See *Clean Water Act: Section 404 Advanced Identification.*)

The federal Section 404 program does not preempt state wetlands regulation. States are free to enact wetlands protection laws as long as they do not affect or impair the authority of the Corps to maintain navigation (Section 404(t)).

The geographic scope of regulatory authority under Section 404 has been the subject of extensive litigation. In 1975 the courts confirmed that Congress had intended that the Section 404 program be broadly applied to all "waters of the United States," not just traditionally navigable waters. This includes wetlands adjacent to interstate rivers and streams and coastal waters. It also includes isolated wetlands, provided that their degradation or destruction could affect interstate commerce (e.g., if they are used by migratory birds).

It should be noted that Section 404 regulates only the discharge of dredged or fill material. Other types of physical alteration, such as drainage or excavation, may also adversely affect wetlands but are not regulated under this program unless they also involve the discharge of dredged or fill material. In addition, under Section 404(f), certain types of discharges are exempt from the permit process. The most important of these are as follows:

- normal (ongoing) farming, silviculture, and ranching practices;
- maintenance, including emergency reconstruction of recently damaged parts of currently serviceable structures such as dikes, dams, levees, and similar specified structures;
- construction or maintenance of farm or stock ponds or irrigation ditches or maintenance (but not construction) of drainage ditches;
- construction of temporary sedimentation basins on a construction site that does not include placement of fill material into U.S. waters; and
- construction or maintenance of farm or forest roads or temporary roads for moving mining equipment if best management practices are followed.

It is important to note that these exemptions do not apply if the discharge is part of an activity whose purpose is to convert an area of waters of the United States to a use to which that area was not previously subject, or where the flow or circulation of waters may be impaired or their reach reduced.

Strengths

- Section 404 provides the most comprehensive federal regulatory protection against activities that degrade wetlands.
- Section 404 provides a mechanism for state assumption (see *Clean Water Act: Section 404 State Assumption*) and can be used by states as a model regulatory program.
- "Advanced identification" of generally suitable and unsuitable discharge areas provides a degree of predictability and certainty.
- The Corps and EPA have resolved to improve implementation of the program and have generated several new initiatives to streamline the program and reduce regulatory delays. Under the current program, the regulatory burden is already modest: many activities are exempt; many

additional activities are allowed under general nationwide permits; and those projects that do require individual permits are approved in the majority of cases.

Challenges

- Protection of wetlands is limited to only those physical alterations (and associated chemical and biological impacts) that result from discharge of dredged or fill materials.
- The permit-by-permit approach makes cumulative impacts difficult to address.
- This program has caused frustration among some sectors of the regulated public that have alleged inconsistent policies and practices among Corps districts and between the Corps and EPA, unreasonably burdensome delays, and failure to account adequately for special circumstances.
- A 1988 General Accounting Office (GAO) review of many aspects of the Section 404 program's implementation concluded that Corps districts do not systematically seek out violators of permit requirements, nor do they always conduct follow-up investigations of suspected violations brought to their attention.
- Limited information exists about the effectiveness of the program.

Users

The Section 404 program is administered by both the Corps and EPA; FWS and the National Marine Fisheries Service play advisory roles. The Clean Water Act also allows states to assume substantial authority for administration of the Section 404 permit program, subject to EPA approval and oversight.

States review Section 404 permits for consistency with their coastal zone management plans and for Section 401 water quality certification. States and local government and the public can comment on proposed permits and potential advanced identification sites and can help bring violations to the attention of the Corps and EPA. Section 505 of the Clean Water Act authorizes "citizen suits" against permit violators or persons who discharge material without a permit.

Resources

EPA can provide grants that states can use to enhance their role in the Section 404 program.

For example, the grants can be used to monitor statewide trends in wetlands. (See *EPA Wetlands Program State Development Grants.*)

Coordination

A primary mechanism for coordination is the mandated public notice-and-comment period. Currently, public notice is sent to interested federal, state, and local government agencies; adjacent landowners; and any other organization or individual who has expressed interest in being on the mailing list.

Under Section 401, states have the authority to review any federal permit or license, including Section 404 permit applications, to ensure that the actions would be consistent with the state's water quality requirements. (See *Clean Water Act: Water Quality Certification.*) States with federally approved coastal zone management plans have the authority to review Section 404 permits in their coastal zones for consistency with the approved plan. (See *Coastal Zone Management Act.*)

To qualify for a Section 404 permit, an activity must not violate the National Environmental Policy Act, the Endangered Species Act, the National Historic Preservation Act, or other federal or state law.

EPA and the Corps encourage permit applicants to request preapplication meetings with agency staff to resolve problems before an application is submitted. Some Corps districts hold regularly scheduled meetings for this purpose. Efforts are underway to increase consistency and efficiency by developing joint federal/state permit processing systems (joint permitting).

As part of its public-interest review, the Corps considers officially adopted state, regional, or local land-use classifications, determinations, or policies for the areas under consideration.

The Section 404(b)(1) guidelines provide for a planning process whereby EPA and the Corps jointly identify wetlands that are generally suitable or unsuitable for discharge permits in advance of any specific permit applications. This process, known as Advanced Identification, provides an important opportunity for coordination and for state involvement. (See *Clean Water Act: Section 404 Advanced Identification.*)

Special Area Management Plans (SAMPs) provide another opportunity for advanced planning and coordination. SAMPs are authorized by the Coastal Zone Management Act and by Corps guidance. (See *Special Area Management Plans.*)

Many people confuse the requirements of Swampbuster and Section 404 of the Clean Water Act. Although the same wetlands fall within the jurisdiction of both programs, the programs treat these wetlands differently. Swampbuster, which is not regulatory, is aimed principally at discouraging the draining of wetlands in agriculture. It provides a strong disincentive for draining by preventing anyone who converts wetlands to cropland from obtaining federal farm benefits. Section 404 in general exempts normal farming and ranching and does not regulate the draining of wetlands if such draining would not involve discharge of dredged or fill material. It may be useful to educate the regulated community as to the requirements of these two programs and their differences and similarities. (See *Farm Programs: Swampbuster.*)

Contacts

U.S. Army Corps of Engineers Wetlands Contacts (see Appendix E)

U.S. EPA Wetlands Contacts (see Appendix E)

References

Want, William. *Law of Wetlands Regulation.* New York: Clark Boardman, 1990.

2. Clean Water Act: Section 404 Advanced Identification
(40 C.F.R. § 230.80 (1991))

States, local governments, and private groups can play a major role in Section 404 Advanced Identification by requesting that the process be conducted, by providing information, and by commenting on wetlands identified as generally suitable or unsuitable for discharge permits. Advanced Identification provides some predictability to wetlands regulation. It also can be helpful in resolving conservation and development conflicts in areas of rapid growth, and in controlling cumulative impacts on wetlands. This program may be subject to change as part of the Clean Water Act reauthorization now underway in Congress.

Section 230.80 of the Section 404(b)(1) guidelines of the Clean Water Act provides for a planning process whereby the U.S. Environmental Protection Agency (EPA) and the Corps of Engineers identify wetlands that are generally suitable or unsuitable for discharge permits in advance of any specific permit applications. Unless tied to general permitting or other regulatory authority, designation of sites as generally suitable or unsuitable for disposal is a guide to but not a guarantee of permit issuance or denial.

Advanced Identification (ADID) requires careful analysis of the ecological conditions and possible impacts of prospective development activities on existing ecosystems. The process generally involves a cooperative effort among state, federal, and sometimes local agencies to inventory, characterize, and map wetlands resources. EPA and the Corps then jointly issue a public notice of the suitable/unsuitable designations for public review. As of June 1991, 20 ADIDs have been completed and 39 are in progress.

Strengths

- ADID is flexible; it can involve any number of parties or any size area.
- The program helps states anticipate problems and increases their information bases about particular areas.
- With this program the permit process becomes more predictable, which helps regulators and developers avoid unnecessary and costly conflicts. The program can also provide a more consistent and efficient framework for permit decisions than a case-by-case basis.
- ADID can bolster public awareness and appreciation of wetlands values.
- Regulatory agencies can assess cumulative impacts over the entire planning area.
- ADID can be readily coordinated with other planning processes and can lead to the development of comprehensive approaches to wetlands protection if undertaken within the context of a broader planning process.

Challenges

- It can be difficult to secure agreement among parties and to coordinate diverse agencies, particularly when they perceive differences in their mandates or authorities.
- ADID can be very time consuming and resource intensive for the individuals and agencies involved.
- Resources to implement ADID may not be available.
- Defining the planning area may be difficult.
- ADID can be used as a guide but not a guarantee of permit issuance or denial.

Users

ADID is the responsibility of the federal government; however, information developed during the ADID process may also be used by state and local agencies and private organizations. Initiated by EPA, ADID generally involves a cooperative effort among state, federal, and local agencies. Public participation is usually encouraged but is not required. Although there is no statutory requirement for state involvement in ADID, states can and do play a key role by requesting that the process be conducted, providing information, and commenting on proposed designations. In addition, states can use the resulting information in their own wetlands protection programs.

Resources

ADID can potentially be funded through EPA's National Estuary Program (NEP) or Near Coastal Waters (NCW) program. ADIDs undertaken in coordination with Special Area Management Plans (SAMPs) could benefit from resources allocated to the SAMP process. (The coastal zone management program provides grants to states for SAMPs; the Corps also funds SAMPs.)

Coordination

Other agencies and private organizations can use the information developed in the ADID process to undertake various federal, state, or local regulatory programs; planning programs such as SAMPs or State Comprehensive Outdoor Recreation Plans (SCORPs); public or private acquisition; and educational campaigns.

EPA and the permitting authority must review available water resources management data in determining whether the identification process complies with Section 404(b)(1) guidelines.

Contacts

U.S. EPA Wetlands Contacts (see Appendix E)

3. Clean Water Act: Section 404 General Permits
(33 U.S.C. § 1344(e) (1986))

General permits allow certain activities to occur without individual federal permit approval, thus streamlining the process. By denying water quality certification or coastal zone consistency, states can in essence veto or condition general permits. Some general permits require that state wetlands permits be obtained.

This program may be subject to change as part of the Clean Water Act reauthorization now underway in Congress. Also, a proposal is pending to amend and modify the regulations for the nationwide permit program.

Under Section 404(e) of the Clean Water Act, the U.S. Army Corps of Engineers is authorized to issue general permits—on a state, regional, or nationwide basis—for categories of activities that are similar in nature and that will cause only minimal individual and cumulative environmental effects. Such activities include minor road crossings, boat-mooring buoys, structures for oil and gas development on the Outer Continental Shelf, and bank stabilization for erosion control. These general permits allow certain activities to occur without individual federal permit approval, thereby streamlining the permitting process. However, several categories do require applicants to notify the Corps district office before commencing activity.

The Corps has issued a series of nationwide general permits and also issues regional general permits (covering a limited, specific geographic area) for activities similar in nature to those covered under the nationwide permits. General permits are issued for five-year periods.

Strengths

- General permits can streamline the regulatory process for activities with minimal impacts.

Challenges

- Public notice for specific projects is not required. Neither the public nor federal or state agencies are given the opportunity to comment on specific projects.
- General permits may not protect against cumulative impacts of many small-scale projects.

Users

The Corps has the lead; states are involved in certifying compliance with water quality standards and consistency with coastal zone management plans and in issuing permits, in the case of certain general permits. Other agencies and the public are involved in commenting on the development of general permits.

Coordination

Under Section 401, states have the authority to review any federal permit or license, including Section 404 general permits, to ensure that the proposed actions are consistent with the state's water quality requirements. For states without certified general permits, specific activities need individual Section 401 certification even though they would not require individual Section 404 permits. (See *Clean Water Act: Water Quality Certification*).

States with federally approved coastal zone management plans have the authority to review Section 404 general permits in the coastal zone for consistency with the approved plan. (See *Coastal Zone Management Act.*)

Some general permits require that a state wetlands permit be obtained. In Maryland, for example, a general permit allows fills of less than five acres of vegetated wetlands subject to certain conditions, which include obtaining a state wetlands permit.

As with individual Section 404 permits, general permits must not violate any state or federal laws, such as the National Environmental Policy Act, the Endangered Species Act, and the National Historic Preservation Act.

Contacts

U.S. EPA Wetlands Contacts (see Appendix E)
U.S. Army Corps of Engineers Wetlands Contacts (see Appendix E)

4. Clean Water Act: Section 404 State Assumption
(40 U.S.C. § 233 (1991))

States can assume administration of the federal program regulating the discharge of dredged or fill material into wetlands. Few states have chosen to assume the program, probably because few federal resources are available to assist states and assumption does not include navigable waters. This program may be subject to change as part of the Clean Water Act reauthorization now underway in Congress.

The Clean Water Act allows the U.S. Environmental Protection Agency (EPA) to approve state assumption of administration of the Section 404 permit program (Section 404(g)). To date, one state (Michigan) has assumed the program and another

(New Jersey) is seriously considering assumption. Sixteen states have formally evaluated assumption.

The act currently does not allow a state to assume permitting responsibility in waters that are navigable, adjacent to navigable waters, or subject to tidal ebb and flow. Jurisdiction over these areas is retained by the Corps.

EPA is responsible for approving state assumption and overseeing assumed programs. EPA can withdraw approval if a state fails to meet standards. States cannot issue permits over EPA's objection, but EPA has the authority to waive its review for categories of permit applications.

Strengths

- States may have more field staff and knowledge of local wetlands than do federal agencies.
- Allowing states to run the regulatory program can increase wetlands protection and efficiency because states already run many regulatory and nonregulatory environmental programs.
- The recent trend has been for states to adopt programs stronger than the federal Section 404 program.
- In the one state that has assumed the program, federal oversight has not been burdensome; EPA reviews only a small percentage of Michigan's permits.

Challenges

- Important federal laws would become inapplicable under state-assumed programs (e.g., Endangered Species Act, National Environmental Policy Act, Fish and Wildlife Coordination Act, Wild and Scenic Rivers Act, Coastal Zone Management Act, National Historic Preservation Act, Equal Access to Justice Act, and others).
- Insufficient resources are available for states to assume wetlands permitting.
- States must still share responsibility with the Corps, which retains authority over wetlands adjacent to navigable waters. These "unassumable" areas are a significant part of many states' waters.
- The act does not provide for partial assumption, and in some states a sharing of authority may be more attractive than assuming total responsibility.
- It may be more difficult for states than for

the federal government to exercise strong political will to protect wetlands, as states may be more vulnerable to pressure from local development interests.

Users

All states are eligible to apply for state assumption. EPA is responsible for approving assumption and oversight of assumed programs. The permitting state is required to provide notice of each permit application to the public and any other state that may be affected, and to provide an opportunity for a public hearing. Other states that may be affected by permitting have the right to comment on permit applications. The permitting state must justify its reasoning if it chooses not to incorporate these comments.

Resources

Significant resources (staff, money, and expertise) are needed for a state to assume the program. Michigan spent $1.3 million in 1989 to protect approximately three million acres of wetlands. Minnesota estimated in 1989 that preparation for program assumption would cost about $67,400 annually and could take at least two years.

EPA can provide grants to states for activities related to state assumption. (See *EPA Wetlands Program State Development Grants*.)

Coordination

Many of the mechanisms for coordination with other tools are the same under state assumption as under the federal Section 404 program. The primary mechanism is the public notice-and-comment period for specific permits. Planning processes such as Advanced Identification and Special Area Management Planning can provide further coordination.

By assuming the wetlands regulatory program, states can better integrate and coordinate various state programs (both regulatory and nonregulatory) that affect wetlands and the environment.

Contacts

U.S. EPA Wetlands Contacts (see Appendix E)

5. Clean Water Act: Water Pollution Control
(33 U.S.C. §§ 1313, 1315, 1329, 1342 (1986 & Supp. 1991))

Federal programs for water pollution control are based on state water quality standards. States can protect wetlands through these programs by developing water quality standards specifically for their wetlands. States can also designate wetlands as Outstanding National Resource Waters in which no degradation of water quality is allowed. Also, states may protect or restore wetlands as part of landscape-based approaches to controlling nonpoint source pollution.

Water pollution control programs may be subject to change as part of the Clean Water Act reauthorization now underway in Congress.

Water quality standards form the basis of programs for point and nonpoint source pollution control, water quality monitoring, and water quality certification. (See *Clean Water Act: Water Quality Certification.*) These programs have considerable potential for protecting wetlands, although they have not been used extensively to do so. By explicitly including wetlands protection in water quality standards, states can ensure that they are providing the same level of protection to wetlands as they do to other surface waters. Also, water quality standards justify protection of wetlands for their own sake as valuable components of the aquatic ecosystem, not just for the protection of adjacent surface waters.

Under Section 402 of the Clean Water Act, point source pollution discharges into waters of the United States, including wetlands, are prohibited unless specifically permitted. Point source discharges of chemical, heavy metal, and biological wastes are regulated by the National Pollutant Discharge Elimination System (NPDES). States can assume responsibility for this program; the U.S. Environmental Protection Agency (EPA) oversees assumed programs.

Effects on wetlands from nonpoint source pollution can be addressed through Section 319 of the Clean Water Act, which requires that states assess nonpoint source pollution impacts on state waters (including wetlands) and implement management programs to control those impacts. These programs must include, among other things, best management practices, state authority for implementation, and a schedule of implementation milestones. In implementing their programs, states may incorporate protection or restoration of wetlands as part of landscape-based approaches to control nonpoint source pollution and to achieve water quality standards.

Various water quality management programs require monitoring to ensure that designated and existing uses are maintained and protected. When

states adopt water quality standards for wetlands, this monitoring results in protection of wetlands.

EPA encourages states to define the protection of water quality broadly to include protection of aquatic life, wildlife, aquatic habitat, vegetation, and hydrology required to maintain the aquatic system.

States must adopt water quality standards and then review and, if necessary, revise them every three years. States have broad authority to adopt standards based on the use and value of their waters for public water supply, fish and wildlife propagation, recreation, and other purposes. State water quality standards are required to designate water uses (at a minimum, protection of fish, shellfish, wildlife, and recreation in and on the water; and in no case lower than existing uses); set criteria to protect the designated uses; and establish a policy to prevent degradation of these uses (antidegradation).

Either narrative or numerical statements of criteria are possible. Criteria are intended to identify the maximum concentrations of pollutants that would not degrade existing uses. It is particularly important that states adopt narrative criteria because impacts on wetlands often cannot be controlled through numeric limits on various parameters. (Examples of such impacts are physical and biological impacts from discharges of dredged and fill material and nonpoint source pollution.) Many states have been successful in protecting wetlands by using narrative criteria.

Antidegradation policies can be particularly useful in wetlands protection. States can use these policies to regulate point and nonpoint source discharges to wetlands. As part of these policies, waters can be designated as Outstanding National Resource Waters in which no degradation of water quality is allowed.

A number of states are developing water quality standards specifically for their wetlands. This is being accomplished by including wetlands in the definition of "waters of the state," designating uses for wetlands consistent with the goals of the Clean Water Act, specifying criteria protective of those uses, and establishing an antidegradation policy and implementation methods.

Strengths

- Some states have been successful in protecting wetlands through water pollution control programs. These programs have considerable potential for use by other states.

- States can tailor programs to their own needs because water quality standards are developed at the state level; moreover, states can require more stringent protection than federal regulations.
- Getting states to include wetlands in their water quality standards is a high priority for EPA.

Challenges
- Narrative criteria must adequately address the wide range of possible impacts on wetlands.
- Incorporating wetlands into water quality standards requires coordination between two different state agents—that is, wetlands managers and water quality managers—which complicates implementation. (For example, water quality managers may be unfamiliar with wetlands and reluctant to change water quality standards to apply to wetlands.)
- Stormwater management poses special challenges. Stormwater can have both positive and negative impacts on wetlands; it can replenish the water supply of wetlands but can also pollute them. Recently passed stormwater regulations have increased the pressure on local municipalities and industries to a find low-cost, alternative treatment of stormwater discharge. Because wetlands act as natural filters, towns and industries are increasingly looking to wetlands as places to discharge stormwater. Certain types of stormwater discharges require NPDES permits.

Users
States have broad authority to adopt standards for surface water quality, which form the basis of several federal water quality management programs.

Authority for permitting industrial and municipal discharges into surface water may be delegated to the states. Nondelegated programs are administered by EPA. States assess, develop, and implement nonpoint source pollution control programs subject to EPA approval.

Local governments and the public can comment on proposed water quality standards and discharge permits.

Resources
EPA has provided guidance to states on how to apply water quality standards effectively to wetlands. EPA plans to compile information on states' experiences in developing and implementing wetlands water quality standards.

States can apply to EPA for wetlands protection grants, which can support the development of water quality standards and improvement of Section 401 water quality certification programs. States can also apply to EPA for grants for implementing their nonpoint source pollution management programs. Grants have been used to protect wetlands from nonpoint source pollution and to restore or create wetlands as part of nonpoint source pollution control. EPA has issued guidance on how to coordinate wetlands programs and those for nonpoint source pollution control.

Coordination
The new Coastal Nonpoint Pollution Program established by the reauthorization of the Coastal Zone Management Act requires the National Oceanic and Atmospheric Administration (NOAA) and EPA to oversee jointly states' development and implementation of programs to protect coastal waters from nonpoint source pollution stemming from adjacent coastal land uses.

States can fill gaps in wetlands protection by coordinating Section 401 certification for wetlands with other state water quality management programs (e.g., coastal zone management, point and nonpoint source pollution programs, and water quality management plans).

Water quality standards can apply to such decisions as landfill siting, fish and wildlife management and acquisition, and best management practices for control of nonpoint source pollution.

Wetlands identified through State Comprehensive Outdoor Recreation Plans as potential sites to acquire may also be suitable for designation as Outstanding National Resource Waters.

Information needed to apply water quality standards to wetlands can be obtained through federal and state wetlands programs, coastal zone management programs, the National Estuary Program, the National Wetlands Inventory of the U.S. Fish and Wildlife Service (FWS), and various other fish, wildlife, and habitat programs administered by FWS.

Contacts
U.S. EPA Wetlands Contacts (see Appendix E)

References
U.S. Environmental Protection Agency. *Water*

Quality Standards for Wetlands: National Guidance. Washington, D.C.: U.S. Environmental Protection Agency, Office of Water, 1990.

——. *National Guidance: Wetlands and Nonpoint Source Control Programs.* Washington, D.C.: U.S. Environmental Protection Agency, Office of Water, 1990.

6. Clean Water Act: Water Quality Certification
(33 U.S.C. § 1341 (1986))

Section 401, which requires that states certify compliance of federal permits or licenses with state water quality requirements, essentially authorizes states to veto or condition federal permits for filling wetlands, permits for point source pollution discharges, and hydropower licenses. This tool may be subject to change as part of the Clean Water Act reauthorization now underway in Congress.

Under Section 401 of the Clean Water Act, states have authority to review any federal permit or license that may result in a discharge to wetlands and other waters under state jurisdiction, in order to ensure that the actions would be consistent with the state's water quality requirements. If a state denies certification, the federal permit or license cannot be issued. States can qualify certifications by specifying conditions that must be met.

Permits or licenses that may result in a discharge (and therefore are subject to state certification) include the following:

- permits for point source discharges under Section 402 and discharges of dredged and fill material under Section 404 of the Clean Water Act;
- permits for activities in navigable waters that may affect navigation under Sections 9 and 10 of the Rivers and Harbors Act; and
- Federal Energy Regulatory Commission (FERC) hydropower licenses.

The U.S. Environmental Protection Agency (EPA) encourages states to define protection of water quality broadly to include protection of aquatic life, wildlife, aquatic habitat, vegetation, and hydrology required to maintain the aquatic system. Certification is based on whether a proposed activity would meet requirements for conventional and nonconventional pollutants, water quality standards, new source performance standards, and requirements for toxic pollutants (and

any more stringent, relevant state law or regulation). (See *Clean Water Act: Water Pollution Control* for background information on water quality standards.) Certification can address physical, chemical, and biological impacts, depending on how a state designs and applies its water quality standards and other appropriate requirements of state law.

Strengths
- Certification provides a mechanism for protecting wetlands against chemical and other alterations that may not be directly covered by other programs. For states without wetlands regulatory programs, Section 401 may be the only way to exert direct control over projects in or affecting wetlands. For states with regulatory programs, Section 401 provides an additional protection for wetlands by requiring maintenance of water quality.
- The program can help states acquire the experience and authority to take on a greater role under Section 404, which may lead to assumption or state general permits.
- Certification provides states with direct control over all wetlands covered by a federal regulatory program, which is often more encompassing than a state's regulatory program.
- This program provides the potential for greatly improving wetlands protection without new legislation or programming.

Challenges
- Section 401 cannot be used to deny or limit the many activities that affect wetlands but do not require a federal permit (e.g., draining); thus, effectiveness is limited if Section 401 is a state's only wetlands tool.
- Most states have not developed specific water quality criteria for wetlands; those states' standards may not be easy to apply to wetlands.
- There are some legal challenges to the scope of Section 401 authority. FERC has asserted that certification conditions on FERC licenses related to fish, wildlife, vegetation, and recreation are inappropriate. Hydropower cases have also challenged the application of designated uses and the antidegradation component of water quality standards. State court deci-

sions have shown mixed results with regard to FERC licenses.

Users

The state in which a discharge originates has the authority to grant, condition, or deny certification for a federal permit or license. If appropriate, an interstate water pollution control agency has the lead. States affected by a discharge can comment on whether their regulations will be met. (EPA takes the lead for states that lack authority.) A state must provide public notice and, at its discretion, a public hearing on certification. Other states that would be affected must be notified and, if they have objections, given a public hearing. The federal permit or licensing agency must condition the license or permit on compliance with other states' water quality requirements.

Resources

States can apply for EPA's Wetlands Protection State Development Grants for developing water quality standards for wetlands and for including wetlands in Section 401 water quality certification programs.

Coordination

States can fill gaps in wetlands protection by coordinating Section 401 certification with other state water quality management programs (e.g., coastal zone management, point and nonpoint source programs, and water quality management plans).

Information needs and the length of environmental studies are potentially significant factors in the hydropower licensing process. States can coordinate with the U.S. Fish and Wildlife Service, National Marine Fisheries Service, and FERC with respect to information needs and study results. Information useful to Section 401 certification may also be obtained from the Advanced Identification and Special Area Management Planning processes.

Contacts

U.S. EPA Wetlands Contacts (see Appendix E)

Reference

U.S. Environmental Protection Agency. *Wetlands and 401 Certification: Opportunities and Guidelines for States and Eligible Indian Tribes*. Washington, D.C.: U.S. Environmental Protection Agency, 1989.

7. Coastal Barrier Resources System
(16 U.S.C. §§ 1301–1305 (Supp. 1991))

The Coastal Barrier Resources Act denies federal subsidies for development within undeveloped coastal barriers designated as units of the Coastal Barrier Resources System (CBRS). Congress designates areas for inclusion in the CBRS. In addition, states, local governments, and conservation organizations owning lands designated by Congress as "otherwise protected" have until May 1992 to add lands under their control to the CBRS. States can complement the benefits of this act by denying state subsidies for development. They can also publicize the location of CBRS units in their state to help ensure that federal flood insurance is denied in these areas.

The Coastal Barrier Resources Act is an attempt to reduce development within units of the CBRS, thereby reducing loss of life, property, and important natural resources as a result of coastal storms. Units of the CBRS are denied major federal development subsidies (such as federal flood insurance, disaster relief, and loans for sewer, water, and highway construction).

In 1990 many wetlands were added to the CBRS. The Coastal Barrier Resources Act had allowed for wetlands, marshes, estuaries, inlets, and near-shore waters adjacent to undeveloped coastal barriers to be included in the system, but many were not. A 1988 Department of the Interior report recommended that existing coastal barrier units be expanded to include these areas and that they be included among all new additions to the system. Even wetlands that are not part of the system benefit from the protection of coastal barriers because these barriers buffer wetlands from storms.

States, local governments, and conservation organizations owning lands designated by Congress as "otherwise protected" have until May 1992 to add lands under their control to the CBRS. ("Otherwise protected" refers to areas within undeveloped coastal barriers that are not part of the CBRS because they are already under some form of protection.) Once the governor, local governmental authority, or conservation organization notifies the Department of the Interior which lands they wish to include, the department will add those lands to the CBRS.

"Otherwise protected" areas are currently denied only federal flood insurance. Once they are included in the CBRS, they will be denied all federal development subsidies, and their development will be discouraged. This "opt-in" process applies to the Great Lakes, and the Atlantic and Gulf coasts.

The Coastal Barrier Improvement Act of 1990, which amends the earlier Coastal Barrier Resources Act, requires the U.S. Fish and Wildlife Service (FWS) to study and map areas along the Pacific coast (excluding Alaska), Hawaii, and the U.S. Pacific territories that qualify for the program and to recommend areas for future inclusion. To be recommended, an area must be considered appropriate for inclusion by the governor of the state.

The 1990 legislation provides that in the future, eligible surplus government land will be included automatically in the CBRS if approved by the Department of the Interior. The legislation has expanded the CBRS to 1.25 million acres and more than 1,200 miles of shoreline along the Atlantic and Gulf coasts and the Great Lakes. Significant expansion of the system has occurred in the Florida Keys, the Great Lakes, Puerto Rico, and the Virgin Islands. Ninety-five percent of the nearly 788,000 acres added in 1990 along the Atlantic and Gulf coasts comprises coastal wetlands and near-shore waters.

Strengths
- By denying federal subsidies, the 1990 act dramatically reduces development on coastal barriers within the CBRS.
- Denial of federal flood insurance in particular is a strong deterrent to development because many loans are conditioned on flood insurance.

Challenges
- If access is easy, market values may rise enough to make development feasible even without federal support.
- Because of a lack of awareness of areas within the system, federal flood insurance is sometimes still sold for areas that are not eligible to receive it.
- Many local governments have been reluctant to incorporate restrictions imposed on CBRS units within their jurisdiction into their planning and permitting processes.

Users
The act allows states, local governments, and conservation organizations to add lands under their

jurisdiction to the CBRS. Governors must endorse proposed new Pacific coast areas as appropriate for inclusion.

FWS is responsible for mapping. Each federal agency is responsible for ensuring that it denies federal subsidies for any areas within the CBRS.

The reauthorization established an 11-member interagency task force, chaired by the Department of the Interior, to develop recommendations to Congress for future federal policies and legislation on both developed and undeveloped coastal barriers.

Resources
The 1990 legislation authorized $1 million annually to implement existing authorities and $2 million over the next two years for the new provisions of the 1990 act. However, no monies have been appropriated, and no funds or technical assistance are available to states.

Coordination
The new interagency task force is required to look at the effects of federal regulatory activities in the CBRS, including wetlands permits under Section 404 of the Clean Water Act and federal tax policy with respect to coastal barrier development. Federal agencies proposing to expend funds within the CBRS under exceptions allowed by Section 6 must consult with FWS before committing any funds.

Contact
U.S. Fish and Wildlife Service
Division of Habitat Conservation
U.S. Department of the Interior
Arlington Square, Room 400
1849 C Street, NW
Washington, DC 20240
(703) 358-2201

8. Coastal Wetlands Planning, Protection and Restoration Act
(16 U.S.C. §§ 3951–3956 (Supp. 1991))

Under the Coastal Wetlands Planning, Protection and Restoration Act, coastal states can apply for matching grants for wetlands acquisition, management, restoration, or enhancement.

This act authorizes the U.S. Fish and Wildlife Service (FWS) to make matching National Coastal Wetlands Conservation grants to coastal states for acquiring, managing, restoring, or enhancing wetlands. Priority is given to projects that are consistent with the National Wetlands Priority Conservation Plan (see *Emergency Wetlands Resources Act*) and that are in states with dedicated funding programs for the acquisition of coastal wetlands, natural areas, and open spaces. Priority is also given to projects in maritime forests on coastal barrier islands. Grants are provided for property acquisition only if the land will be managed for conservation over the long term.

Most of the act's provisions and funding are focused on Louisiana's coastal wetlands. The act establishes a federal task force to prepare a list of high-priority projects for coastal wetlands restoration and a comprehensive restoration plan for Louisiana's coastal wetlands. The Corps of Engineers is the lead agency for these efforts. The act authorizes funding for up to 75 percent of the costs of implementing restoration projects (85 percent if Louisiana agrees to implement a wetlands conservation plan with a goal of no net loss of wetlands, as a consequence of development of coastal areas).

Fifteen percent of the funding available under the act is dedicated to wetlands conservation projects in coastal states through the authority and approval process established by the North American Wetlands Conservation Act. (See *North American Wetlands Conservation Act.*)

Users

Coastal states (including the Great Lakes states) and trust territories are eligible to apply for National Coastal Wetlands Conservation grants, administered by FWS. Many agencies are involved in the Louisiana-related activities.

Resources

Funding comes from a tax on small-engines fuel. Funding for fiscal year 1992 is expected to be approximately $35 million for Louisiana wetlands activities, $6.5 million for National Coastal Wetlands Conservation grants, and $7.5 million for projects undertaken through the North American Wetlands Conservation Act.

A 50-percent state match is required for National Coastal Wetlands Conservation grants. The state share drops to 25 percent if the state has a trust fund for acquisition of coastal wetlands, natural areas, and open spaces.

Contact

U.S. Fish and Wildlife Service

Division of Habitat Conservation
U.S. Department of the Interior
Arlington Square, Room 400
1849 C Street, NW
Washington, DC 20240
(703) 358-2201

9. Coastal Zone Management Act
(16 U.S.C. §§ 1451–1464 (1985 & Supp. 1991))

Participation in the voluntary coastal zone management program requires states to manage coastal wetlands and provides states with some control over these resources by requiring that federal activities be consistent with state coastal zone management plans, which can be more stringent than federal standards. Federal grants, policy guidance, and technical assistance are available to states for developing and implementing their coastal zone management programs. Some grants can be passed through to local governments.

Under the Coastal Zone Management Act (CZMA), coastal states may voluntarily participate in the federal coastal zone management (CZM) program by preparing comprehensive CZM plans, which provide for the conservation and environmentally sound development of coastal resources. For federal approval, state plans must demonstrate that they provide enforceable standards for the protection of specific coastal resources, including tidal and coastal nontidal wetlands.

States may regulate activities that affect wetlands either through state wetlands programs or permits or through federal "consistency" requirements. Under these requirements, applications for federal licenses or permits (including Section 404 permits) to conduct an activity in the coastal zone of a state with an approved CZM plan must demonstrate that the activity is consistent with the plan. Through consistency reviews of Section 404 permits, a state might reject permits that the Corps of Engineers would otherwise have issued or might refuse to certify permits as consistent unless the applicant makes design changes or modifies the application to incorporate state mitigation requirements.

The wetlands components of state CZM programs vary according to the state permitting authority and the coastal zone boundary. Many states have tiered boundaries and exercise different authorities in each tier. For example, a state may issue direct permits in areas containing sensitive coastal resources but may rely on consistency reviews of federal permits and activities outside these areas. In addition to this regulatory component, the CZM program provides opportunities for state-level wetlands acquisition, planning, management, restoration, creation, educational programs, and research.

Currently, all approved CZM programs require state or local approval for alteration of wetlands. Mitigation of wetlands loss is also required in some states. Many states have initiated public education through their CZM programs.

The CZMA also authorizes the National Estuarine Research Reserve System, which provides opportunities for education, research, acquisition, and management. An estuary may be designated a national estuarine reserve if it is a nationally representative estuarine ecosystem, is suitable for long-term research, and is nominated by the governor of the state.

The 1990 CZMA reauthorization established a new, competitive "enhancement grants" program that encourages each coastal state to improve its CZM program continually to achieve one or more of eight objectives. Three of these objectives may be useful for statewide wetlands strategies: (1) protection, restoration, enhancement, or creation of coastal wetlands; (2) assessment and control of the cumulative impacts of coastal development on coastal resources such as coastal wetlands; and (3) preparation and implementation of Special Area Management Plans for important coastal areas. The National Oceanic and Atmospheric Administration (NOAA), in consultation with each state, must determine priorities for improvement for each objective.

The CZMA reauthorization also established a new Coastal Nonpoint Pollution Program, which requires that each coastal state develop a program to protect coastal waters from nonpoint sources of pollution from adjacent coastal land uses. NOAA and the U.S. Environmental Protection Agency (EPA) will implement this program jointly through the CZMA and Section 319 of the Clean Water Act. (See *Clean Water Act: Water Pollution Control*.)

The reauthorization makes it clear that activities subject to consistency requirements include outer continental shelf lease sales and ocean dumping, whether in or outside the coastal zone.

Strengths

- Many states go well beyond federal requirements in terms of the wetlands they include and the activities they regulate. For exam-

ple, states may regulate activities not covered by Section 404 (dredging, farming, ditching).

- The CZMA provides states with some control over federal activities by requiring federal consistency with approved CZM plans, which can be more stringent than federal standards for wetlands protection.
- Coastal zones are often most threatened by growth pressures; this act allows states to pay special attention to these high-priority areas.
- The CZMA provides for a comprehensive, coordinated approach to the protection and management of coastal wetlands by looking at all wetlands in a coastal zone and by considering their protection within the context of a broader CZM program.
- Relative to other federal programs, the CZM program has consistently been fairly well funded.
- Within certain guidelines, states have flexibility to design CZM programs to meet their particular needs. They also have an opportunity and context for land-use planning and regulation undertaken as a state/local partnership.
- The CZM program may provide an important starting point and model for statewide wetlands strategies.
- Interagency coordination achieved through the CZM program can streamline permit reviews.
- The new enhancement grants program provides opportunities for greater efforts to protect coastal wetlands as well as funding for special area management planning, which can help resolve land-use conflicts.

Challenges

- The CZM program requires resources and commitments from states.
- The program addresses only those wetlands in coastal zones; it may be difficult to mesh with a statewide wetlands strategy.
- Because each state has flexibility in choosing the emphasis and elements of its own program, the extent to which CZM plans actually aid wetlands protection and advanced planning varies from state to state.

Users

The CZMA applies to coastal states (35 states and territories are eligible, including the Great

Lakes states) and is a federal mechanism with a large role for states. Congress established national priorities for managing the nation's coastal resources and provided a framework for states to develop coastal programs tailored to local and regional resources, institutions, and needs. Currently, 29 states and territories have received federal approval for their programs and are implementing them. Of those states without approved programs (Minnesota, Illinois, Indiana, Ohio, Georgia, and Texas), three—Minnesota, Ohio, and Texas—are in the process of developing them.

NOAA oversees the program; states are required to involve local and regional government and the public. Local and regional governments can benefit from pass-through grants.

A number of states have found nationwide general Section 404 permits to be inconsistent with their CZM plans. South Carolina, for example, has no direct permitting authority in nontidal wetlands, but its CZM program contains comprehensive freshwater wetlands policies that are far more stringent than those of the Corps. Using its consistency authority, the state reviews all Section 404 permit applications in its coastal counties and routinely denies applications to fill fractions of an acre of wetlands.

Resources

NOAA provides states with grants, policy guidance, and technical assistance for developing and implementing their CZM programs. For fiscal years 1991, 1992, and 1993, grants are authorized for development of CZM programs at a 4-to-1 ratio of federal-to-state contributions, not to exceed $200,000 in any fiscal year. (The amounts actually appropriated may be much smaller.) Federally approved plans are eligible for implementation grants; match ratios vary, depending on when the state's program is approved. No state match is required for the new enhancement grants.

States are eligible for grants for a variety of activities in National Estuarine Research Reserves, including acquisition, operation and management, education, and research. Limits and match requirements apply.

The CZMA authorizes "resource management improvement grants" for specific coastal resources, including wetlands. These grants may be used for acquisition; low-cost construction projects; engineering work; and educational, interpretive, and management costs. Grants must be matched on a 1-to-1 basis and can be passed through to local governments. In addition, NOAA will help

states identify and obtain other sources of funding for these activities.

Coordination

Approval of a CZM program requires that the state possess mechanisms for interagency coordination and for the participation of other agencies. Moreover, federal consistency requirements force coordination between federal and state permitting activities.

The new Coastal Nonpoint Pollution Program requires that NOAA and EPA jointly oversee states' development and implementation of programs to protect coastal waters from nonpoint sources of pollution from adjacent coastal land uses. NOAA and EPA have also agreed on more efficient ways to coordinate the national CZM program with EPA's National Estuary Program (NEP). In addition, regional offices of the National Marine Fisheries Service and state CZM programs are working to coordinate various habitat conservation efforts.

Various interstate CZM efforts are underway, including those in the Great Lakes and the Gulf of Maine. NOAA plans to encourage more such efforts in the future to help protect ecosystems that cross state boundaries.

Contact

Office of Ocean and Coastal Resource
    Management
National Oceanic and Atmospheric
    Administration
U.S. Department of Commerce
1825 Connecticut Avenue, NW
Room 724 N/OR3
Washington, DC 20235
(202) 606-4135

10. Emergency Wetlands Resources Act
(16 U.S.C. §§ 3901–3932 (Supp. 1991))

Activities authorized by the Emergency Wetlands Resources Act can provide states, local governments, and private groups with valuable information on the location of wetlands and on which wetlands should be considered for acquisition. (See also Land and Water Conservation Fund Act.*)*

The purpose of the Emergency Wetlands Resources Act of 1986 is to "promote the conservation of migratory waterfowl and to offset or prevent the serious loss of wetlands by the acquisition of wetlands and other essential habitat, and for other purposes." Under the act, the U.S. Fish and Wildlife Service (FWS) has developed a National Wetlands Priority Conservation Plan to identify the locations and types of wetlands that should be priorities for state and federal acquisition through the Land and Water Conservation Fund (LWCF). To implement the national plan, regional FWS offices prepare Regional Wetlands Concept Plans that include lists of "priority" sites for acquisition. The act authorizes acquisition of wetlands with LWCF monies, consistent with the national plan.

The National Wetlands Priority Conservation Plan may result in acquisition of "priority" wetlands that provide a high degree of public benefit, are representative of rare or declining wetlands types within an ecoregion, and are subject to identifiable threat of loss or degradation. The functions and values of wetlands, as well as historical and potential wetlands loss, are criteria for determining acquisition priorities.

The act requires that each state consider wetlands an important outdoor recreation resource in preparing State Comprehensive Outdoor Recreation Plans (SCORPs) required under the LWCF. (See *Land and Water Conservation Fund Act* for more information on SCORPs.) The wetlands component of SCORPs must be consistent with the national plan. FWS uses the state wetlands component of SCORPs in preparing its Regional Wetlands Concept Plans.

The act also requires continuation of the National Wetlands Inventory (NWI) project to complete preparation of wetlands maps for all the contiguous states by 1998. As of 1991, 71 percent of the contiguous United States, 22 percent of Alaska, all of Hawaii, and all of Puerto Rico had been mapped. Many mapping efforts are being undertaken in conjunction with individual states. The inventory is also developing plant and soil lists, refining a wetlands evaluation system, and digitizing wetlands map data. Mapping done through the NWI project is not directly applicable to regulatory decisions—most mapping is based on aerial photographs and thus needs to be verified in the field.

In addition, the act requires the U.S. Department of the Interior to report to Congress on the status, condition, and trends of wetlands and the effects of federal programs on wetlands in certain regions of the United States. The act also authorizes entrance fees at certain wildlife refuges to pay for refuge operations and the Migratory Bird Conservation Fund.

Strengths

The National Wetlands Priority Conservation Plan provides a coordinated, national process for setting wetlands acquisition priorities.

Challenges

Funds are lacking for the purchase of many "priority" wetlands.

Users

Provisions of the Emergency Wetlands Resources Act are implemented by FWS. In preparing its Regional Wetlands Concept Plans, FWS involves other federal, state, and local agencies and private organizations active in land and water use planning.

Coordination

Each of the regional offices of the U.S. Environmental Protection Agency (EPA) has prepared or is preparing a list of the most valuable and vulnerable wetlands within the region for use in efforts to regulate wetlands under Section 404 of the Clean Water Act. These lists can also be used in determining acquisition priorities under the National Wetlands Priority Conservation Plan and Regional Wetlands Concept Plans. (Also, the national plan and regional plans may be of use to EPA in preparing its lists.)

Other agencies and private organizations can use the information developed by the national plan (and regional plans), the NWI, and the status and trends reports to apply other mechanisms, including federal, state, or local regulatory programs; planning programs such as Advanced Identification or Special Area Management Planning; private acquisition; and education campaigns.

Wetlands identified through Regional Wetlands Concept Plans as potential sites to acquire may also be suitable for designation under the Clean Water Act as Outstanding Resource Waters in accordance with state water quality standards. No degradation of water quality is allowed in Outstanding Resource Waters.

Contacts

U.S. Fish and Wildlife Service Wetlands Contacts (see Appendix E)

For information on ordering NWI maps, call 1-800-USA-MAPS.

Copies of the National Wetlands Priority Conservation Plan are available from:

U.S. Fish and Wildlife Service
Publications Department

U.S. Department of the Interior
Arlington Square, Room 130
1849 C Street, NW
Washington, DC 20240
(703) 358-1171

11. Endangered Species Act
(16 U.S.C. §§ 1531–1544 (1985 & Supp. 1991))

States, local governments, and private groups can use the Endangered Species Act to protect wetlands that provide habitat for endangered or threatened species—by actively supporting the listing of wetlands-dependent species as endangered or threatened and by urging aggressive implementation of the act, including strong recovery plans.

The Endangered Species Act requires federal agencies to conserve endangered and threatened species. It also prohibits any person from "taking" endangered or threatened animal species. (Endangered plants are afforded less stringent protection.) "Taking" is interpreted broadly to include killing, harassing, or harming a protected species. The definition of "harm" includes modifying or degrading a species' habitat such that the change would significantly impair breeding, feeding, or shelter and would result in injury to the species. Currently more than 600 U.S. species are listed as endangered or threatened.

Under Section 7 of this act, all federal agencies must ensure that their actions are not likely to jeopardize the continued existence of any endangered or threatened species or adversely modify or destroy any of their habitat. These requirements apply to all activities carried out, funded, or regulated by a federal agency, including activities in wetlands.

A state can propose or support the listing of wetlands-dependent species, thereby bringing the act's protection to bear on its wetlands. States can identify potential species, petition the federal government to include these species, and conduct the research necessary to justify listing.

The federal government is also supposed to designate "critical habitat" for a species at the time it is listed. As noted, federal agencies are not authorized to modify adversely or destroy critical habitat.

For listed species, the U.S. Fish and Wildlife Service (FWS) is required to prepare "recovery plans" that outline a strategy to conserve and recover the species. States can promote strong recovery plans for wetlands-dependent species. These recovery plans could, for example, call for acquisition of wetlands and restrictions on wetlands development.

At present, permits can be issued that allow the "taking" of endangered or threatened species that occurs incidentally to otherwise lawful activities. Long-term habitat conservation plans (HCPs) must be developed as part of the permit application process. States may wish to initiate or participate in the preparation of HCPs and to advocate for wetlands protection as part of the plans. However, HCPs may be of limited use for wetlands protection because they require the presence of a federally listed endangered or threatened species and because they are expensive and time-consuming to negotiate. In addition, they are intended for activities not subject to federal permits, and many wetlands activities require federal permits.

Strengths
For wetlands that provide habitat for endangered plant and animal species, this act offers protections, proscribing activities that adversely modify that habitat.

Challenges
This mechanism protects wetlands only to the extent that they provide habitat for endangered or threatened species. Due to inadequate resources to implement the endangered species program, there are long delays in listing species and preparing recovery plans. Approximately 40 percent of U.S. listed species do not have approved recovery plans.

Users
For inland species, the program is administered by the FWS. The National Marine Fisheries Service administers and enforces the act for marine species. (This is only a general rule with exceptions; for instance, FWS enforces the program for manatees and California sea otters.) Public involvement in program implementation is required, and the act provides for citizen suits.

The act encourages cooperation with states and provides for implementation of a state's endangered species program if the state meets certain standards.

Resources
If they qualify for cooperative-agreement funding under Section 6 of the act, states can receive federal grants for up to 75 percent of the costs of

particular endangered species conservation projects or up to 90 percent of such costs if two or more states work cooperatively on a project. However, funding is limited.

Using the Land and Water Conservation Fund, land may be acquired to protect endangered or threatened species. (See *Land and Water Conservation Fund Act.*)

Coordination

The Clean Water Act's Section 404(b)(1) guidelines expressly require compliance with the Endangered Species Act. The Corps of Engineers has instructed its districts to stop processing permits for any activities that violate this act.

If the recovery plan for a particular listed species calls for restrictions on development in wetlands, FWS comments on proposed Section 404 wetlands permits are likely to reflect these concerns and result in permit denial or restriction. Moreover, the requirement that an environmental review of federal activities be conducted (under the National Environmental Policy Act) can allow various concerns to be aired about negative effects on endangered species.

Contacts

U.S. Fish and Wildlife Service
Office of Endangered Species
U.S. Department of the Interior
Mail Stop 452
4401 North Fairfax Drive
Arlington, VA 22203
(703) 358-2171

National Marine Fisheries Service
Office of Protected Resources and Habitat
    Programs
1335 East-West Highway
Silver Spring, MD 20910
(301) 427-2319

References

Bean, Michael J. *The Evolution of National Wildlife Law.* New York: Praeger, 1983.

Bean, Michael J., Sarah G. Fitzgerald, and Michael A. O'Connell. *Reconciling Conflicts Under the Endangered Species Act: The Habitat Conservation Planning Experience.* Washington, D.C.: World Wildlife Fund, 1991.

12. EPA Wetlands Program State Development Grants

States can use EPA grants for development and/or enhancement of their wetlands protection programs. The funds can be used for a wide range of activities, both regulatory and nonregulatory.

Beginning in fiscal year 1990, the U.S. Environmental Protection Agency (EPA) made grants available to states for the development of wetlands protection programs. This funding can be used to develop new programs or to refine and enhance existing programs. Priority is given to innovative approaches and to project results that can be transferred. The types of projects likely to be fundable include the following:

- state wetlands conservation plans;
- projects integrating wetlands into traditional water/natural-resource programs;
- multiobjective river corridor management;
- use of water quality standards to protect wetlands;
- incorporation of wetlands into Section 401 programs;
- projects that expand activities covered and/or the geographic jurisdiction of existing regulatory programs; and
- monitoring projects.

Delaware used a $50,000 grant to identify and restore wetlands on marginal agricultural lands. Vermont used a $26,970 grant for a pilot project to coordinate wetlands conservation planning among state agencies, regional planning commissions, and municipal governments, as required by state law. Michigan received a $44,645 grant to develop water quality standards for wetlands, to incorporate them into existing state standards, and to address wetlands better in its Section 401 water quality certification program.

Strengths

States can use development grants to improve their ability to apply other tools. These grants also provide critically needed funding to support various state wetlands efforts.

Users

Grants are available to state wetlands agencies, state water quality agencies, and state agencies with wetlands-related programs. Federally recognized Indian tribes are eligible for grants as well.

Resources

In fiscal year 1990, $1 million was available; in fiscal year 1991, $5 million. States must provide a 25-percent match.

Contacts

U.S. EPA Wetlands Contacts (see Appendix E)

13. Executive Order 11990: Protection of Wetlands

(42 F.R. 26961 as amended by
Exec. Order No. 12608 (1987), reprinted in
42 U.S.C. § 4321 app. at 244–245 (Supp. 1991))

Executive Order 11990 requires each federal agency to

> take action to minimize the destruction, loss or degradation of wetlands, and to preserve and enhance the natural and beneficial values of wetlands in carrying out responsibilities the agency may have for (1) acquiring, managing, and disposing of Federal lands and facilities; (2) providing Federally undertaken, financed, or assisted construction and improvements; and (3) conducting Federal activities and programs affecting land use including but not limited to water and related land resources planning, regulating, and licensing activities.

This executive order does not apply to permits or licenses issued by federal agencies for activities involving wetlands not on federal property. Agencies must avoid undertaking or assisting new construction in wetlands unless the agency head determines that there is no practicable alternative and that the proposed action includes all practicable measures to minimize harm to wetlands.

Agencies must provide opportunities for early public review of plans or proposals for new construction in wetlands, including projects considered not significant enough to require an environmental impact statement under the National Environmental Policy Act.

At Jean Lafitte National Historical Park and Preserve in Louisiana, for example, a federal agency modified its plans for a flood levee that would have adversely affected the park's bayous, freshwater swamps, and marshes. The changes were made in part because of the requirements of the executive order.

14. Farm Programs: Conservation Reserve Program

(16 U.S.C. §§ 3830–3837 (Supp. 1991))

The Conservation Reserve Program provides cost sharing and rental payments to farmers for restoration and protection of farmed wetlands. It has been largely superceded by the newly established Wetlands Reserve Program. The program encourages protection of highly erodible uplands and filter strips along wetlands, which can reduce pesticide and sediment runoff into these wetlands.

With the establishment of the Wetlands Reserve Program in the 1990 reauthorization of the Farm Bill (i.e., the Food, Agriculture, Conservation and Trade Act of 1990), the Conservation Reserve Program (CRP) has less relevance to wetlands protection. In general, the Wetlands Reserve Program will take the place of CRP for wetlands protection. (See *Farm Programs: Wetlands Reserve Program*.)

The CRP was established by the 1985 Farm Bill and expanded in the 1990 version of that bill. Under CRP, landowners who enter into contracts to set aside highly erodible, environmentally sensitive cropland and to implement a conservation plan for the land receive annual payments for 10 to 15 years. No commodity crops can be grown on CRP land. A maximum of 25 percent of a county's eligible cropland may be enrolled in the program. Even after CRP contracts expire, farmers must comply with the conservation plan provisions. Violators of CRP contracts face substantial penalties and can lose a variety of farm program benefits.

The CRP was expanded in January 1989 to allow inclusion of farmed wetlands not subject to erosion. The 1990 reauthorization of the Farm Bill, however, stipulated that farmed wetlands are no longer eligible for CRP. Instead, they are to be enrolled into the Wetlands Reserve Program.

Under a U.S. Fish and Wildlife Service (FWS) initiative, CRP lands can be restored to wetlands if the lands are prior-converted wetlands and are likely to be restored successfully, and if the farmer is willing to protect the restored values. Prior-converted wetlands that were enrolled in CRP before November 29, 1990, may be entered into the Wetlands Reserve Program.

Vegetative filter strips along wetlands, lakes, and rivers can be enrolled in CRP even if not highly erodible. Their purpose is to trap sediment and chemical runoff from adjacent erodible land. These areas can help protect adjacent wetlands.

The 1990 Farm Bill expanded the CRP and made areas important for water quality protection eligible even if they are not highly erodible, which could indirectly result in wetlands protection. As a result of the January 1989 decision to allow farmed wetlands to be enrolled in CRP even if they are not subject to erosion, farmers enrolled 410,000 acres of wetlands in the program in 1989. In 1990, FWS entered into 1,300 agreements to implement wetlands restoration projects on CRP lands.

The Chesapeake Bay region, the Great Lakes region, and Long Island Sound have been designated as conservation priority areas. One goal is to achieve significant enrollment in these areas so as to protect and improve their water quality and wildlife habitat.

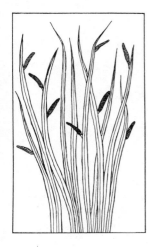

Strengths

Because of financial assistance available for restoring prior-converted wetlands, restoration of these areas may be cheaper than providing other vegetated cover (as required by CRP).

Challenges

The program protects only farmed wetlands already within CRP and prior-converted wetlands that are part of an otherwise eligible field.

Users

The Conservation Reserve Program is administered by the Agricultural Stabilization and Conservation Service (ASCS) of the U.S. Department of Agriculture. The Soil Conservation Service assists ASCS.

Farmers with qualifying cropland can bid for the opportunity to participate. The program is available in all 50 states as well as Puerto Rico and Guam.

Resources

Annual rental payments are provided to participating landowners. Rental payments cannot be higher than local rental rates for comparable land and cannot exceed $50,000 per person annually.

Subject to the availability of funding, cost sharing may be available for restoring prior-converted wetlands. Cost sharing is also available for establishing vegetation on the enrolled areas.

Coordination

State programs can be used to increase incentives for farmers by providing cost-share assistance, rental payments, or tax benefits that supplement federal benefits. For example, farmers may be reluctant to enroll vegetative filter strips in CRP because of the high costs of maintenance, for which there is no federal cost-share support. States could help subsidize these maintenance costs for filter strips that would protect wetlands from sediment or pesticide runoff. For example, Virginia and Maryland provide additional funding to participants with enrolled filter strips. Minnesota, Missouri, Maryland, and Ohio fund additional cost sharing for establishing vegetation in targeted areas.

FWS and private groups such as Ducks Unlimited help restore CRP wetlands in areas targeted by the North American Waterfowl Management Plan. (See *North American Waterfowl Management Plan.*)

State assessments and management plans for nonpoint source pollution control (required by Section 319 of the Clean Water Act) can be used to determine which wetlands could most benefit from filter strips to control runoff.

Contacts

Conservation and Environmental Protection Division
Agricultural Stabilization and Conservation Service
U.S. Department of Agriculture
P.O. Box 2415
Washington, DC 20013
(202) 447-6221

Soil Conservation Service Wetlands Contacts (see Appendix E)

Reference

Walter, John. "Farming in the Flyways." *Successful Farming* 2(1990): 25–40.

15. Farm Programs: Farmers Home Administration Wetlands-Related Programs
(7 U.S.C. §§ 1985, 1997 (Supp. 1991))

The Farmers Home Administration (FmHA) may grant or transfer easements on wetlands in its inventory of repossessed farmland to federal or state agencies for conservation purposes when the land meets certain criteria. FmHA may also forgive loans if the borrower grants a conservation easement. States, local governments, and private groups can help encourage such easements.

Building on an earlier program prompted by Executive Order 11990 on wetlands conservation, the 1990 Farm Bill (i.e., the Food, Agriculture, Conservation and Trade Act of 1990) requires the U.S. Department of Agriculture (USDA) to establish perpetual conservation easements on wetlands in the FmHA inventory of foreclosed farmland. The act also allows for cancellation of borrower debt in exchange for the granting of conservation easements on wetlands. (Debt cancellation is proportional to the area that the owner places in conservation easements, with some restrictions. Debt cancellation is available to new borrowers or those delinquent since December 25, 1985.)

Easement size is restricted to ensure that easements do not jeopardize the continued marketability of a farm: easements are limited to 10 percent of existing cropland for prior-converted wetlands, 20 percent for farmed wetlands, and 50 percent of a parcel's existing forage lands for hayed or grazed wetlands. Easements can be 100 percent of existing cropland for infrequently or noncropped wetlands or for wetlands converted in violation of Swampbuster. Some easements can be reduced or eliminated if USDA determines the easements would limit marketability. Once easements are placed, USDA must protect wetlands values and restore farmed or converted wetlands.

More than 100,000 acres of wetlands conservation easements have been established under this program, which has resulted in the protection, enhancement, and restoration of wetlands and wetlands buffer areas. Many of these areas have been transferred to the U.S. Fish and Wildlife Service (FWS) for inclusion in the National Wildlife Refuge System. In some states, land deemed unmarketable because its special environmental values (e.g., water quality protection, endangered species habitat) limit its agricultural value is routinely transferred to state natural resources agencies.

FmHA loans cannot be used for conversion or other manipulation of wetlands except for maintenance of previously converted wetlands or

for activities initiated before enactment of the 1990 Farm Bill.

Strengths
- FmHA may grant or transfer easements on wetlands in its inventory to federal or state agencies for conservation purposes when the land meets certain criteria.
- Debt reduction provides an incentive for wetlands protection.

Challenges
- FmHA has been reluctant to impose easements on lands in it inventory. Over a recent three-year period, FWS recommended that easements be placed on 225,000 acres of wetlands within the FmHA inventory, but only roughly one-third actually received easements.
- Farmers may be reluctant to grant wetlands easements because debt reduction can be achieved in other ways.

Users
FmHA administers this program. For FmHA inventory lands, FWS has responsibility for proposing areas for easements and may be responsible for restoration, management, and enforcement. For debt reduction easements, FWS helps evaluate land for eligibility and may be responsible for easement management.

Resources
Inventory lands may be transferred free of charge to appropriate federal or state agencies.

Coordination
FWS routinely coordinates with state natural resources agencies in evaluating property for eligibility and appropriateness for easements.

Contacts
State offices of Farmers Home Administration (U.S. Department of Agriculture)

Program Support Staff
Farmers Home Administration
U.S. Department of Agriculture
Room 6039
14th St. and Independence Ave., SW
Washington, DC 20250
(202) 382-9619

U.S. Fish and Wildlife Service Wetlands Contacts (see Appendix E).

16. Farm Programs: Swampbuster

(16 U.S.C. §§ 3821–3824 (Supp. 1991))

By denying federal farm benefits to farmers who drain wetlands, Swampbuster discourages the conversion of wetlands on agricultural lands. States, local governments, and private groups can take advantage of this program by educating farmers about its provisions and can supplement it by denying other benefits to Swampbuster violators.

Under the Swampbuster program, farmers are denied crop subsidies and other agricultural benefits if they:

- drain or otherwise convert wetlands for the purpose of (or to have the effect of) making possible the planting of agricultural commodity crops after November 28, 1990; or
- plant commodity crops on wetlands converted after December 23, 1985.

Until the 1990 reauthorization of the Farm Bill (i.e., the Food, Agriculture, Conservation and Trade Act of 1990), conversion alone did not trigger violations; actual planting of a commodity crop was required. The 1990 reauthorization also established graduated penalties (ranging from $750 to $10,000) if the following conditions apply:

- the violation is inadvertent,
- the producer has not violated Swampbuster more than once in the previous 10 years, and
- the producer restores the wetlands according to a federally approved plan.

These graduated penalties also apply retroactively to violations meeting these criteria and occurring prior to enactment of the 1990 Act. The 1990 act expanded lost program benefits to include payments under the Conservation Reserve Program and other programs.

Under Swampbuster, wetlands conversion is allowed if it will cause only a minimal effect on the hydrological and biological value of the wetlands. The Soil Conservation Service (SCS) and the U.S. Fish and Wildlife Service (FWS) jointly determine whether the conversion will constitute a minimal effect; SCS has the final say. Drainage of frequently cropped wetlands is allowed if the producer provides mitigation by restoring a con-

verted wetlands so as to provide equivalent wetlands value. SCS and FWS also jointly approve restoration plans.

When applying for federal farm program benefits, producers indicate whether they plan to manipulate any wetlands areas. If so, the U.S. Department of Agriculture (USDA) must delineate these wetlands on a certified map. Producers can appeal delineations. In the case of Swampbuster violations, USDA must conduct a site visit before reducing program benefits.

For wetlands farmed prior to December 25, 1985, producers can maintain but not improve upon drainage as it existed at that date.

Strengths

The reauthorized Swampbuster provisions combine broader jurisdiction (drainage, not planting, now triggers violation), with flexibility (graduated penalties and minimal effect/mitigation provisions).

Challenges

Environmental groups have expressed concern that minimal effect determinations and mitigation provisions are overly flexible and may undermine the effectiveness of the program. Swampbuster does not apply to wetlands converted for certain "noncrop" uses (e.g., fruit trees, cranberries, fish production, roads, buildings). However, Section 404 of the Clean Water Act may apply.

Users

Swampbuster applies to any farmer who receives federal crop subsidies. Swampbuster is administered by USDA's Agricultural Stabilization and Conservation Service (ASCS). SCS essentially serves as a technical consultant to ASCS. FWS must be consulted on plans for restoring converted wetlands and to determine whether a conversion will cause a minimal effect.

Resources

No resources are available because this is a disincentive program.

Coordination

The requirements of Swampbuster and Section 404 of the Clean Water Act are often confused. While the same wetlands fall within the jurisdiction of both programs, these programs treat those wetlands quite differently. Swampbuster, though not regulatory, provides a strong disincentive to draining agricultural wetlands; Section 404 in general exempts normal farming and ranching and does not regulate draining of wetlands. It may be useful to educate the regulated community as to the requirements of these two programs, their differences, and their similarities.

Contacts

Conservation and Environmental Protection
    Division
Agricultural Stabilization and Conservation
    Service
U.S. Department of Agriculture
P.O. Box 2415
Washington, DC 20013
(202) 447-6221

U.S. Fish and Wildlife Service Wetlands Contacts (see Appendix E).

Reference

Thompson, Paul, and Karen Tyler. *A Guide to Agricultural Wetlands Protection.* Washington, D.C.: National Governors' Association, 1991.

17. Farm Programs: Water Bank
(16 U.S.C. §§ 1301–1311 (1985))

Although limited in funding and geographic area covered, the Water Bank can provide an important incentive to farmers to protect existing wetlands. States, local governments, and private groups can help publicize this program and can complement it with additional incentives.

Farmers in participating states and counties can receive annual rental payments for up to 10 years for protecting and restoring agricultural, inland fresh wetlands and adjacent uplands that are important to the nesting, breeding, or feeding of migratory waterfowl. Participants must agree not to drain, fill, level, burn, or otherwise damage wetlands; must maintain vegetation on adjacent upland; and must fulfill the terms of an approved conservation plan. To be eligible, wetlands must have been identified in a conservation plan approved by the U.S. Department of Agriculture (USDA).

The Water Bank has protected prairie potholes in the north central United States, bottomland hardwoods in the Southeast, and wetlands associated with irrigated areas in the West. More than 200,000 acres of wetlands are protected by existing landowner agreements.

Strengths

- The Water Bank can be an important complement to the Swampbuster program and Section 404 of the Clean Water Act by providing an incentive for farmers not to convert wetlands in cases where Swampbuster and Section 404 do not apply. (Swampbuster does not apply unless a farmer receives federal crop subsidies or unless conversion is for the purpose of commodity crop production; many farmers do not receive federal program benefits. Section 404 provides several exemptions under which conversions might be allowed.)
- The Water Bank can provide protection of adjacent uplands that are needed to protect the wetlands within the bank.
- For areas that qualify for both the Water Bank and the Wetlands Reserve Program, some farmers may prefer the short-term agreements (10 years) of the bank to the Wetlands Reserve Program's requirement of 30-year or permanent easements.

Challenges

- This program applies only in limited geographic areas.
- The program budget is relatively small.

Users

The Agricultural Stabilization and Conservation Service (ASCS) of USDA administers the program. The Soil Conservation Service provides technical assistance to landowners and assists ASCS, as does the U.S. Fish and Wildlife Service.

The program is available only in 10 states, primarily those in the central and Mississippi River flyways: Arkansas, California, Louisiana, Minnesota, Mississippi, Montana, Nebraska, North Dakota, South Dakota, and Wisconsin. Within these states, only certain counties are eligible. The program is mainly used in Minnesota, North Dakota, and South Dakota.

Resources

In 1990, rental payments ranged from $7 to $66 per acre and averaged $14 per acre. (These rentals are low relative to per-acre payments under the Conservation Reserve Program or payments expected under the new Wetlands Reserve Program.)

Technical assistance is available for developing conservation plans. Cost sharing may be available to eligible producers for various conservation practices, including habitat improvement and bottomland hardwood management. Funding for the Water Bank has increased in recent years.

Contacts
Conservation and Environmental Protection Division
Agricultural Stabilization and Conservation Service
U.S. Department of Agriculture
P.O. Box 2415
Washington, DC 20013
(202) 447-6221

Soil Conservation Service Wetlands Contacts (see Appendix E)

18. Farm Programs:
Wetlands Reserve Program
(16 U.S.C. §§ 3837a–3837f (Supp. 1991))

The important new Wetlands Reserve Program is designed to restore up to one million acres of agricultural wetlands. States, local governments, and private groups can help publicize this program, which provides substantial incentives to farmers, and can complement the program by providing additional incentives.

The 1990 reauthorization of the Farm Bill (the Food, Agriculture, Conservation and Trade Act of 1990) established a Wetlands Reserve Program that provides financial incentives for restoration and protection of up to one million acres of wetlands if producers agree to long-term easements. Priority is given to producers willing to establish permanent easements. The U.S. Department of Agriculture (USDA) is directed to enroll up to one million acres between 1991 and 1995 at a rate of 200,000 acres per year.

Easements are for 30 years or are permanent, or for a maximum amount of time allowed by state law. The landowner must record the easement on the land deed. Easements require that farmers implement conservation plans approved by the Soil Conservation Service (SCS) and the U.S. Fish and Wildlife Service (FWS). Only wetlands uses compatible with protecting wetlands functions are permitted (such as hunting, fishing, and periodic haying or grazing).

This program provides for the restoration and protection of:

- farmed or converted wetlands (converted prior to December 23, 1985);
- croplands adjacent to eligible wetlands that are deemed necessary as buffer areas to protect the functional values of the wetlands being restored (which may result in inclusion of some nonfarmed and nonconverted wetlands); and
- riparian areas that link eligible wetlands.

Lands must have been planted with agricultural commodity crops in at least one of the years from 1986 to 1990.

Farmed and prior-converted wetlands enrolled in the first nine sign-ups of the Conservation Reserve Program are eligible for the Wetlands Reserve Program.

Subject to funding availability, participants receive:

- 10 equal annual payments for less-than-permanent easements (or a single lump sum for permanent easements), with payments not exceeding the difference between the fair market value of the land less the fair market value of the land encumbered by the easement;
- 50-percent cost sharing for less-than-permanent easements (or 75 percent for permanent easements) for implementing conservation measures; and
- technical assistance.

Strengths
This program provides a strong positive financial incentive for restoration and protection of agricultural wetlands.

Challenges
The new program will be expensive to implement.

Users
Any farmer with qualifying wetlands can bid for an opportunity to participate in the program, which is administered by the Agricultural Stabilization and Conservation Service (ASCS) of USDA. SCS essentially serves as ASCS's technical consultant. FWS assists SCS in determining on which wetlands to acquire easements and FWS must concur on the conservation plan for protected wetlands.

Resources
A total of $46.4 million has been appropriated for the Wetlands Reserve Program for fiscal year

1992 for restoration of up to 50,000 acres in five states.

SCS and FWS have developed a course on wetlands restoration techniques that is available to state agency employees. Also available is a 23-minute video for farmers, "The Wealth in Wetlands." A new publication, "Conserving and Restoring America's Wetlands," should be available soon from SCS. For more information, contact Soil Conservation Service Wetlands Contacts (see Appendix E).

Coordination

Farmed and prior-converted wetlands enrolled in the Conservation Reserve Program prior to November 29, 1990, are eligible for the Wetlands Reserve Program.

Contacts

Conservation and Environmental Protection
    Division
Agricultural Stabilization and Conservation
    Service
U.S. Department of Agriculture
P.O. Box 2415
Washington, DC 20013
(202) 447-6221

Soil Conservation Service Wetlands Contacts
(see Appendix E)

19. Federal Aid in Sport Fish Restoration Act (Dingell-Johnson Act)
(16 U.S.C. §§ 777a–777l (1985 & Supp. 1991))

Federal Aid in Wildlife Restoration Act (Pittman-Robertson Act)
(16 U.S.C. §§ 669a–669i (1985 & Supp. 1991))

Under the Dingell-Johnson and Pittman-Robertson acts, states and territories can receive funding for fish and wildlife conservation. Some of this funding has been used for wetlands protection and restoration.

Dingell-Johnson Act funding is distributed to states according to a formula based on the geographic area of the state and the number of state residents with fishing licenses. These monies can be used for up to 75 percent of the cost of fish restoration and management projects and comprehensive plans for fish and wildlife resource man-

agement. A portion of funding under this act can be used for aquatic resource education programs. Since the program began in 1952, roughly $1.4 billion has been given to states. The Dingell-Johnson Act is funded by excise taxes on fishing equipment, import duties on fishing tackle and pleasure boats, and a portion of a tax on motorboat fuels.

Through the Pittman-Robertson Act, states can receive grants for up to 75 percent of the costs of wildlife conservation activities, including acquisition, restoration, and maintenance of wetlands. Since the program began in 1938, more than $2 billion has been given to states. From 1989 to 1990, states acquired nearly 14,000 acres of wetlands. The Pittman-Robertson Act is funded by excise taxes on hunting equipment.

The U.S. Fish and Wildlife Service provides technical assistance to states.

Contact

U.S. Fish and Wildlife Service
Division of Federal Aid
U.S. Department of the Interior
Arlington Square, Room 322
1849 C Street, NW
Washington, DC 20240
(703) 358-2156

20. Federal Wetlands Research and Technical Assistance

U.S. Army Corps of Engineers

The Corps of Engineers is conducting a three-year, $22-million wetlands research initiative aimed at improving wetlands management. Research is being conducted in four areas:
- delineation and evaluation,
- critical processes,
- stewardship and management, and
- restoration and establishment.

The Corps is working in cooperation with several other federal agencies. Information and technology developed through the research initiative will be made widely available.

Contact

Wetlands Research Program (CEWES-EP-D)
U.S. Army Corps of Engineers
Waterways Experiment Station
3909 Halls Ferry Road
Vicksburg, MS 39180-2733

U.S. Environmental Protection Agency

EPA conducts wetlands research on cumulative impacts, water quality functions, and restoration and creation. EPA disseminates the research results and related technology through training programs, a newsletter, and meetings and workshops with state wetlands managers and others.

EPA has many informational materials (including brochures and videos) that explain its wetlands programs. The agency has established a hotline for public inquiries about federal wetlands programs: 1-800-832-7828.

Contacts
U.S. EPA Wetlands Contacts (see Appendix E)

U.S. Fish and Wildlife Service

FWS conducts a variety of wetlands research, including wetlands mapping and analysis of wetlands trends; causes of wetlands loss; value of wetlands as fish and wildlife habitat; and contamination of wetlands.

Contacts
U.S. Fish and Wildlife Service Wetlands Contacts (see Appendix E)

U.S. Soil Conservation Service
Through a variety of its own programs and as a consultant to several programs run by the Agricultural Stabilization and Conservation Service, the Soil Conservation Service provides technical assistance to private landowners in land conservation. This can include assistance in wetlands restoration, creation, and enhancement.

Contacts
Soil Conservation Service Wetlands Contacts (see Appendix E)

21. Fish and Wildlife Coordination Act
(16 U.S.C. §§ 661-668 (1985 & Supp. 1991))

The Fish and Wildlife Coordination Act provides a key role for states in evaluating the impacts on fish and wildlife conservation of water resource development projects or Clean Water Act Sections 402 or 404 permits. This can be a useful tool for protecting wetlands that are important to fish and wildlife conservation.

The Fish and Wildlife Coordination Act requires that federal agencies give wildlife conservation "equal consideration . . . with other features of water-resource development programs." In addition, federal agencies proposing water development projects such as dam construction and reclamation projects or water-modifying activities for which federal permits are required (including Section 404 permits) must consult with the U.S. Fish and Wildlife Service (FWS) or the National Marine Fisheries Service as well as the state agency with jurisdiction over wildlife resources for an evaluation of the proposed project's impacts on fish and wildlife. The goals of this evaluation are to assess the status of affected fish and wildlife resources and to prevent or mitigate their loss and damage. The lead federal agency must include the results of the evaluation (referred to as a "mitigation report") in any report prepared as part of the project and must include in the project plan "such justifiable means and measures for wildlife purposes as the . . . agency finds should be adopted to obtain maximum overall project benefits."

In addition, federal projects must make "adequate provision [consistent with overall project purposes] . . . for the conservation, maintenance, and management of wildlife." This can include acquisition of land or waters.

Strengths
As part of the required consultation, federal and state wildlife agencies can recommend that a permit be denied or be subject to mitigation conditions, on the basis of impacts on fish and wildlife, including wetlands.

Challenges
Mitigation reports are only advisory; the lead agency is not required to follow their recommendations. A 1988 General Accounting Office (GAO) review of many aspects of the Section 404 program's implementation concluded that Corps of Engineers districts in many cases do not require changes to permits to address the recommendations of FWS and other resource agencies.

Users
FWS (or the National Marine Fisheries Service) and the state agency with jurisdiction over wildlife resources perform the required consultations. State wildlife agencies can manage areas set aside for mitigation purposes. Generally, these are areas associated with dams and are west of the Mississippi.

Resources

The act also provides that federal property of value for wildlife conservation can be managed by a state wildlife agency (except for land valuable to migratory bird management). The federal government reserves oil and mineral rights, and the property must continue to be managed for wildlife conservation.

Contacts

U.S. Fish and Wildlife Service Wetlands Contacts (see Appendix E)

22. Fish and Wildlife Service Private Lands Restoration Initiative

The U.S. Fish and Wildlife Service encourages and helps private landowners restore converted and degraded wetlands.

Drawing on several legal authorities, the U.S. Fish and Wildlife Service (FWS) has focused considerable effort for the past few years on encouraging and helping private landowners restore converted and degraded wetlands and associated upland habitat. Roughly one-third of the restorations have occurred on land protected through the 1990 Farm Bill's Conservation Reserve Program or under conservation easements arranged through Farmers Home Administration. (See *Farm Programs: Conservation Reserve Program* and *Farmers Home Administration Wetlands-Related Programs.*) The remainder of the restorations have occurred on private lands for which no other programs provide restoration support. Landowners are required to commit to protecting the restored wetlands for a specified period of time. They are not compensated for loss of land use due to restoration.

Over the first four years of the initiative, FWS restored 142,000 acres of wetlands. Priority is given to areas that are under long-term conservation agreements or easements, that can be of use as habitat for diminishing species, and for which landowners will contribute to restoration.

Strengths

Significant wetlands loss has occurred on private lands. Many areas can be converted back to wetlands relatively easily and inexpensively by restoring their water supply.

Challenges

Land may be converted from wetlands to another use after a landowner agreement expires.

Resources

FWS provides technical advice and assists landowners in restoring wetlands, up to a maximum of $10,000 per person per year.

Contacts

U.S. Fish and Wildlife Service Wetlands Contacts (see Appendix E)

23. Internal Revenue Code
(26 U.S.C. § 170 (1988 & Supp. 1991))

State and local governments can increase wetlands protection by educating landowners about the federal tax benefits of land donation and encouraging the work of private, nonprofit land trusts.

Federal tax law has a major effect on wetlands development and protection. Traditionally, the federal tax code has encouraged wetlands degradation by creating tax incentives that favor real-estate investments and certain agricultural activities (such as cattle grazing) that may have negative effects on wetlands. Although certain laws on federal income and estate tax benefits may encourage landowners to donate land for conservation purposes, the Tax Reform Act of 1986 significantly reduced the income tax advantages of donating property for conservation purposes.

Section 170(f) of the Internal Revenue Code establishes the general parameters within which income tax deductions can be taken for contributing property for conservation purposes. A taxpayer may claim a deduction for contributing a full interest in real estate (i.e., a "fee-simple" interest) or for certain partial interests. An example of a partial interest is a life estate. In this case, a landowner retains a property until his or her death, at which time the property transfers to a conservation organization. The fair-market value of a qualified contribution may be deducted from a landowner's income tax. (The fair-market value is the appraised value for a fee-simple interest or the amount that the full value is reduced by donating a partial interest, such as a conservation easement.)

In addition, the code provides for deductions for bargain sales, allowing a landowner to sell prop-

erty for less than the fair-market value and to claim a deduction for the difference in that value and the sale price. The portion of a donation that a landowner may actually deduct, however, depends on the particular tax situation.

The most significant partial interest for which a landowner may claim a deduction is for a "qualified conservation contribution." Three criteria apply:

- the donation must be made to a government agency, a tax-exempt and publicly supported charity such as a land trust, or a charity controlled by a government agency;
- the donation must be "exclusively for conservation purposes," such as to preserve land for public outdoor recreation or education or to protect fish and wildlife habitat; and
- the donation must be granted in perpetuity and cannot have a limited duration.

Section 170(h)(4) of the Internal Revenue Code defines "conservation purposes" as follows: (1) the preservation of land areas for outdoor recreation or education; (2) the protection of a relatively natural habitat of fish, wildlife, or plants or similar ecosystem; (3) the preservation of open space (including farmland and forest land) where such preservation is for the scenic enjoyment of the general public or pursuant to a clearly delineated federal, state, or local governmental conservation policy and yielding a significant public benefit; or (4) the preservation of a historically important land area or a certified historic structure.

Before acting, taxpayers should see Section 170(g) of the Internal Revenue Code and consult a qualified tax advisor. Less exacting standards apply for estate tax purposes. Donating land for conservation purposes can also provide important estate tax benefits by lowering the taxable value of an estate by the appraised value of the donated interest.

Strengths
- This mechanism provides financial incentives for landowners to donate wetlands for conservation purposes.
- Land trusts often acquire land through donation or at discount rates and then transfer the land at no cost or at discount rates to government agencies.

Challenges
- The Tax Reform Act of 1986 introduced the alternative minimum tax (AMT), which reduces the tax incentives for making substantial gifts of appreciated property. This tax imposes a minimum liability regardless of a taxpayer's deductions, credits, and exclusions. The AMT may prevent a taxpayer from deducting an unrealized appreciation (i.e., the difference between the basis and fair-market value).
- To encourage private donations of wetlands, the tax implications of such contributions must be made explicit, and credibility with the potential donor must be developed. (A local land trust or similar nongovernmental conservation organization is often best suited to overcome this challenge.)

Users
Deductions are available to taxpayers who make qualified conservation contributions. Local land trusts are often involved in using this tool— by educating landowners and encouraging donations.

Resources
Many land trusts have developed information for landowners who are considering such donations.

Coordination
State and local tax benefits (such as reduced property tax assessments) may complement the federal tax benefits of donating wetlands for conservation purposes. Because these tax benefits will rarely if ever be a landowner's primary reason for donation, this mechanism will be more effective if used in coordination with tools that educate landowners and promote a philanthropic interest in wetland values.

Contact
The Land Trust Alliance
900 17th Street, NW, Suite 410
Washington, DC 20006
(202) 785-1410

Reference
Diehl, Janet, and Thomas S. Barrett. *The Conservation Easement Handbook*. Washington, D.C.: Land Trust Alliance, 1988.

The Internal Revenue Service has several relevant publications available at minimal cost by calling 1-800-424-FORM or writing your Regional IRS Forms Distribution Center. Helpful publications include:

Tax-Exempt Status for Your Organization
(publication 557)
Charitable Contributions (publication 526)
Determining the Value of Donated Property
(publication 561)

24. Land and Water Conservation Fund Act

(16 U.S.C. §§ 460l-4 to 460l-11 (1974 & Supp. 1991))

Under the Land and Water Conservation Fund Act, states and local communities can receive federal matching grants for land acquisition and recreation development. States are required to prepare State Comprehensive Outdoor Recreation Plans, including a wetlands component, to qualify for grants. The information in these plans can assist states, local governments, and private groups in applying other wetlands protection tools.

The Land and Water Conservation Fund (LWCF), funded primarily from receipts for offshore oil and gas leasing and development, is used to acquire recreational lands and natural areas, including wetlands. Under the LWCF Act, each state is required to produce a State Comprehensive Outdoor Recreation Plan (SCORP) every five years to be eligible for federal assistance from the LWCF. SCORPs are intended to review state recreation opportunities and outline priorities for land acquisition and development of recreational facilities.

The LWCF Act was amended in 1986 by the Emergency Wetlands Resources Act. The Emergency Wetlands Resources Act recognizes the contribution of wetlands in providing fish and wildlife habitat and offering significant recreational and commercial benefits. The amended LWCF Act requires states to consider wetlands in SCORPs. Specifically, states are expected to identify the agencies and organizations involved in wetlands management, evaluate existing and proposed wetlands protection mechanisms, assess wetlands resources, identify wetlands loss and degradation factors, and establish priorities for protection.

Strengths

- Often, the wetlands component of SCORPs represents a first attempt to assess statewide wetlands resources. The documenting of this effort increases the information available to local, state, and regional planners.
- SCORPs can draw attention to the need for

wetlands protection, thereby prompting more acquisition, and can help target resources on wetlands most in need of acquisition.

Challenges

- SCORPs serve as the basis for acquisition funding under LWCF; however, only lands with recreation opportunities qualify for funding.
- Federal planning requirements can be cumbersome and frustrating for states; although detailed planning is necessary, little funding is available for acquisition.

Users

The National Park Service reviews SCORPs and administers the LWCF grants program. The grant selection process provides for extensive public involvement.

States that produce acceptable SCORPs every five years are eligible for federal matching grants for land acquisition and recreation development. In turn, states can pass grants through to local governments for these same activities.

In revising SCORPs to reflect wetlands needs, states may be able to recommend implementation strategies to a variety of sources, including both public agencies and private organizations.

Resources

LWCF funding available to states was $16.7 million in fiscal year 1990. (Funding has declined dramatically in recent years; $369 million was available in fiscal year 1979.) The National Park Service can provide grants and technical assistance for development of SCORPs, including the wetlands component. The Park Service provides 50-percent matching funds when requested by eligible state agencies.

Coordination

The Emergency Wetlands Resources Act directed the development of a National Wetlands Priority Conservation Plan to identify wetlands for federal and state acquisition. (See *Emergency Wetlands Resources Act.*) The act requires that SCORPs and the national plan be consistent. Also, the state agency preparing the wetlands component of a SCORP must consult with the state's fish and wildlife agency.

Each of the regional offices of the U.S. Environmental Protection Agency (EPA) has prepared or is preparing a list of the most valuable and vulnerable wetlands within its region. EPA will use these lists in its efforts to regulate wetlands under Section 404 of the Clean Water Act. These lists may also be useful to states in preparing SCORPs (and SCORPs may in turn be useful to EPA in preparing its lists).

Other agencies and private organizations can use the information developed by SCORPs to target areas for applying other mechanisms, including federal, state, or local regulatory programs; planning programs (such as Advanced Identification or Special Area Management Planning); private acquisition; and education campaigns.

Wetlands identified through SCORPs as potential acquisition sites may also be suitable for designation as Outstanding Resource Waters in accordance with a state's water quality standards. No degradation of water quality is allowed in such waters.

Contact

SCORP Program Manager
Recreation Resources Assistance Division
National Park Service
P.O. Box 37127
Washington, DC 20013-7127
(202) 343-3780

25. Migratory Bird Conservation Fund
(16 U.S.C. §§ 718–718j (1985 and Supp. 1991))

The Migratory Bird Conservation Fund finances acquisition of land for the national wildlife refuge system. In addition, easements or fee-simple title can be acquired for wetlands in the prairie pothole region for use as federal waterfowl production areas.

The Migratory Bird Conservation Fund was established by the Migratory Bird Hunting and Conservation Stamp Act, commonly known as the Duck Stamp Act. The act required all waterfowl hunters over 16 years of age to purchase federal hunting stamps (currently $15 per stamp). In addition to revenue from duck stamp sales, the fund includes refuge entrance fees, import duties on arms and ammunition, and other miscellaneous revenues. Fund income for fiscal year 1992 is expected to be $35.2 million. The fund is used to acquire land for the national wildlife refuge system and for federal waterfowl production areas.

Federal authority for refuge land acquisition and a system for making refuge acquisition deci-sions was established by the Migratory Bird Conservation Act (16 U.S.C. §§ 715–715s (1985 & Supp. 1991)). The act established a Migratory Bird Conservation Commission to review acquisition proposals. State approval is required before the Secretary of the Interior can recommend an area for purchase or rental.

The Fish and Wildlife Service Small Wetland Acquisition Program uses the fund to acquire fee-simple title or easements on wetlands in the prairie pothole region. FWS then manages the acquired wetlands as federal waterfowl production areas. Easements prohibit the draining, burning, or filling of wetlands. When the wetlands are dry, land-owners can crop, hay, graze, plow, or work them. Landowners can open or close their lands to hunting or trapping and can retain the right to develop minerals. Fee-simple title is acquired mostly for permanent water areas. Adjacent uplands that are important as nesting habitat can be acquired; drained wetlands that can be restored may also be eligible.

Strengths

The easement program provides protection for wetlands but also allows landowners to use the areas when they are dry and of little value for waterfowl production.

Users

FWS administers these programs.

To be eligible for easements, wetlands must be valuable to waterfowl production and in a county approved for the program.

Resources

Landowners receive one-time lump-sum payments for easements. Cost-sharing funds for restoring wetlands may be available, and restored wetlands may then be eligible for easements.

Purchase price under the Small Wetland Acquisition Program is based on the market value of comparable land.

As of the end of fiscal year 1989, over 23,000 easements were placed on more than 1.2 million acres of wetlands at a cost of roughly $49 million under the Small Wetland Acquisition Program. In addition, fee-simple title was acquired for almost 564,000 acres at a cost of $102 million.

Contacts

U.S. Fish and Wildlife Service Wetlands Contacts (see Appendix E)

26. National Environmental Policy Act
(42 U.S.C. §§ 4321–4375 (1977 & Supp. 1991))

The National Environmental Policy Act allows states, local governments, and private groups to ensure that the environmental impacts of federal actions affecting wetlands are considered. Federal agencies are obligated to consider additional state or local environmental analysis requirements as long as these requirements do not conflict with this act. Environmental review is required for all federal actions, including permits, licenses, loans, and other subsidies.

The National Environmental Policy Act (NEPA) requires that environmental impacts be considered in federal decision making. Federal agencies must prepare environmental impact statements (EISs) on major federal actions significantly affecting the quality of the human environment. Major federal actions may include construction projects, permits, licenses, loans, and other subsidies. An environmental assessment (EA) is undertaken to determine whether a full EIS is necessary.

Preparing an EIS is a costly, lengthy process that requires extensive comment from the public and various governmental agencies. NEPA review must consider direct, indirect, and cumulative effects as well as alternatives to the proposed actions.

Individual Section 404 wetlands permits require review under NEPA. EAs are undertaken for most individual Section 404 permit applications; EISs are done for only a small percentage of applications. General permits require NEPA review only for the overall permit. Other wetlands alterations that involve federal activities require NEPA review and the preparation of either EAs or EISs.

Strengths
- NEPA review ensures that the environmental impacts of all federal activities affecting wetlands are considered.
- This mechanism requires extensive public and agency comment on EISs during preparation and on drafts.

Challenges
The preparation of an EA and/or EIS does not prevent adverse effects. It merely requires that possible impacts be considered fully.

Users
NEPA review is the responsibility of the federal agency conducting the major activity. States can take a "joint lead" with a federal agency in preparing an EIS.

The U.S. Environmental Protection Agency (EPA) reviews and comments on all federal draft and final environmental regulations and other proposed major federal actions of other agencies. EPA's comments are available to the public. The public and other government agencies may also comment during the evaluation process.

Coordination
NEPA is triggered by implementation of many other federal laws, including Section 404 wetlands permits. In the case of Section 404, NEPA review is built into the process.

A number of states have adopted NEPA-like laws. Federal agencies are obligated to consider additional state or local environmental analysis requirements as long as these do not conflict with NEPA requirements. If a federal activity would be inconsistent with a state or local plan or law, the environmental impact analysis needs to discuss the inconsistency and how the agency plans to reconcile the conflict.

Contacts
Council on Environmental Quality
722 Jackson Place, NW
Washington, DC 20006
(202) 395-5750

U.S. Environmental Protection Agency
Office of Federal Activities
Mail Code A-104
401 M Street, SW
Washington, DC 20460
(202) 260-5053

References
Council on Environmental Quality. *Forty Most Asked Questions Concerning CEQ's National Environmental Policy Act Regulations* (46 F.R. 18026, 1981).

Mandelker, Daniel A. *NEPA Law and Legislation.* Wilmette, Ill.: Callaghan & Co., 1984.

U.S. Environmental Protection Agency. *Facts About the National Environmental Policy Act.* Washington, D.C.: U.S. Environmental

Protection Agency, Office of Enforcement and Compliance Monitoring, 1989.

27. National Estuary Program
(33 U.S.C. § 1330 (Supp. 1991))

The National Estuary Program provides impetus, funding, and technical assistance for the management of nationally significant estuaries, of which wetlands are an important component. Governors can nominate estuaries for inclusion in the program.

Authorized by the Water Quality Act of 1987, the National Estuary Program (NEP) targets nationally significant estuaries for research, planning, and management. For each estuary in the program, the U.S. Environmental Protection Agency (EPA) provides technical assistance and facilitates a planning process that results in a strategy for cleanup, called a Comprehensive Conservation and Management Plan. Plan participants must commit to specific financial, institutional, and political actions. High-priority "demonstration" projects can be undertaken before completion of the plan.

Estuaries in the program as of 1991 are: Buzzards Bay and Massachusetts Bay in Massachusetts; Narragansett Bay in Rhode Island; Long Island Sound in Connecticut and New York; New York-New Jersey Harbor; Delaware Bay in New Jersey, Pennsylvania, and Delaware; Delaware inland bays; Albemarle/Pamlico Sounds in North Carolina; Sarasota Bay, Indian River Lagoon, and Tampa Bay in Florida; Galveston Bay in Texas; Santa Monica Bay and San Francisco Bay in California; Puget Sound in Washington; Casco Bay in Maine; and Barataria-Terrebone Bays in Louisiana. A Comprehensive Conservation and Management Plan has been completed and approved by EPA and the state for Puget Sound; the plan for Buzzards Bay is expected to be completed soon.

Other estuaries can be added to the program by congressional action or by EPA in response to nomination by a governor.

Strengths
- The program focuses attention and funding on protecting the living resources of high-priority estuaries, of which wetlands are an important component.
- The program coordinates and capitalizes on other programs and encourages innovative management approaches.
- NEP takes a comprehensive approach to

problem solving by looking at entire estuaries instead of isolated problems. It can include consideration of all affected interests so that the resulting plan is a consensus document. Moreover, NEP increases the information base about a particular area.

Challenges
- Resources to implement NEP may not be available.
- NEP is limited to only some of the more than 100 estuaries throughout the nation.
- The program requires the cooperation of many parties, and securing agreement may be difficult.
- NEP can be very time-consuming and resource-intensive, and the individuals involved may change over time.

Users
EPA has lead responsibility for the program. The law requires broad participation in NEP Management Conferences. Representatives of citizen and user groups, scientific and technical institutions, and federal, state, and local government must participate.

Governors can nominate estuaries (in whole or in part) in their states for inclusion in the program. Nomination requires a commitment to action by the state.

Resources
Roughly $15 million per year in federal funding is available for the development of plans. State and local governments together must provide a 25-percent match. No federal funds are directly earmarked for implementation.

Coordination
EPA works closely with the National Oceanic and Atmospheric Administration in implementing the National Estuary Program, particularly in conducting research to assess ecosystems and setting up comprehensive water quality sampling programs.

Contact
U.S. Environmental Protection Agency
Office of Wetlands, Oceans, and Watersheds
Oceans and Coastal Protection Division
Coastal Management Branch
WH-556F
401 M Street, SW

Washington, DC 20460
(202) 260-6502

28. National Flood Insurance Program
(42 U.S.C. §§ 4001–4128 (1977 & Supp. 1991))

The National Flood Insurance Program can benefit wetlands by (1) designating "floodways" along rivers and streams (thereby severely restricting any development within that area), and (2) encouraging communities to protect open space and limit floodplain development by offering advantageous flood insurance rates for communities that exceed minimum federal standards. (This program is subject to change due to pending legislation.)

The federal government plays two roles in floodplain management: limiting its own activities and making flood insurance available in local communities that have adopted floodplain management regulations. Federal floodplain policy calls for protecting the natural and beneficial functions of floodplains (including wetlands) in addition to protecting public safety and property.

Executive Order 11988, "Floodplain Management" (May 24, 1977, 42 F.R. 26951, as amended by Executive Order 12608, September 9, 1987, 52 F.R. 34617), requires federal agencies to avoid the adverse impacts associated with the modification or development of floodplains and to avoid the direct and indirect support of floodplain development if there is a practicable alternative.

While floodplain regulations are designed to reduce flood damages, many of the regulations incidentally protect other values and functions of floodplains such as wetlands. In addition, the Federal Emergency Management Agency (FEMA) has implemented a community rating system (CRS) that offers advantageous insurance rates to communities exceeding minimum federal standards for open-space preservation and new development.

More than 18,000 communities nationwide have adopted floodplain management regulations in order to qualify for federally supported flood insurance. More than 2.5 million local policies are in effect.

Strengths
- Communities are required to restrict development in "floodways" (a designated portion of river floodplains in which further development would increase flood heights). Floodway designation therefore results in wetlands protection along rivers. Roughly five million acres of floodways have been designated along 40,000 stream and river miles. Some states and local communities have adopted more restrictive floodway requirements, thereby bringing a greater portion of the floodplain into the floodway.
- The National Flood Insurance Program has provided impetus for much of the existing state and local floodplain planning and regulation.
- An estimated 80 percent of the nation's wetlands are located in floodplains, often in the most hazardous (and thus most likely to be regulated) portions. Wetlands in some floodplains have been credited with reducing downstream flood peaks by 80 percent. This fact motivates the protection of wetlands through floodplain management programs.

Challenges
- Some communities have resisted the land-use planning "strings" attached to the availability of federally backed floodplain insurance.
- Local community compliance with federal regulations has also been a problem.

Users
FEMA administers the National Flood Insurance Program. State enabling legislation is often required for local governments to regulate land use in flood hazard areas. Often, states prepare model floodplain management ordinances that are then adopted by local communities.

Property owners qualify for flood insurance if the community enacts minimum floodplain management regulations.

Resources
FEMA provides technical and financial assistance to state and local communities with regard to adopting and complying with floodplain management regulations. FEMA has mapped the flood hazard areas of every flood-prone community and makes these maps available to the public.

Coordination
The floodplain executive order requires that the "public interest review" required of Section

404 wetlands permit applications include a consideration of effects on floodplains.

Federal flood insurance is not available for new or substantially improved structures in areas within the Coastal Barrier Resources System. In many areas, however, development has continued.

Some communities have integrated floodplain and wetlands planning.

Contact

Federal Insurance Administration
Federal Emergency Management
    Administration
500 C Street, SW
Washington, DC 20472
(202) 646-2781

29. Near Coastal Waters Program

The Near Coastal Waters Program seeks to improve management of the environmental quality of near coastal waters, which include tidal inland waters and those ocean waters affected by pollution from the land.

In 1986 the U.S. Environmental Protection Agency (EPA) began the Near Coastal Waters Program by developing a 10- to 15-year strategic plan for near coastal waters. A number of joint EPA–state demonstration projects were funded, including marsh restoration projects in Louisiana.

Strengths

This program focuses attention and resources on coastal areas and their important habitats, including wetlands, which face many pressures from urbanization and agriculture.

Challenges

The program has no earmarked funding source. Because funding must be obtained from a variety of other programs, it has been erratic.

Users

EPA regional offices have the lead and are preparing near coastal water strategies. States can play a key role in preparation of these strategies, including ensuring that coastal wetlands protection is included. The Great Lakes are included in the program.

Resources

EPA regional offices can pass funding through to states in the form of grants or cooperative agreements. Also, EPA transfers technology and information through conferences and publications to a network of government water quality managers, scientists, and private groups.

Coordination

There is overlap between the near coastal waters program and the National Estuary Program (NEP) (see *National Estuary Program*), which funds in-depth planning for select estuaries. The near coastal waters program takes a broader perspective, looking at more than the estuaries in the NEP program and at more waters than estuaries alone. A specific intent of the program is to improve coordination among federal, state, and local agencies.

Contact

U.S. Environmental Protection Agency
Office of Wetlands, Oceans, and Watersheds
Oceans and Coastal Protection Division
Coastal Management Branch
WH-556F
401 M Street, SW
Washington, DC 20460
(202) 260-6502

30. North American Waterfowl Management Plan

By participating in "joint-venture" partnerships under the North American Waterfowl Management Plan, states, local governments, and private groups can benefit from the resources of other partners as well as from research and educational information developed under this program. The program encourages partnerships for protection, enhancement, or restoration of wetlands that are important to waterfowl and other migratory birds.

The North American Waterfowl Management Plan was initiated by a 1986 agreement between the United States and Canada. The plan responds to the decline of waterfowl and other wetlands-dependent species in the past 10 years. Its goal is to protect, enhance, restore, and create in North America six million acres of wetlands and upland crucial to waterfowl survival. The plan is implemented through partnerships: in areas identified as critical for waterfowl, the U.S. Fish and Wildlife Service (FWS) coordinates "joint ventures" of public and private partners. Currently, eight joint ventures are underway in the United States, and three more are in the planning stages.

The plan entails research on wetlands restoration and the effects of contaminants on wetlands, wetlands status surveys, and wetlands inventories. Moreover, the plan encourages regional planning, involvement of farmers as primary partners, and citizen advocacy for wetlands conservation.

The North American Wetlands Conservation Act broadened the focus of the plan to include protection of wetlands habitat that is important to species beyond waterfowl. (See *North American Wetlands Conservation Act.*)

Principal U.S. areas targeted by the plan are California's Central Valley; the prairie pothole regions of Minnesota, North Dakota, South Dakota, and Iowa; the lower Mississippi River region; the Gulf Coast; the Atlantic Coast from Maine to South Carolina; the lower Great Lakes-St. Lawrence River basin; and the playa lakes of Texas, New Mexico, Oklahoma, Kansas, and Colorado. Future joint ventures are planned for the intermountain West, the Great Plains, the Pacific Coast, the Rainwater Basin, the upper Mississippi River-Great Lakes region, and other areas.

Strengths

- Joint habitat ventures in the United States have succeeded in protecting, restoring, or enhancing more than 650,000 acres of wetlands in a recent two-year period.
- Joint ventures leverage the strengths of the various groups involved and target resources for maximum impact.
- Implementation of the North American Wetlands Conservation Act will probably lead to increased funding for the plan and increased emphasis on protecting habitat that is important to species in addition to waterfowl.
- Plan participants have created an informal network for sharing technical information.
- The plan can serve as a model for similar efforts at the state level.

Challenges

- The plan's emphasis on waterfowl management may limit projects focusing on habitat that is important for other species.

- A challenge for the plan is to integrate the habitat needs of a wide array of wetlands-dependent species with a continuing emphasis on waterfowl.

Users

FWS and the Canadian Wildlife Service jointly administer the plan. An international management committee coordinates implementation. The committee includes a state representative from each of the four migratory bird flyways. Nineteen private conservation, agricultural, and timber organizations constitute the U.S. Implementation Board. Nearly 200 public and private organizations participate in plan programs in various capacities.

Resources

Full implementation of the plan, targeted for completion in 2000, is estimated to cost $1.5 billion. The North American Wetlands Conservation Act of 1989 authorized up to $30 million a year for North American wetlands conservation projects. In 1990 the U.S. government's contribution to the plan of $40 million was supplemented by $78 million from states, the Canadian government, Canadian provinces, private organizations, corporations, and individuals in the United States and Canada. The plan encourages private-sector fund raising.

Coordination

The North American Wetlands Conservation Act of 1989 provides additional funding and encouragement for wetlands conservation under the plan.

Contact

U.S. Fish and Wildlife Service
North American Waterfowl and Wetlands Office
U.S. Department of the Interior
Arlington Square, Room 340
1849 C Street, NW
Washington, DC 20240
(703) 358-1784

Reference

U.S. Fish and Wildlife Service and Canadian Wildlife Service. *North American Waterfowl Management Plan—Progress Report: A New Beginning.* Washington, D.C.: U.S. Fish and Wildlife Service, 1991.

31. North American Wetlands Conservation Act

(16 U.S.C. §§ 4401–4413 (Supp. 1991))

Under the North American Wetlands Conservation Act, states and private groups or individuals can receive matching grants for wetlands conservation projects if the projects further the goals of the North American Waterfowl Management Plan and international migratory bird treaties and if they entail public/private partnerships. Grants are available for acquisition of land or water rights and for restoration, management, or enhancement of wetlands. (See also North American Waterfowl Management Plan.)

The North American Wetlands Conservation Act encourages partnerships among federal agencies and others to protect, restore, enhance, and manage wetlands and other habitats for migratory birds, fish, and wildlife. It is intended to support implementation of the North American Waterfowl Management Plan.

Federal matching grants are available to acquire land and water rights and for restoration, management, or enhancement of wetlands. The act requires biennial assessments of progress.

Land acquired must become part of the National Wildlife Refuge System unless approved by the Migratory Bird Conservation Commission for conveyance without cost to a state or private organization. For such conveyance to occur, the state or private organization must ensure that it can provide long-term protection of the wetlands.

Strengths

The act provides increased funding for wetlands and other wildlife habitat protection under the North American Waterfowl Management Plan and broadens the plan to include habitat important to species in addition to waterfowl.

Challenges

During economically difficult periods, the program may not be well funded.

Users

The U.S. Fish and Wildlife Service (FWS) administers the act. Any federal, state, or private organization or individual may apply for matching grants.

A nine-member North American Wetlands Conservation Council evaluates and recommends projects for funding. The council includes a state representative from each of the four migratory bird flyways. The Migratory Bird Conservation Commission (which oversees acquisition of migratory bird habitat) reviews the recommendations of the council and decides which projects to fund.

Resources

The act authorized up to $30 million per year for North American wetlands conservation projects. Because roughly half this amount depends on congressional appropriation, funding may vary considerably from year to year. At least 50 percent of the funding for the act must be used for projects in Canada and Mexico.

As of September 1991, 61 U.S. projects had been approved, affecting nearly 200,000 acres of wetlands and associated uplands. Nearly $16 million was expended on U.S. projects in fiscal year 1991.

The Coastal Wetlands Planning, Protection and Restoration Act of 1990 provided funding for wetlands conservation projects in coastal states approved under the North American Wetlands Conservation Act.

Coordination

Wetlands conservation projects receive more favorable consideration if they further the purposes of the North American Waterfowl Management Plan and international treaties on migratory birds, are consistent with the National Wetlands Priority Conservation Plan, provide habitat for listed or candidate endangered or threatened species, and entail public/private partnerships.

Contact

U.S. Fish and Wildlife Service
Coordinator, North American Wetlands
    Conservation Council
North American Waterfowl and Wetlands Office
U.S. Department of the Interior
Arlington Square, Room 340
1849 C Street, NW
Washington, DC 20240
(703) 358-1784

32. Ramsar Convention

(September 1972, 11 I.L.M. 963–976)

The Ramsar treaty can result in increased wetlands protection.

The Convention on Wetlands of International Importance Especially as Waterfowl Habitats, known as "Ramsar," is an intergovernmental treaty that obligates its 45 signatory nations to consider wetlands conservation in their land-use planning, to promote wise use of their wetlands, to establish wetlands nature reserves, and to encourage wetlands research and data exchange. In addition, each country must designate at least one site for inclusion in a List of Wetlands of International Importance. Countries are also required to promote the conservation of these sites.

Sites on the Ramsar list in the United States as of 1991 are the Izembek Lagoon National Wildlife Refuge and State Game Range, Alaska; Forsythe National Wildlife Refuge, New Jersey; Okefenokee National Wildlife Refuge, Georgia/Florida; Ash Meadows National Wildlife Refuge, Nevada; Everglades National Park, Florida; Chesapeake Bay Estuarine Complex, Maryland/Virginia; Cheyenne Bottoms State Game Area, Kansas; Cashe-Lower White Rivers Joint Venture Area, Arkansas; Horicon Marsh, Wisconsin; and Catahoula Lake, Louisiana. The total acreage of these wetlands is nearly 2.8 million.

Some countries prepare a "shadow list" of sites eligible for listing. The United States may do so in the near future.

Strengths

Including wetlands on the Ramsar list focuses attention on them and can result in greater protection.

Challenges

The United States adds to the Ramsar list only those sites that are already protected by other laws or programs. Designation of areas not already protected could have a greater impact. The treaty entails few legally binding conservation obligations.

Users

The U.S. Fish and Wildlife Service (FWS) is the lead federal agency.

The U.S. National Ramsar Committee, a nonprofit, nongovernmental organization, monitors and comments on Ramsar implementation.

Contact

U.S. Fish and Wildlife Service
Office of International Affairs
U.S. Department of the Interior
Arlington Square, Room 860
1849 C Street, NW
Washington, DC 20240
(703) 358-1763

33. River Conservation and Management
(16 U.S.C. §§ 1271–1287 (1985 & Supp. 1991))

States can initiate designation of rivers as wild and scenic, which results in federal consultation, coordination, and protection, particularly from impacts of water resources development projects. State and local governments and private organizations are eligible for technical assistance for conservation and management of rivers, including those not in the Wild and Scenic Rivers system. Wetlands are often located along rivers, so these federal programs can afford significant protection, particularly in the arid West, where wetlands along rivers are often critical habitats.

The Wild and Scenic Rivers Act authorizes the designation of rivers with outstanding scenic, recreational, geologic, fish and wildlife, historical, cultural, or similar values. The act provides protection of these rivers from adverse impacts of water resource development projects, effectively guaranteeing that they remain free flowing.

Public lands with wild and scenic rivers running through them must be managed to protect and enhance the important values of these rivers. This can result in restrictions on logging, mining, and corridor developments, which may degrade river resources. Most wild and scenic rivers are in Oregon, Alaska, and California. As of 1991, 124 rivers had been included in the National Wild and Scenic Rivers system—a total of 9,358 miles.

Potential wild and scenic rivers also receive some protection in the form of federal policy measures to avoid or mitigate adverse effects. These rivers are identified in the National Park Service's Nationwide Rivers Inventory. As of 1991, 1,500 potential national wild and scenic river segments were included, totaling 62,000 miles.

Also, the National Park Service provides assistance in river conservation planning and management to state and local governments, private groups, and landowners. This assistance also applies to rivers not within the Wild and Scenic Rivers system. Two common projects, statewide river assessments and river corridor planning, can result in wetlands protection. The National Park Service serves as a facilitator and technical resource for these efforts.

Strengths
- Wetlands are often located along rivers, so these federal programs can afford significant protection. In the arid West, wetlands

along rivers are particularly critical habitats.

- Designation of a river as wild and scenic may spur significant land acquisition efforts along the river corridor.
- Including wetlands in a statewide river assessment and in river corridor plans are ways in which a state can emphasize their value and justify their protection.

Challenges

- The Wild and Scenic Rivers system covers a limited area; only 0.3 percent of U.S. rivers are so designated.
- It can be difficult and expensive to control development on private lands within river corridors.

Users

Additional rivers or river segments are added to the Wild and Scenic Rivers system through congressional action or by the Secretary of the Interior in response to a state request. States can initiate designation of a river as wild and scenic by passing state legislation designating that river as a state scenic river, preparing a management plan for permanent protection and compatible uses of the river and adjacent lands, and requesting a federal designation. The Secretary of the Interior is authorized to add the river to the system, without congressional approval, if the designation does not require federal funds. States maintain management responsibility for the river. As of 1991, 13 rivers within the system were state-administered. Several other states have taken steps toward designating rivers.

Rivers within the Wild and Scenic Rivers system are administered by either a state department of natural resources or, at the federal level, by the Forest Service, the National Park Service, the Bureau of Land Management, or the U.S. Fish and Wildlife Service.

State and local governments and the public can participate in the Wild and Scenic Rivers program by recommending rivers for designation, providing information leading to designation, monitoring and commenting on the administration of rivers, and participating in the development and implementation of river management plans for designated rivers.

State and local governments, other federal agencies, private groups, and landowners are eligible for technical assistance in planning for the conservation and management of rivers (including those not in the Wild and Scenic Rivers system).

Resources

Subject to availability of funding, the National Park Service provides technical assistance for development of river conservation and management plans, studies, and other activities leading to designation of wild and scenic rivers, and for river conservation education. Funding preference is given to cooperative efforts, those complex enough to warrant federal involvement, and those including rivers identified as eligible for further study or inclusion as wild and scenic.

Coordination

Other agencies and private organizations can use the information developed by river management plans to apply other conservation mechanisms. These could include federal, state, and local regulatory programs, public or private acquisition, and educational campaigns.

Contact

National Park Service
Recreation Resources Assistance Division
P.O. Box 37127
Washington, DC 20013-7127
(202) 343-3780

34. Special Area Management Plans
(16 U.S.C. §§ 1452–1453 (1985 & Supp. 1991))

States, local governments, and private groups can play a major role in preparing Special Area Management Plans (SAMPs). SAMPs provide some predictability for wetlands regulation, can be helpful in resolving conservation and development conflicts in areas of rapid growth, and can help control cumulative impacts on wetlands. Funding is available to states for preparation and implementation of SAMPs in coastal zones.

Coastal Zone Special Area Management Plans

One of the policies of the Coastal Zone Management Act (CZMA) is to encourage the preparation of SAMPs. (See *Coastal Zone Management Act* for a description of the CZM program in general.) A SAMP is defined in the CZMA as

> a comprehensive plan providing for natural resource protection and reasonable economic growth containing a detailed and comprehensive statement of policies, standards, and criteria to guide public

and private uses of lands and waters; and mechanisms for timely implementation in the specific geographic areas within the coastal zone.

States have employed SAMPs to address a wide range of coastal resource management problems, ranging from the protection of historic river corridors from excessive boat traffic to comprehensive management plans for entire estuaries. The 1990 reauthorization of the CZMA reemphasized the importance of SAMPs by making their preparation and implementation eligible for 100-percent funding through competitive "coastal zone enhancement grants."

One goal of SAMP development is the incorporation of results into state coastal zone management programs. Enforceable policies developed through a SAMP, once incorporated, can be the basis for state permitting decisions and consistency reviews of federal activities and permits.

Corps of Engineers Special Area Management Plans

The Corps of Engineers has adopted the SAMP concept and incorporated it into its own policies. A Corps Regulatory Guidance Letter (issued October 2, 1986, by the Office of the Chief of Engineers) requires that four criteria be met before the Corps will begin a SAMP process:

1. The area should be environmentally sensitive and under strong development pressure.

2. Ideally, there should be strong public involvement throughout the process.

3. There should be a sponsoring local agency to ensure that the plan fully reflects local needs and interests.

4. All parties must be willing at the outset to conclude the process with definitive regulatory products.

CZM-sponsored SAMPs focus on coastal zones. Corps SAMPs are not restricted to coastal zones. The wetlands addressed depend on the boundary of the particular SAMP area. Beyond the general guidance that SAMPs provide for natural resource protection and reasonable economic growth, the SAMP process is undefined. It can potentially address all causes of wetlands loss.

Strengths
- SAMPs can be tailored to meet the needs and resources of a particular area and can

provide a more consistent and efficient framework for permit decisions than can a case-by-case framework. SAMPs can also provide for regulatory predictability and local involvement.
- This proactive process addresses conservation and development conflicts and focuses strongly on the most environmentally sensitive and most threatened areas.
- SAMPs can lead to the development of comprehensive approaches to wetlands protection within a planning area and within the context of broader planning approaches. The process may serve as an important starting point and model for state-wide wetlands strategies.
- Regulatory agencies can assess the cumulative impacts of isolated fills on an entire planning area.
- SAMPs can include consideration of all affected interests so that the resulting plan is a consensus document.
- SAMPs can increase the information base for particular areas and can bolster public awareness and appreciation of wetlands values.
- The process can be coordinated with other planning processes, acquisition efforts, and so forth.

Challenges
- The process is intended to accomplish a very difficult task: planning for both resource protection and development.
- Limits on staff and funding dictate that federal agencies limit the number of SAMPs in which they participate.
- SAMPs can be very time-consuming and resource-intensive, and the individuals involved may change over time.
- Resources to implement SAMPs may not be available.
- It may be difficult to define the SAMP planning area.
- The process does not guarantee permit issuance or denial (unless tied to a regulatory decision, such as a decision regarding zoning or a Section 404 general permit).
- SAMPs have not been used much to date; it is difficult to evaluate their success in cases where they have been tried.
- It may be difficult to coordinate diverse

agencies, particularly when those agencies perceive differences in their mandates or authorities.

Users

For SAMPs prepared under CZMA authority, states play the lead role (with federal oversight and participation), as the SAMP is intended as an extension of a state CZM program. For Corps SAMPs, the Corps takes the lead.

SAMPs typically involve federal, state, and local government as well as the public. The Corps requires that there be a sponsoring local agency "to ensure that the plan fully reflects local needs and interests." States can and do play key roles in requesting that SAMPs be done, in providing information, and in commenting on draft plans. In addition, states can use the resulting information in their own wetlands protection programs.

Resources

Although no earmarked funding is available for SAMP development under the CZMA, states may use program implementation and program enhancement funds for SAMPs. States can pass these grants through to local or regional governments. The Corps has funded SAMPs through a "special studies" segment of its overall regulatory budget.

Coordination

The SAMP process directs all relevant local, state, and federal agencies to coordinate permit programs in implementing SAMPs. The comprehensive nature of the process provides many opportunities for coordination with other tools and programs. Other agencies and private organizations can use the information developed by SAMPs to undertake federal, state, or local regulatory programs; planning programs such as Advanced Identification; public or private land acquisition; and educational campaigns.

Contacts

Office of Ocean and Coastal Resource Management
National Oceanic and Atmospheric Administration
U.S. Department of Commerce
1825 Connecticut Avenue, NW
Room 724 N/OR3
Washington, DC 20235
(202) 606-4135

U.S. Army Corps of Engineers Wetlands Contacts (see Appendix E)

35. Surplus Federal Property Transfer
(40 U.S.C. §§ 471–544 (1986 & Supp. 1991))

Surplus federal property can be "assigned" to the U.S. Department of the Interior, which may then transfer it to state or local government at no or low cost.

Properties transferred to state or local government through the National Park Service must be used for parks and recreation, which can include nature preserves and open space used for such passive activities as birdwatching and nature study. Parcels are typically 20 acres or less. Many are subsequently improved through the Land and Water Conservation Fund. The National Park Service assists state and local governments in applying for property transfers.

Property can be transferred to state or local government through the U.S. Fish and Wildlife Service for wildlife conservation. These properties are primarily used for management of upland species, but some wetlands may be involved.

Contacts

Recreation Resources Assistance Division
National Park Service
P.O. Box 37127
Washington, DC 20013-7127
(202) 343-3780

U.S. Fish and Wildlife Service
Division of Realty
U.S. Department of the Interior
Arlington Square
1849 C Street, NW
Washington, DC 20240
(703) 358-1713

36. Water Resources Development
Acts of 1986 (33 U.S.C. §§ 2201–2316 (Supp. 1991, amended 1990))
and 1990 (33 U.S.C. §§ 2201–2324 (Supp. 1991))

The Water Resources Development Acts of 1986 and 1990 include numerous provisions that relate to wetlands protection, primarily in connection with water resources development projects.

These omnibus measures authorized construction or study of hundreds of new water resources development projects, to be undertaken by the Corps of Engineers. In addition, these acts added new restrictions that specifically require wetlands protection. Provisions requiring protection of fish and wildlife habitat may result indirectly in wetlands protection. The acts also authorized several regional environmental restoration projects, some with a goal of significant wetlands restoration.

The 1986 act requires that mitigation plans accompany all project proposals unless it can be shown that the project will have negligible effects on fish and wildlife. It also requires that mitigation be undertaken simultaneously with other project activities.

The 1990 act requires that the goal of the Corps's water resources development program be "no overall net loss" of wetlands. The act also requires the Corps to develop an action plan to achieve this goal and to identify any new authorities it needs to meet the goal. The action plan must be prepared in consultation with the U.S. Environmental Protection Agency (EPA) and the U.S. Fish and Wildlife Service (FWS).

The 1990 act also authorizes the training and certification of wetlands delineators as well as a demonstration program to determine the feasibility of wetlands restoration, enhancement, and creation as a means of contributing to no net loss. Federal and state land-owning agencies and private parties may contribute land to the demonstration areas.

Finally, the act also establishes environmental protection as one of the primary missions of the Corps in water resources projects.

Contacts
U.S. Army Corps of Engineers Wetlands Contacts (see Appendix E)

37. Watershed Protection and Flood Prevention Act
(16 U.S.C. §§ 1001–1009 (1985 & Supp. 1991))

The watershed protection program provides financial and technical assistance to local organizations.

The Soil Conservation Service (SCS) provides financial and technical assistance to local organizations in planning and carrying out projects for watersheds not larger than 250,000 acres. The purposes of the program include flood prevention, agricultural water management, recreation, municipal and industrial water supply, and fish and wildlife development.

The 1990 Farm Bill (i.e., the Food, Agriculture, Conservation, and Trade Act of 1990) amended the watershed protection program to allow cost sharing (federal funding of 50 percent or more) for acquiring perpetual wetlands or floodplain easements for conservation or flood prevention. Other projects can indirectly benefit wetlands. For example, wetlands restoration or creation is often required as mitigation for project construction. Loans and funding advances may be available for these projects. Eligible organizations include Indian tribes, state or local governments, soil or water conservation districts, flood prevention or control districts, nonprofit water users' associations, and similar organizations that can carry out and maintain improvement projects.

Contacts
Soil Conservation Service Wetlands Contacts (see Appendix E)

State Mechanisms

S tates can choose from numerous available programs for implementing their wetlands protection strategies. This section discusses the mechanisms listed below.

ACQUISITION

REGULATION

Wetlands Regulatory Programs

Area-Specific Programs
Floodplain Management Programs
Shoreline Protection Programs
Wild and Scenic Rivers Protection Programs
Endangered Species Protection Programs
Water Rights Programs

Activity-Specific Programs
Point Source Pollution Control Programs
Nonpoint Source Pollution Control Programs
State Environmental Policy Acts (SEPAs)

PLANNING

Statewide Land-Use Plans
Special Area Plans
Greenway/River Corridor Plans
Special Purpose Plans

RESTORATION, CREATION, AND MANAGEMENT

INCENTIVES

Financial Incentives
Nonfinancial Incentives

TECHNICAL ASSISTANCE, EDUCATION, AND OUTREACH

Local Government Assistance
Landowner Assistance
Curricula Development
Outreach

RESEARCH

ACQUISITION

Although many states don't have specific wetlands acquisition programs, natural resource management agencies typically can acquire wetlands as part of their mandates to preserve natural areas, maintain habitats, provide parks, and so on. States with specific wetlands acquisition programs often support these efforts with dedicated funding sources such as conservation or waterfowl stamps, as in New Jersey and Alaska.

States can use acquisition programs to protect wetlands in a variety of ways. Traditionally, acquisition involves the state agency purchasing all the legal rights associated with a given parcel of land; this is known as "fee-simple" acquisition. Another form of acquisition allows the agency to purchase a "less-than-fee-simple" interest, granting the agency the right to prohibit or control certain activities on the land without owning the property itself.

Strengths

- *Control.* Acquisition programs can provide a state with a high level of influence over the resources acquired.
- *Flexibility.* States can use a variety of acquisition mechanisms, ranging from fee-simple acquisition to conservation easements, to address different situations (available options may be limited by state law or public opinion).
- *Cost-sharing possibilities.* Acquisition programs often involve joint ventures among multiple agencies as well as the private sector.
- *Resolution of land-use disputes.* Acquisition can help resolve public-interest and private-equity issues in land-use disputes. For example, California's Coastal Conservancy has fostered land assembly projects in subdivisions containing wetlands. In a land assembly, individual lots are purchased, and the property is replotted and restricted to protect environmental features. Then the property is resold, and funds generated from the sale can be used to subsidize additional land assembly projects.

Challenges

- *Costliness.* Acquisition tends to be much more expensive than other resource protection techniques; therefore, it typically can play only a limited role in an overall wetlands protection strategy.
- *Delay.* State acquisition processes often entail time-consuming requirements, such as lengthy approval processes that reduce the state's ability to purchase key wetlands when they enter the market.
- *Land management responsibilities.* The acquired land needs to be managed, requiring additional state resources and personnel.

Users

State acquisition programs are usually implemented through natural resources agencies. States also can form partnerships with other government agencies and the private sector. A few states have created special nonregulatory agencies with acquisition powers to resolve local environmental disputes. California's Coastal Conservancy, for example, complements the state regulatory agency in coastal areas. The Conservancy provides acquisition grants and loans to local governments and land trusts to protect coastal resources, including wetlands. Similarly, the recently created Florida Communities Trust provides grants to assist local governments in achieving their conservation goals, including wetlands protection.

Resources

Expertise is necessary for developing a system to determine which wetlands to acquire, for coordinating with other relevant agencies and programs, for carrying out acquisitions cost-effectively, and for managing sites. But the principal need is funding.

- *Dedicated funding sources.* Many acquisition programs are funded by earmarked revenues. All or part of the revenues from waterfowl stamps, for example, can be statutorily assigned to wetlands acquisition. A dedicated funding source can provide a relatively stable source of revenue.

  Bonds remain one of the most common sources of funding for wetlands acquisitions.

  Many funding sources are in some way related to real-estate property sales, for example:
  —Florida's documentary stamp tax (a $.55 tax on each $100 worth of property sold in the state),
  —Maryland's real-estate transfer tax (a percentage of the purchase price in land sales), and
  —Vermont's land gains tax (a capital gains tax on sales of undeveloped land held for less than six years).

  Taxpayer-choice funding sources include:
  —state income-tax checkoffs (over 30 states have a checkoff to fund open-space acquisition),
  —lottery revenues (Iowa and Colorado fund state parks with the proceeds), and

—special automobile license plates ("vanity" plates in California provide funding for land acquisition).

Other dedicated funding sources include:
—severance taxes or royalties paid on the extraction of oil and minerals (as in Michigan, Florida, Montana, and Tennessee),
—revenues from state forests, and
—proceeds from state parks (such as entry fees or a portion of concession revenues).

- *Enabling local revenue measures.* States can authorize local governments to use a variety of revenue sources. For example, Massachusetts has enabled Nantucket and other local governments to levy real-estate transfer taxes. Florida allowed Monroe County (the Florida Keys) to pass a special "tourist tax" on temporary accommodations to fund acquisition of ecologically important areas. Some states may need to form special tax districts for areas that will particularly benefit from a park or conservation project.
- *Long-term revenue-generating ability.* The ability of a funding source to generate revenues on a long-term basis should be considered. In Florida, a tax on the filing of legal documents (such as deeds) continues to provide significant funding for land acquisition; however, a California fishery enhancement program once funded by taxes on motor-boat fuel suffered with the decline in power boating.

Coordination

- *Coordinated funding for acquisition.* Many state acquisition programs have historically involved cooperation with the federal government through the Land and Water Conservation Fund. States also work through multiple agencies with local governments and nonprofit groups to acquire lands. For example, acquisitions along North Carolina's Roanoke River were funded through these sources:
—private donations of land,
—direct appropriations from the state legislature,
—proceeds from the nongame species preservation income-tax checkoff,
—earned interest from the state's Wildlife Endowment Fund,
—funds from Ducks Unlimited, and

—interest-free loans from The Nature Conservancy.
- *Comprehensive resource management plans.* Acquisition is often one of several mechanisms used to implement a large resource protection plan. For example, in New Jersey's Pinelands, planning, acquisition, and regulation help protect ecologically unique communities, including wetlands, and provide recreation. About 75 percent of the land identified for acquisition is in the preservation area, the most environmentally sensitive and tightly controlled portion of the Pinelands plan.

Examples
New Jersey
The Green Acres program, created and funded through a 1961 state bond issue, was designed to acquire lands for open space and recreation. Since its establishment, the program has received $710 million in bond issues. The Department of Environmental Protection uses these funds to finance direct state acquisitions as well as grants and loans for local governments. Although not targeted specifically to wetlands protection, the Green Acres program has facilitated the acquisition of 4,300 acres of wetlands in Cape May, in addition to thousands of acres of wetlands in the Pinelands and throughout the state.

Tennessee
The Natural Resources Agency surveys, appraises, and purchases wetlands using dedicated funds from the state's property transfer tax. The tax is $0.32 per $100, with $0.0325 going directly into the Wetlands Acquisition Fund for the purchase of wetlands; the fund receives nearly $4 million each year. By August 1991 the program had acquired more than 17,000 acres of wetlands for approximately $9.8 million.

Reference
Lincoln Institute of Land Policy. *Funding and Land Conservation: Update and Innovation.* Cambridge, Mass.: Lincoln Institute, 1988.

REGULATION

Wetlands Regulatory Programs

To date, 20 states have enacted wetlands regulatory programs. The extent of wetlands protection depends on each statute's specific criteria for defining wetlands and the activities subject to regulation. Wetlands statutes generally require permits for specific activities that have adverse effects on wetlands. Most state statutes include exemptions for activities such as farming, ranching, timber, irrigation, and recreation. Classification and ranking systems, mitigation requirements, and minimum jurisdictional sizes of wetlands also determine the amount of protection provided.

Strengths

- *Adaptability.* State regulatory programs can be designed to address factors particular to each state, such as the political and regulatory structure, number and type of wetlands, and appropriate type of monitoring and enforcement.
- *Broad scope.* State wetlands regulations can cover more activities or more wetlands areas than the federal regulatory program, significantly expanding the protection granted to wetlands.

Challenges

- *Unpopularity.* Passing wetlands protection legislation can be difficult. Citizens often oppose any increase in the government's regulatory powers; environmental protection laws may also raise economic concerns.
- *Enforcement.* Regulatory programs require extensive monitoring and enforcement. The administering agency often lacks sufficient staff to monitor and enforce the state wetlands regulations effectively.

Users

State, regional, county, or municipal governments, agencies, or planning boards may be involved in implementing state regulations, depending on the delegation of responsibility. The entity responsible for reviewing and permitting projects is the key player. In some states, such as Rhode Island and New Jersey, a state agency retains all wetlands regulatory authority. In others, the state requires local governments to adopt wetlands regulations that meet state standards, as in Connecticut and Massachusetts, which are strong "home rule" states. Other states retain authority unless local governments want to gain certification to conduct their own permitting; these local entities must have sufficient regulations and staff to satisfy the state requirements for certification. In New York, for instance, only three local governments have become certified.

Resources

New Jersey's Department of Environmental Protection and Energy administers the state's wetlands regulatory programs (described below). The freshwater wetlands program has about 40 staff members and an annual budget of $1.9 million. Less than one-quarter of its budget comes from state general funds; fees from permits generate the remainder of the program's revenue.

Coordination

State regulatory programs can coordinate with both federal and local regulatory requirements to streamline the permitting process and increase the overall efficiency of all the regulatory programs. In Louisiana, for example, the state Coastal Management Division and the Army Corps of Engineers issue joint public notices for permit applications and hold joint public hearings.

Examples

New Jersey

Tidal wetlands are delineated on official maps and subject to the Wetlands Act of 1970 (N.J. Stat. Ann. §13:9A-1 et seq. [West 1970]). Inland wetlands are subject to the Freshwater Wetlands Protection Act of 1987 (N.J. Rev. Stat. §13:9B-1 et seq. [West 1987]) unless located within the jurisdiction of the Hackensack Meadowlands Commission or the Pinelands Commission, two special districts established by the state with separate regulatory powers. The state uses the federal three-criteria method of identifying and delineating freshwater wetlands. The state's Department of Environmental Protection has permitting jurisdiction for both tidal and freshwater wetlands.

The Freshwater Wetlands Act has several important features:

- The law regulates more activities than the federal regulatory program does. These activities include removal, excavation, disturbance, or dredging of soil and drainage or disturbance of the water level.
- Most activities in buffer zones around wetlands areas are also regulated; buffer zone size varies according to the resource value of the wetland.
- Mitigation is required with all individual permits to replace lost wetlands with wetlands of "equal ecological value."

Vermont

The Vermont Wetlands Act of 1986 (Vt. Stat. Ann. title 10, §905:7, 8, 9 [1986]) protects functions and values of wetlands instead of the land itself. To qualify as a wetland, the area must perform or provide at least one of the 10 values and functions protected by the act; these include water storage for runoff, water quality protection, wildlife habitat, educational resources, aesthetic values, economic benefits, and other wetlands characteristics. Wetlands that meet at least one of the criteria are considered sufficiently significant to warrant protection under the act. There is no permit program; specified activities are listed as "allowed uses," and all other uses must be authorized through "conditional use determinations."

References

Note: The *National Wetlands Newsletter,* published bimonthly by the Environmental Law Institute in Washington, D.C., provides current information on state regulatory programs.

O'Brien, Catherine L. "Vermont Adopts Wetlands Rules." *National Wetlands Newsletter* 3 (1990): 8–9.

Want, William. *Law of Wetlands Regulation.* New York: Clark Boardman Company, Ltd., 1990.

Area-Specific Programs

Some state regulatory efforts do not specifically protect wetlands but provide incidental protection as part of a broader program. The following examples discuss state programs that regulate particular *geographic areas* often containing wetlands.

Floodplain Management Programs

Thirty-four states authorize and require the adoption of local floodplain regulations to control activities in the 100-year floodplain to reduce flood loss. (Local governments must also adopt floodplain regulations to qualify for National Flood Insurance; see Part III.2, "National Flood Insurance Program"). Most riverine, estuarine, and coastal wetlands lie within the 100-year floodplain.

The state regulatory agency establishes standards for local regulations, provides technical assistance to local governments, monitors compliance of local regulations, and, in many states, directly regulates the floodplain if local governments fail to adopt and enforce regulations meeting state standards.

Strengths
- *Wetlands protection in floodplains.* Fill restrictions in floodplain management programs can provide considerable protection for wetlands in "floodways" (designated portions of river floodplains in which further development would increase flood heights).
- *Ability to establish stringent standards.* States can require communities to exceed the minimum standards of the National Flood Insurance Program. Several states have done this through a variety of measures, such as accounting for future watershed conditions in mapping floodplains, defining more restrictive floodways (e.g., a zero rise floodway), and prohibiting a broader range of activities than the federal program.

Challenge
- *Lack of wetlands focus.* Floodplain programs are often staffed by engineers and planners who adhere rigorously to their primary goal of reducing flood loss and perceive wetlands protection as entirely incidental to flood loss reduction. Education of state and local floodplain managers with regard to wetlands values and functions can help overcome this problem.

Coordination

Floodplain managers can promulgate combined ordinances for flood loss reduction and wetlands protection. State/local watershed management plans can be prepared that incorporate flood loss reduction and wetlands protection goals and objectives.

Users

State natural resources or water management agencies and local governments are chiefly involved in floodplain management programs.

Resources

In Wisconsin, the state floodplain management program (described below) employs 18 full-time staff members and has an annual budget of $1 million. The state works with 565 local communities in its program to prevent flood damages.

Examples
Wisconsin
The legislature directed the Department of Natural Resources to work with local governments

in a coordinated effort to manage the state's floodplains, shorelines, and wetlands. The state has four major responsibilities:

- to set and maintain minimum statewide zoning and mapping standards for floodplains, shorelines, and wetlands;
- to provide technical assistance to local governments in ordinance adoption, administration, and enforcement;
- to conduct information and education programs; and
- to adopt ordinances for noncomplying communities.

Washington

The floodplain management program integrates federal, state, and local plans to reduce flood damages. This program provides technical assistance to local governments in identifying and mapping critical wetlands areas within floodplains. It also includes a Flood Control Assistance Account Program, administered by the state Department of Ecology, which allocates matching funds to local governments for the development of comprehensive flood control management plans, including wetlands management strategies.

Reference

Wisconsin Department of Natural Resources. *Floodplain & Shoreland Management Guidebook.* Wisconsin Department of Natural Resources, March 1988.

Shoreline Protection Programs

Some states have programs regulating activities in and around shorelines, typically through a permit process. The regulated area sometimes specifically includes wetlands, as in Washington state, but often simply covers areas within a certain distance of the shore. Depending on the state, shoreline protection programs can include both coastal wetlands and wetlands adjacent to rivers, streams, lakes, or ponds.

State shoreline regulatory programs often rely heavily on local involvement; the state adopts standards which must be adopted and implemented by local governments (as in Wisconsin, Washington, and Minnesota). In most cases the state adopts shoreline regulations for local governments that fail to act. Other states assume direct regulatory responsibilities in shoreline areas. In Rhode Island, for example, state permits are needed for certain activities along shorelines. Incentives or acquisi-

tion efforts, particularly for greenways (which are often located along rivers or other surface waters), sometimes supplement shoreline program regulations.

Strengths

- *Integrated resource protection.* Shoreline programs provide opportunities to protect wetlands as part of a larger natural resource conservation program. Many states have adopted wetlands preservation programs in the course of broader standard-setting efforts to protect shoreline areas.
- *Opportunity for local involvement.* Delegation of authority on state regulations provides a strong role for local efforts to protect natural resources.
- *State-established minimum standards.* State standards serve as minimum criteria for local actions, facilitating a consistent shoreline management program statewide.

Challenges

- *Exclusion of isolated wetlands.* Only wetlands along rivers, lakes, or other surface waters are included in shoreline protection programs.
- *Exemption of some wetlands.* Wetlands associated with smaller surface waters may be exempt from regulation and protection in some programs.

Users

Both state natural resources agencies and affected local governments (when delegation of authority exists) are involved in shoreline protection programs.

Resources

Washington's Department of Ecology program on shoreline management (described below) has about 20 staff members in its wetlands regulation section. These employees assist local governments in preparing master programs for wetlands protection in their jurisdictions, and they also review all permits issued at the local level to verify their compliance with local and state wetlands protection policies.

Coordination

Shoreline protection regulations can be effectively combined or closely coordinated with wetlands regulations (as in Wisconsin). Coordinating shoreline regulatory mechanisms with acquisition and incentive programs can greatly increase the protection of these shoreline areas.

Example

Washington

Under the Shoreline Management Act (Wash. Rev. Code §90.58 [1971]), the state oversees the program and local governments have primary responsibility for implementation, allowing for regional flexibility within the regulatory program. The state assists local governments with significant shorelines in developing master programs to protect lands within 200 feet of the shore. The local government grants permits for land uses within the regulated zone, and the state reviews these permits to ensure that they comply with both state law and the local master program. Also, the state must approve any variances or conditional uses. Although all activities along shorelines are subject to the act, some are exempt from the permitting process, such as agriculture and repairs to existing structures. In response to an executive order, the state's Department of Ecology has heightened its scrutiny of the permitting process and increased its focus on mitigation when wetlands impacts occur.

Reference

Want, William. *Law of Wetlands Regulation.* New York: Clark Boardman Company, Ltd., 1990.

Wild and Scenic Rivers Protection Programs

The purpose of wild and scenic rivers programs is to preserve rivers in their free-flowing condition, to protect rivers and adjacent lands from development, and to preserve ecological, aesthetic, and recreational values. In addition to the federal Wild and Scenic Rivers Act, many states have initiated their own river protection programs. The degree of protection provided in state programs varies. In some cases the state has the authority to acquire land, prohibit the construction of dams, and establish minimum stream flows. The statute may also authorize the use of condemnation, or it may enable local governments to implement Special Area Management Plans to protect wild or scenic rivers. Wetlands located in the designated river corridor (the size of the corridor varies but often includes one-quarter of a mile on each side of the river) are protected as part of the river resource.

Strengths

- *Protection of range of values.* A wild and scenic rivers program can protect aesthetic, recreational, and other values of designated rivers and associated wetlands.
- *Geographic flexibility.* Protection can vary, from individual rivers, to a system of rivers, to all the waterways in the state.
- *Land-use regulation.* Unlike the federal scenic rivers program, state programs can regulate land use.

Challenges

- *Lack of regulatory authority.* These mechanisms are often little more than designation programs with no "teeth" to protect the rivers and their associated wetlands.
- *Narrow geographic scope.* Since wild and scenic rivers programs apply only to wetlands within the immediate river corridor, many ecologically significant wetlands may remain without protection.
- *Protection of aesthetic values.* Because aesthetic values are not among those usually regulated by state police powers (e.g., powers to protect the health, safety, and welfare of the public), states often are reluctant to use condemnation powers to promote aesthetic goals.

Users

State natural resources agencies or recreation agencies typically administer wild and scenic rivers programs.

Resources

Oregon's Scenic Waterways Program (described below) currently operates on a relatively small budget drawn from state general funds. However, the program is working to secure a dedicated funding source through upcoming initiatives to enhance the budget of the state park service, the agency in charge of the Scenic Waterways Program. These initiatives would provide a gas tax directed to the park service and also grant the park service bonding authority to raise funds.

Coordination

- *Private organizations.* Nonprofit groups often provide great assistance in promoting wild and scenic river designation and in organizing land or easement purchases.

- *Federal government.* States can request that the Secretary of the Interior include state-protected waterways in the National Wild and Scenic Rivers System; the federal legislation can provide additional protection for these rivers and associated wetlands.
- *Nonregulatory programs.* Regulatory measures in wild and scenic rivers programs can be coordinated with acquisition and incentive programs to encourage landowners to protect designated areas.

Example
Oregon

The Scenic Waterways Program establishes a planning policy for management of scenic rivers and their associated wetlands. It prohibits dam building and other development incompatible with the values of these rivers. The current program lacks the authority of the federal Wild and Scenic Rivers Act, however, and must rely on the willing participation of property owners along scenic waterways. Despite this lack of regulatory strength, the program has been generally successful in preserving the values of scenic rivers. In the past 10 years, the agency has issued more than 700 notices of conflict and in only two cases have property owners refused to cooperate with the policy.

References
Oregon State Parks and Recreation Department. *The Oregon Scenic Waterways Program: A Landowners' Guide.* Salem, Oreg.: Oregon State Parks and Recreation Department, 1988.

Morrison, Charles C. "Protecting Rivers and Their Environs: The New York State River Program." *National Wetlands Newsletter* 6 (1987): 2–5.

Endangered Species Protection Programs

Many states have laws that provide protection for species threatened with extinction in their regions. States typically classify protected species in one of three categories: endangered, threatened, or "of special concern." As in the federal Endangered Species Act, state legislation typically prohibits "taking" or harming threatened or endangered species. In the federal act, the definition of harm includes destruction or conversion of critical habitat; occasionally this provision exists in state laws as well and can be used to protect wetlands that provide endangered species habitat.

The lists of species protected by state laws typically overlap with the federal inventory. Exceptions include plants and animals that may be rare in one state but more common elsewhere, or species at the limits of their range that constitute an important, genetically distinct population.

Strengths
- *Link between wetlands and endangered species habitat.* Since wetlands harbor more than one-third of all endangered and threatened species in the United States, these state laws can provide opportunities to protect wetlands through prohibitions on critical habitat destruction.
- *Coordination with federal law.* State laws often mesh with federal endangered species legislation, which can provide additional protection for wetlands that provide habitat for endangered and threatened species.

Challenges
- *Lack of protection for habitat.* Many state endangered species acts, while protecting the individual species, do not adequately protect habitat. Modification of the statutory language to include habitat protection increases the utility of state laws in wetlands protection.
- *Limited applications.* Endangered species statutes can only protect wetlands that host listed species.

Users
States generally have a department of conservation or a fish and game division that implements the state law.

Resources
Adequate funding is essential if endangered species programs are to achieve their potential as habitat protection tools. Various states have experimented with tax checkoffs and license surcharges to raise revenues for nongame and endangered species programs, with mixed success.

Coordination
Section 6 of the federal Endangered Species Act encourages states to develop their own parallel legislation and nominally provides appropriations for implementation at the state level. Generally,

cooperative projects and agreements between the U.S. Fish and Wildlife Service and individual states are the most successful and well funded of all endangered species protection programs.

Examples

Colorado

The state purchased several hundred acres of marsh in 1982 as a habitat for protected shore-birds in cooperation with the U.S. Fish and Wildlife Service.

Massachusetts

The recently enacted Massachusetts Endangered Species Act (Mass. Gen. L. ch. 131A [1990]) includes a habitat protection provision that can be used to protect wetlands. The state natural resources agency is currently developing regulations; the prohibitions on habitat alteration will go into effect in 1992.

Reference

Newsome, Pat. *State Endangered Species Programs: From Alligators to Zebras.* Report No. BG048902. Lexington, Ky.: Council of State Governments, 1989.

Water Rights Programs

Water rights are uses of water recognized and protected by law. The creation, definition, and control of water rights is regulated (in most cases) by state law. There are two basic types of water rights—*riparian* and *appropriative*. As a general rule, eastern states follow the riparian doctrine of water rights and western states follow the appropriative doctrine, although some states use a combination of both.

Riparian water rights reserve waters for the benefit of the lands along the stream. Landowners adjacent to or containing a water body have the right to make "reasonable use" of the water as long as the rights of downstream riparian landowners are not interfered with. Although riparian systems did not originally involve a process for allocating or distributing the water (allowing each riparian owner to make "reasonable use" of the water), many states now require water users to obtain permits because of increasing demands on water use in these areas.

Appropriative water rights are not tied to the ownership of riparian lands but are generally owned by the state, which then appropriates the

water to users. Often referred to as "first in time, first in right," the appropriation doctrine grants the most senior water right to the first person to divert the water and put it to beneficial use. States following the prior appropriation doctrine administer an allocation system, permitting specific quantities of water to specific users for specific purposes.

Riparian systems, by recognizing the right of riparian owners to a living stream, can provide protection for wetlands by ensuring that there is sufficient flow in the stream to protect the aquatic habitat. Under the appropriation doctrine most states have adopted policies to maintain sufficient instream flows to protect environmental values, which can include protecting adjacent wetlands.

Strength

- *Explicitly links water quantity to wetlands protection.* States' control over water rights laws and the amount of water diverted from streams can provide an important opportunity to limit water diversions that may adversely affect wetlands.

Challenges

- *Limited geographic scope.* Water rights laws can only help to ensure sufficient quantities of water for wetlands with direct hydrologic connections to surface water flows.
- *Competing uses.* In areas with scarce water supplies, human-oriented water uses such as diversions for agriculture and public water supplies often compete and conflict with the need to maintain adequate instream flows to protect wetlands.
- *Lack of specific wetlands protection provisions.* Most instream flow programs (under appropriative systems) do not provide adequate protection for wetlands (i.e., minimum flows are usually based on fisheries rather than wetlands protection; wetlands protection is often incidental to other resource protection).

Users

State legislatures, state water agencies, and state courts are involved in the use of water rights laws to protect wetlands.

Resources

Water rights permitting programs are typically administered by state water or natural resource agencies. In Montana, the Department of Natural

Resources has a budget of $2.6 million and approximately 75 employees (located in the state capital and nine regional offices) to administer the state's water rights program.

Coordination

Efforts to protect wetlands through water rights programs should be closely coordinated with other regulatory programs that may affect riparian wetlands, including wetlands regulatory programs, shoreline and floodplain management programs, and point and nonpoint source water quality programs. In addition, regulatory control can be enhanced through acquisition programs that purchase water rights specifically for wetlands.

Examples

Montana

Montana's water rights law includes fish and wildlife and recreation as "beneficial uses," allowing water rights permits to be obtained for these purposes. The Montana Department of Fish and Wildlife, for example, holds several water rights to protect state wildlife management areas, including a water right for Black Butte Swamp to protect marshy habitat important for bears.

Nevada

In many states, water rights are being transferred from consumptive uses to wetlands protection. In Nevada, for example, The Nature Conservancy and the U.S. Fish and Wildlife Service are acquiring irrigation water rights and transferring these rights to provide water to maintain the wetlands in the Stillwater National Wildlife Refuge.

References

MacDonnell, Lawrence, et al. *Wetlands Protection and Water Rights.* Boulder, Colo.: Natural Resources Law Center, 1990.

Wright, Kenneth, ed. *Water Rights of the Fifty States and Territories.* Denver, Colo.: American Water Works Association, 1990.

Activity-Specific Programs

Many regulatory programs incidentally protect wetlands as part of broader regulations of specific activities.

Point Source Pollution Control Programs

(See Part III.2, "Clean Water Act: Water Pollution Control.")

Nonpoint Source Pollution Control Programs

(See Part III.2, "Clean Water Act: Water Pollution Control.")

State Environmental Policy Acts (SEPAs)

Modeled after the National Environmental Policy Act, SEPAs require the preparation of environmental impact statements (EISs) to assess the environmental effects of proposed public agency actions. EISs typically contain descriptions of unavoidable impacts, assessments of alternatives to the proposed action that might reduce the impacts, and discussions of mitigation measures. About one-quarter of all states have some form of a SEPA.

Some states, such as New York and California, include local government actions in their SEPA requirements; others, like Wisconsin, include only state agencies. The activities covered also vary. Thus, in some states a SEPA may cover private development if it reaches certain thresholds or requires the approval of a public body.

Although SEPAs mandate a process, not an outcome, information derived from a review frequently affects state decision making. In the case of wetlands, state projects have been modified or their effects mitigated because of such information-gathering.

Strengths

- *Increased protection.* SEPAs provide additional environmental protection through the EIS review process, which considers the impacts on wetlands of proposed public actions.
- *Early assessments.* Potential wetlands losses and other negative impacts can be identified before they occur through the EIS review process.

Challenges

- *Cost and delay.* The review process can be time consuming, resource intensive, and subject to legal challenges.
- *Obtaining unbiased data.* Applicants usually provide the data, which may result in biased information. However, many SEPA programs require agency review and acceptance of data, which helps alleviate this problem.

Users

A state natural resource or environmental protection agency typically administers the SEPA process. In addition to the state and local agencies regulated under SEPAs, citizens often can use these laws to enjoin government actions; they are among the most frequently litigated of state environmental legislation.

Resources

For a SEPA to be effective, the reviewing agency needs staff, funding, and expertise. Even though the applicant usually provides the data, the reviewing agency must have a staff that is technically sophisticated enough to conduct a critical assessment.

Coordination

Reviews frequently involve the participation of experts from various agencies and programs in assessing impacts and recommending alternatives or mitigation strategies. Implementing a common wetlands mitigation strategy may also involve interagency participation to identify appropriate mitigation sites and approaches.

Example

California

The California Environmental Quality Act (CEQA) requires mitigation of significant adverse impacts of projects. Implementing these requirements has involved cooperation among various agencies and nonprofit organizations. For example, mitigation for wetlands lost in the development of a geothermal power site at the Geysers involved both public and private participation. The Department of Water Resources paid for the mitigation; the Energy Commission developed the mitigation requirements; and the Sonoma Land Trust acquired the mitigation site.

Reference

Anderson, Frederick R., Daniel R. Mandelker, and A. Dan Tarlock. *Environmental Protection: Law and Policy.* Boston: Little, Brown and Co., 1984.

PLANNING

States develop and implement plans for a variety of purposes, including natural resource protection, economic development, and transportation. These planning efforts are generally under-

taken to anticipate and address future needs and problems. Wetlands protection may be the primary goal or just one objective in a broader planning effort.

Statewide Land-Use Plans

Since the 1960s, many states (including Hawaii, Vermont, Florida, Oregon, Colorado, North Carolina, New Jersey, Maine, Georgia, and Washington) have enacted an array of planning laws that provide an opportunity for the state to influence land-use decisions (traditionally the realm of local governments). Several states have statutorily adopted comprehensive plans or statewide planning goals that set forth state interests in protecting wetlands and other natural resources.

Strengths

* *Links wetlands protection to land-use planning.* Statewide planning can provide a comprehensive and effective mechanism for ensuring adoption and implementation of land-use plans that incorporate wetlands-related goals and policies. For example, Florida, Oregon, Washington, and Georgia have included among their statewide planning goals the protection of natural resources and specifically wetlands.
* *Promotes local consistency.* The mandated adoption of local land-use plans consistent with a statewide plan or goals ensures that state interests will be protected or upheld at the local level.

Challenges

* *Lack of wetlands-specific focus.* Planning mandates may be too broad and may not adequately address wetlands issues.
* *Extensive resource needs.* Developing and implementing statewide planning mandates requires staff and ongoing state funding.

Users

Adopting a statewide plan involves government agencies, elected officials, and the public. Implementing a land-use plan primarily involves the state planning agency, regional planning agencies and commissions, and local government planning offices.

Resources

Statewide land-use planning requires a state office or agency with adequate staffing and funding to implement planning mandates and monitor the adoption and implementation of local or regional plans. States that have adopted comprehensive land-use plans have made large, ongoing financial investments to implement these efforts. Oregon, for example, created the Department of Land Conservation and Development (DLCD) to oversee the implementation of state planning goals as well as the preparation and implementation of local plans. Since its inception in 1973, DLCD's budget has averaged $3.6 million per year (over 50 percent of the budget is grants made to local governments). DLCD currently has 40 full-time staff.

Coordination

Land-use plans can reinforce and promote the objectives of regulatory and nonregulatory programs by designating areas for development or protection. Implementing statewide plans also requires and promotes partnerships between state and local governments.

Example

Florida

Florida's Local Government Comprehensive Planning and Land Development Regulation Act (Florida Statutes, Chapter 163) requires each local government to adopt a comprehensive plan in compliance with minimum criteria, including conservation and protection of wetlands, development of a land-use map identifying wetlands, and conservation of coastal resources. In addition, local governments must adopt regulations in conformance with their adopted comprehensive plans. These plans must also be compatible with neighboring local plans (addressing cumulative impacts) as well as the comprehensive regional policy plan of the governing regional planning council, according to the State and Regional Planning Act (Chapter 186, Florida Statutes).

Reference

DeGrove, John M. *Land Growth and Politics.* Chicago: American Planning Association Press, 1984.

Special Area Plans

Special area plans target specifically defined geographic areas rather than jurisdictional areas. Special areas (often referred to as "areas of critical concern," "areas of state interest," or "areas of critical environmental concern") have unique characteristics of statewide interest. Special area plans are designed to provide policies and guidelines for interjurisdictional protection and management of an area. This planning technique protects state interests by subjecting land use and development in the area to special planning and regulatory requirements; often approval is required from a designated state agency or oversight committee.

States typically initiate special area plans through statutory mandates. Such mandates often specify steps in the process, a time frame for completion, and representation on the committee developing the plan. Representation normally includes affected local governments, affected landowners, special-interest groups, and area representatives of state agencies.

Special area plans have been used frequently for areas containing wetlands, such as Florida's Green Swamp, and Big Cypress Swamp, Maryland's Chesapeake Bay area, and Oregon's Amazon Creek Drainage Basin.

Strengths

- *Follow ecological boundaries.* The planning area can be based on ecological rather than jurisdictional boundaries.
- *Provide opportunities for conflict resolution.* These plans typically are designed to meet the needs of both natural resources protection and economic development.
- *Include regional and local participation.* A regional board or commission of local representatives can be appointed to implement the plan, which may diminish local resistance to state intervention in local matters.

Challenges

- *Generate controversy.* Special area plans can create controversy between natural resources protection and economic development interests. For example, environmentalists may view such a plan as prodevelopment. Local opposition to state intervention in the area of concern may also develop.
- *Resource needs.* Special area plans require detailed site-specific information about the planning area.

Users

Any state can require the development and implementation of special area plans. The following parties may be involved:

- affected state agencies, such as a state planning agency, natural resources agency, and environmental regulation agency;
- affected local governments;
- affected landowners; and
- special-interest groups.

Such planning usually involves certain federal agencies, such as the Army Corps of Engineers, U.S. Fish and Wildlife Service, and EPA.

Resources
- *Technical studies and data.* Data and studies on issues within the area of concern are needed to serve as a basis for the plan. The development of critical area plans in Florida has often relied on regional agencies, such as the governing water management district or regional planning council, to provide technical as well as staff support.
- *Staffing support.* This type of planning requires a facilitator (often a state agency representative) to coordinate the plan development process and keep the effort in focus and on track. Special area plans are usually developed according to a state-imposed schedule.
- *Funding.* Special area planning requires state funding as well as local contributions. Because the development of such plans often relies on the participation of many different interests, the process can use the resources of each participant, particularly state agencies and landowners who may have privately financed studies of resources in the areas.

Coordination
Adopted special area plans can be included in the land-use plans of affected local governments, and incorporated into the plans and policies of regional and state agencies.

Examples
Maryland
Maryland enacted the Chesapeake Bay Critical Area Protection Law (Nat. Res. Article § 8–1801–1816) in 1984 to foster more sensitive development activity along the Bay's shoreline in order to minimize damage to water quality and natural habitats. The act established the Critical Area Commission, composed of local and state officials and various private interests, to develop criteria for future development within the special

area. These criteria, approved by the General Assembly, guide local governments in developing land-use programs within the critical area. The criteria address wetlands-related issues such as shore erosion, water-dependent facilities, and habitat protection.

Florida
Chapter 380 of Florida Statutes mandates the use of two special area planning processes, Areas of Critical State Concern and Resource Planning and Management Committees, when areas containing environmental or natural resources of regional or statewide significance are under threat of deterioration. Florida has used both processes in developing resource protection and management plans for a number of areas, including Charlotte Harbor, the Lower Kissimmee River Basin, and the Everglades National Park/East Everglades. In each case the plan established guidelines for the protection of water resources (including wetlands) from inappropriate land uses and development activity in the area.

References
DeGrove, John M. "Critical Area Programs in Florida: Creative Balancing of Growth and the Environment." *Journal of Urban and Contemporary Law* (1988), 51–97.

Sullivan, J. Kevin, and Lee R. Epstein. "The Race to Protect the Chesapeake Bay." *National Wetlands Newsletter* 6 (1990): 10–14.

Greenway/River Corridor Plans

A greenway is a linear open space established along a natural corridor, such as a riverfront or stream valley, for recreational or protective purposes. A greenway plan identifies the most important features of the corridor, describes ways in which they can be maintained, and assigns responsibility for their protection and use. Many greenways are established along river corridors that either encompass wetlands or have wetlands in adjacent areas.

Strengths
- *Follow ecological boundaries.* Greenway planning respects the geographic boundaries and landscape of the resource; corridors are easy to identify and isolate.
- *Provide coordination opportunities.* A green-

way or corridor plan can serve aesthetic, historic, habitat, and recreational purposes and thus can be coordinated with other programs related to these purposes.

- *Gathers public support.* This type of plan is a highly visible conservation measure that typically gains widespread public support.

Challenges

- *Lack of wetlands focus.* Wetlands protection may be one of many objectives in a greenway plan, resulting in inadequate protection of wetlands resources.
- *Encouragement of incompatible uses.* Intensive use of greenways for recreation may be incompatible with wetlands protection (i.e., use may destroy wetlands vegetation and disturb wildlife).
- *Involving multiple interests.* Greenway planning may involve a large number of affected interests, as these corridors can wind through many jurisdictions.

Users

Any state can adopt a greenway or corridor plan. A state's planning agency, parks and recreation agency, and natural resources protection agency as well as affected local governments, affected landowners, special interests, federal agencies, and private land trusts and conservancies may all be involved in some aspect of greenway planning.

Resources

- *Informational resources:*
  —Maps outlining the extent of the corridor
  —Identification of affected government entities and property owners within the corridor
  —Inventories of natural resources and facilities within the corridor
- *Funding.* Opportunities for funding include the federal Land and Water Conservation Fund, and state and local bond issues. Delaware, for instance, is funding its state greenway program through monies from a statewide open-space bond issue passed in 1990.
- *Technical assistance.* The National Parks Service's State and Local Rivers Conservation Assistance Program provides assistance in identifying greenway values and preparing conservation plans.

Coordination

A greenway plan can be coordinated with various other efforts such as parks and recreation plans, floodplain plans, and land acquisition. Such a plan might also be coordinated with related private-land acquisition efforts, such as private land trusts and conservancies.

Examples

Oregon

Goal 15 of Oregon's statewide planning program establishes the Willamette River Greenway. The purpose of the greenway is to protect, conserve, enhance, and maintain the natural, scenic, historical, agricultural, economic, and recreational qualities of lands along the Willamette River. State agency plans and plans of local governments within the corridor must be consistent with this goal; they must respect the corridor's setback line, within which any change of use of the riparian lands (including wetlands) is forbidden.

Georgia

The Georgia legislature passed the Metropolitan River Protection Act in 1971 and charged the Atlanta Regional Commission with adopting a plan for land and water use for a 46-mile length of the Chattahoochee River corridor, which encompasses extensive wetlands areas. Local development actions affecting the corridor must be consistent with the regional plan; the Atlanta Regional Commission determines consistency. Any local action deemed inconsistent by the Commission must seek approval from the state's Environmental Protection Division.

Reference

Little, Charles E. *Greenways for America.* Baltimore, Md.: The Johns Hopkins Press, 1990.

Special Purpose Plans

States can develop statewide plans to serve a specific purpose, such as enhancing recreational opportunities or water quality. Special purpose plans can specifically address wetlands protection or can encompass wetlands protection as a policy or an objective that is part of a broader single purpose, such as highway improvement or port development and expansion.

Strength

- *Specificity.* Because of their narrow focus, special purpose plans can include more specific policies than a broader comprehensive planning effort.

Challenge

- *Limited scope.* A special-purpose plan may not provide a comprehensive approach to wetlands protection and management. For example, State Comprehensive Outdoor Recreation Plans assess and identify wetlands for their recreational benefits but do not address other benefits, such as flood control and water recharge.

Users

Various state agencies, affected local governments, special interests, and the public are involved in developing special purpose plans. The plans are typically implemented by one or more state and local agencies.

Resources

Data, maps, and accurate information regarding the purpose of the plan are required for plan development. The budget for implementing the Puget Sound Water Quality Management Plan (described below) for 1991–93 is $37 million. This budget, funded by state general funds and several special fees and taxes, provides support for the 11 agencies involved in implementing the plan.

Coordination

Special purpose plans can be included as elements of broader, more comprehensive plans. They can be used to guide both regulatory and nonregulatory programs within the plan area.

Example

Washington

The Puget Sound Water Quality Authority was created by the Washington state legislature in 1985 to address the cumulative, wide-ranging impacts that contribute to the degradation of Puget Sound. The authority was directed to develop a comprehensive plan for water quality protection to be implemented by state and local governments. The 1991 plan recommends that each local government in the Puget Sound region adopt a comprehensive wetlands protection program, including comprehensive land-use planning, a preservation

program, a restoration program, an education program, and a regulatory program with a no net loss goal.

RESTORATION, CREATION, AND MANAGEMENT

States administer programs (unrelated to any mitigation requirements of their wetlands regulations) aimed at improving and expanding the state's wetlands base through wetlands restoration, creation, and effective management of wetlands areas. Some programs include wetlands projects among many other resource enhancement efforts, such as dune restoration and revegetation along shores, or as a part of an overall strategy to improve surface water quality. Other programs are designed specifically to improve degraded wetlands or ensure good management of wetlands on state and private land.

Strengths

- *Models.* State-sponsored restoration/creation/management programs can provide models for private efforts.
- *Partnership opportunities.* Many restoration projects are undertaken as joint efforts with the participation of various government agencies and the private sector.
- *Widespread support.* Programs aimed at enhancing or improving the environment through proactive voluntary measures typically enjoy broad-based public and political support.

Challenges

- *Uncertain success.* Due to the complexity of wetlands systems and the uncertainty of the science, the long-term success of restoration or creation techniques is in most cases unknown.
- *Ongoing monitoring of sites.* Restoration/creation projects should be closely monitored to help ensure that projects are successful; such monitoring requires staff and technical support.
- *Long time frames.* Results from these programs may not be realized immediately (a restored wetland may require many years to regain all its functions). Management, restoration, or creation activities may need to be structured so that interim goals are established to help gauge progress.

Resources

Funding, staff, technical expertise, and research are needed to undertake wetlands restoration, creation, and management strategies. In 1991, New York's restoration/management program, through the North American Waterfowl Management Plan, restored 1,016 acres at 152 sites for a cost of $420,000.

Coordination

State programs should be coordinated with similar federal, local, and private programs to enhance effectiveness of all restoration/creation/management efforts. In addition, acquisition programs can be targeted to areas with restoration potential.

Examples

California

The California Coastal Conservancy often facilitates implementation of restoration plans involving multiple agencies. For example, it provided funding for the acquisition and restoration of wetlands in Huntington Beach to carry out a mitigation plan approved by the state Fish and Game Department and the Coastal Commission as part of a larger mitigation plan for three public-works projects.

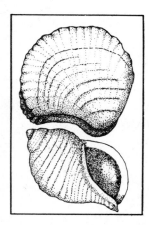

Florida

In Florida, wetlands restoration has frequently been part of a strategy to restore and protect lakes, rivers, and bays through the Surface Water Improvement and Management program. Wetlands have been recreated to help clean the waters of Lake Apopka, once thought to be a dead lake. Farms that relied on perimeter dikes, interior drainage canals, and pump stations to prevent inundation have been purchased along the Oklawaha River. The pumps are being idled, which is restoring the marshy floodplain.

New York

Adopt-a-wetland programs encourage good management of privately owned wetlands areas. Under New York's program, adopted in 1990, citizens enter into agreements with the state to keep a particular wetland in its natural condition. The program specifies the activities (such as cleanup after vandalism or trail maintenance) that may occur in the wetland and allows the state to rescind the agreement if it is breached by the landowner. To recognize wetlands stewards, the program also issues press releases, certificates, and a newsletter.

References

Kusler, Jon A., and Mary E. Kentula, eds. *Wetlands Creation and Restoration: The Status of the Science.* Washington, D.C.: Island Press, 1990.

Berger, John J., ed. *Environmental Restoration: Science and Strategies for Restoring the Earth.* Washington, D.C.: Island Press, 1990.

INCENTIVES

Financial Incentives

Financial incentives for wetlands protection include reductions in taxes (income, estate, and property) and subsidy payments to landowners. Some incentives, such as Minnesota's counterpart to the federal Conservation Reserve Program and Iowa's property tax abatement, apply only to wetlands. Other incentives apply to conservation actions in general.

Strengths
- *Public support.* Both development and protection interests typically support incentive programs.
- *Specific protection.* Incentives can be targeted to protecting unregulated (e.g., isolated or small) wetlands and wetlands threatened by exempted activities (e.g., agriculture).

Challenges
- *Creating effective rewards.* Incentives alone are unlikely to protect wetlands in the face of strong development pressure.
- *Structuring the incentive.* Particularly for tax incentives, the conditions under which a landowner is granted an incentive must be considered carefully:
  —Must the landowner commit to maintain the land as wetlands for a specified period of time?
  —If so, for how long, and how is that commitment made?
  —How and by whom is the presence of a wetlands documented?
- *Loss of revenue.* If local property taxes are affected, loss of local revenue may result in demands for reimbursement by the state. For example, Iowa, New York, Pennsylvania, Minnesota, and Vermont reimburse

local governments for lowered property taxes that result from participation in incentive programs.

Users

State and local property tax reductions or state income tax reductions for donations of land or conservation easements on wetlands require, at a minimum, the involvement of a state's department of revenue and possibly local property tax assessors. Subsidies usually require the involvement of the state's natural resources agency.

Resources

The majority of funding for the Reinvest in Minnesota easement program has been raised through state bond issues. Over six years, $28 million was spent to secure easements.

Coordination

Incentive programs can be used to complement regulatory programs by targeting programs at wetlands exempt from regulatory control (i.e., in many cases, small isolated wetlands). Incentive programs can also be used to promote the goals of acquisition programs by encouraging private landowners to protect specific wetlands in lieu of purchasing these areas.

Examples

Tax incentives

Property tax reductions are offered in these states (this is not a comprehensive list):

- Iowa, Minnesota, and New Hampshire (specifically for landowners who preserve their wetlands);
- New York (for landowners denied permits on their wetlands);
- Connecticut, Delaware, Maine, New Hampshire, North Carolina, Rhode Island, Tennessee, Vermont, New Jersey, Illinois and Virginia (for landowners who protect open space);
- Delaware, Maryland, New Jersey, Rhode Island, and South Carolina (for landowners who grant conservation easements).

Subsidies

Most subsidy programs address wetlands in agricultural areas. Minnesota's Wetland Reserve Program (part of Reinvest in Minnesota) pays landowners for a permanent easement on wetlands. In some of the California Coastal Conservancy's enhancement projects, the Conservancy enters into agreements with farmers and ranchers to protect streams and watersheds. The Conservancy typically pays for the costs of improvements (e.g., fencing or crossings that keep cattle out of stream corridors) that the farmer maintains.

References

Bingham, Gail, ed. *Issues in Wetlands Protection: Background Papers Prepared for the National Wetlands Policy Forum.* Washington, D.C.: Conservation Foundation, 1990.

Lincoln Institute of Land Policy. *Funding and Land Conservation: Update and Innovation.* Cambridge, Mass.: Lincoln Institute, 1988.

Nonfinancial Incentives

Nonfinancial incentives are designed to recognize individuals, companies, or government agencies that have voluntarily protected wetlands. Many nonfinancial incentives, such as conservation award programs, apply to general conservation actions and include but are not limited to wetlands protection.

Example

Maine

Under Maine's Critical Areas Program, established by the state legislature in 1974, a statewide inventory was conducted to identify areas of special zoologic, botanic, scenic, and geologic significance. The inventory specifically identified the state's coastal peat lands, ribbed fens, and eccentric peat lands. Owners of these areas are contacted and encouraged to include their property on the state registry of special resource areas. By educating the landowner about the values of these areas through reports and site visits, the state encourages voluntary protection of these important resources. In conjunction with the registry program, the governor also presents Critical Area Awards to recognize exemplary stewardship of these areas.

TECHNICAL ASSISTANCE, EDUCATION, AND OUTREACH

Local Government Assistance

States provide technical assistance primarily to local governments and landowners. Such assistance can include furnishing data, maps, and other informational materials, as well as expert knowledge and advice regarding options for protecting and managing the resource and for complying with state and federal regulations.

Technical assistance to local governments helps to improve implementation of regulations, plans, and policies for wetlands protection at the local level.

Strengths

- *Augmenting local resources.* Technical assistance programs give local governments the expertise and resources they often lack but need in order to comply with state wetlands regulations and planning requirements. Local governments may be more willing to undertake voluntary efforts regarding wetlands protection if necessary resources are provided.
- *State involvement.* These programs provide a direct avenue for states to become involved in shaping and influencing local wetlands policies, ordinances, and plans.

Challenge

- *Acquiring and maintaining resources.* Providing comprehensive technical assistance entails acquiring and maintaining necessary information and staff resources.

Resources

Accurate and current data and information regarding wetlands are needed. In addition, a staff with expertise in educating others on technical issues and a network of contacts or liaisons at the local level who are conversant in wetlands issues are also helpful.

Users

State agencies and affected local governments are typically involved in establishing and using technical assistance tools.

Coordination

Technical assistance needs to be coordinated with other local assistance programs—particularly planning programs, which require the preparation of local plans in compliance with state criteria. For example, the Florida Department of Community Affairs provides technical assistance to local governments in developing the floodplain portions of their comprehensive plans and provides a model land development code, including regulations for land uses in floodplains.

Examples

Maryland

Maryland's Department of Natural Resources offers training sessions on wetlands plant identification and wetlands classification to local officials, state agency officials, and private consultants.

Georgia

Georgia's Department of Community Affairs is currently in the process of compiling a statewide geographic information system (GIS) to assist local governments in the preparation of required local plans, which must set policies for wetlands protection.

Pennsylvania

The Pennsylvania Department of Environmental Resources provides a guidance manual, *Wetlands Protection: A Handbook for Local Officials,* which outlines the key roles that local governments play in wetlands protection. The manual discusses the values and functions of wetlands and the planning, regulatory, and acquisition techniques that local governments can use to protect wetlands.

Landowner Assistance

State agencies can provide technical assistance to landowners through guidebooks, workshops, personal communications, and seminars designed to educate landowners about the resource that a property encompasses, state and federal regulations affecting its use, and available options for managing and protecting the property.

Strengths

- *Promotes compliance.* Technical assistance to landowners helps ensure that private property owners comply with wetlands regulations.
- *Provides information on options.* Technical assistance programs provide an opportunity for the state to inform landowners of the value of wetlands and the options available for protecting wetlands areas.

Challenges

- *Reaching landowners.* Identifying and establishing contact with landowners can be difficult—wetlands may be widespread throughout the state and information linking wetlands locations with property ownership may not be available.

- *Communication.* Technical wetlands regulations and policies need to be communicated in a clear and straightforward manner.

Users

Any state agency and affected landowner can be involved in technical assistance programs.

Resources

These projects require staff skilled in educating landowners who may have limited knowledge of wetlands regulations and issues.

Examples

Alaska/Washington

Alaska's Department of Environmental Conservation has developed a handbook to assist landowners who are planning projects in wetlands areas. Similarly, Washington's Department of Ecology offers three publications to educate landowners about available options for wetlands protection and preservation and regulations affecting use of their lands: *Wetlands Preservation: An Information and Action Guide, Wetlands Regulation Guidebook,* and *At Home with Wetlands.*

New Jersey

The New Jersey Pinelands Commission has published a landowner's guide, *Pinelands Development Credits.* It details an incentive program that encourages landowners to shift development from wetlands areas to more appropriate areas.

Curricula Development

Various interdisciplinary environmental curricula have been developed in public and private schools. These curricula can include wetlands and can emphasize their natural and socioeconomic values, to foster a clearer understanding among school-aged children of the importance of the wetlands resource.

Strengths

- *Flexibility.* Each state can design environmental education curricula to suit the environmental issues it faces. The curriculum can be updated continually.
- *Reach.* Such curricula can reach a broad and captive audience.
- *Expansion of humanities education.* An environmental component can be integrated into both arts and sciences curricula in addition to courses devoted specifically to environmental issues including wetlands.

Challenge

- *Support for wetlands education.* Environmental education is often considered a lower priority than the educational "basics." Curricula in public schools are already deemed overcrowded with required courses, and teachers often lack knowledge of fundamental environmental concepts and require training.

Users

Public and private elementary and high schools are typically involved in educational curriculum development. State agencies can provide wetlands information and educational materials; state education departments, local school boards, and statewide teachers' organizations are also likely to be involved.

Resources

- *Staff.* Teachers are needed who are qualified to provide wetlands/environmental education.
- *Educational materials.* Textbooks, films, monthly newsletters, and suggested classroom activities are all important resources.
- *Communication.* An ongoing working relationship between the agency and the state's school system is necessary.

Coordination

Educational programs concerning wetlands can be coordinated with broader community education efforts. Also, broad curricula can be enhanced by specific materials and programs of universities and private organizations. Curriculum and program development should be coordinated with a state's teacher certification program to ensure that teachers are adequately qualified in environmental/wetlands education.

Examples

Missouri

The Missouri Department of Conservation offers three separate programs—"Conservation Seeds," "Learning with Otis," and the "Conservation Education Series"—for use in public and private schools. Each program addresses wetlands issues and is designed to target a different level of students.

New Jersey

The Public Programs Office of the New Jersey Pinelands Commission provides for grades 6–12 a self-contained audiovisual program presenting an overview of the ecology and history of this wetlands-rich area and describing its protection program. In addition, New Jersey's Hackensack Meadowlands Development Commission provides a natural sciences program, "Ecology of an Estuary," for grades 2–12. Activities of the program include field trips to wetlands within the Hackensack Meadowlands region and discussion of the values of wetlands and human influences on wetlands.

Washington

Washington's Department of Ecology has developed an interdisciplinary wetlands curriculum for grades 4–8 entitled "Discover Wetlands." The curriculum includes posters, traveling displays, and a teacher's guide with ideas for classroom activities. A teacher's workshop program is also provided to train teachers.

Outreach

Outreach includes information, materials, and programs designed to inform the community at large about a particular issue. Pamphlets and other reading materials, television commercials, radio announcements, newspaper editorials, videos, traveling exhibits, lectures, guided tours, field trips, and annual events are all forms of outreach. Any of various community outreach techniques can be used to educate and inform state residents about the wetlands resources within the state and their functions and values.

Strengths

- *Education.* Wetlands issues and needs can be communicated to the broadest audience possible in order to create a clearer public understanding of the critical functions of wetlands.
- *Support.* Outreach can generate widespread support for future wetlands protection efforts, particularly the passage of bond issues for wetlands acquisition.
- *Marketing.* Outreach allows for use of creative marketing and advertising strategies to promote wetlands policies, programs, legislation, and funding.

Challenges

- *Costliness.* Outreach can be an expensive mechanism, depending on the type of program or medium used.
- *Communication.* It can be difficult to communicate specific or technical wetlands issues on an "at-large" basis to an audience that is largely nontechnical.

Users

Outreach involves state agencies concerned with wetlands protection, management, and regulation as well as the public information and public relations offices of these agencies.

Resources

For outreach to be successful, accurate information about wetlands is imperative. Funding needs depend on the scope (state- or area-wide) and depth of the outreach effort and the medium used.

Coordination

Outreach can clearly be used in conjunction with K–12 environmental education. In addition, outreach actions can be coordinated with certain activities of state and national parks systems, such as guided tours of wetlands areas and habitats. State agencies can make outreach mechanisms available to the general public through such public facilities as libraries, parks and recreation systems, schools, and universities.

Examples
Kentucky

The Kentucky Division of Water administers the state's Water Watch program. One component of this multifaceted program is the adoption program, in which citizens can adopt lakes, streams, and wetlands. The adoption program personally involves sponsors in educating users about their adopted wetlands through field guides and in-field training sessions. In addition, the program helps sponsors enlist public and private support in protecting their wetlands.

Missouri/Maryland

The Missouri Department of Conservation holds an annual Day on the River on the banks of an Ozark stream. The program includes a guided tour through forested wetlands areas and lectures about Missouri rivers and the surrounding areas and wildlife. Similarly, the Maryland

Water Resources Administration sponsors an annual Chesapeake Bay Appreciation Day, which includes a tour of wetlands within the bay area.

References

Burke, David G., et al. *Protecting Nontidal Wetlands.* Planning Advisory Service Report No. 412/413. Chicago: American Planning Association Press, 1988.

Washington State Department of Ecology. *Environmental Education Resources.* Publication No. 90-72. Olympia, Wash.: Washington State Department of Ecology, 1990.

RESEARCH

States often fund research through grants to individuals, college or university departments, or private organizations that will then undertake the research and report results to the state agency. In some cases state agencies may perform individual research projects themselves. In addition, states support many research efforts indirectly through the general support of state universities. State research can be either policy-related or scientific in nature and could range from studying the impact on wetlands of a new government program to studying the nutrient retention at a specific site. Some state agencies have funded graduate students or faculty to research and develop wetlands plans for a particular area in the state. Other agencies have funded wetlands newsletters that include information on current wetlands research.

Strengths

- *Basis for policies.* Research can provide critical information to guide the development and implementation of a state's wetlands protection policies and programs.
- *Support for wetlands programs.* Research can provide data that can help justify wetlands efforts and help garner political and public support.

Challenges

- *Resource needs.* Research can be time- and resource-intensive, and may need to be repeated as conditions and circumstances change.

Example

Louisiana

In 1991, the Coastal Ecology Institute at Louisiana State University undertook a follow-up study on wetlands. The initial research project, funded by the Louisiana Department of Natural Resources, began more than five years earlier with the goal of determining the effectiveness of filling previously dredged channels by documenting the long-term benefit to the health of the marsh. In a two-year effort, the Institute performed one detailed site study and 30 general site studies along the coast. The results of the initial project were submitted to the state (as will the on-going research), to be used in further developing wetlands policy in the area.

Local Mechanisms

L ocal governments have numerous mechanisms that can be used to protect and manage wetlands as part of a statewide wetlands strategy.

ACQUISITION

REGULATION AND ZONING

Flexible Zoning Techniques
Special Permits
Cluster Zoning and Planned Development
Performance-Based Zoning
Overlay Zones
Large Lot Zoning

In 1989, The Conservation Foundation (now incorporated into World Wildlife Fund) prepared *Creating Successful Communities: A Guidebook to Growth Management Strategies* (Island Press). Much of the material for this section is drawn from that publication. Interested readers may want to consult *Successful Communities* and the companion volume, *Resource Guide for Creating Successful Communities*, for more detailed information on ways in which local governments can better protect wetlands.

Other Regulatory Techniques
Subdivision Regulations
Transfer of Development Rights

PLANNING

RESTORATION, CREATION, AND MANAGEMENT

INCENTIVES
Capital Improvements Programming
Use-Value Taxation for Wetlands

TECHNICAL ASSISTANCE, EDUCATION, AND OUTREACH

ACQUISITION

Acquisition is the most direct and effective method available to a local government for controlling the use or development of wetlands. The traditional method is to purchase and retain all the legal rights to a parcel of land (to acquire the parcel in "fee simple"). A local government may also acquire a "less-than-fee interest," such as an easement prohibiting any undesired development.

Local governments acquire land for multiple

purposes (parks, schools, landfills, etc.). Wetlands may be acquired because they are in a floodplain, wellhead, or groundwater recharge area, or for recreational purposes. Acquisition of wetlands is typically included in an overall local program to acquire property of natural, cultural, or recreational significance. Local land acquisition is an important complement to land-use regulations.

In several towns (including Nantucket, Massachusetts; Block Island, Rhode Island; and Davis, California), local governments have established local land trusts as public or quasi-public entities. These land trusts participate in the private real-estate market as representatives of the public interest.

Strengths
- *Control.* Ownership provides a local government with a high level of managerial control over the wetlands resource.
- *Flexibility.* Local governments can use a variety of acquisition mechanisms, ranging from fee-simple acquisition to easements, to address different situations.
- *Partnering possibilities.* Multiple agencies and the private sector often undertake acquisition programs as joint ventures.
- *Resolution of land-use disputes.* Acquisition can help resolve public interest and private-equity issues in land-use disputes.

Challenges
- *Costliness.* Acquisition is expensive. In addition to substantial acquisition costs, fee-simple acquisition removes property from local tax rolls and can result in significant management and maintenance costs. Less-than-fee interests in wetlands can be acquired at much lower costs.
- *Off-site impacts.* Acquisition fails to protect wetlands from off-site impacts, particularly water quality degradation due to upstream activities. Acquisition and watershed-wide regulatory controls must thus be coordinated.

Users
Acquisition decisions typically involve both the local governing bodies and the voters, who must often approve funds for capital outlays by referendum.

Resources
Funds for acquisition can be raised through sales taxes, "tourist taxes," set-aside funds, real-estate transfer taxes, property taxes, excise taxes, and other mechanisms.

- In 1989, citizens of Boulder, Colorado, voted by a 3-to-1 margin to increase the percentage of sales tax revenues dedicated to open-space acquisition from 40 percent to 73 percent to speed the acquisition of critical lands.
- Residents of Glastonbury, Connecticut, approved a $2 million "Reserve for Land Acquisition and Conservation" in 1988, allowing the town to set aside money for future land acquisitions.
- In the Florida Keys in March 1988, voters approved a "tourist impact tax"—a 1 percent increase in hotel and motel room taxes; half of this fund will be used for land acquisition.
- Howard County, Maryland, uses a real-estate transfer tax to fund purchases of development rights to agricultural land. The county offers interested sellers tax-free, zero-coupon bonds. The bonds allow some owners to receive a greater financial return than they would through sale to a developer.
- Fourteen of 15 towns in Cape Cod, Massachusetts, collectively spent $115 million between 1985 and 1989 to buy natural lands, with a heavy emphasis on wetlands. Each town's acquisition program was approved by a two-thirds vote at a town meeting.
- In 1989 the New Jersey legislature authorized counties to levy permanent property taxes for open-space acquisition if approved by county voters in a referendum. To date four counties have approved the tax; this approach allows counties to avoid interest payments on bonds.
- Two small Rhode Island towns, Little Compton and New Shoreham (Block Island), collect a real-estate transfer tax to fund land acquisition. Nantucket, Massachusetts, also imposes a real-estate conveyance tax to fund a local open-space acquisition program.
- The Washington state legislature has authorized each county to increase an existing

local-option excise tax on real-estate sales to fund acquisition of open space if the county has adopted an open-space plan and capital improvement program.

Example

In *James City County, Virginia,* the Department of Development Management has been working with landowners to secure conservation easements in the Powhatan Creek watershed. This area, under intense development pressure, contains important natural resources, including a blue heron rookery and two rare and endangered plant species. Although the county set aside funds to acquire land based on a study of the natural features of the area, it has been successful in securing protection through conservation easements rather than acquisition. As development activity (such as rezoning) is proposed, the county works with landowners to secure the specific easements.

REGULATION AND ZONING

All states have delegated the authority to regulate land use to local governments. On the basis of this authority, local governments implement and fund regulatory programs to protect public health, safety, and welfare. Many state constitutions or statutes also permit a degree of local "home rule," allowing local governments to draft charters determining the scope of local powers.

Local governments can employ a wide variety of regulatory tools to protect wetlands, including zoning, subdivision regulations, and mandatory cluster development. In many cases regulatory authority is not delegated explicitly to protect wetlands but can be used for that purpose. Many localities also use home rule authority to provide more protection for wetlands than would be provided by state legislation. For example, New York has detailed legislation authorizing local governments to regulate wetlands. However, in 1988 the Westchester County Soil and Water Conservation District prepared a "Model Ordinance for Wetland Protection," which recommends that local governments rely on home rule authority to adopt a wetlands protection ordinance rather than on the explicit state legislation. In relying on home rule authority, local governments need not accept state statutory

provisions exempting certain activities from regulation.

Local regulations can protect wetlands by targeting specific problems or needs, including:

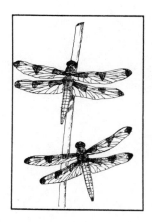

- protection of water quality (e.g., regulating the percentage and amount of developed land within a watershed or limiting accelerated stormwater runoff);
- prevention of dredging, filling, draining, flooding, and other activities detrimental to wetlands;
- prevention of wetlands fragmentation (e.g., controlling pressures for incidental degradation of wetlands caused by adjacent residential or commercial uses);
- creation of buffers;
- minimization of ancillary intrusions (e.g., minimizing physical intrusions, such as roads, driveways, and utility rights-of-way, and incidental degradation of wetlands ancillary to private development;
- mitigation of unavoidable impacts;
- provision of long-term stewardship (e.g., creating a regulatory framework before development in order to better control the potentially harmful, long-term by-products of that development);
- linkages of wildlife habitats (e.g., protecting critical wetlands and wetlands corridors to improve wildlife habitat values and encourage the integrated, professional management of wetlands); and
- regulation of forestry and agricultural practices.

Zoning is the most frequently used local device for land-use regulation. Zoning regulates both the use of land and structures and the characteristics of permitted uses, such as minimum lot sizes and location of structures on lots. In addition, zoning ordinances regulate nondimensional aspects of development, such as design, landscaping, public infrastructure, and mitigation of the impacts of development on natural resources.

A comprehensive regulatory program to protect wetlands should involve some or all of the following seven steps, depending on local conditions:

- development of a statement of purpose explaining the values of local wetlands and the need to protect them;
- development of clear, comprehensive, and

defensible definitions of wetlands and regulated activities;

- provision of an objective and defensible method of mapping or delineating wetlands;
- clear specification of uses and impacts permitted within wetlands;
- establishment of appropriate buffers and setbacks;
- development of comprehensive provisions governing existing nonconforming uses with negative impacts on wetlands values; and
- development of a policy addressing mitigation of inevitable impacts.

Strengths

- *Minimum standards.* Local regulations provide a minimum code of conduct for development of private land.
- *Broad acceptability.* Local regulations provide a framework for regulating land use that is politically and legally acceptable and that can be adapted to the conservation of wetlands.
- *Scope.* Local regulations can address types of wetlands and activities not regulated at the federal or state level.

Challenges

- *Obtaining a substantial long-term commitment.* A local government needs a professional staff with expertise in land-use and environmental planning along with the political will to enforce land-use controls to make effective use of its regulatory authority. Funding to implement and enforce regulations is also needed.
- *Incorporating wetlands protection into zoning.* Many zoning provisions promote sprawling development that increases the degradation of wetlands. A conventional zoning ordinance will do little to protect wetlands unless it includes measures specifically designed to accommodate wetlands constraints.

Users

Developing and implementing local regulatory tools involves several parties:

- The governing board of a local government is responsible for adopting the regulations.
- A separate development review commission, typically the planning or zoning commission (or, less often, a local conservation commission), shares responsibility with the governing body for administering land-use regulations.
- Private landowners are typically responsible for delineating wetlands on specific parcels.
- Local governments and private landowners frequently enlist professional soil scientists or environmental consultants to delineate wetlands and assist in designing developments.
- Concerned citizens interested in local conservation help ensure that adequate attention is paid to wetlands protection.
- State agencies responsible for natural resource conservation and technical assistance to local governments can provide technical information to support local regulatory programs.

Resources

Adequate staffing and funding for consistent implementation of regulations is important. Many towns with populations of less than 2,500 are able to rely on volunteers, consultants, and other government offices to run their regulatory programs; towns of 2,500 to 10,000 generally need at least one professional staff member with some support. Towns with more than 10,000 residents may need to add a professional staff person for every additional 5,000 to 10,000 people.

Coordination

Even with the most effective program, a local government alone cannot ensure adequate protection of wetlands within its borders. Therefore, local regulations should coordinate with:

- local planning efforts, in order to identify:
  —levels of development within a watershed that would exceed the capacity of its wetlands to accommodate change,
  —opportunities for wetlands restoration, and
  —areas unsuitable for development;
- other local decisions, such as those to improve roads, extend sewers, acquire open space, or locate public facilities; and
- state and federal wetlands protection programs, particularly Section 404 of the Clean Water Act (see Part III.2).

Flexible Zoning Techniques

Local land-use control has evolved into a system of techniques designed to balance the predictability of conventional zoning with the flexibility needed to review individual developments. The most promising zoning techniques for protecting wetlands are special permits, cluster zoning and planned development, zoning based on performance standards, overlay zones, and large-lot zoning. Each of these techniques, discussed in the sections that follow, enables local governments to analyze the effects of a development proposal on a parcel and, based on this site-specific analysis, to avoid, minimize, and compensate for impacts on wetlands.

Strengths

Flexible zoning techniques enable individual discretionary reviews of development proposals, denials of inappropriate development, and approvals conditioned on site-plan revisions designed to protect wetlands. Discretionary reviews can also help localities avoid "takings" challenges.

Challenges

The flexibility necessary to ensure site-sensitive decisions must be balanced with the need for administrative standards that guide local decisions, inform landowners about acceptable activities, and ensure that decisions are predictable.

Users

Most local governments have the authority to use flexible zoning techniques; however, there may be limitations on certain techniques. The governing body and the development review commission are always involved, and professional staff may also be necessary.

Resources

Flexible zoning techniques need not be complex or difficult to administer. Local resources needed are often insignificant if the jurisdiction has a zoning ordinance.

Coordination

In order to prevent conflicting standards, flexible zoning regulations must be carefully integrated into the existing zoning ordinance and coordinated with other regulations rather than merely tacked onto existing provisions.

Special Permits

Special permits, also known as conditional uses or special exceptions, are a widely used zoning device. In zoning ordinances, uses are permitted either "by right," in which case there is no individual review, or by special permit, in which case a board reviews the individual proposal to determine whether it complies with criteria set forth in the ordinance. For example, a locality may require a special permit for a proposed shopping center in many or all zoning districts, whereas a single-family residence could be built on the site without further review.

Many localities use special permits to review clearing and grading plans for intensive development and to review and influence other aspects of a proposed site development plan. Although the local board has discretion in considering a proposed use, a special permit must be granted if the proposal complies with the criteria set forth in the ordinance. The board is generally authorized to grant approvals with conditions necessary to achieve compliance.

A special permit should be distinguished from a variance, which is an individual exemption from zoning requirements. Variances typically are allowed when a zoning requirement would impose undue hardship on a landowner because of certain unique features of a parcel.

Criteria for approval of a special permit can be tailored specifically to protect wetlands. Special-permit criteria can require development proposals to minimize direct intrusion into wetlands; provide on-site buffers; and minimize the effects of such ancillary intrusions as road cuts. Special permits can also regulate postconstruction activities to protect wetlands. For example, many Massachusetts communities use special permit criteria to limit the use of lawn fertilizer within designated environmentally sensitive districts.

Example

Local governments often use broad special permit standards to vest the development review commission with considerable discretion and to strengthen the legal defensibility of land-use decisions. Section 7 of Washington's "Model Wetlands Protection Ordinance," promulgated in 1990 by the Department of Ecology, provides an example of broad and inclusive standards:

> a permit shall only be granted if the permit, as conditioned, is consistent with the provi-

sions of this chapter. Additionally, permits shall only be granted if:

(1) a proposed action avoids adverse impacts to regulated wetlands or their buffers or takes affirmative and appropriate measures to minimize and compensate for unavoidable impacts;

(2) the proposed activity results in no net loss [of wetland acreage and function]; or

(3) denial of a permit would cause an extraordinary hardship on the applicant.

Cluster Zoning and Planned Unit Development (PUD)

Cluster zoning (also known as open-space zoning) and planned unit development (PUD), a more complex form of cluster zoning, are land-use controls that allow flexible design and clustering of development on the most appropriate portion of a parcel to provide increased open space. The layout of a project is negotiated, rather than dictated by static regulations, as in conventional zoning. For example, if a 100-acre parcel is zoned for half-acre residential lots that could be developed into 200 buildable lots, under cluster zoning the developer could concentrate the 200 units on 50 acres and permanently protect the other 50 acres.

Clustering is most often used with residential development. It often does not allow for increased overall development density but simply rearranges development to preserve open land and improve site design. Many cluster ordinances will, however, grant a density bonus to encourage clustering.

Cluster zoning can protect wetlands by:

- requiring development to avoid wetland areas and concentrating development on less sensitive portions of a parcel; and

- setting aside entire wetland areas, including buffers, as permanent open space, thereby preventing the fragmentation of wetlands into numerous parcels and minimizing road crossings and other ancillary intrusions.

This tool also provides a mechanism for addressing the long-term management of private facilities, such as on-site wastewater treatment systems and stormwater management facilities, which can degrade wetlands if not adequately maintained. The developer of a planned development often creates a homeowners' association, or a "common interest community," to manage certain property (e.g., dedicated open space, sewage treatment plants). Regulations can authorize the local government to review the proposed project to ensure long-term protection of wetlands and other environmental resources.

Cluster zoning faces two principal challenges: (1) the opposition of neighbors who may believe that smaller lots will reduce property values; and (2) the need to ensure that dedicated open space remains so in perpetuity. Well-drafted criteria and sensitive site planning can address both of these issues. Numerous fiscal studies have shown that well-designed cluster developments with dedicated open space in some instances appreciate more rapidly than do conventional subdivisions. Conservation easements are frequently used to provide security that dedicated open space will remain undeveloped.

Example

Boulder County, Colorado, has a simple PUD ordinance to protect wetlands and other resource lands. The county's nonurban PUD provisions authorize greater density in exchange for a commitment to keep a certain percentage of the parcel undeveloped in perpetuity. In the county's rural zoning districts, the maximum permissible density is one dwelling unit per 35 acres. However, PUD provisions allow this density to be increased to two units per 35 acres if the landowner agrees to place the new structures on less than 25 percent of the parcel and to maintain the balance of the parcel in its undeveloped state.

Performance-Based Zoning

Performance standards base zoning restrictions on the permissible impacts of a proposed use rather than specifically enumerating permitted uses, dimensions, and so forth. Proposed uses whose effects would exceed specified standards are prohibited. Performance standards were first used widely in industrial zones to set standards on noise, dust, emissions, and other impacts.

Performance controls can protect wetlands by establishing maximum levels of runoff or land disturbance throughout an entire watershed. For example, an ordinance may limit the percentage of a parcel that may be covered by structures or other impervious surfaces, such as buildings, asphalt driveways, and sidewalks. An increasing number of local governments are adopting no net loss of wetlands acreage and function as a performance standard to evaluate development proposals affecting wetlands.

Performance-based zoning is relatively difficult and time consuming to monitor and enforce. A local government must commit the funding, expertise, and institutional resources necessary to ensure that approved uses continue to comply with performance standards and to take action against violations.

Example

Medford Township, New Jersey, has adopted a development ordinance with performance standards to protect the township's wetlands and other natural features. Section 160-57 of the ordinance prohibits all forms of development in or on any wetlands as well as development within 300 feet of wetlands if one or more of the following negative consequences is likely to occur:

- an increase in surface water runoff discharging into a wetland;
- a change in the normal seasonal flow patterns in the wetland;
- an alteration of the wetland's water table;
- an increase in erosion resulting in increased sedimentation in the wetlands;
- a change in the natural chemistry of the ground or surface water in the wetlands;
- a loss of wetlands habitat or a reduction in habitat diversity;
- a change in wetlands species composition; or
- a significant disturbance of areas used by indigenous and migratory wildlife for breeding, nesting, or feeding.

Overlay Zones

An overlay zone applies a common set of standards to a designated area that may cross several preexisting zoning districts. These "overlaying" standards apply in addition to those of the underlying district. Unlike conventional zoning districts, an overlay zone may not be mapped precisely on the local zoning map; rather, the district is described in the text of the zoning ordinance. The location of the overlay district depends on the specific physical characteristics of a parcel and is determined on a case-by-case basis when development applications are filed.

Two well-known types of overlay zones are historic districts and the flood zones created under the National Flood Insurance Program. Flood zones are often described in local zoning ordinances but not mapped initially on the zoning map. The ordinances provide that flood district regulations apply to areas within the 100-year floodplain, as designated in Flood Insurance Rate Maps. The overlaying flood zone may not affect the uses and densities permitted in the underlying

zone but may impose additional construction requirements. (See Part III.2, "National Flood Insurance Program," and Part III.3, "Floodplain Management Program.")

Overlay zones provide a mechanism to prohibit development and limit other activities in wetlands, impose wetlands buffers, or require measures to reduce the effects of development in wetlands without affecting development outside the designated wetlands area and adjacent buffer zones.

Example

Chapel Hill, North Carolina, has enacted a Resource Conservation District to protect wetlands and water courses as an overlay zone. The objective approach and clear language of the ordinance are noteworthy:

> A Resource Conservation District Elevation is hereby established, and defined to be that elevation two (2) feet above the 100-year floodplain elevation, as said 100-year elevation is delineated in the official Town floodplain maps.
>
> The Resource Conservation District is hereby established as a district which overlays other zoning districts. . . . The Resource Conservation District shall consist of the area bounded by the Resource Conservation District Elevation and the areas within buffer zones established as follows:
>
> (a) Fifty (50) feet from the bank of a perennial stream draining less than one square mile, plus land with a slope greater than fifteen percent (15%) up to seventy-five (75) feet from such a bank, and
>
> (b) Fifty (50) feet from the bank of a perennial stream draining one square mile or more, plus land with a slope greater than fifteen percent (15%), up to one hundred (100) feet from such a bank.

Large-Lot Zoning

Large-lot zoning—which requires that lots in a residential subdivision include, for example, at least 3 acres and sometimes more than 40 acres—is often used to reduce the density of residential development. As a result, it may also protect wetlands and other environmentally sensitive resources by reducing both the density and number of residential structures. Used judiciously, large-lot zoning can help avoid physical alterations of wetlands, provide buffers around wetland areas, and reduce incidental incursions into wetlands resulting from residential development. This type of zoning can be simple to adopt and easy to administer.

Large-lot zoning can, however, encourage low-density sprawl that unduly degrades wetlands across a larger landscape. Local governments should not rely extensively on large-lot zoning to protect wetlands without closely examining local conditions to determine whether the benefits outweigh the risks.

Examples

Large-lot zoning is widely used by suburban and rural communities. Courts have upheld a minimum lot size of 160 acres in rural *McHenry County, Illinois.* Five-acre minimum lot sizes have been upheld in several states. However, courts have invalidated minimum lot sizes of less than 5 acres and even less than 1 acre when there is little justification for them.

Other Regulatory Techniques

Subdivision Regulations

Almost all local governments use subdivision regulations to regulate the conversion of land into building lots. Subdivision ordinances can:

- regulate the physical layout of new lots;
- influence the design and physical characteristics of on-site public improvements such as streets, utility systems, sidewalks, curbs and gutters, and stormwater management facilities;
- regulate land planning and landscaping; and
- require dedication of open lands.

Subdivision regulations can be used to require that development avoid wetlands or dedicate wetlands for conservation uses. Subdivision regulations can prevent the physical alteration of wetlands by requiring that new subdivisions be laid out in a manner that avoids wetland areas or minimizes road crossings and other encroachments. In addition, these regulations offer options for local governments seeking to protect surface water quality by improving stormwater runoff controls and drainage requirements in new subdivisions. For example, drainage standards can address the maintenance of catch basins, controls on the types of catch basins authorized for various uses, and controls on lawn fertilizers.

Example

The subdivision regulations for *East Lyme, Connecticut,* contain several provisions designed to protect wetlands. The regulations require that "existing features which would add value to residential development or to the Town of East Lyme as a whole, such as trees, wetlands and water-

courses, beaches and similar irreplaceable assets, shall be preserved in the design of the subdivision." In addition to requiring avoidance of wetlands, the ordinance requires that:

- clearing of vegetation be minimized and limited to areas delineated for clearing;
- the subdivision be designed to maintain groundwater recharge and quality; and
- stormwater runoff be managed so that it will not adversely affect natural streams or wetlands.

Transfer of Development Rights

Transfer of development rights (TDR) is an innovative and sophisticated growth-management technique that offers substantial promise for protecting wetlands and other sensitive lands on a regional scale. With a TDR system, landowners are able to retain undeveloped land but sell or otherwise transfer the right to develop the land to other property whose development potential is greater. This technique preserves open land, pays the landowner for its development potential, and uses private rather than public funds.

Under a typical TDR program, a local government awards development rights to each parcel of developable land in the community or in selected districts, based on the land's acreage, zoning, or value. Individuals can then sell their development rights on the open market if they do not want to develop their property or are prohibited by regulations such as wetlands protection regulations or those governing agricultural districts from developing the property at the desired density. Land from which development rights have been sold cannot be developed.

TDR offers considerable potential for protecting wetlands; however, it is seldom used explicitly for this purpose. Rather, TDR is used to protect large areas of open space and natural resource lands, including wetlands.

Example

Island County, Washington, has enacted a revision to its zoning ordinance that places wetlands into a wetlands overlay zone with very restrictive development controls and authorizes the sale or transfer of development rights from property within the wetlands overlay zone to receiving areas, which are designated in previously developed villages and town sites. Land within the wetland overlay zone can be developed at a density no greater than one unit per five acres. Land within a designated receiving area can be developed at one unit per every two and one-half acres without a density transfer and one unit per acre with a density transfer.

PLANNING

A comprehensive plan sets forth how a local government will attain specific goals and objectives for addressing social, economic, aesthetic, and natural resource concerns. The plan is an overall policy guide for public and private land-use decisions, including decisions on regulations, spending, and other land-use and resource conservation efforts. A plan can include specific directions for protecting wetlands or can include wetlands in broader natural resource protection goals and objectives.

Strengths

- *Sound decision making.* A comprehensive plan helps to ensure that local land-use decisions are made with sufficient knowledge of local wetlands resources, threats to these resources, and the costs and benefits of various courses of action.
- *Legal defense.* Comprehensive planning not only informs wetlands protection decisions but also contributes substantially to the legal defense of wetlands protection decisions. Courts are more likely to uphold regulatory decisions when they are based on sound research and planning.

Challenges

- *Inconsistency.* In many states, zoning ordinances and decisions on individual development applications are often inconsistent with local comprehensive plans. (Even when states require that local land-use decisions are consistent with a comprehensive plan, the requirement is often ignored.)
- *Resource needs.* Effective comprehensive planning requires a substantial long-term commitment of resources, staff including funds, and public involvement.

Users

Planning is a tool available to all local governments. Citizen groups or landowners can also initiate planning efforts if local officials fail to act. Planning processes typically involve the following parties:

- citizens and various sectors of the public, such as developers and conservation advocates;
- elected officials who typically direct planning processes;
- planning commission members who advise decision makers; and
- planning professionals, including staff members or outside consultants.

Coordination

Planning provides the framework for regulation, acquisition, private activities, and other efforts and decisions to protect wetlands.

Example

The *City and Borough of Juneau, Alaska,* have prepared a wetland management plan to decrease the time required for obtaining federal Section 404 permits and to better allocate wetlands throughout the city and borough to various uses. To prepare such a plan, the city and borough created an interagency technical advisory committee including local, federal, and state representatives. The city and borough appropriated $250,000 for this planning effort. Wetlands throughout the city and borough were mapped and evaluated through the use of the WET technique (see Part IV.2). Community meetings were also held to determine public preferences and gain feedback. An analysis of "practicable alternatives" was undertaken. This information was then combined in a wetland management plan.

RESTORATION, CREATION, AND MANAGEMENT

Local governments typically undertake wetlands restoration, creation, and management projects through natural resource protection or parks and recreation programs. Local governments can also integrate wetlands restoration or creation into other municipal activities by using natural or constructed wetlands to treat wastewater. Wetlands treatment often costs one-tenth to one-half that of conventional treatment systems and provides other benefits, including wildlife habitats and recreational opportunities.

Examples

Through its Emergent Grasses Program, *Anne Arundel County, Maryland,* provides up to $2,000 worth of free wetlands plants to county residents.

The purpose of the program is to encourage residents to stabilize shorelines by reestablishing emergent wetlands vegetation rather than using riprap or other structural solutions. The wetlands vegetation also enhances the habitat and improves water quality. In addition to providing the plants, the county visits the site to help with design and provides planting instructions. Since the program began in 1987, 35,000 plants have been distributed and planted on 16,000 feet of shoreline.

Arcata, California, a coastal town of 15,000, constructed a 154-acre marsh, pond, and lagoon system to treat wastewater discharges. Combined with some conventional technology, the total system cost $5 million; in contrast, a completely conventional system would have cost $12 million. Maintenance costs are also lower. Arcata's system discharges water cleaner than the receiving water, turns solids into mulch used in city parks, provides habitat for waterfowl and muskrats, supplies nutrient-rich water to a salmon hatchery, and is used by birdwatchers and nature enthusiasts. The marsh plants are harvested and burned to generate electricity and heat.

Orlando, Florida, reclaimed 1,200 acres of wetlands that had been converted to cattle pasture as a discharge point for treated wastewater. Wastewater is piped 16 miles to the new Orlando Wilderness Park, where it takes 30 days to wind through a wet prairie, a marsh, and a hardwood swamp. The total cost exceeded $20 million, but the wetlands option was chosen over 20 other options because of lower maintenance and operating costs and better public acceptance.

INCENTIVES

The most important local incentives for protecting wetlands are local spending decisions and tax policies.

Capital Improvements Programming

Local decisions on extending or expanding public utilities or facilities, such as roads and sewers, strongly influence the economic feasibility of many private development proposals. A decision not to extend or expand public services to an area with high wetlands values can make development prohibitively expensive or limit growth of the area.

The extension or expansion of such facilities is generally governed by a local capital improvements program (CIP)—a program by which a local government determines the timing and level of public services (such as sewer and water service) that it intends to provide over a specific period of time. Generally, a CIP covers a 5- to 10-year period.

Strengths

CIPs can coordinate local capital spending decisions with resource assessments and comprehensive planning to ensure that local public investments do not undermine wetlands protection goals.

Challenges

CIPs require a substantial commitment of resources for coordinating the plans, budgets, and activities of several local agencies.

Users

This mechanism is available to any local government that undertakes comprehensive planning and long-term capital budgeting. CIP involves a number of local agencies, including planning, budgeting, and engineering.

Example

Ramapo, New York, used a CIP and limits on residential development not served by public utilities to control the town's growth rate by requiring a special permit for new residential development. Special permit criteria required that development have access to municipal sanitary sewers, drainage facilities, public parks, roads, and firehouses.

Use-Value Taxation for Wetlands

One property taxation program widely used to influence land development decisions is use-value assessment (also referred to as "preferential assessment" of real property). In use-value assessment, the tax assessor, at the request of a landowner, values a parcel solely on the income-producing capacity of its existing use. This differs from the usual method of tax assessment, which considers the market value of the parcel for its highest and best use and accounts for the full development potential of the property.

The principal goal of use-value assessment is to reduce the tax burden on certain land uses that produce less income than other more intensive uses. This reduced property tax burden may reduce the pressure on the owner of land with a low-intensity use to convert it to a more profitable and more intensive use.

Most states either authorize or mandate local governments to assess certain property at its use value rather than its full market value. Almost every state authorizes use-value assessment for farmland. In addition, many states provide for use-value assessment of other low-intensity land uses such as forest land, open-space land, land available for public recreational use, and land of scenic or ecological significance, such as wetlands.

Strengths

Use-value taxation can to some extent reduce pressure to develop wetlands by reducing the local property tax burden of qualifying property.

Challenges

A local property tax burden is typically only one element in a landowner's decision to develop or conserve property. Such programs also reduce the local tax base and therefore are unpopular with local officials.

Users

Use-value assessment is a local policy and must be authorized explicitly by state law. Landowners participate voluntarily in use-value assessment. This tool can be implemented largely by the property tax assessor.

TECHNICAL ASSISTANCE, EDUCATION, AND OUTREACH

Although local governments often receive technical assistance from state and federal agencies, they also play an important role in providing information. Through zoning and permitting programs, local governments are typically on the "front line" and have extensive contact with landowners. Local governments often provide on-site assistance as well as publications to help landowners understand wetlands programs.

Examples

To help alleviate some of the confusion caused by wetlands regulatory programs, the Conservation District of *Bradford County, Pennsylvania,* delineates wetlands for landowners and helps with the permitting process. This service is funded jointly by state and local governments.

New York's Westchester County Soil and Water Conservation District has prepared and published a Model Wetlands Protection Ordinance. *King County, Washington,* has worked with the state's Department of Ecology to develop a model wetlands preservation program and "how-to" guidebook

explaining the process to other local jurisdictions. Also, the *Chesapeake Bay* Local Government Advisory Committee, which provides technical assistance to local governments in the Chesapeake Bay watershed, has published a compilation of successful local programs that improve the Chesapeake Bay ecosystem.

REFERENCES

Babcock, Richard F., and Charles L. Siemon. *The Zoning Game Revisited.* Boston: Lincoln Institute of Land Policy, 1985.

> An updated version of a classic book on zoning and the land-use regulatory process. Provides case studies of 11 local and regional land-use programs and their origins, development, legal aspects, and political history.

Brower, David J., et al. *Managing Development in Small Towns.* Chicago: American Planning Association Press, 1984.

> A comprehensive overview of the use of growth-management measures in small towns, including techniques based on local land acquisition, public spending, taxation, and regulatory powers. Provides practical guidance in assessing the need for growth management and in implementing specific techniques.

Chapin, F. Stuart, and Edward J. Kaiser. *Urban Land Use Planning,* 3rd ed. Urbana, Ill.: University of Illinois Press, 1979.

> A leading land-use planning textbook.

Chesapeake Bay Local Government Advisory Committee. *Chesapeake Bay Restoration: Innovations at the Local Level.* Washington, D.C.: U.S. Environmental Protection Agency, Chesapeake Bay Program, 1991.

> Provides short examples of steps taken by local governments to restore the Chesapeake Bay ecosystem.

Clark, John. *The Sanibel Report: Formulation of a Comprehensive Plan Based on Natural Systems.* Washington, D.C.: The Conservation Foundation, 1976.

> Explains the process of developing a performance-based comprehensive planning process and overlay zoning program

for Sanibel Island, Florida. The basis for the program is mitigating the impacts of development on the vegetation, wildlife, coastal process, geology, and hydrology of the barrier island.

Diamont, Rolf, J. Glenn Eugster, and Christopher J. Duerksen. *A Citizen's Guide to River Conservation*. Washington, D.C.: The Conservation Foundation, 1984.
> Provides an introduction to the protection of rivers and river corridors. Specific chapters focus on threats to rivers; strategies for organizing communities to protect rivers; tools for protecting rivers (such as zoning, easements, and tax incentives); private nonprofit mechanisms for river conservation; and local, state, and federal programs for river conservation.

Diehl, Janet, and Thomas S. Barrett. *The Conservation Easement Handbook: Managing Land Conservation and Historic Preservation Easement Programs*. Alexandria, Va.: Trust for Public Land and Land Trust Exchange, 1988. (Available from the Land Trust Exchange, 1017 Duke Street, Alexandria, VA 22314.)
> An authoritative book providing solid information on establishing and managing easements programs.

Dunford, Richard W. "A Survey of Tax Relief Programs for the Retention of Agricultural and Open Space Lands." *Gonzaga Law Review* 15 (1980): 675.
> Includes citations to the various state statutes or constitutional amendments authorizing use value assessment.

Getzels, Judith, and Charles Thurow, eds. *Rural and Small Town Planning*. Chicago: American Planning Association Press, 1988.
> An introduction to the role of planners in rural towns as well as basic aspects of planning, including use of natural resources as the basis for planning; zoning and development permitting; subdivision regulations; infrastructure planning; and provision of rural transportation and housing services. Includes numerous examples of ordinance language from rural communities nationwide.

Kusler, Jon A. *Regulating Sensitive Lands*. Washington, D.C.: Environmental Law Institute, 1980.
> Thoroughly discusses regulatory programs to protect floodplains, lake and stream shores, coastal zones, wetlands, rivers, areas of scientific interest, and similar sensitive areas. Also discusses state resource protection programs and cases.

Mantell, Michael A., Stephen F. Harper, and Luther Propst. *Creating Successful Communities: A Guidebook to Growth Management Strategies* and *Resource Guide for Creating Successful Communities*. Washington, D.C.: Island Press, 1990.
> Developed for civic activists, policy makers, and planners, this guidebook and its companion resource guide explain how to use growth-management strategies to protect specific natural resources, including wetlands, open space, and rivers. Also contains 31 case studies and specific ordinance language.

McHarg, Ian. *Design with Nature*. Garden City, N.Y.: Natural History Press, 1969.
> A pioneering introduction to regional land-use planning based on the development constraints and opportunities presented by natural systems. Contains case studies showing how environmental and scenic inventories can be combined to indicate where development should be directed.

Meshenberg, Michael J. *The Administration of Flexible Zoning Techniques*. Planning Advisory Service Report No. 318. Chicago: American Society of Planning Officials, 1976.
> Introduces and analyzes flexible zoning techniques.

Roddewig, Richard J., and Cheryl A. Inghram. *Transferable Development Rights Programs*. Planning Advisory Service Report No. 401. Chicago: American Planning Association, 1987.
> Explains transfer of development rights (TDR) and their legal foundation and analyzes the conceptual and practical strengths as well as the weaknesses of key TDR programs around the country.

Sanders, Welford. *The Cluster Subdivision: A Cost-Effective Approach*. Planning Advisory Service Report No. 356. Chicago: American Planning Association, 1980.

>Provides detailed guidance on the design of cluster subdivision ordinances. Includes legal guidance and excerpts from several local zoning ordinances.

Smith, Herbert H. *The Citizen's Guide to Planning*. Chicago: American Planning Association Press, 1979.

>A general introduction to planning written by an experienced planner.

——. *The Citizen's Guide to Zoning*. Chicago: American Planning Association Press, 1983.

>A general introduction to zoning written by a veteran planner.

Thomas, Ronald L., Mary C. Means, and Margaret A. Grieve. *Taking Charge: How Communities Are Planning Their Futures*. Washington, D.C.: International City Management Association, 1988.

>Discusses how successful community-based planning efforts work and offers several examples of these programs.

Thurow, Charles, William Jones, and Duncan Early. *Performance Controls for Sensitive Lands: A Practical Guide for Local Administrators*. Planning Advisory Service Report Nos. 307 and 308. Chicago: American Society of Planning Officials, 1975.

>An early, comprehensive discussion of the use of performance standards to protect environmental resources, including wetlands, streams and lakes, aquifers, woodlands, and hillsides. Includes excerpts of illustrative performance-control ordinances.

U.S. Environmental Protection Agency. *Constructed Wetlands and Aquatic Plant Systems for Municipal Wastewater Treatment*. Cincinnati, Ohio: U.S. Environmental Protection Agency, Center for Environmental Research Information, 1988.

>A design manual for constructing wetlands and aquatic plant systems.

Yaro, Robert D., et al. *Dealing with Change in the Connecticut River Valley: A Design Manual for Conservation and Development*. Amherst, Mass.: University of Massachusetts, Center for Rural Massachusetts, 1988.

>Discusses the advantages of clustered development, provides practical planning standards for preserving natural resources while accommodating economic development, includes sample ordinance language for clustered development, and provides excellent aerial graphics showing various landscapes before and after conventional development and creative site-sensitive development. Builds a convincing argument for clustered development regulations.

Private Mechanisms

rivate organizations, including nonprofit conservation groups as well as businesses and corporations, have at their disposal numerous programs for protecting wetlands that can be included in a state wetlands strategy.

ACQUISITION

Techniques for private land acquisition complement public wetlands protection measures and can be an effective method for protecting wetlands not adequately protected through regulation. The most important private voluntary tools for acquiring and protecting wetlands are as follows:

- conservation easements;
- donations or bargain sales of fee-simple or less-than-fee interests;
- options to buy property if it is to be sold;
- rights of first refusal to buy property;
- preacquisition and resale of land to a public agency; and
- limited or controlled development.

Owning all the rights associated with the title to a parcel of land constitutes a "fee-simple" interest. If the rights associated with a land title are sold separately, the various parties own "less-than-fee" interests. Private organizations and individuals can acquire both fee-simple and less-than-fee interests in land.

Conservation Easements

Easements are among the distinct property rights that may be sold independently. The holder of an easement can control or conduct activities on property belonging to someone else. Easements can be used to ensure the protection of a resource while the landowner retains most or all other ownership rights and usually continues to assume management and maintenance costs. Because easements can be acquired more readily and cheaply than fee-simple interests, they are particularly useful and economical tools for land trusts.

Donations or Bargain Sales

Often, nonprofit groups can acquire fee-simple or less-than-fee interests in land through donations. As tax-exempt organizations, many nonprofits are eligible to receive tax-deductible contributions.

A bargain sale involves a purchase at less-than-fair-market value. An owner essentially donates the difference between the full value and the sale price and is often entitled to a tax deduction for the value of this contribution (see Part III.2, "Internal Revenue Code").

Options

Private organizations often facilitate land protection by acquiring options to purchase property. An option is a widely used real-estate contract device that provides a party with the exclusive right to purchase a property at a specified price within a specified time. The party is not obligated to purchase the land; however, the landowner is prevented from accepting offers from other potential purchasers during the term of the option. Options can be acquired at a fraction of the ultimate purchase price, or they may be donated by the landowner. The deadline imposed by an option may be useful to marshal the funds necessary to purchase a parcel or find a suitable private purchaser.

Rights of First Refusal

A right of first refusal is an agreement between a landowner and a second party in which the landowner agrees that if he receives a legitimate offer from a third party to buy the property, he will notify the second party and give that party a specified period of time in which to match the third-party offer under similar terms before the landowner will accept the offer from the third party. Private conservation groups can acquire such rights by purchase or donation.

Pre-Acquisition

Conservation organizations often acquire wetlands with the intent of reselling them to a public agency. These transactions, known as pre-acquisitions, have administrative and financial benefits for both private and public entities. Public agencies often realize substantial savings by repurchasing land previously acquired by conservation groups. A private organization can often negotiate and undertake the necessary steps for acquisition faster and more adeptly than the public agency. After land is conveyed to a public agency, public land management agencies can often manage additional adjacent land more economically than a private organization. Ownership by a public agency also confers more protection against condemnation by other public agencies, such as a state highway department, than does private land trust ownership.

Limited or Controlled Development

Increasingly employed by innovative land trusts, limited or controlled development typically entails development of a portion of a parcel in order to finance the acquisition and preservation of the balance of the parcel. Development is generally limited to nonsensitive or previously disturbed portions of a parcel. Limited development can permit land protection in situations in which donation or acquisition for full preservation is not possible. It is often made feasible by the increased property value of lots or houses adjacent to restricted open space.

Strengths
These private acquisition tools facilitate:
- quick and efficient action relative to government-initiated acquisition efforts;
- cooperation among private landowners and private organizations;
- income, estate, and gift tax deductions to persons or entities making qualified donations;
- local initiatives for resource protection; and
- the coexistence of traditional private land ownership and wetlands protection (less-than-fee acquisitions).

Challenges
The principal challenge is raising funds to acquire and manage wetlands. In addition to

private fundraising efforts, private groups can mobilize state and local resources.

Users

While any private organization can use these land acquisition tools, land trusts are particularly suited for protecting wetlands through land acquisition. Land trusts are private, tax-exempt, non-profit organizations that seek to preserve significant natural resources through land acquisition.

Examples

The Nature Conservancy (TNC) has purchased 70,000 acres of pristine tidal wetlands along Florida's Gulf Coast in the Big Bend region. TNC acquired the property from Buckeye Cellulose, a division of Procter and Gamble, at a bargain sale. Florida later acquired the property with funds from its Save Our Coast land acquisition program.

The *Trust for Public Land* (TPL) assisted New York in acquiring Sloop Hill, a 102-acre parcel on the Hudson River containing critical wetlands and shorelands. The state and the owner had negotiated fruitlessly, unable to agree upon a price. TPL, a national land trust, acquired the property for $13.3 million. The state was then able to purchase the parcel from TPL using $12.65 million in state funds plus funds raised privately by three nonprofit conservation organizations.

References

Browne, Kingsbury, Jr. *Federal Tax Incentives and Open Space Preservation*. Lexington, Mass.: Lexington Books, 1982.

Diehl, Janet, and Thomas S. Barrett. *The Conservation Easement Handbook: Managing Land Conservation and Historic Preservation Easement Programs*. Alexandria, Va.: Land Trust Exchange and Trust for Public Land, 1988.

Hoose, Phillip M. *Building an Ark: Tools for the Preservation of Natural Diversity Through Land Protection*. Covelo, Calif.: Island Press, 1981.

Land Trust Alliance. *Starting a Land Trust: A Guide to Forming a Land Conservation Organization*. Washington, D.C.: Land Trust Alliance, 1990. (Available from Land Trust Exchange, 900 17th Street NW, Suite 410, Washington, DC 20006, 202/785-1410.)

Wilkins, Suzanne C., and Roger Koontz. *Connecticut Land Trust Handbook*. Middletown, Conn.: Land Trust Service Bureau, 1981. (Available from Land Trust Service Bureau, Box MMM, Wesleyan Station, Middletown, CT 06456.)

REGULATION

Although regulations are carried out by government authorities, private organizations and individuals can play an important role. Private contributions to wetlands regulation include:

- political action (influencing the formulation of laws, participating in hearing and comment processes);
- litigation (filing suits against government authorities charged with implementing wetlands regulations);
- watchdog activities (aiding government authorities in the enforcement of regulations); and
- technical assistance and scientific expertise (participating in hearing and comment processes or on independent panels formed by governments to evaluate the effects of various regulatory efforts).

Examples

The *National Wildlife Federation* (NWF) encourages its members to participate in the federal regulatory process. NWF's Environmental Hotline is a telephone recording, updated weekly, that provides current information on pending legislation, proposed regulations, and the outcome of congressional votes. NWF contracts a toll-free phone-based service that, for a small fee, sends an overnight mailgram to a targeted legislator or government official. NWF's "activist members" receive action alerts with detailed information and guidance on targeting Congress and submitting comments. These programs are used for wetlands and other issues. (National Wildlife Federation, 1400 16th Street NW, Washington, DC 20036, 202/797-6800; hotline 202/797-6655.)

The *Passaic River Coalition* (PRC) established its Floodplain Watch program in 1985. This program has trained hundreds of citizen volunteers to monitor wetlands development in and around their communities. Suspicious activities are checked against the PRC's database of stream encroachment permits, Section 404 permits, and wetlands maps. Violations are reported directly to the violations division of the Army Corps of Engineers and the Bureau of Floodplain Management of the New

Jersey Department of Environmental Protection (NJDEP). All but four of the 134 violations reported between 1985 and 1989 have been verified by the NJDEP and prompted follow-up actions. (Passaic River Coalition, 246 Madisonville Road, Basking Ridge, NJ 07920, 908/766-7550; see the *National Wetlands Newsletter*, March/April 1991.)

PLANNING

Vigorous community participation is essential if local planning efforts are to produce workable plans supported by a broad spectrum of interests. Individuals and private organizations provide the vision and priorities that shape a comprehensive plan and help ensure its success in protecting wetlands.

Individuals and private organizations can participate in the planning process by:
- attending public hearings;
- seeking appointment to the local planning commission;
- initiating the development of a new element in the local land-use plan dealing specifically with wetlands;
- undertaking a natural resource inventory or wetlands inventory with private funds; and
- developing brochures and other information explaining alternatives to development practices that harm wetlands values.

Strengths

Local government attention to wetlands protection almost always results from efforts of concerned citizens to establish wetlands protection as an important local goal. Planning provides the framework for private conservation organizations and concerned citizens to make wetlands protection a recognized priority.

Challenges

Getting all the concerned nongovernmental parties to negotiate and reach a consensus is the greatest challenge to the development of comprehensive plans. The involved parties may include individuals and organizations representing diverse agendas and interests; reconciling these concerns can be a lengthy and demanding process.

Users

Planning processes typically involve three principal parties:

- citizens and various sectors of the public, such as developers and conservation advocates;
- elected officials, who typically direct planning processes; and
- planning professionals, either staff members or outside consultants.

Examples

The *Dutchess Land Conservancy* in New York acquires land for governments and civic groups to facilitate improvements in local land-use planning and land-use controls and to encourage more responsible land development practices. The conservancy advocates land-use patterns that concentrate populations in existing centers of settlement at relatively high densities to divert development pressures away from wetlands and other sensitive areas. The conservancy also encourages all towns to map wetlands and other ecologically important areas and to require clustering of development away from these areas.

The *Brandywine Conservancy* developed a Natural Features Conservation Ordinance for Lower Merion Township in Montgomery County, Pennsylvania. The ordinance integrates measures to protect wetlands with standards for stormwater management facilities, woodland protection, trail development, and tree planting.

INCENTIVES

Incentive programs carried out by private organizations include:
- leases and management agreements that can provide income to landowners in exchange for the right of the lessee, usually a conservation organization, to manage and occupy the property or to specify the terms and restrictions under which the landowner continues to manage the property; and
- programs that work toward "greening" public attitudes and increasing the motivation of private companies to address environmental issues for public-relations reasons.

Examples

The National Wildlife Federation established the *Corporate Conservation Council* (CCC) in 1982. Consisting of delegates from a maximum of 20 major corporations, the CCC provides a forum for discussing responsible use of natural resources. The CCC gives an annual Environmental Achievement Award to a corporation that goes beyond regulatory requirements to protect the environment. Of the six awards given to date, three have been for projects involving wetlands.

The *Wildlife Habitat Enhancement Council* (WHEC) is a nonprofit organization formed by corporations and conservation organizations to promote the protection and enhancement of wildlife habitats on corporate lands. In addition to its programs offering technical assistance, WHEC initiated the Corporate Wildlife Habitat Certification Program in July 1990. This program publicly recognizes corporations involved in wildlife enhancement on their lands; WHEC maintains a national register listing these certified properties. Landowners receive a Certificate of Recognition and are entitled to post WHEC Corporate Wildlife Habitat signs at their site. (Wildlife Habitat Enhancement Council, 1010 Wayne Avenue, Suite 1240, Silver Spring, MD 20910, 301/588-4629; see *Environment, Science and Technology*, vol. 25, no. 5, 1991.)

RESTORATION, CREATION, AND MANAGEMENT

Private landowners, nonprofit organizations, and corporations are successfully involved in the restoration of destroyed or degraded wetlands, creation of wetlands where none existed previously, and management of existing wetlands. Partnerships between two or more organizations, often including governments, are common. Private landowners, including corporations, are especially important in identifying significant wetlands areas and making their lands available for inclusion in restoration, creation, and management programs.

Examples

The *Michigan Wildlife Habitat Foundation*, a private, statewide conservation group, is working with the U.S. Fish and Wildlife Service to restore privately owned wetlands in lower Michigan. Landowners and volunteers cooperate in identifying wetlands enhancement projects, such as blocking drainage ditches to restore wetlands habitats. Landowners may obtain free assistance in exchange for entering into a 10-year conservation agreement.

In North Carolina, E. I. DuPont de Nemours & Company, in cooperation with the nonprofit *Wildlife Habitat Enhancement Council* (WHEC), has conserved 450 acres of its Kinston plant site, including a substantial bald cypress wetland. As part of the broader land management plan, DuPont also created a shallow one-acre pond and enhanced habitat for wildlife and plant species in both wetlands and terrestrial ecosystems. (WHEC, 1010 Wayne Avenue, Suite 1240, Silver Spring, MD 20910, 301/588-4629.)

The National Wildlife Federation, Ducks Unlimited, and many private landowners are cooperating with various local, state, and federal agencies in South Dakota's *Lake Thompson Watershed Project* (LTWP). Governor George Mickelson initiated the LTWP after the watershed area experienced extensive and increasing flooding. The project has three phases: (1) restoration and protection of wetlands and enhancement of private lands; (2) acquisition of flooded private lands from willing sellers in the Lake Thompson Basin; and (3) management of important small wetlands in the watershed. The LTWP addresses flood control, water quality, soil erosion, waterfowl habitat, and socioeconomics. Private landowners are major participants in the project, as most of the restoration work is being done on private land.

The *American Crystal Sugar Company*, a cooperative owned by sugar beet growers, is nearing completion of a 160-acre wetlands complex built to treat the plant's wastewater discharge. The wetlands complex, created at the company's Hillsboro, North Dakota, plant, includes seven nesting islands for waterfowl and will be able to treat 1.5 million gallons per day of wastewater containing high concentrations of organic materials. Waterfowl have moved rapidly into the new wetlands habitat. This wetlands treatment system, used as a tertiary treatment system, is costing American Crystal less than one-half of what a comparable, more traditional treatment system would cost (see *Ducks Unlimited*, May/June 1991).

TECHNICAL ASSISTANCE, EDUCATION, AND OUTREACH

Technical Assistance

Private organizations provide technical assistance to both private and governmental bodies interested in protecting wetlands. This assistance includes guidebooks, reports, workshops, newsletters, and ecological evaluations of specific sites. Private technical assistance efforts can give individuals, small citizens' organizations, and local and state government agencies access to information that they might not otherwise be able to obtain.

Examples

The *Izaak Walton League of America* offers a "Partners for Wetlands" protection kit with information on restoring wetlands, particularly waterfowl habitats. The program focuses on enhancing farmers' efforts to manage their lands for wetlands and wildlife protection. The kit includes wetlands fact sheets, fundraising and public relations ideas, and summaries of individual projects. (The Izaak Walton League of America, Inc., 1401 Wilson Boulevard, Level B, Arlington, VA 22209, 709/528-1818.)

The *Land Trust Alliance* is an organization whose members include land trusts, government agencies, conservation professionals, and individuals. In addition to providing technical information and organizing conferences, the Land Trust Alliance maintains the Conservation Lawyer's Network, a nationwide listing of lawyers experienced in land conservation transactions who counsel landowners and land trusts on land preservation. The Land Trust Alliance also publishes a newsletter, *Exchange.* (The Land Trust Alliance, 900 17th Street NW, Suite 410, Washington, DC 20006, 202/785-1410)

Education and Outreach

Nongovernment organizations play an important role in environmental education. These organizations produce educational materials that can be used by school districts or individual educators, including activity books, teachers' guides, maps, posters, slide shows, and videos. Private organizations also run field schools, camps, and other extracurricular educational activities for school-aged children.

Private organizations are involved in more general public education or outreach efforts as well. These programs can include newsletters, newspaper editorials, lectures, workshops, citizen activism, guided tours or nature walks through wetlands, TV specials, and videos.

Examples

The Environmental Concern has published a curriculum guide for teachers of grades K through 12. *Wow! The Wonders of Wetlands* presents 40 classroom and field lessons designed to prepare students to make environmentally responsible decisions about wetlands, water quality, and land use. The final section of the nearly 200-page teachers' manual is a guide to conservation and restoration

activities that includes plans for a variety of projects, such as creating a small pond or marsh for study or planting wetlands plants to enhance the habitat. These projects build on the skills and knowledge gained in the lessons. (The Environmental Concern, P.O. Box P, St. Michaels, MD 21663, 301/745-9620.)

Wetlands Institute of Stone Harbor, located in New Jersey's South Shore region, is a nonprofit organization dedicated to educating the public and fostering scientific research on intertidal salt marshes and other coastal ecosystems. The institute offers programs for school groups and other youth groups, including presentations and activities in the marshes. The Wetlands Institute maintains an education center and museum with saltwater aquaria, exhibits depicting life in the salt marsh, a children's discovery room, and an observation tower offering a panoramic view of the surrounding wetlands. Among other programs are summer nature classes for children in preschool through sixth grade, family programs, a public lecture series, natural history courses, and internships. (Wetlands Institute of Stone Harbor, Stone Harbor Boulevard, Stone Harbor, NJ 08247, 609/368-1211.)

The *Port Blakely Mill Company,* a timber company in Washington state, formed a partnership with a local school district to provide wetlands education to the children and community of Bainbridge Island. The company is planning to preserve nearly half of a 1,153-acre site (which includes wetlands) as open space, recreation areas, and wildlife habitats. An access agreement with the Bainbridge Island School District will allow area schools to use the site as an outdoor classroom for studying wetlands. The Port Blakely Mill Company also provided the school district with a $10,000 grant to expand its natural resources curriculum. The staff, faculty, and students of Captain Blakely Elementary School celebrated the new partnership with the first annual Wetlands Day in 1990. (Port Blakely Mill Company, 151 Modrone Lane North, Winslow, WA 98110, 206/842-3088.)

The *National Audubon Society* distributes a "tool kit" to would-be activists. The package includes several fact sheets on topics such as common myths about wetlands and Section 404; where to address letters voicing concerns about wetlands protection; a sample letter to a newspaper editor; ideas for community projects; a copy of the special wetlands issue of *Audubon Activist*; and a list of other wetlands materials available from Audubon, including a slide show and a tape-recorded public announcement. (National Audubon

Society, 950 Third Avenue, New York, NY 10022, 212/832-3200.)

RESEARCH

Nonprofit organizations, corporations, academic institutions, and individuals are involved with wetlands research efforts of several different types:

- research as a component of a larger project (for example, a wetlands inventory done as part of a land-acquisition program);
- post-project evaluations (such as an evaluation of the effects of a restoration effort);
- policy research (studies or reports on the effectiveness of policies, regulations, etc.); and
- scientific research (for example, studies of ecological, botanical, zoological, or chemical features).

Examples

Ducks Unlimited (DU) initiated its Habitat Inventory and Evaluation program in 1984. The program uses satellite data from LandSat Thematic Mapper and Spot as well as digital wetlands data from the U.S. Fish and Wildlife Service's National Wetlands Inventory program. These remote-sensing and geographic information systems help DU biologists select the most effective sites for wetlands preservation, enhancement, and restoration; monitor changes in the availability of waterfowl habitats; and evaluate the effectiveness of waterfowl management plans.

Wetlands Research, Inc. (WRI), is a nonprofit organization that provides opportunities for applied wetlands research. WRI owns 440 acres of riparian lands along the Des Plaines River in northern Illinois, most of which has been previously farmed or mined. Scientists are creating wetlands as living laboratories, enabling them to study various restoration and management techniques and to learn more about restoring functions of degraded wetlands. Scientists from various universities perform most of the research; results are published in WRI's series of technical reports. (Wetlands Research, Inc., 53 West Jackson Boulevard, Suite 1015, Chicago, IL 60604, 312/922-0777.)

The *Society of Wetlands Scientists* (SWS) promotes the exchange of scientific information related to wetlands. Members include scientists from local, state, and federal government agencies; the academic community; and consulting firms. SWS holds annual meetings to present scientific papers and publishes a biennial journal, *Wetlands*, featuring articles on biology, regulation, management, and other wetlands issues. (Society of Wetland Scientists, P.O. Box 296, Wilmington, NC 28402.)

PART IV
Wetlands Data Sources and Collection Methods

Introduction

To identify problems leading to wetlands loss and the best mechanisms for dealing with those problems, a state needs to address a series of questions regarding the following basic issues:

- the location, quantity, type, condition, and functions of the wetlands resource, and
- the resource's status and trends (e.g., causes and rate of loss, areas where the loss is concentrated).

To assist strategy developers, Part I of this manual presents and discusses these questions as they relate to the choice of appropriate protection mechanisms to include in a wetlands strategy. The questions are repeated below, along with suggested sources of data and data-collection methods that may help strategy developers answer the questions. These data sources are not exhaustive but are introduced as a guide or sampling. They are reviewed in detail in Part IV.2 (which also includes a review of data sources and wetlands evaluation methods that are *not* addressed here).

The data sources introduced below (with their associated questions) are divided into three levels. **Level 1** sources yield information at relatively low cost, usually with lower overall accuracy and precision and at larger scales. **Level 2** and **Level 3**

sources entail considerably greater costs but may yield greater accuracy and precision. It should be noted that Level 1 information is adequate in many instances; more is not necessarily better.

Data sources at each level are keyed, by part number/section letter, to the detailed review of sources in Part IV.2 (see the outline of reviewed sources on page 172). Users can thus proceed to the question(s) of interest, find the appropriate data-source level(s), and go to the relevant part and section in the review of data sources (which also begins on page 172).

Examples of several states' approaches to data collection are given during the introduction of the data sources. State wetlands managers and other decision makers will undoubtedly appreciate, after reading these examples, the state-specific nature of data needs and methods of meeting those needs. Also interspersed are short discussions of topics relevant to data collection, such as using rapid assessment techniques (for function/value assessments), assessing wetlands condition, using remotely sensed data, and understanding cumulative impacts.

Following the introduction to the data sources is a brief discussion of criteria for selecting appropriate data-collection methods.

How many wetlands does a state have, and where are they located?

Level 1 data base:

Obtain National Wetland Inventory (NWI) maps to determine locations (II,A).*

Obtain data from STATSGO digital soils maps and attribute files to estimate amount and general distribution (II,C). (*Note:* The use of hydric soil maps alone to identify the location and extent of wetlands may lead to inaccurate results. There is no direct correlation between hydric soils and wetlands.)

Level 2 data base:

Obtain digital NWI maps (II,A).

Obtain SSURGO digital soil maps (II,B).

Obtain floodplain maps (II,E) and SCS

***Parenthetical notations refer to sections in Part IV.2.**

"Swampbuster" maps (II,D); digitize if possible.

Level 3 data base:

Update NWI maps, perhaps through use of TM and SPOT imagery, and/or field-check existing NWI maps.

What kinds of wetlands are they?

Level 1 data base:

Use NWI maps to identify and classify wetlands (I).

Level 2 data base:

Field-check wetlands, using vegetation or other criteria for classification (I).

What are the wetlands' functions?

Level 1 data base:

Examine existing literature reviews; consult with experts.

Wetlands Inventories

Many state legislatures have directed their natural resources agencies to conduct inventories and produce maps showing the location, acreage, and (in some cases) types of wetlands statewide. In Oregon, for example, the Division of State Lands is directed to compile and maintain a comprehensive statewide wetlands inventory based on uniform identification standards and criteria at a scale practicable for planning and regulatory purposes. New York State's Freshwater Wetlands Act calls for the identification and mapping of all freshwater wetlands of at least 12.4 acres and the preparation of maps delineating the boundaries of those wetlands.

Many wetlands inventory efforts begin with a "paper inventory," a compilation of probable wetlands locations and boundaries determined from existing maps and other available information (Granger, 1989). National Wetlands Inventory (NWI) maps, soil maps, and floodplain maps are the primary sources for a paper inventory. The maps provide fairly reliable information on potential wetlands, cover most of the country, and are readily available.

Where more detailed information is required, existing maps can be improved through a variety of techniques, including field checks and aerial photographic interpretation. In Thurston County, Washington, for example, field verification was conducted to determine the accuracy of the paper inventory. The location and extent of a sampling of wetlands in each township were checked by biologists through field reconnaissance.

In New York, the Adirondack Park Agency conducted an extensive update of NWI maps in conjunction with its regulatory program. NWI methodologies were intensified to ensure that statutorily defined wetlands were mapped. Modifications included mapping to one-acre units, increasing covertype resolution by using large-scale backup photography, and conducting intensive field checks (Curran et al., 1989). Wetlands boundaries were plotted on 7.5-minute maps prepared from the photo overlays. Landowners with wetlands on their properties were notified, and public hearings were conducted. Based on the results of the hearings, final regulatory maps were prepared.

Level 2 data base:

Apply rapid assessment field techniques for functional evaluations to a representative sample of each wetlands type (IV).

Link SOILS5 attribute files with STATSGO or SSURGO spatial data on hydric soils to classify wetlands by hydrologic and water quality functions.

Level 3 data base:

Directly measure functions of representative wetlands (V).

What condition are the wetlands in?

Level 1 data base:

Examine wetlands-related trends data such as Breeding Bird Surveys (III,H) and Clean Water Act Section 305(b) state water quality reports.

Review FWS Status and Trends reports (III,A).

Level 2 data base:

Overlay land cover maps (II,F) or data (III,B) with NWI or hydric soil maps to quantify land uses with potential impacts.

Consult local, regional, and state growth planning studies to identify where impacts from growth may have occurred.

Level 3 data base:

Directly measure functions (e.g., biological surveys, hydrologic instrumentation) of representative wetlands or wetland watersheds (V,A through C).

Compare sets of aerial photographs to locate where growth or wetlands alterations have occurred over time (e.g., changes in vegetation cover can indicate degradation of wetlands; wetlands in developed areas are more likely to be degraded than wetlands in undeveloped areas).

How rapidly are wetlands disappearing, and where is most of the loss concentrated?

Level 1 data base:

Obtain state or regional data from FWS Status and Trends reports (III,A), which provide a basic picture of both recent and long-term trends.

Level 2 data base:

Sponsor intensified estimations of FWS Status and Trends reports in more localized areas by using aerial photographs, TM and SPOT remotely sensed data, and field-based updating of 1970s NWI maps.

Analyze permit data files to compare permitted losses with replacement requirements (III,G).

Estimate some other types of loss by reviewing USDA drainage statistics data (III,D).

Examine the National Resources Inventory (III,B) or the Forest Inventory and Analysis database (III,C).

Review local, regional, and state growth planning studies to identify where losses are occurring or may occur in the future.

Level 3 data base:

Use digitized NWI maps to estimate loss by subtracting wetlands acreage from hydric soil acreage of SOILS6 database (county level) (III,F). For more localized estimates, use STATSGO or SSURGO maps to approximate hydric soils (II,B and C).

Which activities are most responsible for wetlands degradation and loss?

Level 1 data base:

Discuss threats with regulatory staff and scientists; review government statistical reports, particularly the Clean Water Act Section 305(b) reports published annually by states and FWS Status and Trends data (III,A).

Level 2 data base:

Identify conversions from a time series of representative aerial photographs.

Assessing the Condition of Wetlands

There are diverse ways of measuring the condition of wetlands. At a broad watershed or regional level, information on trends in wetlands-related resources may reveal changes in quality or condition. A comparison among data from several years of Christmas Bird Counts or Breeding Bird Surveys, for example, may show a decline in migratory water birds. Although a direct correlation between wetlands degradation and declining bird populations is not explicit, this trend may be a preliminary indication of a decline in wetlands quality.

Wetlands condition can sometimes be assumed based on proximity to potential threats. Although these conclusions are not definitive, they can serve as initial screening tools. Small, isolated wetlands located along major roadways will probably show signs of impairment of their wildlife and fisheries functions but usually not of their flood storage function.

Directly determining condition may involve in-depth studies of water quality and other biological parameters on an individual wetland level. Specific sampling techniques and information on indicators of wetlands condition are included in Adamus and Brandt (1990).

Using Remotely Sensed Data

Remotely sensed data (i.e., satellite imagery and aerial photographs) are useful for mapping wetlands and monitoring resource changes. Satellites equipped with multi-spectral scanners—such as LANDSAT and the French equivalent, SPOT—are frequently used to map wetlands, although current satellite technology may result in incomplete wetlands mapping. Wetlands that are frequently flooded or continually wet are most readily detected; temporarily or seasonally flooded areas, particularly forested types, are difficult to distinguish from upland areas. Furthermore, the resolution of satellite data is not fine enough to allow detection of many small wetlands areas. As the resolution improves and scanner devices become more advanced, imagery may provide more reliable data for identifying wetlands.

Color infrared photography is used for wetlands inventories because wetlands vegetation is easily identified by its signature color combination. Remotely sensed data are not a substitute, however, for intensive field reconnaissance, although for the purposes of monitoring changes in regional wetlands acreage, remotely sensed data may be an economical means of detecting gross changes from year to year. Data can be used to assess the status of the resource, detect changes over time, and identify more obvious impacts such as encroachment and sedimentation.

Analyze permit data files to determine which types of activities are associated with permitted losses (III,G).

Overlay land cover maps (II,F) or data (III,B) with NWI or hydric soil maps, to quantify land uses with potential impacts.

Correlate population, economic, and agricultural statistics with wetlands loss data.

Level 3 data base:

Conduct a field inventory of representative wetlands and adjacent land uses to quantify observable stress/response situations.

Directly measure impairment of wetland functions (e.g., bioindicator species, sediment contamination) and correlate with surrounding land cover (IV and V,A).

Apply well-calibrated exposure models to quantify potential impacts on biological functions (e.g., Brody and Pendelton, 1987).

What are the consequences of loss?

Level 1 data base:

Using technical literature or experts, compile accounts of wetlands species disappearance,

---

Measuring Wetlands Trends in Lake George, New York

Recognizing the important role that wetlands play in maintaining surface water quality, state and local agencies were concerned about possible wetlands loss and changes in function due to development. A study was conducted to assess recent trends in wetlands loss and to document land-use changes to determine whether current New York laws were effective in protecting wetlands in the Lake George area.

Using aerial photographs from 1948 through 1986, the study compared land-use patterns and wetlands acreage over the 38-year period. Photographic stereo pairs were interpreted, and wetlands boundaries and applicable land-use changes were identified and drafted on acetate overlays. The information was entered into a GIS for analysis.

The analysis revealed that roughly half the wetlands in the Lake George Basin had been altered since 1948. Furthermore, the study was able to determine the types of conversions and changes in land-use patterns over the 38-year period. The study also revealed that most of the wetlands alterations occurred prior to 1978 (wetlands protection laws and a slower growth rate contributed to the decline in wetlands conversions).

Understanding Cumulative Impacts

For more than two centuries, human activities have affected the quality and abundance of wetlands in the United States. Despite fairly stringent environmental regulations, the cumulative impacts of isolated projects continue to alter the character of the overall landscape.

Measuring cumulative impacts is a challenge. In many instances, such effects are synergistic: interactions among disturbances produce secondary effects that differ from those of the original disturbances taken discretely. Moreover, disturbances can have indirect effects that are difficult to measure. These effects can accumulate over time without producing a measurable impact until later.

Recent research efforts have concentrated on developing methods for addressing cumulative impacts by focusing on entire landscape units rather than individual wetlands sites. The synoptic method, for example, ranks watersheds or other landscape units by their condition in relation to hydrologic, water quality, and life support functions (see Part IV,A,3). In addition, techniques are being developed to measure the effects of cumulative impacts on the biotic community (Brooks et al., 1991)

To evaluate the effects of incremental impacts, wetlands protection and management must be approached from a *landscape perspective*. Individual wetlands are often affected by events beyond their boundaries, either in adjacent uplands or in more distant areas within the same watershed. Understanding how a wetland fits into its surrounding landscape is the first step in assessing potential impacts over time.

- Where in the watershed is the wetland located?
- What are the historic losses of wetlands area/type in the region?
- If the wetland is altered, how will local or regional biodiversity be affected?
- What will be the impacts on water quality and quantity within the watershed?
- What effects will increased flooding or reduced water supplies upstream have on the wetland?

Perhaps the simplest way to assess cumulative impacts is to examine changes in the landscape that have occurred over time—such as changes in land-use patterns, vegetative cover, or wetlands acreage. (An increase in roadbuilding in a watershed, for instance, is likely to result in increased runoff, sedimentation, and habitat fragmentation.) Documenting landscape changes helps establish the relative level of impact among watersheds statewide.

A direct loss of wetlands acreage can be used to determine a watershed's vulnerability to subsequent loss. The greater the historic wetlands loss, the greater the susceptibility to cumulative impacts. In addition to direct loss, wetlands are subjected to a number of stresses, including alteration of hydrologic patterns; point and nonpoint source discharges of nutrients, toxics, and sediment; and timber and peat harvesting. These activities often contribute to a watershed's degradation. By documenting both wetlands loss and the activities that directly or indirectly cause degradation, a relative level of impact can be assessed.

Various readily available sources of information can be used to assess wetlands loss, to identify activities potentially detrimental to wetlands, and to document increases in those activities. For example, aerial photographs show changes in vegetation, development, and agricultural activities, and discharge permits for industrial facilities provide information on point source stressors. Also useful are comparisons of affected wetlands with reference wetlands, which serve as a standard (Hughes et al., 1986). From a landscape perspective, reference sites can be entire watersheds whose stream networks and associated wetlands are relatively intact. Comparisons of reference hydrologic or biological conditions with those of areas being altered can inform decisions as to whether the ecological integrity of the ecosystem is being maintained. For example, if stream-side wetlands within the lower reaches of a watershed are already receiving abnormally high amounts of sediment as compared to the reference wetland, continued development in the headwaters of the watershed should be discouraged.

Although methods have not yet been developed to predict accurately the impacts of the ''next'' project on the ecological integrity of a watershed, it is possible to identify and observe areas within a state that have undergone significant alteration, determine what activities are causing loss, and target areas requiring management attention. Knowing that a watershed has been exposed to significant alteration over time allows certain assumptions to be made about future activities. This qualitative information provides important guidance for management decisions.

increased flooding, and other landscape functional losses.

Level 2 data base:

Correlate long-term changes in wildlife, water pollution, and/or stream flow regime with measured losses of wetlands (III,H).

Compile economic data on resources (e.g., timber, hay, waterfowl hunting licenses), hazards (e.g., downstream flooding, water quality degradation), and economic hardships suffered by industry (e.g., fishing) related to wetlands loss.

Level 3 data base:

Measure a large enough sample of wetlands to eliminate nonwetlands factors that may confound the interpretation of correlation analyses just described; link to economic losses where appropriate.

Selecting a Data-Collection Method

Level of Detail

There is inevitably a trade-off between accuracy and timeliness in determining what data-collection methods to use. Some methods provide general, "broad-brush" information that is readily obtained but may not offer enough detail; others take longer but provide greater accuracy. The appropriate level depends on specific data requirements and particular situations, as the following two examples illustrate.

Snohomish County, Washington, conducted an in-depth inventory of its wetlands, including detailed assessments of physical and biological characteristics. Assessment information was collected so that staff would have reliable information on which to base preliminary decisions about the potential impacts of proposed projects on wetlands values. The county produced an atlas of wetland maps and a computerized data base of inventory information. Compiling this inventory required 15 full-time biologists, technicians, and Corps of Engineers members who worked for six months.

The information is being used to establish a wetlands protection program; in addition, county agencies use the atlas to review development projects and their relation to county ordinances and laws.

In contrast, San Juan County, Washington, needed general guidance on wetlands location in order to alert staff, during permit reviews, to projects that might affect wetlands. In preparing a field-verified inventory, the county first conducted a paper inventory that consisted of hydric soils superimposed onto NWI maps. This effort required the work of one planner for one week.

Appropriateness of the Method

Here are several questions to consider:
- Is the information already available?
- Does the method provide the information needed?
- Does it produce a useful product?
- What are the costs associated with the method in terms of time, personnel, expertise, money, equipment, and training?
- Is the technique easy to use?
- Are there any alternatives to this method?

Data Validity

Data-collection techniques must be defensible, especially when they are tied to regulations. When choosing a method, it is important to be aware of its potential shortcomings and specifically to consider these questions:
- Are the results obtained by the method replicable?

Some methods require considerable subjective judgment. As a result, different users may arrive at different ratings, thus defeating the purpose of a standardized evaluation tool.
- Is the method well-documented?

While all methods contain assumptions, the method should have strong ties to the technical literature base.
- Does the method account for temporal dynamics of wetlands?

Wetlands are changing ecosystems, varying both seasonally and over time. The method should account for the potentially large temporal differences.

Review of Sources and Methods

What follows is a detailed review of sources of wetlands information and evaluation methods. A narrative on each source or method describes its uses and limitations. Some subjectivity was required in drafting these narratives. The authors or data base managers respon-

Part IV.2 has been funded by the U.S. Environmental Protection Agency (EPA) and conducted through Contract 68-C8-006 to ManTech Environmental Technology, Inc. It was written by:

Paul R. Adamus
ManTech Environmental Technology, Inc.
U.S. EPA Environmental Research Laboratory
200 SW 35th Street
Corvallis, OR 97333

This material was prepared for the U.S. Environmental Protection Agency's Wetlands Research Program and World Wildlife Fund. It has been subjected to EPA's peer review. The opinions expressed herein are those of the author and do not necessarily reflect those of EPA; an official endorsement of the agency should not be inferred. Mention of trade names of commercial products does not constitute endorsement or recommendation for use.

sible for the methods and sources reviewed here were given an opportunity to comment on the narratives; most responded, and changes were made as appropriate. No recommendation is made, however, as to which method or source is "best"; this should be determined by individual users who are aware of the objectives, budgets, and schedules associated with particular applications.

Public decisions often must be made that require information on the location, status, trends, and valued functions of wetlands. However, as public interest in wetlands has increased, so have the number of information sources. One consequence is that decision makers are confronted with many evaluation methods and data sources to choose from but sometimes lack the time or resources to examine and compare these methods and sources in detail. The following pages represent the results of such an effort. Table 1 at the end of this material compares various rapid evaluation methods with regard to the indicators they use.

Considerable effort was made to keep this analysis as objective as possible. Both strengths and weaknesses of each method or source are discussed. To better describe the possible (and quite diverse) contexts for the use of particular methods, a set of factors (e.g., time and labor requirements) was consistently applied to each. These factors are assumed to be important to users of this guide and were derived from wetlands-related issues encountered by the author during the last decade (i.e., in workshops and correspondence with users and reviewers of some of the methods and data sources as well as previous reviews published by other authors).

Nonetheless, there is some subjectivity inherent in the choice and application of these particular factors. Because the methods were not evaluated with a specific management objective in mind, no attempt was made to establish a standard for "adequacy," and methods and sources were *not* reviewed with their own individual objectives in mind. (A method that appears, on the basis of the following narratives, to be one of limited use in developing a statewide wetlands strategy could thus be more than adequate for its intended use.)

The review of sources and methods is organized as follows:

I. WETLANDS CLASSIFICATION SCHEMES

    A. Cowardin et al. Classification
    B. Hydrogeomorphic (Brinson) Classification

II. MAPS AND NATIONAL DATA BASES

    A. National Wetlands Inventory (NWI) Maps
    B. SCS County Soil Survey Maps (SSURGO)
    C. SCS STATSGO and NATSGO Maps
    D. SCS "Swampbuster" Maps
    E. FEMA Flood Hazard Maps
    F. USGS Land-Use Land Analysis (LUDA) Maps
    G. NOAA Coastal Ocean Program/Coastwatch: Change Analysis Program Data Base
    H. Forest Inventory and Analysis (FIA) Data Base
    I. National Resources Inventory (NRI) Data Base

III. DATA SOURCES ON WETLANDS STATUS AND TRENDS

    A. FWS Status and Trends Reports
    B. National Resources Inventory (NRI) Data Base
    C. Forest Inventory and Assessment (FIA) Data Base
    D. USDA Drainage Statistics Data
    E. Environmental Monitoring and Assessment Program (EMAP) Data Base
    F. Wetlands Loss Calculated by "Hydric Acreage" Minus "NWI Acreage"
    G. Wetlands Loss Calculated from Examination of Permit Files

    H. Trends in Wetlands-Related Resources
    I. NOAA Coastal Ocean Program/Coastwatch: Change Analysis Program Data

IV. RAPID METHODS FOR EVALUATING, RANKING, OR CATEGORIZING WETLANDS

Methods Intended for Use in Any of the Coterminous States
    A. HAT (Habitat Assessment Technique)
    B. HEP (Habitat Evaluation Procedures)
    C. Synoptic Approach for Wetlands Cumulative Effects Analysis
    D. WET (Wetland Evaluation Technique)

Methods Developed for Particular Regions or Wetlands Types
    E. Bottomland Hardwood Forest Habitat Evaluation Model
    F. Connecticut/New Hampshire Method
    G. HES (Habitat Evaluation System)
    H. Hollands-Magee (Normandeau) Method
    I. Larson/Golet Method
    J. Minnesota Wetland Evaluation Methodology (WEM)
    K. Ontario Method

V. INTENSIVE METHODS FOR INDIVIDUAL WETLANDS

    A. Biological Functions
    B. Hydrologic Functions
    C. Water Quality Functions
    D. Cumulative Functions

I. WETLANDS CLASSIFICATION SCHEMES

This section examines two schemes for classifying wetlands: (1) the U.S. Fish and Wildlife Service (FWS) classification (Cowardin et al., 1979), which is reviewed because it is the most widely used and officially adopted scheme; and (2) the "hydrogeomorphic" classification scheme, which is reviewed because the Wetlands Research Program of the U.S. Army Corps of Engineers (COE) is currently considering its development and use as an organizing paradigm. Other wetlands or aquatic classification schemes currently receiving less use or attention include the "Circular 39" classification, once used by the Soil Conservation Service

(SCS) and FWS (Shaw and Fredine, 1956), and schemes investigated or proposed by Gosselink and Turner (1978), Novitzki (1979), O'Brien and Motts (1980), Winter (1977), Adamus (1983), Rosgen (1985), and Hollands (1987).

Numerous other wetlands classification procedures or criteria have been or are being developed by agencies. Some of these include wetlands value as a criterion. However, in the context of this appendix, we use the term "classification" to describe schemes that are almost purely descriptive and value neutral.

A. Cowardin et al. Classification

Explained in:
> Cowardin, L. M., V. Carter, F. C. Golet, and E. T. LaRoe (1979), *Classification of Wetlands and Deepwater Habitats of the United States*, FWS/OBS-79/31, U.S. Fish and Wildlife Service, Washington, DC.

Available from:
> National Wetlands Inventory, U.S. Fish and Wildlife Service, Washington, DC. Training in its use is available from National Wetlands Inventory, U.S. Fish and Wildlife Service, 9720 Executive Center Drive, Monroe Building, Suite 101, St. Petersburg, FL 33702.

How developed:
> This classification scheme was developed and tested throughout the United States by a group of wetlands scientists over a five-year period.

Categories:
> This classification applies to deepwater and unvegetated aquatic areas as well as vegetated wetlands habitats. The following wetlands types are included:

1. Marine systems
   - Aquatic bed
   - Reef
2. Estuarine systems
   - Emergent
   - Scrub-shrub
   - Forested
   - Aquatic bed
   - Reef
3. Riverine systems
   - Emergent
   - Aquatic bed
4. Lacustrine systems
   - Emergent
   - Aquatic bed
5. Palustrine systems
   - Moss-lichen
   - Emergent
   - Scrub-shrub
   - Forested
   - Aquatic bed

To the extent that site data allow, users can include secondary categories that further describe plant forms (for example, deciduous vs. evergreen forested wetlands), water regime, water chemistry, general soil type (organic vs. mineral), origin (manmade vs. beaver vs. other natural), and other "modifiers" (for example, species dominance type). As optionally developed by users, these can be combined in more than 100,000 ways to describe wetlands.

General description:
> This classification scheme has been officially adopted by FWS and most other federal agencies. A wetland (or a spatially discrete biological community within a wetland) is placed in one of the foregoing hierarchical categories, based on interpretation of aerial imagery and/or ground-level observation.

Rationale for categories:
> The categories were developed to achieve consistency in classifying and mapping wetlands habitats. To some extent they were defined to represent habitats that can be distinguished by aerial imagery.

Feasibility of mapping:
> Highly feasible (see below).

Extent of use:
> The Cowardin classification scheme is the most extensively peer-reviewed and used wetlands classification system. This scheme is the official basis for the National Wetlands Inventory (NWI) maps (described in part II below) and FWS Status and Trends reports (described in part III below).

Extent of validation:
> This classification scheme is the most extensively validated one currently in use. That is, comparisons of groupings of wetlands using this classification have been found to corres-

pond well with those arrived at through independent expert judgment and/or statistical analysis of hydrologic and vegetation data.

Primary strengths:

The scheme is used extensively in connection with the largest source of wetlands mapping data (the NWI maps). It appears to have a high degree of internal consistency and objectivity; as a result, the precision of application is relatively high (that is, independent users generally assign the same class to the same wetland).

Primary limitations:

The classification categories are not explicitly intended to represent differences that may be significant in terms of wetlands function. Important indicators of function that are not included in the scheme include wetlands gradient (shoreline and inlet-to-outlet), basin size and shape, water source and transport vector, interspersion of open water with vegetation, and, especially, position and condition relative to that of other wetlands, land uses, and landform types. Also, some classification rules seem counterintuitive to some users (for example, forested floodplain wetlands cannot be classified as "riverine" when using the Cowardin scheme). This makes the scheme less capable of addressing basic questions such as this: How many wetlands are associated with flowing water?

B. Hydrogeomorphic (Brinson) Classification

Explained in:

Brinson, M. M., personal communication, (Biology Department, East Carolina University, Greenville, NC).

Available from:

Scheduled for release in 1992 from the Wetlands Research Program, U.S. Army Corps of Engineers, Waterways Experiment Station, WESER-W, Vicksburg, MS 39180 (601/634-2571).

How developed:

This classification scheme was expanded by Dr. Mark Brinson from a scheme proposed in the early 1980s by Dr. Ariel Lugo and others (1990). The hydrogeomorphic classification was the focus of a three-day technical

peer-review workshop held in February 1991 in Stone Mountain, Georgia, and sponsored by the COE Wetlands Research Program.

Categories:

1. Water source and transport vector
   - Mainly sustained by precipitation (atmospheric vector)
   - Mainly sustained by flows from upstream/upslope (lateral-surface or near-surface vector)
   - Mainly sustained by groundwater (phreatic vector)
2. Geomorphic setting
   - Fringe of lake or ocean
   - Riverine
   - Depressional
3. Hydrodynamics
   - Mainly unidirectional flow
   - Mainly bidirectional flow
   - Little flow; mainly vertical water-level fluctuations
4. Water chemistry
   - Salinity
   - Turbidity
   - Conductivity
   - Fulvic/humic content

General description:

A wetland is classified according to each of the foregoing indicators, which are sometimes redundant or highly intercorrelated. This information represents a "profile" of wetlands from which the wetlands' probable functions are postulated by an experienced professional. To validate these postulations, detailed measurements of both indicators and function are implemented in reference wetlands sites. The reference wetlands must be representative of natural or quasi-natural wetlands that either occur currently in the region or occurred there prior to major settlement (e.g., as described in historic surveys or paleoecological analyses). See also Brinson (1989) and Brinson and Lee (1989).

Rationale for categories:

Wetlands scientists generally agree that the hydrogeomorphic classification scheme includes factors important to wetlands functions, particularly the abiotic functions. It relies on generally accepted hydrologic and geomorphic principles.

Feasibility of mapping:

The hydrogeomorphic classification scheme initially requires ground-level measurements to determine function, indicators, and their spatial and temporal variability within a region. With research, these measurements might eventually be statistically correlated to mapping categories used by the National Wetlands Inventory (NWI) (see above) as well as to other features discernable from aerial photographs, topographic maps, and soil surveys. At that point, application of the classification scheme to regionwide wetlands mapping could become practical.

Extent of use/validation:

This classification scheme is newly proposed and untested but appears promising.

Primary strengths:

The hydrogeomorphic classification scheme is the only *functionally based* simple scheme that has drawn widespread interest. It is based on factors that may be important not only to predicting function but also to sustaining wetlands function over time. The scheme does not represent a compromise between what might be important to wetlands function and what is practical to identify and map.

Primary limitations:

The scheme does not rank wetlands and is not intended to be used as the primary means of assigning wetlands to value-based protection or mitigation categories. This classification scheme indicates that some wetlands have certain functions while others do not. Such a yes/no functional determination may be unrealistic in some situations because a wetland rarely lacks a particular function (e.g., flood regime alteration) completely, and thresholds for defining when a function occurs "meaningfully" are absent or site specific. Consequently, subjectivity is required in determining when the magnitude of function of a particular wetland class is so insignificant that the class is considered to lack the function. In addition, the elegant simplicity of the hydrogeomorphic classification scheme may limit its sensitivity. Its primary strength is in distinguishing among broad classes of wetlands on a national or regional level; on a local level, it could tend to indicate large similarities among wetlands.

In the short term, use of the scheme will be limited by the significant costs and time required for measuring the indicators in a replicable manner (particularly the "water source" indicators). Even greater cost and time will be required to validate the scheme with measurements of function from a sufficient number of regional reference wetlands (part V lists some methods for doing so). However, in the long term the result of making detailed measurements of functions will be a much-improved understanding of functions and a technically robust, ecologically meaningful classification scheme.

Another uncertainty concerns the hydrogeomorphic classification scheme's use of just a few indicators. Given the tremendous functional variability among wetlands types, it is uncertain whether so few indicators are sufficient to categorize the functions of individual wetlands with a level of accuracy acceptable to scientists, regulators, and the public. For example, other important indicators of function include wetlands gradient (shoreline and inlet-to-outlet), management history, basin size and shape, soil physics and chemistry, interspersion of open water with vegetation, position in watershed, and, especially, position and condition relative to that of other wetlands, land uses, and landform types. To some extent these additional indicators might be correlated with or subsumed by indicators already contained in this hydrogeomorphic classification. If so, their inclusion in the scheme might be unnecessary because it would add little new information. However, there is no evidence that this is the case, and the extent and nature of correlations will surely vary by region and landscape type.

II. MAPS AND NATIONAL DATA BASES

Maps and national data bases may potentially be used both to locate wetlands and to assess their functions, particularly in a landscape context. However, statistical comparisons have seldom been made (or described in published reports) among the various map types and data bases to determine their degree of overlap and variability. Thus, the narratives given below are somewhat subjective.

Some individual state and local agencies have mapped wetlands and/or compiled acreage and trends of wetlands. Also, some regional COE and

EPA offices have mapped jurisdictional wetlands at a fine scale in local areas. Information about such efforts can be obtained by contacting the National Wetlands Inventory Coordinator in the regional office of the U.S. Fish and Wildlife Service.

A. National Wetlands Inventory (NWI) Maps

Available from:
> Earth Science Information Center, U.S. Geological Survey, 507 National Center, Reston, VA 22092 (1-800/USA-MAPS).

Scale(s) and minimum map unit size(s):
> Most maps are at fine scales (1:24,000 and 1:62,500); some (less often) are at coarse scales (1:100,000 and 1:250,000). These are the same scales used in corresponding U.S. Geological Survey (USGS) topographic maps. Minimum wetlands size mapped on the fine-scale maps is mostly one to three acres (less than an acre in some prairie pothole areas). Very narrow wetlands in river corridors may also be missed.

Coverage:
> Currently, NWI maps are available for over 70 percent of the coterminous United States (especially in the eastern, north central, and southwestern states) and 20 percent of Alaska. The remainder will be completed by 1998. Digital versions, importable into many geographic information systems (GIS), are currently available for about 13 percent of the United States.

Cost:
> Maps are usually $2.50 each for a printed copy and $25 per quadrangle for a completed digital version.

Date(s):
> In most cases each map represents only one time period. Some maps were prepared using 1970s or 1980s remote imagery; others are being prepared from more current data.

How wetlands classified:
> Wetlands are classified according to the Cowardin et al. (1980) classification scheme (see section I,A).

How developed:
> Maps are developed from interpretations of available aerial photographs.

Extent of acreage/type compilation:
> Acreage data have generally not been compiled from these maps; exceptions are compilations (generally by quad sheet) that have been completed for Delaware, Florida, Georgia (Kundell and Woolf, 1986), Illinois, Indiana, New Jersey, Maryland, Rhode Island, and Washington as well as most coastal areas (see section II,G).

Extent of use:
> NWI maps are the most commonly used wetland maps and are applied extensively.

Extent of validation:
> A minority of the maps have been ground-truthed, but nationwide efforts to validate the accuracy of the maps have been extensive. Accuracy varies upward from about 60 percent, with most maps being at least 90 percent accurate.

Primary strengths:
> The maps' spatial resolution (often to within 1 acre) is relatively good. NWI maps not only identify wetlands but also indicate wetlands type (using the Cowardin et al. classification scheme; see section I,A).

Primary limitations:
> Wetlands that were cultivated (cropped) at the time of mapping are generally not depicted, and forested wetlands are poorly discriminated. In some regions these two wetlands types are a major portion of the wetlands resource. Particularly in areas of rapid growth and accelerated wetlands loss, many maps have become quickly outdated. Derived mainly from aerial imagery, the mapped boundaries of wetlands do not necessarily reflect jurisdictional boundaries (as would be determined if the federal delineation manual were used on the ground).

B. SCS County Soil Survey Maps (SSURGO)

Available from:
> U.S. Department of Agriculture (USDA) Soil Conservation Service (SCS) field offices (generally located in the county seat of each county).

Scale(s) and minimum map unit size(s):
Scales range from 1:15,840 to 1:31,680, and the minimum map unit is less than one acre.

Coverage:
About 70 percent of the counties of the coterminous United States are covered (usually excluding federal land). SCS has digitized about 10 percent of these maps (termed SSURGO, for Soil Survey Geographic Data Base), and these data are importable into many GIS systems.

Cost:
There is no cost for limited copies of the survey reports. Digital versions cost about $500 per county or soil survey area.

Date(s):
Soil mapping is ongoing, and the dates of existing maps vary widely. Most comparable SCS soil surveys have been completed since 1960.

How wetlands classified:
Wetlands themselves are not delineated; rather, their presence is inferred from the occurrence of soils officially considered "hydric" (as listed in USDA Soil Conservation Service, 1991). From accompanying soil interpretation record data (contained in the SCS national data base "SOIL5" and describing the physical properties of each soil series), wetlands might cautiously be classified by function. (To obtain computer tapes, contact Dr. Harvey Terpstra, Statistical Laboratory, Iowa State University, Ames, IA 50011.)

How developed:
Trained soil scientists examine vertical soil profiles at regular intervals along ground transects and generalize subjectively from them to the surrounding landscape on the basis of landform, vegetation, and other factors.

Extent of acreage/type compilation:
These maps do not specify wetlands type (other than soil type). Most published soil surveys include a table that reports the acreage of each soil series in the survey area. The map unit use file (contained in the SCS national data base "SOIL6") includes these tables from all soil surveys in the United States and is also available from Iowa State University (see

above). From the County Soil Survey reports, an acreage subtotal can be calculated for those series that are hydric and thus likely to be wetlands (state/county lists of officially designated hydric soil series can be obtained from the same SCS office).

Extent of use:
County Soil Surveys are extensively used as a secondary data source for wetlands mapping.

Extent of validation:
Hydric soil inclusions (i.e., patches of hydric soil too small to map) are probably common in many soils mapped as nonhydric, but the extent to which this occurs is unknown.

Primary strengths:
Soil surveys are sometimes available in areas that currently lack NWI maps. Soil surveys might be used, with caution, to (a) infer locations of cropped wetlands not included in NWI maps; (b) differentiate among some wetlands functional types (e.g., alluvial seasonally flooded vs. isolated seasonally flooded) when linked with SCS's SOIL5 database; and (c) categorize hydrologic and water purification functions of specific wetlands.

Primary limitations:
Many small but cumulatively significant areas that often are wetlands (with hydric soil inclusions) are not mapped because the soil classification systems used in soil survey maps classify soils in landscape groupings. Aquatic bed and many tidal or permanently flooded wetlands are typically mapped as open water, not wetlands, on SCS maps. Areas classified as having hydric soils are not always wetlands, in part because they may have been drained (either prior to or after the soil survey was conducted). This can lead to overestimation of current wetlands acreage. Many drained hydric soils can retain sufficient "hydric" features to result in their being classified (by soil mappers) as hydric even after decades of continuous drainage. Conversely, not all wetlands contain soils that are classified as hydric, and this can lead to underestimation of wetlands acreage. Wetlands may be the result of recent impoundment (e.g., by beaver, highways); in such areas, it typically takes at least a decade

for hydric soil features to appear. Moreover, even the soils of some wetlands that have existed for decades and that have hydric characteristics do not appear on the SCS hydric soil list.

C. SCS STATSGO and NATSGO Maps

Available from:
> National Cartographic Center, USDA Soil Conservation Service, P.O. Box 6567, Fort Worth, TX 76115 (817/334-5559).

Scale(s) and minimum map unit size(s):
> STATSGO (State Soil Geographic Data Base): 1:250,000 scale (about 100 acres minimum resolution)
> NATSGO (National Soil Geographic Data Base): 1:3,000,000 scale

Coverage:
> STATSGO: All 50 states will have digital coverage by late 1993. Currently, digital data have been compiled for about 12 states, but the maps have not yet been released. Maps include soils on federal land.
> NATSGO: Maps are currently available showing the entire United States. They do not include federal land.

Cost:
> NATSGO: $500 for the entire United States.
> STATSGO: $500 per state. STATSGO is distributed as a complete coverage for a state, in one-degree by two-degree quadrangle units.

Date(s):
> The age of the data used varies greatly but is mostly based on soil surveys completed since 1960.

How wetlands classified:
> Wetlands themselves are not delineated; rather, their presence is inferred from the presence of soils officially considered "hydric." From accompanying SOIL5 data, wetlands landscapes might cautiously be classified by function.

How developed:
> SCS has determined the map unit composition (i.e., the groupings of soil types mapped as a single polygon or unit) by transecting or sampling areas on the more detailed SCS County Soil Survey maps (see section II,B) and expanding the data statistically to characterize each whole map unit. For NATSGO the map units are the polygons of SCS's Major Land Resource Area (MLRA) map. The sample points of the National Resources Inventory (NRI) (see section II,H) are statistically aggregated within each MLRA unit. Each NRI record has a pointer to the soil interpretation record (SOIL5) data base so that soil attributes relevant to wetlands function are available for each of the 300,000 NRI sample points.

Extent of acreage/type compilation:
> No compilations related specifically to wetlands have yet been done, but they are technically feasible.

Extent of use:
> These maps are relatively new. For a general explanation, see Bliss and Reybold (1989); for an example of applications to nonwetlands resource issues, see Bleecker et al. (1990).

Extent of validation:
> The maps have not yet been tested extensively against wetlands field data.

Primary strengths:
> These are the only currently available maps from which the landscape-level water purification and flood control functions of wetlands might be inferred for all areas of the United States. (This might be accomplished by cautiously linking STATSGO map data to parameters in the SOIL5 data base that indicate or predict wetlands function).

Primary limitations:
> These maps cannot be used to infer the functions of an individual wetland. Inferences of wetlands functions at the landscape level would be based on hydric soils, but not all hydric soils are wetlands (see section II,B). In the case of the STATSGO data, the soil mapping units do not necessarily coincide with physical boundaries that are relevant to defining landscape functional units (e.g., watersheds). This could lead to some imprecision in estimates compiled on that basis. Soil totals from coastal areas are especially likely to be inaccurate because shorelines and large areas of open water have been inconsistently digitized. The generation and compilation of

thematic STATSGO and NATSGO maps requires a mainframe computer with adequate storage, advanced data base management and GIS software, and a skilled computer technician. STATSGO will not be complete for the entire nation until 1993.

D. SCS "Swampbuster" Maps

Available from:
SCS state offices (generally located in the state capital or the city of a land grant university). For general information, contact Norm Kempf, Soil Conservation Service, P.O. Box 2890, Washington, DC 20013 (202/382-1839).

Scale(s) and minimum map unit size(s):
Mostly at about 1:12,000 or 1:20,000.

Coverage:
The maps cover primarily cropland and areas closely associated with cropland.

Cost:
The maps are not for sale. Delineations of wetlands, drawn on aerial photographs, can be viewed at SCS state offices.

Date(s):
Most maps were completed since 1987. They represent a mostly one-time assessment; about 5 percent may be reassessed annually.

How developed:
Wetland boundaries were hand drawn on recent aerial photographs. The delineations were based on (a) overlay of hydric soil maps; (b) hydrophytic vegetation and presence of surface water (as visible in aerial photographs from multiple years); and, in some cases, (c) field-checking to confirm wetlands status.

Extent of acreage/type compilation:
Acreages have been compiled for few areas; compilations would need to be done manually because digital versions do not exist.

Extent of use:
These maps are relatively new and not widely used because of limited distribution.

Extent of validation:
This is perhaps the most detailed, up-to-date, extensive map source for wetlands in certain areas.

Primary strengths:
These maps are a useful complement to NWI maps because they include many of the wetlands that NWI misses—specifically, cropped and very small wetlands.

Primary limitations:
Because wetlands boundaries were drawn on aerial photographs not printed for mass distribution, these maps are difficult to access and compile. They often do not include "prior converted" wetlands (T. Dahl, National Wetlands Inventory, personal communication).

E. FEMA Flood Hazard Maps

Available from:
Flood Map Distribution Center, Federal Emergency Management Agency (FEMA), 6930 San Tomas Road, Baltimore, MD 21227-6227 (1-800/333-1363).

Scale(s) and minimum map unit size(s):
The scale varies depending on locality and ranges from 1 in. = 2000 ft to 1 in. = 200 ft. A small subset of the maps (some of the first ones prepared) were also printed on USGS quadrangles at a scale of 1:24,000 or 1:62,500; printed copies of these are no longer available for purchase but can be obtained on microfiche or reviewed in government map libraries.

FEMA has budgeted for the eventual digitization of all its floodplain maps. Digital versions for about 40 densely populated counties will be available beginning in mid-1992. Some state and local agencies have independently digitized a limited number of floodplain maps.

Coverage:
Maps are available for about 22,000 communities throughout the United States. Maps are printed in "panels," each about 0.5 x 0.5 mile.

Cost:
The cost per panel is $0.60 with a $5 base fee. Digital versions, when available, will cost about $200 per county (contact Dan Cotter at FEMA, 202/646-2757).

Date(s):
Maps show floodplains of 100- and 500-year

storm events based on analyses conducted since 1968.

How developed:
Floodplains were delineated from topographic maps, stream flow data, channel cross-sectional measurements, and aerial photographs supplemented with limited hydraulic modeling and ground-checking.

Extent of acreage/type compilation:
Acreage of floodplains in each of the 22,000 communities has been compiled by the Risk Studies Division of the Federal Insurance Administration office of FEMA. These data might be useful in assessing the status of some types of riparian wetlands.

Extent of use:
The maps are not used extensively in wetlands studies.

Extent of validation:
Floodplain boundaries represent preliminary estimates. Validation by comparison to actual long-term flood data has been limited.

Primary strengths:
These maps might be used to help identify dominant water sources and transport vectors for specific wetlands located near rivers (see section I.B). They also might be used to identify wetlands that, if they store floodwater, are likely to have greater social value because they help protect downstream properties that otherwise are likely to be flooded.

Primary limitations:
In most cases FEMA floodplain maps are available only for urban and developed areas. The 100- and 500-year floodplains do not have any particular ecological or geomorphic significance (annual, two-year, and five-year floodplains are probably more functionally important), and their correlation with wetlands or hydric soil extent or function is unknown. Their accuracy may be reduced in areas with very wide, flat floodplains and backwater flooding. Boundaries may be outdated on maps of communities that have experienced rapid development since mapping.

F. USGS Land-Use Land Analysis (LUDA) Maps

Available from:
Earth Science Information Center, U.S. Geological Survey, 507 National Center, Reston, VA 22092 (1-800/USA-MAPS).

Scale(s) and minimum map unit size(s):
LUDA maps are mostly at a scale of 1:250,000; some are at 1:100,000. The minimum map unit size for the former is 40 acres (generally) and ten acres for open water.

Coverage:
Both digital (raster and vector) and hard-copy maps are available for nearly the entire coterminous United States. Digital versions are importable on many GIS systems.

Cost:
Digital data costs $7 per quadrangle (one degree by two degrees) plus a base fee of $90.

Date(s):
Each map represents only one time period, ranging from the late 1960s to the present. USGS plans to update the maps have thus far not been broadly implemented.

How wetlands classified:
These maps recognize only two types of wetlands: "forested" and "nonforested" wetlands. They also include categories for streams, lakes, reservoirs, and estuaries. Classification is described in Anderson et al. (1976).

How developed:
The maps are based on interpretation of aerial photographs at a scale of 1:62,500.

Extent of acreage/type compilation:
No effort has been made to use the digital versions of these maps to compile wetlands or other land cover acreages nationwide or regionwide.

Extent of use:
These maps are seldom used in wetlands studies.

Extent of validation:

Testing of the accuracy of the wetlands categories has been limited.

Primary strengths:

These maps are the only source of digital wetlands data for nearly the entire United States. They are the only map data source that includes all landscape components, not just wetlands. This allows for better integration of wetlands data with other landscape data when interpreting the role of wetlands in the landscape.

Primary limitations:

These maps grossly underestimate wetlands, in part because the minimum map unit size is too coarse and in part because a consistent, modern definition of wetlands was not used during the mapping. In particular, forested, cropped, and aquatic bed wetlands appear to be ignored or severely underestimated.

G. NOAA Coastal Ocean Program/Coastwatch: Change Analysis Program Data Base

Source:

Field, D. W., A. J. Reyer, P. V. Genovese, and B. D. Shearer (1991), *Coastal Wetlands of the United States: An Accounting of a Valuable National Resource*, Strategic Assessment Branch, National Oceanic and Atmospheric Administration, Washington, DC.

Scale(s) and minimum map unit size(s):

The maps are at fine scales (1:24,000 and 1:62,500), with some (less often) at coarse scales (1:100,000 and 1:250,000). The minimum wetlands size mapped on the fine-scale maps is mostly one to three acres (less than an acre in some prairie pothole areas). Very narrow wetlands bordering tidal channels might be underestimated.

Coverage:

The status report (cited above) is currently available and provides acreage summaries for 507 counties and 92 estuaries.

Date(s):

The aerial imagery used was from various years between 1972 and 1985.

How wetlands classified:

Coastal wetlands were classified as salt marsh (brackish or unspecified); fresh marsh (tidal, nontidal, or unspecified); forested and scrub-shrub (nontidal fresh, tidal fresh, fresh unspecified, and estuarine); and tidal flats.

How developed:

The analysis was based on grid sampling of NWI maps using 45-acre grid cells; there are about 900 sampling points per map.

Primary strengths:

This represents the most extensive compilation of coastal wetlands acreage.

Primary limitations:

These maps suffer the same limitations as the NWI maps, including a limited ability to delineate certain types of palustrine wetlands (e.g., nontidal forested, cropped wetlands) (see section II,A).

H. Forest Inventory and Analysis (FIA) Data Base

See section III,C.

I. National Resources Inventory (NRI) Data Base

See section III,B.

III. DATA SOURCES ON WETLANDS STATUS AND TRENDS

This section focuses on national data bases that provide (or can be analyzed to provide) estimates of wetlands status and trends. Various agencies have sometimes analyzed regional, state, and local trends, but these reports are not reviewed here. Few statistical comparisons of the following methods/sources and their variability have been published; hence, the narratives below are somewhat subjective.

A. FWS Status and Trends Reports

Available from:

National Wetlands Inventory, U.S. Fish and Wildlife Service, Room 400 Arlington Square, 1849 C Street NW, Washington, DC 20240 (703/358-2201). Reports by the following authors should be requested: Dahl (1990), Frayer et al. (1989), Tiner (1984), and Tiner and Finn (1986).

Coverage and resolution:

Wetlands acreage changes were compiled by type of change (natural or obviously human-induced) and wetlands type; they were reported by region and (as statistically supportable) by state. The reports cover the coterminous United States. Changes in wetlands as small as one acre can be detected.

Basis for calculations:

FWS selected a stratified, weighted random sample of 3,635 plots nationwide, each four square miles in size. Mid-1950s and mid-1970s aerial photography was interpreted from all study plots. All changes to wetlands and deepwater habitats within these areas were identified as either natural or human-induced changes.

The procedure was repeated in 1990, comparing wetlands in mid-1980s aerial photography with those in mid-1970s photography. Release of a report describing that comparison is imminent. FWS is mandated to produce reports on future trends at 10-year intervals. Intensified sampling is planned for some regions; also, in a very few areas FWS intends to determine wetland trends more accurately by completely re-mapping wetlands (rather than basing trends on a probability sample as described above).

Primary strengths:

Wetlands definition and photo interpretation protocols are standardized. All wetlands types (except cropped wetlands) are included.

Primary limitations:

Trend data deal only with trends in wetlands acreage, not trends in quality. The data collected so far are too coarse to allow determination of local, watershed, or even (in most cases) statewide trends. Where actual trends are expected to have been less than the usual error associated with photographic distortion and interpretation, meaningful trend detection is not feasible. Wetlands fills or dredging occupying less than one acre probably are undetectable. (See section II,A, National Wetlands Inventory Maps, for a discussion of other limitations.)

B. National Resources Inventory (NRI) Data Base

Available from:

Resources Inventory Division, USDA Soil Conservation Service, P.O. Box 2890, Washington, DC 20013. Also available from the Statistical Laboratory, Iowa State University, Ames, IA 50011 (Statistical Bulletin No. 756).

Coverage and resolution:

A successor of the "Conservation Needs Inventory" conducted in the 1960s, the NRI was initiated in 1977. Generally comparable wetlands data sets have been included since 1982, and wetlands trends have been calculated by region (using 1982 versus 1987 estimates of acreage) for the coterminous United States. Under certain circumstances, statistically significant trends might be calculated at the level of a state or an MLRA (Major Land Resource Area). (See George and Choate, 1989, for some examples of types of trend data available from the NRI.)

Basis for calculations:

SCS field personnel visited a portion of the 300,000 randomly selected points on non-federal land throughout the United States for the 1982 and 1987 estimates. Information for sample points that were not visited was estimated from aerial photographs. The NRI is scheduled to be repeated every five years, with increased reliance on remote sensing.

Primary strengths:

Trends in other land cover uses and conservation practices can be paired with wetlands trend data based on the same plots. Where data are sufficient to allow for statistically significant analysis, this provides opportunities to quantify threats to wetlands and to interpret causes of changes in wetlands.

Primary limitations:

Apparent trends must be examined carefully

to determine if they are due only to (a) between-period changes in NRI protocols or (b) a change in ownership of wetlands between survey periods (because the NRI inventories only those wetlands on nonfederal land). NRI data generally cover rural land. The variability of identification skills of the field personnel who compiled the inventory is unknown; also, certain wetlands types (such as open water wetlands, lacustrine and riverine emergent wetlands, and aquatic beds) are underestimated because of seasonal factors. Misclassification is also a potentially large source of error because NRI protocols require that an area be placed in a limited number of categories. Thus, for example, it is not clear whether a wetland on saline soil would be classified as a wetland or as a saline soil (T. Dahl, National Wetlands Inventory, personal communication).

NRI trend estimates of wetlands are likely to be less accurate in areas where wetlands constitute only a small portion of the landscape, and standard errors generally cannot be calculated. Data are too coarse to allow determination of local, watershed, or even (in most cases) statewide trends.

Finally, the compilation and accurate statistical interpretation of NRI data require a mainframe computer with adequate storage, advanced data base management software, and a skilled computer technician and statistician.

C. Forest Inventory and Analysis (FIA) Data Base

Source:
U.S. Forest Service experimental stations (Fort Collins, CO; Ogden, UT; St. Paul, MN; Broomall, PA; Portland, OR; Berkeley, CA; Asheville, NC; New Orleans, LA). For general information, contact Richard Birdsey, U.S. Forest Service, Washington, DC (202/ 382-9341).

Coverage and resolution:
Data in the RPA (Renewable Resources Planning Act of 1974) timber data base are available on the status of forest types commonly associated with forested wetlands (e.g., oak-gum-cypress), beginning in the late 1920s, for much of the commercial forest land in the United States. The FIA uses a systematic grid of sample plots spaced 4.8 kilometers apart.

Basis for calculations:
Data on acreage (and volume, basal area, and weight) of forest cover types/species are based on field measurements from a probability sample of forest in each region (i.e., continuous forest inventory projects). Trends must be calculated from data drawn from many reports but collected using similar methods at 10-year intervals.

Extent of acreage/type compilation:
The only compilations relevant to wetlands accomplished using this database so far appear to be those of Abernethy and Turner (1987) and McWilliams and Rosson (1990), completed in the southeastern United States.

Primary strengths:
This data base can be used to estimate forested wetlands trends at a state (and perhaps in some instances, a substate) level for time periods not covered by the NWI's trend analyses.

Primary limitations:
No nationally consistent, centralized data base exists, and state and regional data bases use somewhat different conventions for estimating acreages and grouping forest types. This data base is limited to forested wetlands. Forest types indicative of forested wetlands do not correspond entirely to jurisdictional wetlands. The compilation and accurate statistical interpretation of FIA data also requires a mainframe computer with adequate storage, advanced data base management software, and a skilled computer technician and statistician.

D. USDA Drainage Statistics Data

Source:
Surveys of the U.S. Department of Agriculture, as cited in Pavelis, G. A. (ed.) (1987), *Farm Drainage in the United States: History, Status, and Prospects* (Miscellaneous Publication No. 1455), USDA Economic Research Service, Washington, DC.

Coverage and resolution:
County-level data preceding 1970 are available for most states.

Basis for calculations:
Trends must be calculated manually from tabular data. These data are based on volunteer reports by farmers.

Extent of acreage/type compilation:
Trends cannot be calculated by wetlands type.

Primary strengths:
Some changes in wetlands quality (and perhaps extent) that are not noticeable through the use of aerial imagery may be roughly quantified using this approach. It represents a useful complement to other sources of trends data.

Primary limitations:
The data are very coarse and outdated, and their accuracy is largely unknown.

E. Environmental Monitoring and Assessment Program (EMAP) Data Base

Source:
EPA-sponsored estimates of status and trends in wetlands' ecological condition will become available in the late 1990s. For information, contact Technical Director, U.S. EPA Research Laboratory, 200 SW 35th Street, Corvallis, OR 97333 (503/757-4666) (FTS/420-4666).

Coverage and resolution:
The data bases will be available for all regions of the United States. Trends will be reported by region and wetland type.

Basis for calculations:
Ecological indicators (e.g., plant communities, sediment characteristics) will be measured in about 3,000 wetlands nationally during repeating four-year periods. These wetlands represent a probability sample of 16 wetlands types, thus allowing results to be extrapolated to entire wetlands populations within each region.

Primary strengths:
Once developed, the EMAP data bases may be the only source of nationwide data on status and trends in the ecological condition of wetlands (e.g., changes in extent of exotic species, sedimentation, percent cover). The data bases will be compiled concurrently and congruently with trends data for upland ecosystems, thereby allowing wetlands losses to be placed in context. The data bases are being coordinated with NWI analysis of wetlands acreage trends (see above).

Primary limitations:
The data bases are not currently available.

F. Wetlands Loss Calculated by "Hydric Acreage" Minus "NWI Acreage"

Source:
This is not a compiled source but rather an approach, as demonstrated by Tiner (1985) and Abbruzzese et al. (1990). (See, under this heading, the narratives for SCS County Soil Survey Maps, section II,B, and NWI Maps, section II,A.)

Coverage and resolution:
See, under this heading, the narratives on SCS County Soil Survey Maps and NWI Maps.

Basis for calculations:
The acreage and location of hydric soils, as officially listed (SCS, 1991) and compiled from SCS County Soil Survey maps, are assumed to represent the acreage of nonpermanently flooded wetlands prior to human settlement. The acreage and location of wetlands (as compiled from NWI maps) are assumed to represent the current acreage of wetlands. The difference between the two figures is assumed to estimate loss or gain in nonpermanently flooded wetlands. (The NWI figure should exclude deepwater, aquatic bed, and other nonpermanently flooded wetlands, as these are usually not mapped as hydric soils by SCS.)

Extent of acreage/type compilation:
Such compilations have been done only for limited areas.

Primary strengths:
This calculation can provide an estimate of wetlands loss in areas that presently do not have data on trends. Possible causes of loss (i.e., the type of land use to which former wetlands were converted) for specific wetlands types can be estimated site specifically. This approach may be the only source of quantified data on long-term wetlands loss other than anecdotal accounts.

Primary limitations:
The validity of this approach is untested. It requires that both soil survey and NWI maps be available (preferably in digital/GIS format)

for the same area. The limitations and errors of the two respective map data bases (see sections II,A and II,B under this heading) are compounded.

Trends in acreage of wetlands that were formerly permanently flooded are poorly accounted for because these areas were probably not mapped as soil. Data on trends calculated using this approach may be least accurate in urban and coastal areas, where wetlands have been lost mostly through filling and thus are no longer classified as hydric (as opposed to drained wetlands, which usually are). Moreover, the time period during which wetlands losses occurred cannot be specified with this approach.

G. Wetlands Loss Calculated from Examinations of Permit Files

Source:
    This is not a compiled source but an approach.

Basis for calculations:
    Citizens and agencies wishing to alter wetlands through deposition of dredged or fill material must apply for permits to the COE. The annual incidence of such requests and the acreage of wetlands cumulatively involved can be compiled from records in COE district offices. Some state agencies also require permits for land drainage, stream alteration, aquatic weed control, farm chemical use, and mosquito control. These can be compiled similarly to estimate certain types of wetlands losses or impacts.

Extent of acreage/type compilation:
    EPA's Wetlands Research Program has compiled data on Section 404 permit-related wetlands losses by type for all or part of the resource in the following states: Alabama, Arkansas, California, Louisiana, Mississippi, Oregon, Texas, and Washington.

Primary strengths:
    The data compiled using this approach relate directly to monitoring the success of existing laws to protect wetlands. Secondary objectives, such as determining the extent of compliance monitoring of constructed wetlands, can easily be pursued simultaneously. EPA has developed and extensively tested a simple, user-friendly software program for entering, sorting, and querying a compiled set of permit data (Holland and Kentula, 1991).

Primary limitations:
    Deducing previous wetlands losses from Section 404 permit records means that only losses attributable to dredge and fill activities are identified, and these are usually a minority of losses. This approach excludes previous losses of wetlands that fall under "general permits" (e.g., many isolated headwater wetlands). Also, caution is required to determine if trends are due to changes or errors in recordkeeping protocols rather than real changes in wetlands acreage. If a previous record of permitting activities has been kept, its compilation is very labor-intensive (the average cost is about $25,000 to $75,000 per state); however, initiation of ongoing permit monitoring (related to non-Section 404 activities as well) is relatively simple and inexpensive using the EPA software.

H. Trends in Wetlands-Related Resources

A variety of national and regional automated data bases do not estimate wetlands trends directly but describe trends of resources related to the abundance and distribution of wetlands. These data bases also contain data that could be used to help compare areas and establish reference conditions for metrics related to wetlands function and value (e.g., bird species richness and density, average water quality).

Breeding Bird Survey Data Base
Trends in wetlands species have been calculated at state and ecoregional levels based on 2,000 roadside survey routes conducted annually since 1966. Computer files containing raw or calculated trend data are available from the Breeding Bird Survey, Patuxent Wildlife Research Center, U.S. Fish and Wildlife Service, Laurel, MD 20708. Data from New England states are being analyzed rigorously by the University of Maine (Dr. Raymond O'Connor).

Christmas Bird Count Data Base
Trends in selected species have been calculated nationwide based on winter counts conducted in thousands of nonrandomly distributed, 15-mile-diameter circles inventoried annually since before 1960. Computer files containing raw data may be purchased from the Cornell Laboratory of Orni-

thology, Sapsucker Woods Road, Ithaca, NY 14850. Data from New England states is being analyzed in detail by the University of Maine (Dr. Raymond O'Connor).

Waterfowl Parts Data Base

Species-level data pertaining to the annual harvest of hunted waterfowl are reported by county, state, and region from state agency surveys. Computer files containing raw data and a data base interface are available from the Patuxent Wildlife Research Center, Waterfowl Harvest Surveys Section, U.S. Fish and Wildlife Service, Laurel, MD 20708.

Water Quality and Streamflow Trends from USGS Sampling Stations

Regional and station-specific trends in parameters often affected by the cumulative acreage of wetlands in a watershed are calculated periodically by the Office of Water Quality, U.S. Geological Survey, Reston, VA 22092. See also Lettenmaier et al. (1991).

I. NOAA Coastal Ocean Program/Coastwatch: Change Analysis Program Data

Source:
Field, D. W., A. J. Reyer, P. V. Genovese, and B. D. Shearer (1991), *Coastal Wetlands of the United States: An Accounting of a Valuable National Resource*, Strategic Assessment Branch, National Oceanic and Atmospheric Administration, Washington, DC. For information, contact Ford A. Cross, Program Manager, NMFS/NOAA Beaufort Laboratory, Beaufort, NC 28516-9722. See also Kiraly et al. (1990).

Scale(s) and minimum map unit size(s):
Maps are mostly at a scale of 1:100,000.

Coverage:
The status report (cited above) is currently available, and trends (change) monitoring is beginning. Initial change analyses will be completed in 1991 and 1992 for the Chesapeake Bay. Ongoing change analysis will be expanded to cover the entire U.S. coastline and immediately adjacent inland areas within the NOAA Estuarine Drainage Boundary (or, in some cases, farther inland, until the lowest water quality monitoring station is reached).

Date(s):
Ongoing efforts will compare coastal wetlands area changes over one- to five-year periods. Completed prototypes compared wetland changes in the Chesapeake Bay between the mid-1970s (multispectral scanner data), 1980s (thematic mapper data), and more current time periods.

How wetlands classified:
These maps classify coastal wetlands as estuarine emergent (high), estuarine emergent (low), palustrine forest, or palustrine emergent.

How developed:
The status analysis is based on grid sampling of NWI maps using 45-acre grid cells with 900 cells per map. Wetlands acreage between time periods is digitally compared, cell by cell.

Primary strengths:
When fully developed, this program will be a consistent source of trends information for coastal areas. It will allow a comparison of wetlands change rates with the change rates of other land cover types.

Primary limitations:
The maps are not currently available. In addition, the ability to delineate certain types of palustrine wetlands (e.g., nontidal forested, cropped wetlands) may be limited, as with the NWI (see section II,A).

IV. RAPID METHODS FOR EVALUATING, RANKING, OR CATEGORIZING WETLANDS

The following pages provide reviews of each of the 11 methods used for rapid assessments of wetlands. The first four methods (A-D) are applicable to the entire coterminous United States, while the remainder (E-K) were developed for use in more geographically restricted areas. Methods reviewed are those that, on the basis of the author's experience and published descriptions, appear to have been used in a large number of wetlands assessments.

This review updates and expands previous reviews of rapid assessment methods by Lonard et al. (1981), Kusler and Riexinger (1986), and Adamus (1989a). A few methods mentioned in those reviews are not examined here because they appear to be seldom used.

Recently, a number of states have developed (or are attempting to develop) more simplified criteria for categorizing or ranking wetlands. (Among them are Maine, Maryland, New York, North Carolina, Oregon, Vermont, and Washington.) These criteria were not reviewed in detail and are not described, although information on the indicators they use is included in table 1. A trend among these state-level categorization criteria is that they tend not to evaluate specific functions, and they use a smaller number of indicators to evaluate function than are used in most of the methods described below. The scientific basis for such a strategy has not been tested. Also, various state, federal, and private agencies and institutions have identified (and in some cases, protected) specific wetlands considered "significant" or have assigned special designations to larger landscapes that may include wetlands. Information on such priority listings can be obtained from EPA regional offices (e.g., "Advanced Identification" project reports), FWS regional offices (e.g., Regional Wetlands Concept Plans), offices of The Nature Conservancy and state heritage programs, and an EPA report (Southerland et al., 1991).

In terms of the extent of use and flexibility, the rapid assessment method most widely used is "best professional judgment." Nonetheless, for reasons of scientific, legal, and public credibility, some states have developed or used standardized procedures for assessing wetlands. Of the many standardized "rapid" methods that have been developed, none enjoys widespread, daily use. Methods that estimate the functions of individual wetlands do not differ substantially in terms of time and labor required; all can be completed in a few hours for most wetlands, although some are more difficult to use than others. Currently, no method appears to please a majority of users.

The prospects for future development of simpler, even more rapid techniques that are technically valid are limited by these factors:

- the considerable complexity of processes that support wetlands functions;
- the lack of information about these processes and their thresholds;
- the characteristically large variability among wetlands, even within a particular class;
- the many components of wetlands value that must be accounted for; and
- the diversity of assessment objectives.

Most currently available methods require the ability to delineate watersheds accurately from a topographic map, and most use readily available data sources such as wetlands maps, soil surveys, and aerial photographs. All require a degree of subjective judgment, but some attempt to limit this and enhance replicability by allowing users to choose from among several prespecified conditions that may or may not be technically supported.

None of the methods has been validated extensively. Attempts have been made to validate a few (e.g., HEP, WET) in selected instances. "Validation" is used in this sense to mean accuracy (i.e., the degree to which assessment results reflect the real-world occurrence of a function [Usher, 1986] in either absolute or relative terms). "Real-world" condition is generally based on the results of a detailed, long-term measurement of function. Validation is seldom performed because of the expense of measuring functions intensively. More commonly, field-testing of methods has involved examining their precision (replicability). Doing this commonly involves comparing the assessment results (or responses to individual questions) of different users of a method or of the same user visiting the same wetland at different times. If individuals respond similarly, or at least if their final ranking of a series of wetlands is similar, replicability is considered adequate. Methods also have sometimes been evaluated in terms of their comparability. This has involved comparing the results of different rapid assessment methods that purport to assess the same functions to see if they rank a series of wetlands similarly.

Although a few of the methods infer relative condition of a wetland (i.e., probable degree of degradation and functional impairment) by requesting information on surrounding land uses, none of the methods rigorously uses biological or physico-chemical indicators, such as the presence of exotic plants or evidence of contamination, to document the condition of a wetland, probably because of the difficulty of collecting such data rapidly. Moreover, none of the methods is capable of assessing wetlands suitability for particular uses, generating performance standards (such as best management practices) for particular uses, or predicting the impacts of particular uses. In some cases, if structural changes (e.g., decline of the percentage of open water after drainage) can be predicted by mechanistic models, analogies, or other means, most methods listed below can suggest the effects that such changes might have on wetlands functions and values.

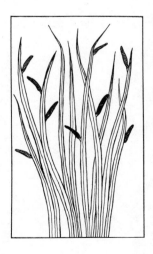

By the ratings they provide, all the methods can be used to suggest qualitatively the degree of mitigation that could be required if a wetland is altered. Some (e.g., the Connecticut method, HEP, HES) also quantify this, using the generally unsupported assumption that acreage and function can be traded off in linear calculations. The unfortunate result, especially when such methods are used as part of a mitigation bank program, may be that attempts are made to "compensate" for the losses of large wetlands with gains in the combined total of habitat units from many smaller wetlands. The fallacy of this is that some of the rarest wetlands species occur only in large wetlands; consequently, such an approach can lead to declines in regional biodiversity.

None of the methods was developed for use in the functional design of constructed wetlands, although Marble (1990) attempted to adapt some of the criteria used in the WET method for this purpose. In other cases, some methods have been applied erroneously in mitigation planning. Users have assumed that environmental factors that lead to a high wetlands rating when used in an assessment method can be used as design standards for constructing a high-functioning wetland. However, certain factors (i.e., predictors, elements, indicators, and attributes) used by the methods are simply indicators of function, whereas others are determinants. For example, the presence of substantial accumulations of fine sediment within a wetland suggests that the wetland may be effective in retaining sediment—a function that is valuable in terms of protecting aquatic areas farther downslope. However, creating a wetland with a thick sediment layer surely would not lead to increased sediment retention. In a similar fashion, activities such as dredging, which affect an indicator used by an assessment method, may have no real effect on function, but activities that affect a determinant are much more likely to affect function. None of the methods adequately distinguishes which of its questions or indicators are truly indicators and which refer to determinants.

Nearly all the drafts of these methods indicate that they are "developmental," "evolving," or "operational." A few have demonstrated institutional commitments toward making future revised versions a reality. Notable perhaps are three- to five-year programs proposed by the COE (Waterways Experiment Station, Vicksburg, Mississippi) and EPA (Environmental Research Laboratory, Corvallis, Oregon) to develop new rapid methods of wetlands assessment—primarily for site-specific application in the case of the COE and for landscape-level application by EPA. The COE methods will be developed by regional panels of scientists for particular wetlands hydrogeomorphic types (see section I.B) and functions.

Methods differ in what they assess. Four methods (HAT, HEP, HES, and the Bottomland Hardwood Forest Habitat Evaluation Model) assess only the habitat functions of wetlands; one (the synoptic approach) assesses the cumulative effects of wetlands loss; and the remainder address multiple functions of individual wetlands. Methods also differ in the number and types of indicators they use and the degree to which they demonstrate technical support for the indicators used. Table 1 summarizes the indicators used by various methods.

Finally, methods differ in the degree and manner in which they integrate a large amount of indicator data into a few ratings. Some methods (e.g., HEP, Hollands-Magee) use mathematical formulas and flexible indicator weights to generate a wetland's "score," whereas others (e.g., WET) use verbal models that result in ratings of high, moderate, or low. Most methods assign ratings simply to individual functions, but a few (e.g. Ontario) also combine all functional ratings into a single rating for a wetland. If this is done, public input should be sought in determining functional weights and combination formulas. Also, if fundamentally different wetlands types are being compared (e.g., salt marsh vs. pocosin), it may be inadvisable to combine each wetland's function scores into a single score for that wetland (Brinson, 1991). A good discussion of the assumptions, advantages, and limitations of various data integration strategies is contained in Smith and Theberge (1987).

One decision that can profoundly affect the outcome of every wetlands assessment, regardless of the method used, concerns the choice of the boundaries of the area being assessed and the scale at which the area is assessed. "Bounding" relates to decisions regarding the functional boundaries of (a) the wetland itself, (b) landscapes expected to affect the function of the wetland, and (c) the region and temporal context within which the wetland's rarity or functional contribution is to be assessed. The boundary that yields the most accurate estimates of function and value cannot be assumed to be simply the jurisdictional boundary of the wetland or the portion of the wetland proposed for alteration.

The decision of where and how to draw boundaries is problematic. For example, consider a series of wetlands connected by surface water or existing as a complex. Should two such wetlands in close proximity or separated only by a narrow culverted road be considered the same wetland? How close must they be to be considered the same? When deciding whether to assess, for example, wetlands' size individually or collectively, does it matter whether the wetlands are hydrologically connected or connected by a corridor of undeveloped habitat?

A similar "bounding" issue concerns the assessment of subunits within a wetland, such as a parcel where fill is actually being placed (e.g., the "project area") or a distinct cover type. Some assessment methods attempt to assess the functions of these discrete areas apart from the characteristics of the surrounding wetland. Methods seldom state which functions and indicators can be assessed accurately at such a limited scale.

Such issues can drastically affect the determination of functional ratings as well as whether particular wetlands fall below an administrative size threshold. Thus, unless a method contains specific criteria for bounding the assessment areas, two wetlands evaluators may end up looking at two different areas, and the results may differ. This problem is common to all assessment methods, although some do not acknowledge it or provide guidance in dealing with it.

Deriving appropriate bounding criteria is thus one of the largest challenges of wetlands science because it involves determining quantitative linkages between a wetland and its adjoining landscape as well as the rate at which these linkages diminish as one moves farther from the wetland. In the absence of strong technical support for using particular bounding or scale criteria (e.g., as derived from use of tracers, radiotelemetry, or energetics models), bounding protocols should at least be standardized so that results will be more replicable.

Differences among methods with regard to this issue are described in each narrative below under the heading "Consideration of bounding/scale issues." Other differences become apparent when reading the following narratives, which contain these headings:

Method explained in:
Available from:
Applicable to which wetland types:
Function(s)/values addressed:
Summary of procedures and output:

General features/assumptions:
Inclusion of essential indicators:
Documentation from technical literature:
Documentation of procedures for derivation of results:
Consideration of temporal dynamics:
Consideration of bounding/scale issues:
Consideration of hierarchical relations among indicators:
Consideration of physical/landscape context:
Consideration of social context:
Time and labor requirements:
Duration:
Personnel needed:
Technical expertise needed:
Preliminary results obtainable without site visit:
Effort collecting background data:
Effort collecting primary data:
Data analysis effort:
Extent of peer review/use:
Sensitivity:

These headings are mostly self-explanatory, although a few require elaboration, as given below. (Bounding/scale issues were discussed earlier.)

Inclusion of Essential Indicators

There is no consensus among wetlands scientists as to how many (and which) indicators are necessary to predict various wetlands functions. Much depends on the desired degree of accuracy and precision, which in turn depends on the planning context in which the results are to be used. On the one hand, a proliferation of indicators in an assessment method does not necessarily imply technical sophistication or make a method valid. On the other hand, use of a very limited set of indicators may be attractive in terms of ease of use and interpretation but may also be technically irresponsible regardless of the intended application context. Use of fewer indicators also makes a method less sensitive to variability among different types of wetlands. (As indicated in Table 1, wetlands assessment methods vary widely in the number and type of indicators used to predict each function.)

The number of indicators used by a method was not the sole criterion used in reviewing methods for this appendix. Rather, the basis for each review was the inclusion of indicators (a) related to all ecosystem processes important to controlling a function, (b) highly correlated with the level of function, and (c) related to social value or recognition of a function. This evaluation is thus unavoidably subjective.

Consideration of Temporal Dynamics

This addresses the degree to which seasonal and annual variability is accounted for. For example, many methods ask the evaluator to record the dominant type of vegetation, but this often varies by season. During winter months woody vegetation may be spatially dominant, but in late summer, areas that were previously open water may be temporarily filled with floating-leaved and submerged herbaceous macrophytes. Unless the method specifies the season at which an indicator is to be assessed, replicability and accuracy will be low. In a similar fashion, the way in which each method's models use the seasonal information is important. If herbaceous vegetation is assumed to benefit water quality function more than woody vegetation, for example, its dominance in winter may be irrelevant if most runoff occurs during summer.

Consideration of Hierarchical Relations Among Indicators

This addresses the degree to which context-specific interactions (for example, synergisms) among indicators are realistically accounted for. Some methods assign a score to each indicator condition, reflecting the importance attached by the indicator to the function. This overlooks indicator interactions, particularly the degree to which the occurrence and nature of these interactions vary by wetlands type. False predictions of function can result. For example, in the case of nitrogen removal, an assessment method might assume that the function is predicted by four indicators—wetlands organic matter, dominant vegetation class, water level fluctuation, and type. Corresponding scores might be as follows:

Organic matter	*Points*
>20 mg/l	10
5–20 mg/l	5
<5 mg/l	1

Dominant vegetation class	
Woody vegetation	10
Emergent	5
Aquatic bed or moss	1

Water level fluctuation (greater than one foot) throughout most of the wetland

Monthly or more often	10
Annually or seasonally	5
Less often than annually	1

Wetlands type	
Palustrine, lacustrine, or estuarine	10
Riverine	5
Marine	1

Many methods at this stage would simply add the scores, and the wetland with the most points would be assumed to be the most capable of removing nitrogen. However, a closer examination of technical literature might show the following:

- woody vegetation cannot occur (by the Cowardin definition) in marine or riverine wetlands;
- water-level fluctuations in natural marine and estuarine wetlands can never be less than daily, as these systems are tidally influenced; and
- organic matter may exhibit a threshold effect on nitrogen removal—if concentrations are above, say, 5 mg/l, this indicator exerts no influence on function and becomes immaterial in the hierarchy of the four indicators.

Failure to account for indicator interactions can thus implicitly bias an assessment method.

Consideration of Physical/Landscape Context

Wetlands do not function in a vacuum; they have intimate functional connections with adjoining landscapes. A wetland's level of function as well as its perceived value is determined not only by intrinsic characteristics but also by exchanges of organisms and materials with surrounding areas. Thus, function cannot be assessed accurately without taking these exchanges into account. Methods vary in their attempts to do this.

Consideration of Social Context

In a similar fashion, if an assessment is intended to address value, the proximity and positioning of a wetland relative to areas that may benefit from that wetland's functions is an important criterion. For example, some assessment protocols for the flood storage function ignore social context and rank two physically similar wetlands the same even though one is located immediately above a town that has experienced chronic flood damage.

Although social context is an important component of the evaluation, it is important to recognize that social context, like wetlands function, is temporally dynamic. For example, a wetland that currently is rated low because no residences are located in floodplains downstream may become more valuable as regional growth spills into downstream areas, even if the wetland itself is unchanged.

Effort Collecting Background Data

For some methods the accuracy of a large portion of the required information will be improved dramatically if substantial time is spent contacting other agencies, obtaining maps, and reviewing reports before actually visiting a wetland. This naturally requires more effort.

Effort Collecting Primary Data

For some methods the accuracy of a large portion of the required model information will be improved dramatically by making detailed on-site measurements as opposed to visual observations. This, too, requires more effort.

Sensitivity

This addresses the degree to which model outputs (scores or qualitative ratings) are likely to change in response to varying the indicators (that is, "robustness") (Usher 1986). Methods that are highly sensitive are more likely to indicate subtle differences among wetlands; whether these differences are scientifically supportable or functionally or socially significant must be determined by other means. Thus, a highly sensitive method is not necessarily a sound method, and an insensitive method is not necessarily a poor one.

Methods Intended for Use in Any of the Coterminous States

A. HAT (Habitat Assessment Technique)

Explained in:
Cable, T. T., V. Brack, Jr., and V. R. Holmes (1989), "Simplified Method for Wetland Habitat Assessment," *Environmental Management 13*, 207–213.

Available from:
Same publication.

Applicable to which wetlands types:
All.

Function(s)/values addressed:
Breeding bird habitat is addressed, although in theory habitats of other organisms could be addressed as well as bird habitats used during migration and winter. However, these would require compilation of considerably more background data.

Summary of procedures and outputs:
An ornithologist (or competent birder) comprehensively inventories birds during the breeding season in a study wetland. One score that reflects diversity and uniqueness of the species present is calculated, based in part on a comparison of site-specific data with background data about the regional status of each species.

General features:
HAT is based on the premise that habitats containing larger numbers of species and uncommon species are of greater regulatory concern. HAT standardizes comparisons among wetlands by dividing diversity parameters by wetlands acreage; however, the assumed lognormal relationship may not be ecologically appropriate for some diversity-area relationships. Standardization according to habitat quality rather than acreage might be more appropriate, but the data would be costly and subjective. Species that are inflexible in their need for wetlands are treated the same as those that tolerate substitute habitats. Although inflexibly wetlands-dependent species can often be assumed to be associated more with wetlands of larger size or greater quality, additional data might be needed before weighting species according to dependency.

Inclusion of essential indicators:
Bird presence and wetlands size are the only indicators. Rather than relying on habitat indicators, evaluators survey birds directly (or compile existing presence/absence data). Birds, especially nonbreeding individuals, may sometimes occur in wetlands that are subop-

timal habitats (i.e., cannot sustain populations over the long term) because of traditional use patterns or because there is a regional deficit of suitable habitats. Under such conditions, bird community composition could be a poor indicator of true habitat quality, and comparisons among wetlands may be inaccurate if habitat loss has not been evenly distributed throughout the evaluation region.

Documentation from technical literature:
Overall assumptions are documented, but assumptions of specific applications must be developed by user.

Documentation of procedures for derivation of results:
The computational approach is adequately explained.

Consideration of temporal dynamics:
These are not considered. Because the index is based directly on bird presence, rankings of wetlands are more likely to vary from year to year as bird populations fluctuate than if structural features were used to estimate habitat suitability.

Consideration of bounding/scale issues:
Procedures for defining the functional boundaries of the study habitat are not defined.

Consideration of hierarchical relations among indicators:
Not applicable.

Consideration of physical/landscape context:
This method assumes that at least one critical life function of a species is met within the wetland. However, the occurrence of some species may be attributable more to factors external to the wetland.

Consideration of social context:
Not applicable.

Time and labor requirements:
Duration:
Hours to weeks per wetland, depending on size, access, availability of background information, and desired accuracy and precision.

Personnel needed:
At least one evaluator.
Technical expertise required:
Advanced skills in bird identification (i.e., auditory recognition of all species).
Preliminary results obtainable without site visit:
None (unless historic data exist).
Effort collecting background data:
The method requires quantitative estimates of the abundance category for each species and acreage of the largest wetland in the region or state. It also requires establishing an "optimum" wetland size, which is likely to be highly subjective.
Effort collecting primary data:
Except in rare cases where data of sufficient quality already exist, use of HAT requires at least three visits to a wetland to inventory enough species to detect rarer ones that contribute most to biodiversity and the HAT score. The method can be applied accurately only during the 6 to 10 weeks of the year that generally constitute the breeding season.
Data analysis effort:
Final scores are simple to calculate (using a hand-held calculator or personal computer).

Extent of peer review/use:
Use by parties other than the authors of this method has been limited, perhaps in part because of its newness (it has been in use only since about 1985).

Sensitivity:
This method is probably least sensitive when comparisons are being made among small, fairly monotypic wetlands.

Other comments:
Because HAT uses all available information on species occurring in a particular wetland, it avoids the biases of indicator-species selection that can be a problem with some other methods (see HEP below). HAT is most likely to be useful in the few states with wetlands whose breeding avifauna have been extensively inventoried and are expected to be relatively stable on an annual basis (e.g., Maine, Massachusetts, Delaware).

B. HEP (Habitat Evaluation Procedures)

Explained in:

U.S. Fish and Wildlife Service (1980), *Habitat Evaluation Procedures (HEP) Manual* (102ESM), U.S. Fish and Wildlife Service, Washington, DC.

Available from:

Same.

Applicable to which wetlands types:

This method applies to all types containing at least five animal species for which seasonally and geographically appropriate "habitat suitability models" have been published by FWS and are available from the FWS National Ecology Research Center in Fort Collins, Colorado.

Function(s)/values addressed:

Habitats of selected fish, wildlife, or invertebrates.

Summary of procedure and output:

A team of biologists selects a few species (indicators) that could potentially use a habitat unit (e.g., a study wetland or one of its cover types). The team then visits the wetland and measures or visually estimates habitat structural features that are believed to indicate or correlate with the density of these species. Separate FWS publications (dealing with habitat suitability models) provide the list of habitat features that should be measured for each indicator species, guidelines for selecting indicator species, and protocols for measurement of habitat structural features. The team of biologists arrives at a habitat suitability score (1 = most suitable, 0 = least) for each species, and these are pooled to give one score for the wetland or other habitat unit. Wetlands can be compared using each wetland's product of this score multiplied by the acreage of the wetland or other habitat unit.

General features/assumptions:

This is generally the most accurate and well-documented of the methods used for rapid assessment of habitat values. However, its application to wetlands assessments is limited by the small number of supporting models available for wetlands species. Users may encounter difficulty in interpreting a HEP score from a single wetland alone; individual scores are best placed in the context of scores from a series of wetlands. HEP assumes that animal density is correlated with measurable habitat quality (suitability) and generally ignores (as do all assessment methods) the influence of species' demographic characteristics, predation, competition, and other interspecific relationships. HEP's approach of combining the indicator values linearly, and particularly of making the final score equal to the product of acreage times functional value, may not truly reflect the nonlinear behavior of natural processes. One consequence is that large but otherwise unremarkable wetlands may score higher than small wetlands that function exceptionally well. There also is a danger in over-interpreting HEP scores; fine distinctions (such as might be suggested by HEP scores) may not be technically supportable, and differences of a few points between wetlands should not be considered significant.

Inclusion of essential indicators:

For the species that it covers, HEP addresses most of the essential structural indicators of habitat suitability. However, for some applications, published habitat suitability models may not be available for a sufficient number of species to allow analysis.

Documentation from technical literature:

For the species that it covers, HEP models are thoroughly documented from the literature.

Documentation of procedures for derivation of results:

The computational approach is adequately explained.

Consideration of temporal dynamics:

The preferred season for measuring habitat structural indicators is generally noted in the habitat suitability models.

Consideration of bounding/scale issues:

These are recognized, but no specific guidance is given.

Consideration of hierarchical relations among indicators:

These are adequately recognized and incorporated in most models.

Consideration of physical/landscape context:

Most of the HEP suitability models consider landscape-scale indicators of habitat suitability.

Consideration of social context:

Integrated FWS procedures are available for incorporating the economic value of wildlife into HEP scores.

Time and labor requirements:

Duration:

Hours to weeks per wetland, depending on size, access, and whether the "short HEP" or "full HEP" version is used. The "short HEP" is a version requiring fewer data inputs.

Personnel needed:

At least three evaluators.

Technical expertise needed:

Schooling in field biology. (Graduation from the HEP training course offered by FWS/Colorado State University probably increases the accuracy and replicability of results but is not essential.)

Preliminary results obtainable without site visit:

None.

Effort collecting background data:

If habitat suitability models are available for enough potentially occurring species, background data collection is usually minimal. However, it may not be possible to assess many wetlands because expected species have not yet been the subject of model development by FWS.

Effort collecting primary data:

Moderate to large. The effort will be moderate if visual estimation ("short HEP") is used, but many habitat suitability models include indicators that require a large effort to measure. This method is generally more time-consuming than other rapid assessment methods.

Data analysis effort:

Usually small. Optional computer software can be purchased.

Extent of peer review/use:

This is the most extensively funded, tested, and used method for assessment of habitat values of wetlands; it has been in use since the mid-1970s.

Sensitivity:

In most cases HEP will be highly sensitive to differences among wetlands. HEP results are very sensitive to the particular assemblage of indicator species used in the assessment; hence, an objective selection of indicator species is crucial. Use of species that are habitat generalists can result in wide ranges in scores for suitable habitats.

C. Synoptic Approach for Wetlands Cumulative Effects Analysis

Explained in:

Abbruzzese, B., S. G. Leibowitz, and R. Sumner (1990), *Application of the Synoptic Approach to Wetland Designation: A Case Study in Washington*, EPA/600/3-90/072, U.S. EPA Environmental Research Lab, Corvallis, OR.

Abbruzzese, B., S. G. Leibowitz, and R. Sumner (1990), *Application of the Synoptic Approach to Wetland Designation: A Case Study in Louisiana*, EPA/600/3-90/066, U.S. EPA Environmental Research Lab, Corvallis, OR. (The approach is still evolving, and the foregoing represent initial pilot tests only.)

Available from:

Scott Leibowitz, U.S. EPA Environmental Research Laboratory, 200 SW 35th Street, Corvallis, OR 97333 (503/757-4666). Also available from Brooke Abbruzzese, ManTech Environmental Technology, Inc., U.S. EPA Environmental Research Laboratory, 200 SW 35th Street, Corvallis, OR 97333 (503/757-4666).

Applicable to which wetlands types:

All.

Function(s)/values addressed:

Hydrologic, water quality, and life-support functions.

Summary of procedures and output:

The evaluator prepares maps showing rankings of watersheds or other landscape units. These are developed from measures or compilations of synoptic (broad-scale, holistic) spatial data from existing maps and data sources. No site visits are required. The output maps, prepared for a region, state, or major watershed, show the condition of all landscape units (e.g., watersheds or river basins) with regard to each indicator. These maps portray indicators of wetlands capacity, cumulative loss (i.e., prior and projected future loss of wetlands acreage), and landscape input to wetlands. Formulas are suggested for combining the indicators into assessments of hydrologic, water quality, and life-support functions (input and/or capacity) as well as wetlands loss. Because existing data seldom have been compiled by watershed, the user employs map-sampling procedures and/or prorates county data to watersheds to obtain estimates at a watershed scale.

General features/assumptions:

This method differs from all others in that it categorizes entire landscape units (e.g., watersheds) rather than ranking individual wetlands. Landscape units may either be ranked (first, second, etc.) or placed in broad categories (high, moderate, low, etc.). The numerical criteria that define these are specified by the user. The method does not indicate the functions or values of a particular wetland but rather is intended to complement site-specific information by providing a landscape perspective. It is the most rapid technique for ranking landscapes and can help focus later site-specific analyses using other techniques.

Inclusion of essential indicators:

In the initial pilot tests, the data compiled by watershed or other landscape unit have consisted of information on the following indicators: wetlands acreage, hydric soil acreage, watershed acreage, annual precipitation, land cover, slope, main channel length, length of polluted streams, number of threatened/endangered species, and agricultural and population growth rates. Data on other indi-

cators may be compiled at the discretion of the user. EPA intends that future development and refinement of the synoptic approach will involve use of (and comparison of results from use of) landscape data at several levels of detail, from coarsely estimated to finely measured.

Documentation from technical literature:

Tests are ongoing to determine the validity of using the synoptic approach's particular short list of indicators to indicate the relative ranking of a watershed for the named functions. Some publications on the synoptic approach include a brief rationale and a limited number of citations of technical literature to support the choice of these indicators and the formulas used for combining them.

Documentation of procedures for derivation of results:

The computational approach is adequately explained.

Consideration of temporal dynamics:

The appropriate season for assessing each indicator is not specified, but most of the indicators used are resistant to major temporal change.

Consideration of bounding/scale issues:

For hydrologic and water-quality functions, bounding is well based (watershed boundaries are used). For life-support functions, watershed boundaries are assumed to be appropriate. Procedures for identifying the appropriate scale at which to delineate watersheds are left to the discretion of the user (e.g., for ranking purposes, should a state be divided into eight large river basins or 80 smaller component ones?).

Consideration of hierarchical relations among indicators:

Not currently addressed.

Consideration of physical/landscape context:

Landscape inputs are considered on a basin-wide basis.

Consideration of social context:

Some recognition is given to watersheds where

loss of wetlands is more likely to reduce certain benefits to society.

Time and labor requirements:
Duration:
Weeks to months for assessment of an entire state, depending in part on the desired resolution (i.e., number of landscape units) and preferred number of indicators.
Personnel needed:
At least one evaluator.
Technical expertise needed:
Schooling in environmental sciences. GIS skills are needed if mapping or analysis is to be facilitated using digital map data.
Preliminary results obtainable without site visit:
Yes; the synoptic approach depends exclusively on existing data.
Effort collecting background data:
Compared to site-specific methods, the time requirements of this method are relatively extensive. However, when the method is applied to entire regions, states, or river basins, the initial time investment pays off, making this the least time-consuming of all methods on a per-wetland basis.
Effort collecting primary data:
Not applicable.
Data analysis effort:
Relatively time-consuming but fairly simple.

Extent of peer review/use:
This method was reviewed by 10 to 20 scientists. Applications have been limited mostly to those described in the reports cited above; use by parties other than the authors of this method is ongoing. The method is relatively new (in use since 1989).

Sensitivity:
Can be adjusted by the user.

D. WET 2.0 (Wetland Evaluation Technique)

Explained in:
Adamus, P. R. et al., (1987a), *Wetland Evaluation Technique (WET)*, vol. II, Technical Report Y-87, U.S. Army Corps of Engineers, Waterways Experiment Station, Vicksburg, MS.

An earlier version, termed by some the "Adamus" or "Federal Highways" method, was published as follows:

Adamus, P. R. (1983), *A Method for Wetland Functional Assessment*, report nos. FHWA-IP-82-23 and 24, Federal Highway Administration, U.S. Department of Transportation, Washington, DC.

Available from:
The manual containing the 1987 version of WET can be obtained by requesting Report ADA 189968 and sending $27.50 to the National Technical Information Service (NTIS), Springfield, VA 22161.

The optional computer program for analyzing the data can be obtained by sending a formatted diskette to Dan Smith, WESER-W, P.O. Box 631, Vicksburg, MS 39180.

Applicable to which wetlands types:
All. A version of WET modified specifically for bottomland hardwood wetlands of the southeast (Adamus, 1987) was published as a review draft and had limited distribution. It is currently being revised and is scheduled for release by the Waterways Experiment Station (see above) in 1992.

Function(s)/values addressed:
Eleven functions plus habitat suitability (at a very coarse level) for selected wetlands fish and birds are addressed. Functions include groundwater recharge, groundwater discharge, floodflow alteration, sediment stabilization, sediment/toxicant removal, nutrient removal/transformation, production export, aquatic diversity/abundance, and wildlife diversity/abundance.

Summary of procedures and output:
The user first collects and reviews existing data sources to determine whether a wetland is likely to be of particular value or to have special social significance by virtue of its landscape position, loss rate, present designations, and other factors. (This method can be used as a screening or risk-assessment process to limit the number of wetlands in a region requiring more time-consuming analysis.) Topographic maps and aerial photographs are then used in conjunction with a field visit to estimate

qualitively the effectiveness (capacity) of the wetland and its opportunities (e.g., landscape inputs) to perform a function. The user's yes-no responses to questions addressing about 80 indicators of function and value (more, if detailed data are available) are analyzed manually by reference to flow charts or (more typical) are transferred from field sheets to a computer file and analyzed. The result is a categorization of a wetland as "high," "moderate," or "low" for social significance, effectiveness, and opportunity for each of the 11 functions. Flow charts are available in the report for determining the basis for a particular rating. No procedures are specified for combining the ratings of the individual functions (or their significance, opportunity, or effectiveness components) into a single overall rating for the wetland.

General features/assumptions:

WET is unique in that it places a wetland into one of only three broad categories (high, moderate, low). This limited sensitivity (as opposed to that of scoring methods) may result in several wetlands being rated similarly. Placement of a wetland's functions into any of these categorical ratings can occur as a result of the wetland's possessing any of several possible combinations of characteristics (i.e., question responses or indicator conditions). The categories are unique in that they are intended to represent the qualitative probability of various functions occurring in a wetland as opposed to the value of the functions. Functional categories are not converted to scores and multiplied by wetlands acreage to give a final rating because a scientific consensus was considered lacking with regard to whether current technical knowledge of wetlands is sufficient to support such an approach. Thus, a large wetland of a type mostly ineffective for a function on a per-unit area basis (e.g., a peat bog for phosphorus retention) may be undervalued if the user were interested in defining function in terms of total loading capacity. (For example, a large bog, although ineffective, may remove more phosphorus than a small wetland of a type that is characteristically a poor phosphorus retainer.)

Inclusion of essential indicators:

This is probably the most technically comprehensive method for assessment of multi-

ple wetlands functions. The selected indicators were based on a three-year review of most of the entire body of North American, peer-reviewed literature on wetlands. The number of indicators is cumulatively large and conceptually redundant (deliberately) in places, but for any particular function the number of highly influential indicators is probably small.

Documentation from technical literature:

Technical literature is used as background or support for all the individual questions (indicators) whenever such literature has been published.

Documentation of procedures for derivation of results:

Explicit descriptions are provided of the combinations of wetlands and landscape characteristics (indicators) that result in assignment to a high, moderate, or low category. However, the authors of this method have used judgment in developing criteria for assigning particular combinations to one category or another. That judgment attempts to reflect information in the technical literature that implied that certain combinations of indicators occur in wetlands that are highly functioning, as defined absolutely by the net direction of flow or substances (e.g., groundwater, water quality functions) or by intuitive comparisons with other wetlands in the nation (e.g., aquatic and wildlife diversity/abundance).

Consideration of temporal dynamics:

The method's response forms allow users to account for the seasonal variability of indicators. This variability is also accounted for in the criteria used to generate the categorical ratings.

Consideration of bounding/scale issues:

This is one of the few methods that addresses bounding issues explicitly and provides guidelines.

Consideration of hierarchical relations among indicators:

Hierarchical relations are addressed in the structuring of the interpretation keys, where (for example) the criteria used for lacustrine wetlands differ from those used for palustrine wetlands for some functions.

Consideration of physical/landscape context:

Regional factors and landscape inputs that are inseparable determinants of wetland's function are considered throughout. Final ratings sometimes reflect the contribution of adjoining uplands and deepwater more than the capacity of a wetland itself, or the contribution of an entire wetland's rather than merely a project area within a wetland. Some users may find this a disadvantage for their particular applications.

Consideration of social context:

Added recognition is given to wetlands that are positioned upstream from social/cultural features (i.e., features especially likely to benefit from functions of those wetlands).

Time and labor requirements:

Duration:

Hours to days for assessment of a wetland, depending on size, access, availability of background information, and desired accuracy and precision. The list of questions that must be answered by the evaluator is the most comprehensive of any wetlands assessment method, and considerable practice is required to become skilled at using WET correctly. On average, experienced users can assess two to four wetlands daily.

Personnel needed:

At least one evaluator.

Technical expertise needed:

Schooling in environmental sciences. Use of a multidisciplinary team is desirable but not essential; graduation from the WET one-week training course (offered by federal agencies and private wetlands training institutes) probably increases the accuracy and replicability of results but is not essential.

Preliminary results obtainable without site visit:

Yes.

Effort collecting background data:

Moderate to large, depending on desired accuracy. Some necessarily pivotal questions require information that can be estimated accurately only with prior experience with the particular wetland. This is in part due to WET's optional consideration of wetlands temporal dynamics (e.g., effect of changing seasonal and tidal conditions on function).

Effort collecting primary data:

Small to moderate, depending on desired accuracy.

Data analysis effort:

Relatively small if using the available optional software; laborious if not.

Extent of peer review/use:

WET is probably the most extensively reviewed technique for assessing multiple functions of wetlands. It is also probably the most commonly used standardized technique, applied regionally as part of several EPA Advance Identification projects and COE Special Area Management Plans. Under development since 1980, the 1983 version was reviewed by over 100 scientists and users nationwide, and their comments were incorporated into the 1987 version.

Sensitivity:

Categories (high, moderate, low) reflect only the gross degree of sensitivity believed to be supported by the technical literature. As a result, comparisons among wetlands of similar geomorphic and vegetation type may show few differences and thus limit WET's utility for some purposes. However, sensitivity is context specific, and in some cases changing only one answer to a WET question can alter functional ratings. The available software expedites the conduct of sensitivity analyses, which are used to determine which indicators have the greatest influence on a particular assessment and which could cause the greatest errors if their associated questions were misinterpreted.

Other comments:

The phrasings of several questions to be answered by the user are tedious, awkward, and/or ambiguous, which leads to an initially high level of frustration. A few procedural errors may exist, suggesting further need for verification.

Methods Developed for Particular Regions or Wetland Types

E. Bottomland Hardwood Forest Habitat Evaluation Model

Explained in:

O'Neil, L. J., T. M. Pullen, Jr., and R. L. Schroeder (1991), *A Wildlife Community*

Habitat Evaluation Model for Bottomland Hardwood Forests in the Southeastern United States, U.S. Army Corps of Engineers, Waterways Experiment Station, Vicksburg, MS.

Available from:
Scheduled for distribution in 1992.

Applicable to which wetlands types:
Bottomland hardwoods of the southeast, probably excluding backwater, spring-fed, and bog systems.

Function(s)/values addressed:
Wildlife habitat, specifically the suitability of habitat for maintaining regional diversity of amphibian, reptile, bird, and mammal species.

Summary of procedures and output:
Information on landscape-level indicators (e.g., tract size and configuration, isolation, expected water quality, disturbance factors) is collected from maps and aerial photographs. Data on plot-level indicators are collected using field plots. The range of conditions of each indicator is assigned a value on a scale of 0 (poor habitat) to 10 (habitat conditions "needed to support the highest numbers of native wildlife species on a regional scale over a long time period"). As with HEP, the scores of individual indicators are combined mathematically. The result is a pair of values for two indices—plot suitability and tract suitability—which are then multiplied to give a single, numerical "tract habitat suitability index."

General features/assumptions:
This method is generally similar to its predecessor, HES (see IV.G below), but differs in part because of its greater incorporation of regional biodiversity values, greater standardization of procedures for measuring and weighting indicators, and omission of fish habitat suitability. In contrast to HEP (and a related method for southeastern wetlands, the Wildlife Habitat Appraisal Guide or WHAG, developed by the Missouri Department of Conservation and SCS in 1990), the Bottomland Hardwood Forest Habitat Evaluation Model does not use individual species as indicators of overall habitat quality. Rather, it assumes that some wetlands contribute more to regional biodiversity (i.e., the total number of species in a region) than others and that

such wetlands can be identified with a series of indicators related both to site-specific and landscape-level factors. Bottomland hardwood forests considered by this method to be least suitable for supporting regional biodiversity will probably be of small patch size, isolated, young, and homogeneous. As with other scoring methods, there is a danger in over-interpreting the scores. Although the scoring mechanisms used by this method appear scientifically reasonable, they have not always been confirmed by empirical data. Thus, slight differences in scores may be of little biological significance.

Inclusion of essential indicators:
Probably all the major indicators of community diversity in bottomland hardwoods are included.

Documentation from technical literature:
Assumptions are thoroughly documented by literature citations throughout.

Documentation of procedures for derivation of results:
The computational approach is adequately explained.

Consideration of temporal dynamics:
The model was constructed to take into consideration the year-round needs of wildlife. Primary seasons for data collection are specified.

Consideration of bounding/scale issues:
Relatively little guidance is given for determining the boundaries of assessment areas (e.g., how wide a bisecting river or levee must be before the tract through which it passes should be evaluated as two areas instead of as one).

Consideration of hierarchical relations among indicators:
These appear to be adequately recognized and incorporated in the model.

Consideration of physical/landscape context:
Considerable attention is given to landscape indicators of suitability.

Consideration of social context:
Wildlife social and economic values are not considered in the assessment of habitat.

Time and labor requirements:
Duration:
Hours to days to assess a wetland, depending on size, access, availability of background information, and desired accuracy and precision.
Personnel needed:
At least one evaluator.
Technical expertise needed:
Schooling in field biology.
Preliminary results obtainable without site visit:
None.
Effort collecting background data:
Moderate to large, depending on desired accuracy.
Effort collecting primary data:
Small to moderate, depending on desired accuracy.
Data analysis effort:
Simple and straightforward.

Extent of peer review/use:
Comments of many regional experts are incorporated, but the method is relatively new and untested.

Sensitivity:
The model is expected to be highly sensitive to slight differences in wetlands (tract) area and, to a lesser degree, to differences in wetlands habitat quality.

F. Connecticut/New Hampshire Method

Explained in:
Ammann, A. P., R. W. Franzen, and J. L. Johnson (1986), "Method for the Evaluation of Inland Wetlands in Connecticut" Bulletin No. 9, Connecticut Department of Environmental Protection and USDA Soil Conservation Service, Hartford, CT.

Ammann, A. P., and A. L. Stone (1991), *Method for the Comparative Evaluation of Nontidal Wetlands in New Hampshire*, NHDES-WRD-1991-3, New Hampshire Department of Environmental Services, Concord, NH.

Available from:
New Hampshire Department of Environmental Services, Water Resources Division, Wetlands Bureau, P.O. Box 2008, Concord, NH 13302 (603/271-2147).

Applicable to which wetlands types:
Nontidal wetlands in Connecticut and New Hampshire and possibly other areas of the northeast.

Function(s)/values addressed:
Fourteen functions or values are addressed: ecological integrity, wetlands wildlife habitat, finfish habitat, educational potential, visual/aesthetic quality, water-based recreation, flood control potential, groundwater use potential, sediment trapping, nutrient attenuation, shoreline anchoring, urban quality of life, historical site potential, and noteworthiness.

Summary of procedures and output:
The conceptual approach is nearly identical to that of the Hollands-Magee method, which preceded it (see IV.G below), except that (a) no provision is made for combining functional scores to produce a single score for each wetland, and (b) functional scores are optionally multiplied by acreage to give a total wetland score for each function (as in HEP). The criteria for scoring "urban" wetlands are different from those for other wetlands.

General features/assumptions:
This method is conceptually similar to the Hollands-Magee method. Being a scoring technique, the Connecticut/New Hampshire method is not suitable for assessing a single wetland. Rather, the method ranks a series of wetlands and does not place them in specific categories (e.g., high, moderate, low). Fine distinctions (such as are suggested by this method's scores) may not be technically supportable, and differences of a few points between wetlands should not be considered significant. Also, the approach of linearly combining the indicators, and particularly of making the final score equal to the product of acreage multiplied by functional value, may not truly reflect the nonlinear behavior of natural processes. One consequence is that large but otherwise unremarkable wetlands may be scored higher than small wetlands that function exceptionally well. There are also important statistical objections to using ordinal data in integrative mathematical operations (see Smith and Theberge, 1987).

Some users may find inconvenient the method's failure to suggest which score thresholds define the "high" or "low" level of a particular wetlands function. For example, if this method indicates that a wetland is in the eighth percentile for water quality maintenance, can it be assumed that it does or does not maintain water quality (e.g., as indicated by net annual phosphorus balance)? For other users, this scoring approach allows a wetland's optimal, attainable, or cost-effective condition to be defined by the user, based on scores from reference wetlands (e.g., pristine or functionally enhanced wetlands) or policy considerations. Thus, a wetland could be compared (ranked) with other wetlands in any wetland population (e.g., all wetlands in county X, all forested wetlands, all isolated headwater wetlands, or combinations of these).

Inclusion of essential indicators:
> For the flood control function, a proven mechanistic model is used and documented. For other functions, the indicators included are technically sound and important, but many essential, easily observed indicators are not included, thereby weakening the technical rigor of the analysis.

Documentation from technical literature:
> A rationale is given for each indicator. Evidence that the choice of indicators is supported by technical literature is seldom given. The manner of combining the indicators (i.e., weights assigned to the indicators in various instances) appears not to be mechanistically based (except for the flood control function) and is weakly documented.

Documentation of procedures for derivation of results:
> The computational approach is adequately explained.

Consideration of temporal dynamics:
> Functions are assessed only as they exist at the season during which the wetland is visited. The appropriate season for assessing each indicator and function is usually not specified, and the field sheet does not allow users to enter multiple responses to reflect seasonally changing conditions.

Consideration of bounding/scale issues:
> Procedures are clearly specified for bounding the assessment areas.

Consideration of hierarchical relations among indicators:
> These are generally not considered in detail. An exception is that different indicators and scoring are used for stream vs. lake fish habitats and urban vs. nonurban wetlands.

Consideration of physical/landscape context:
> Some landscape context factors that determine wetlands function are considered.

Consideration of social context:
> In the case of some of the physical functions, wetlands positioned close to an area that benefits from their function would usually receive no higher rating than those farther away. However, the method includes proximity to users in its assessment of historical site potential, noteworthiness, education, and visual/aesthetic quality functions. In addition, the method includes an "urban quality of life" function, which considers separately wetlands that are likely to be most heavily used.

Time and labor requirements:
> Duration:
>> Hours to days to assess a wetland, depending on size, access, availability of background information, and desired accuracy and precision.
> Personnel needed:
>> At least one evaluator.
> Technical expertise needed:
>> The intended user is a town official. Schooling in environmental sciences and use of a multidisciplinary team is probably desirable. Some questions require the ability to delineate a watershed.
> Preliminary results obtainable without site visit:
>> None.
> Effort collecting background data:
>> Moderate to large, depending on desired accuracy.
> Effort collecting primary data:
>> Small to moderate, depending on desired accuracy.
> Data analysis effort:
>> Relatively small; use of a hand-held calculator or personal computer (optional) facilitates the analysis.

Extent of peer review/use:
> The method was reviewed extensively within

New Hampshire and Connecticut. It has been used primarily by its authors, reviewers, sponsoring agencies, and town officials in the two states. The method has been under development since about 1984.

Sensitivity:
In most cases, this method will be highly sensitive to differences among wetlands.

Other comments:
The format is very attractive and user friendly.

G. HES (Habitat Evaluation System)

Explained in:
U.S. Army Corps of Engineers, Lower Mississippi Valley Division (1980), Vicksburg, MS.

Available from:
Environmental Analysis Division, Planning Directorate, Lower Mississippi Valley Division, U.S. Army Corps of Engineers, P.O. Box 80, Vicksburg, MS 39180.

Applicable to which wetlands types:
Forested wetlands (wooded swamps, streams, and bottomland hardwoods) of the lower Mississippi River Valley and perhaps similar areas/types.

Function(s)/values addressed:
Habitats of fish and wildlife.

Summary of procedures and output:
This method is conceptually similar to HEP (described in section IV,B). However, rather than selecting species as indicators of wetlands function and assessing their habitats, the user assesses a series of prescribed structural indicators of habitat (e.g., number of snags). HES does not explicitly link these indicators to the needs of particular species, although an orientation toward game species seems implicit. Moreover, although HES calls for assigning different weights to different structural indicators, that task is relegated to the user's judgment. The output is a wetlands score termed the habitat quality index.

General features/assumptions:
In contrast to HEP, HES does not require multiplication of habitat quality by wetlands acreage to yield a final value for the habitat quality index. Thus, a large wetland of a type that is mostly a poor habitat on a per-unit area basis (e.g., some high-graded hardwood stands) may be undervalued if function were to be defined in terms of population density or total richness of wildlife. HES assumes that animal density is correlated with measurable habitat quality (suitability) and generally ignores (as do all assessment methods) the influence of species' demographic characteristics, predation, competition, and other interspecific relationships. HES's approach of combining the indicator values linearly may not truly reflect the nonlinear behavior of natural processes. Users may encounter difficulty in interpreting an HES score on the basis of a single wetland; individual scores are best placed in the context of scores from a series of wetlands. However, there is a danger in overinterpreting HES scores; fine distinctions (such as might be suggested by HES scores) may not be technically supportable, and differences of a few points among wetlands should not be considered significant.

Inclusion of essential indicators:
Although the included indicators are technically sound and important, some essential, easily observed indicators are not included, thereby weakening the technical rigor of the analysis.

Documentation from technical literature:
A rationale is given for each indicator but is weakly supported by literature citations. Of greater concern is the fact that the manner of combining the indicators is not explicitly justified; that is, no literature is cited to support the weights assigned to the indicators in various instances.

Documentation of procedures for derivation of results:
The computational approach is adequately explained and very flexible.

Consideration of temporal dynamics:
No specific guidance is given.

Consideration of bounding/scale issues:
No specific guidance is given.

Consideration of hierarchical relations among indicators:
These are mostly not accounted for by this method.

Consideration of physical/landscape context:
Some information on surrounding habitat features is included in the assessment of a wetland.

Consideration of social context:
Not considered.

Time and labor requirements:
Duration:
Hours to weeks per wetland, depending on size, access, availability of background information, and desired accuracy and precision.
Personnel needed:
At least one evaluator.
Technical expertise needed:
Schooling in environmental sciences. Use of a multidisciplinary team is desirable but not essential.
Preliminary results obtainable without site visit:
None.
Effort collecting background data:
Moderate to large, depending on desired accuracy.
Effort collecting primary data:
Moderate to large, depending on desired accuracy.
Data analysis effort:
Usually small and fairly simple (optionally undertaken with a hand-held calculator or personal computer).

Extent of peer review/use:
This method was used primarily by its authors and reviewers and by COE staff, mostly during the early 1980s. Recently, the COE Waterways Experiment Station and others have developed an assessment method with a similar purpose (see IV,E).

Sensitivity:
In most cases HES will be highly sensitive to differences among wetlands.

H. Hollands-Magee (Normandeau) Method

Explained in:
Hollands, G. G., and D. W. Magee (1985), "A Method for Assessing the Functions of Wetlands," in J. Kusler and P. Riexinger (eds.), *Proceedings of the National Wetland Assessment Symposium* (1985), Association of Wetland Managers, Berne, NY.

Available from:
Dennis Magee, Normandeau Associates, 25 Nashua Road, Bedford, NH 03102-5999 (603/472-5191). Distribution may be limited due to the method's proprietary nature.

Applicable to which wetlands types:
Nontidal wetlands in New England and some midwestern states, possibly other areas.

Function(s)/values addressed:
Ten functions and values are addressed: biological function, hydrologic support, groundwater function, storm and floodwater storage, shoreline protection, water quality maintenance, cultural and economic function, recreational function, aesthetics function, and educational function.

Summary of procedures and output:
The user visits a study wetland and answers multiple-choice questions pertaining to the condition of structural indicators ("elements") of the 10 wetland functions. Each condition has an associated numerical score (e.g., 3 = best condition for that indicator, 0 = worst condition for that indicator). Each of the indicators also has an associated numerical weight (e.g., 3 = most important contributor to a function, 1 = least important contributor to a function). After returning from the field, the user multiplies each score by the indicator weight and totals these products, thereby deriving a weighted score for each function. The 10 functions themselves are also assigned weights or are ranked in comparison with ratings from other wetlands. From the ranking, each wetland is assigned a decile score. Functional scores are not multiplied by wetlands acreage to give a final score for each wetland. Thus, a large wetland that is of a type that is mostly ineffective for a function on a per-unit area basis (e.g., peat bogs for phosphorus retention) might be undervalued if function were to be defined in terms of total loading capacity.

General features/assumptions:
This method is generally similar to the Ontario method (see IV,K), developed at about the same time, and the Connecticut/New Hampshire method (see IV,F), developed several years later. The method does not place wetlands in categories of high, moderate, or low. Instead, the method explicitly provides for

assigning each scored wetland to a decile group, which expresses its functional uniqueness relative to all other wetlands that the evaluator has assessed. This requires that the evaluator assess several dozen other wetlands (or use scores from wetlands included in the Normandeau Associates data base). If the other assessed wetlands are selected randomly and/or are truly representative of wetlands in the region, the assignment to a particular decile is easier to interpret. As with most scoring approaches, however, fine distinctions (such as are suggested by this method's scores) may not be technically supportable, and differences of a few points between wetlands should not be considered significant. The Hollands-Magee method's grouping of scores into deciles mitigates this problem somewhat. Also, the approach of linearly combining the indicators, may not truly reflect the nonlinear behavior of natural processes. One consequence is that large but otherwise unremarkable wetlands may be scored higher than small wetlands that function exceptionally well.

The method's procedure for representing the multiplication of function scores by ordinal weights (e.g., 1, 2, 3) in integrative mathematical operations would be considered invalid by many statisticians and planners (see Smith and Theberge, 1987). This can be a significant issue if users infer that slight differences in the resulting scores of a group of assessed wetlands indicate real differences in function among the wetlands. Also, in the trading off of functions and values that is implicit in the process of assigning weights to functions, the method does not specify any role for the public; weights are assigned solely by the user.

Some users may become frustrated by the method's failure to suggest which score thresholds define a "high" or "low" level of a particular wetlands function. For example, if this method indicates that a wetland is in the eighth percentile for water quality maintenance, can it be assumed that it does or does not maintain water quality (e.g., as indicated by net annual phosphorus balance)? For other users, this scoring approach allows optimal, attainable, or cost-effective conditions to be defined by the user, based on scores from reference wetlands (e.g., pristine or functionally enhanced wetlands) or policy considerations. Thus, a wetland could be compared (ranked) with other wetlands in any wetlands population (e.g., all wetlands in a county, all forested wetlands, all isolated headwater wetlands, or combinations of these).

Inclusion of essential indicators:
Although the included indicators are technically sound and important, many essential, easily observed indicators are not included, thereby seriously weakening the technical rigor of the analysis.

Documentation from technical literature:
A rationale is given for each indicator (element) but is weakly supported by literature citation. Of greater concern is the fact that the manner of combining the indicators and functions is not explicitly justified; that is, no literature is cited to support the weights assigned to the indicators or functions in various instances.

Documentation of procedures for derivation of results:
The computational approach is adequately explained and is fairly simple; a hand-held calculator or personal computer can be used.

Consideration of temporal dynamics:
Functions are assessed only as they exist at the season during which the wetland is visited. The appropriate season for assessing each indicator and function is usually not specified, and the field sheet does not allow users to enter multiple responses to reflect seasonally changing conditions.

Consideration of bounding/scale issues:
Not specified.

Consideration of hierarchical relations among indicators:
Not accounted for.

Consideration of physical/landscape context:
Wetlands that receive significant inputs from the landscape are generally treated no differently from those that do not. A few indicators deal generally with watershed position.

Consideration of social context:
Topographic position is used in a general manner to infer opportunities for performing some functions.

Time and labor requirements:
Duration:
Hours to days per wetland, depending on size, access, availability of background information, and desired accuracy and precision.
Number of personnel needed:
Two evaluators.
Technical expertise needed:
A geologist/hydrologist and botanist/ecologist.
Preliminary results obtainable without site visit:
Partial results are obtainable.
Effort collecting background data:
Moderate, depending on desired accuracy.
Effort collecting primary data:
Small to moderate, depending on desired accuracy.
Data analysis effort:
Relatively small, optionally using a hand-held calculator or personal computer. (However, data interpretation requires calculation of or access to the scores of many other wetlands.)

Extent of peer review/use:
Use by parties other than the authors of this method is unknown. This method has been in use since about 1982.

Sensitivity:
In most cases, this method will be highly sensitive to differences among wetlands.

I. Larson/Golet Method

Explained in:
Larson, J. S. (ed.) (1976), *Models for Assessment of Freshwater Wetlands*, Publication No. 32, Water Resources Research Center, University of Massachusetts, Amherst, MA.

Supporting academic documents that provide more detailed explanations include these:

Golet, F. C. (1973), "Classification and Evaluation of Freshwater Wetlands as Wildlife Habitat in the Glaciated Northeast," Ph.D. dissertation, University of Massachusetts, Amherst, MA.

Heeley, R. W. (1973), "Hydrogeology of Wetlands in Massachusetts," M.S. thesis, University of Massachusetts, Amherst, MA.

Smardon, R. C. (1972), "Assessing Visual-Cultural Values of Inland Wetlands in Massachusetts," M.L.A. thesis, University of Massachusetts, Amherst, MA.

Available from:
Water Resources Research Center, University of Massachusetts, Amherst, MA 01003 (413/545-2842).

Applicable to which wetland types:
Nontidal wetlands of Massachusetts and perhaps other nontidal wetlands in the northeast.

Function(s)/values addressed:
Wildlife value (Golet submodel), groundwater potential (Heeley-Motts submodel), and visual-cultural value (Smardon-Fabos submodel).

Summary of procedures and output:
The conceptual approach is nearly identical to that of the Hollands-Magee method (see IV,H), except that no provision is made for combining functional scores to produce a single score for each wetland.

General features/assumptions:
Being a scoring technique, the Larson/Golet method is not suitable for assessing a single wetland. Rather, the method ranks a series of wetlands and does not place them in specific categories (e.g., high, moderate, low). Fine distinctions (such as are suggested by this method's scores) may not be technically supportable; thus, differences of a few points among wetlands should not be considered significant. Also, the approach of linearly combining the indicators may not truly reflect the nonlinear behavior of natural processes. There are important statistical objections as well with regard to using ordinal data in integrative mathematical operations (see Smith and Theberge, 1987).

Some users may become frustrated by the method's failure to suggest which score thresholds define "high" or "low" levels of a particular wetlands function. For example, if this method indicates that a wetland is in the eighth percentile for water quality maintenance, can it be assumed that it does or does not maintain water quality (e.g., as indicated by net annual phosphorus balance)? For other users, this scoring approach allows optimal, attainable, or cost-effective condition to be defined by the user, based on scores from reference wetlands (e.g., pristine or functionally enhanced wetlands) or policy considerations. Thus, a wetland could be compared (ranked) with other wetlands in any wetland population (e.g., all wetlands in a county, all forested wetlands, all isolated headwater wetlands, or combinations of these).

Inclusion of essential indicators:
Although the included indicators are technically sound and important, some essential, easily observed indicators are not included, thereby weakening the technical rigor of the analysis. Wetlands science and knowledge of indicators has advanced greatly in the 20 years since these models were developed.

Documentation from technical literature:
A rationale is given for each indicator (element) but is weakly supported by literature citations in the summary reports. Additional documentation is available in theses that support this work. Of greater concern is the fact that the manner of combining the indicators is not explicitly justified; that is, no literature is cited to support the weights assigned to the indicators in various instances.

Documentation of procedures for derivation of results:
The computational approach is adequately explained and fairly simple.

Consideration of temporal dynamics:
Functions are assessed only as they exist at the season during which the wetland is visited. The appropriate season for assessing each indicator and function is usually not specified.

Consideration of bounding/scale issues:
Not specified.

Consideration of hierarchical relations among indicators:
Not accounted for.

Consideration of physical/landscape context:
Some questions address the landscape matrix, but corridors are generally not considered.

Consideration of social context:
Proximity to users is considered somewhat in the assessment of visual-cultural and ground-water functions.

Time and labor requirements:
Duration:
Hours to days to assess a wetland, depending on size, access, availability of background information, and desired accuracy and precision.
Personnel needed:
At least one evaluator.
Technical expertise needed:
Schooling in environmental sciences. Use of a multidisciplinary team is desirable but not essential.
Preliminary results obtainable without site visit:
None.
Effort collecting background data:
Moderate to large, depending on desired accuracy.
Effort collecting primary data:
Small to moderate, depending on desired accuracy.
Data analysis effort:
Final scores are simple to calculate (optionally using a hand-held calculator or personal computer).

Extent of peer review/use:
This was the first method developed for rapid assessment of inland wetlands. It has been used extensively in Rhode Island.

Sensitivity:
In most cases this method will be highly sensitive to differences among wetlands.

J. Minnesota Wetland Evaluation Methodology (WEM)

Explained in:
U.S. Army Corps of Engineers, St. Paul District (1988), *The Minnesota Wetland Evaluation Methodology for the North Central United States*, Minnesota Wetland Evaluation Methodology Task Force and Corps of Engineers, St. Paul District.

Available from:

St. Paul District, U.S. Army Corps of Engineers, 1135 U.S. Post Office and Custom House, St. Paul, MN 55101.

Applicable to which wetlands types:

All types in Minnesota and perhaps other north-central states.

Function(s)/values addressed:

Eleven functions and values are addressed: peak flow reduction, sediment trapping, nutrient trapping, wildlife diversity and productivity, warmwater fish, northern pike spawning habitat, shoreline anchoring, visual variety, visual importance, visual integrity, and special features.

Summary of procedures and output:

This method is conceptually similar to WET (see IV,D), from which it was partly adapted. However, WEM includes an option for the user to proceed farther and assign scores (e.g., 3, 2, 1) to the generated categorical ratings (high, moderate, low) and to assign weights (subjectively chosen) to the individual functions. The method then specifies that scores be multiplied by function weights to arrive at an overall wetlands score. WEM also differs from WET in that it (a) uses a more mechanistically based procedure for assessing flood storage, (b) uses a generally narrower set of indicators, and (c) includes procedures for assessing visual values.

General features/assumptions:

WEM's generation of categorical ratings has the same strengths and weaknesses of WET (see IV,D). Specifically, WEM places a wetland into one of only three broad categories (high, moderate, low). Such placement can occur as a result of a wetland's having any of several possible combinations of characteristics (i.e., question responses or indicator conditions).

WEM's option of representing qualitative ratings (high, moderate, low) by ordinal numbers (e.g., 1, 2, 3) in integrative mathematical operations would be considered invalid by many statisticians and planners (see Smith and Theberge, 1987). This can be a

significant issue if users infer that slight differences in the resulting scores of a group of assessed wetlands mean real differences in function among the wetlands. Also, WEM's option for assigning weights to functions is likely to be subjective because little specific guidance is given as to how to do this. Moreover, in the trading off of functions and values implicit in this process, WEM does not specify any role for the public; weights are assigned solely by the user.

Although WEM assigns scores to functions and wetlands, these scores (unlike the HEP) are not multiplied by wetlands acreage to give a final wetlands rating. Thus, a large wetland of a type that is mostly ineffective for a function on a per-unit area basis (e.g., peat bogs for phosphorus retention) may be undervalued if users are interested in defining function in terms of total loading capacity. For example, a large bog, although ineffective, may remove more phosphorus than a small wetland of a type that is characteristically a poor phosphorus retainer.

Inclusion of essential indicators:

Some essential, easily observed indicators are not included, thereby weakening the technical rigor of the analysis.

Documentation from technical literature:

For the flood flow function, a proven mechanistic model is used and documented. For other functions, a rationale is given for each indicator (element) but is weakly supported by literature citations.

Documentation of procedures for derivation of results:

Explicit descriptions are provided of the combinations of wetlands and landscape characteristics (indicators) that result in assignment to a high, moderate, or low category. As in the case of WET (which was used as a template), however, the authors of this method have exercised judgment in developing criteria for assigning particular combinations to one category or another.

Consideration of temporal dynamics:

Functions are assessed only as they exist at

the season during which a wetland is visited. The appropriate season for assessing each indicator and function is usually not specified, and the field sheet does not allow users to enter multiple responses to reflect seasonally changing conditions.

Consideration of bounding/scale issues:
Not specified.

Consideration of hierarchical relations among indicators:
These are especially well accounted for in the portion assessing the flood flow function. For other functions, interactions among predictors are addressed in the detailed structuring of the interpretation keys.

Consideration of physical/landscape context:
Regional factors and some landscape context factors that contribute to wetlands function are considered.

Consideration of social context:
Added recognition is given to wetlands that are positioned upstream from some types of social/cultural features that are especially likely to benefit from functions of those wetlands.

Time and labor requirements:
Duration:
Hours to days to assess a wetland, depending on size, access, availability of background information, and desired accuracy and precision.
Personnel needed:
At least one evaluator.
Technical expertise needed:
Schooling in environmental sciences. Use of a multidisciplinary team is desirable but not essential.
Preliminary results obtainable without site visit:
None.
Effort collecting background data:
Moderate to large, depending on desired accuracy.
Effort collecting primary data:
Small to moderate, depending on desired accuracy.
Data analysis effort:
Relatively small if using the available optional software; difficult if not using the

software. The software (which requires a math coprocessor in the user's computer) *must* be used to determine the peak flow-reduction function.

Extent of peer review/use:
The method has been reviewed extensively within Minnesota. Its use by parties other than its authors and reviewers is unknown. The method has been under development since about 1985.

Sensitivity:
The sensitivity of the categorical procedure is probably low to moderate.

Other comments:
Compared to other methods, the format of this one is very attractive, but it lacks adequate forms for recording data and summarizing ratings.

K. Ontario Method

Explained in:
Euler, D. L. et al. (1983), *An Evaluation System for Wetlands of Ontario South of the Precambrian Shield*, Ontario Ministry of Natural Resources and Canadian Wildlife Service, Ontario, Canada.

Available from:
Wildlife Branch, Ontario Ministry of Natural Resources, Whitney Block, Queen's Park, Toronto, Ontario, Canada.

Applicable to which wetland types:
All types in Ontario and perhaps immediately adjoining parts of the United States.

Function(s)/values addressed:
Fifteen functions and values are addressed: flow stabilization, water quality improvement, erosion control, biological productivity, biological diversity, marketable resources, recreation, aesthetics, education, rarity/scarcity, special habitat features, ecological age, size, ownership, and proximity to urban areas.

Summary of procedures and output:
The conceptual approach is nearly identical to that of the Hollands-Magee method.

General features/assumptions:

This method is similar to the Hollands-Magee method (see IV,H), which was developed about the same time. Being a scoring technique, the Ontario method is not suitable for assessing a single wetland. Rather, the method generates scores that permit a ranking of a series of wetlands and does not place wetlands in specific categories (e.g., high, moderate, low). Fine distinctions among wetlands (such as are suggested by this method's scores) may not be technically supportable; differences of a few points among wetlands should not be considered significant. Also, the approach of linearly combining the indicators, and particularly the approach of making the final score equal to the product of acreage multiplied by functional value, may not truly reflect the nonlinear behavior of natural processes. One consequence is that large but otherwise unremarkable wetlands may be scored higher than small wetlands that function exceptionally well.

The method's procedure for representing the multiplication of function scores by ordinal weights (e.g., 1, 2, 3) in integrative mathematical operations would be considered invalid by many statisticians and planners (see Smith and Theberge, 1987). This can be a significant issue if users imply that slight differences in the resultant scores of a group of assessed wetlands mean real differences in function among the wetlands. Also, in the trading off of functions and values that is implicit in the process of assigning weights to functions, the method does not specify any role for the public; weights are assigned solely by the user.

Some users may become frustrated by the method's failure to suggest which score thresholds define "high" or "low" levels of a particular wetland function. For example, if this method indicates that a wetland is in the eighth percentile for water quality maintenance, can it be assumed that it does or does not maintain water quality (e.g., as indicated by net annual phosphorus balance)? For other users, this scoring approach allows optimal, attainable, or cost-effective conditions to be defined by the user, based on scores from reference wetlands (e.g., pristine or functionally enhanced wetlands) or policy considerations. Thus, a wetland could be compared (ranked) with other wetlands in any wetland population (e.g., all wetlands in a county, all forested wetlands, all isolated headwater wetlands, or combinations of these).

Inclusion of essential indicators:

Some essential, easily observed indicators are not included, thereby weakening the technical rigor of the analysis.

Documentation from technical literature:

A rationale is given for each indicator but is seldom supported by literature citations. Of greater concern is the fact that the manner of combining the indicators is not explicitly justified; that is, no literature is cited to support the weights assigned to the indicators or functions in various instances.

Documentation of procedures for derivation of results:

The computational approach is adequately explained.

Consideration of temporal dynamics:

The importance of temporal dynamics is acknowledged in the introduction, but the method does not specify the appropriate season for assessing each indicator, and the field sheet does not allow users to enter multiple responses to reflect seasonally changing conditions.

Consideration of bounding/scale issues:

This is one of the few methods that addresses all aspects of the bounding issues explicitly and provides guidelines, although these are subjective.

Consideration of hierarchical relations among indicators:

These are mostly not accounted for by this method. An exception is the flow stabilization assessment protocol, which scores a wetland's size according to its position in the watershed.

Consideration of physical/landscape context:

Regional factors and landscape inputs are considered.

Consideration of social context:

Added recognition is given to wetlands positioned above some types of social/cultural features especially likely to benefit from functions of the upstream wetlands.

Time and labor requirements:
Duration:
Hours to days to assess a wetland, depending on size, access, availability of background information, and desired accuracy and precision.
Personnel needed:
At least one evaluator.
Technical expertise needed:
Schooling in environmental sciences. Use of a multidisciplinary team is desirable but not essential.
Preliminary results obtainable without site visit:
None.
Effort collecting background data:
Moderate to large, depending on desired accuracy.
Effort collecting primary data:
Small to moderate, depending on desired accuracy.
Data analysis effort:
Relatively small (optionally using a handheld calculator or personal computer).

Extent of peer review/use:
This method has been reviewed extensively within Ontario and has been under development since about 1980.

Sensitivity:
In most cases this method will be highly sensitive to differences among wetlands.

V. INTENSIVE METHODS FOR INDIVIDUAL WETLANDS

Occasionally a need arises for measuring a wetland's function definitively rather than with the use of indicators (as described in part IV) to infer the level of function with less certainty. Detailed measurements are most often requested where an administrative action concerning a wetland or a wetland watershed is likely to be litigated or where a need exists to develop a detailed management plan for multiple uses of an individual wetland or wetland watershed. Moreover, in certain situations it is desirable to assess directly the extent to which wetlands functions or biological communities have been affected by human activities. In such instances, methods requiring multiple visits to wetlands and costly monitoring equipment are needed.

Some intensive methods used to measure wetlands functions or community structures are slight adaptations of methods used in the measurement of other surface waters; others have been developed specifically for a particular type of wetland. As a whole, intensive methods used to measure wetlands functions are too numerous and diverse to describe. For this reason, only a brief listing of sources is presented here.

A. Biological Functions

A recent EPA report (Adamus and Brandt, 1990) presents methods for intensive sampling and analysis of biological communities and processes of inland wetlands. The report cites and briefly describes detailed methods and indicator taxa that have been used in community studies of wetlands microbes, algae, vegetation, aquatic invertebrates, fish, amphibians, reptiles, birds, mammals, and ecological processes. It also provides an overall discussion of considerations for intensive studies of wetlands biological condition. There is no comparable compendium for coastal wetlands, but the report by Simenstad et al. (1989) represents a starting point.

B. Hydrologic Functions

There is no standard reference that describes detailed methods for measuring wetlands hydrologic functions. Measurement of selected indicators pertinent to some of the hydrologic functions is discussed by Gunderson (1989), Heliotis and DeWitt (1987), Kadlec (1984), Kadlec (1988), LaBaugh (1986), Rosenberry (1990), EPA (1983, 1985), Welcomme (1979), Winter (1981), and Zimmerman (1988). Data-intensive, mechanistic, hydrologic models for site-specific use are proposed by Hammer and Kadlec (1986), Guertin et al. (1987), and Chescheir et al. (1988), for example. Some of the available hydrologic models are reviewed according to their potential relevance to inland wetlands by Brunner (1988).

C. Water Quality Functions

In a similar fashion, no standard reference exists for detailed studies of wetlands water purification functions. Soil measurement techniques relevant to these functions are discussed by Faulkner et al. (1989). Useful information is also contained in the reports by Kadlec (1984) and EPA (1983, 1985). A data-intensive, mechanistic model for site-specific use is proposed by Kadlec and Hammer (1988). Procedures for measuring a wetland's ability to remove nitrogen are reviewed by Tiedje et al. (1981) and Tiedje (1982).

D. Cumulative Functions

Most of the methods reviewed in part IV deal with functions of individual wetlands. Only a few detailed methods have been developed for assessing the aggregate contribution of wetlands to landscape function throughout an entire region or river basin (see Adamus, 1989b, for a partial review).

Where relationships between indicators and functions are relatively well understood, the procedure of Bain et al. (1985) may be useful for organizing available knowledge. Where quantitative data exist from a landscape unit (e.g., historic streamflow data from a watershed), the papers by Burdick et al. (1989), Gosselink et al. (1990), and Childers and Gosselink (1990) demonstrate a data analysis and interpretation approach useful for preparing case histories of cumulative effects of wetlands loss. Mapping approaches (termed "gap analyses") that identify areas likely to contribute the most to regional biodiversity (based on GIS overlay and analysis of vegetation maps and species range maps) have also been demonstrated (Scott et al., 1987, 1990; Crumpacker et al., 1988). Where a statistically robust analysis of wetlands cumulative contributions is required (and resources and time allow for it), more data-intensive regression procedures as demonstrated by Jones et al. (1976), Brown and Dinsmore (1986), or Johnston et al. (1988, 1990) might be used to document the proportion, pattern, and characteristics of wetlands needed to ensure maintenance of landscape functions such as water purification, biodiversity, and flood storage. Simulation approaches for estimating the relative role of wetlands in landscape function are demonstrated by Frederick (1983), DeVries (1980), Ogawa and Male (1983), Cowardin et al. (1988), and Dreher et al. (1989). Attempts to develop mechanistic models of wetlands are discussed by Mitsch et al. (1988), Costanza and Sklar (1985), and Brunner (1988).

REFERENCES

Abbruzzese, B., S.G. Leibowitz, and R. Sumner. 1990a. "Application of the Synoptic Approach to Wetland Designation: A Case Study in Louisiana." EPA/600/3-90/066. U.S. EPA Environmental Research Lab, Corvallis, Ore.

———. 1990b. "Application of the Synoptic Approach to Wetland Designation: A Case Study in Washington." EPA/600/3-90/072. U.S. EPA Environmental Research Lab, Corvallis, Ore.

Abernethy, Y., and R.E. Turner. 1987. "U.S. Forested Wetlands: 1940–1980." *BioScience* 37:721–727.

Adamus, P.R. 1983. *A Method for Wetland Functional Assessment*. Report No. FHWA-IP-82-23 and 24. Federal Highway Administration, U.S. Department of Transportation, Washington, D.C.

———. 1989a. "A Review of Technical Information Sources for Support of U.S. EPA Advanced Identification Projects." U.S. EPA Environmental Research Laboratory, Corvallis, Ore.

———. 1989b. "Determining the Cumulative Effects of Forested Wetlands: EPA's Research Program and Choices for Research and Monitoring Designs." In *Best Management Practices for Forest Wetlands: Concerns, Assessment, Regulation, and Research*, pp. 36–47. National Council of the Paper Industry for Air and Stream Improvement, Inc. (NCASI), Corvallis, Ore.

Adamus, P.R., and K. Brandt. 1990. *Impacts on Quality of Inland Wetlands of the United States: A Survey of Indicators, Techniques, and Applications of Community Level Biomonitoring Data*. EPA/600/3-90/073. U.S. EPA, Cincinnati, Ohio.

Adamus, P.R., and L.T. Stockwell. 1983. *A Method for Wetland Functional Assessment*. Volume I: *Critical Review and Evaluation Concepts*. Report FHWA-IP-82-24. U.S. Department of Transportation, Federal Highway Administration, Washington, D.C.

(continued on p. 220)

Table 1
Indicators Used in Rapid Methods for Assessing Multiple Functions of Wetlands

Only those functions that are assessed by more than one method are included below. Listing of an indicator should not be interpreted as suggesting either a positive or a negative relationship to the named function. These methods sometimes differ in the specific way in which they define each function and in the rankings they assign to indicator conditions (for example, some methods that use the indicator "permanent flooding" consider it detrimental to the nutrient retention function while others consider it beneficial). To facilitate comparisons, some of the functions and indicators have sometimes been generalized from the definition used in the listed methods, whereas others occasionally have been disaggregated. Although several methods sometimes appear to use the same indicator, the methods may differ in the specific way they define the indicator or in the intensity, objectivity, and accuracy of techniques they use for measuring it. Methods are abbreviated as follows and are reviewed in detail in the accompanying text (section IV) unless otherwise noted.

Methods Reviewed in Section IV

WET: Wetlands Evaluation Technique

BLH: Bottomland Hardwood Forest Habitat Evaluation Model

CT/NH: Connecticut/New Hampshire method

HES: Habitat Evaluation System

H-M: Hollands-Magee method

L-G: Larson-Golet method

WEM: Minnesota Wetland Evaluation Method

ONT: Ontario Wetlands Evaluation System

SA: Synoptic Approach for Wetlands Cumulative Effects Analysis

Methods Not Reviewed in Section IV

MD: Maryland WET (Wetland Evaluation Technique for Nontidal Wetlands in the Coastal Plain of Maryland), Nontidal Wetlands Division, Maryland Department Natural Resources (October 1990 draft).

ME: Maine Wetland Protection Rules, Natural Resources Protection Act, Chapter 310, Maine Department of Environmental Protection (June 1990).

NC: North Carolina Wetland Rating System Manual, North Carolina Department of Environment, Health, and Natural Resources (January 1991).

NY: New York Freshwater Wetlands Act (Curran et al. 1989).

WA: Washington State Wetlands Rating System, Washington Department of Ecology (May 1991).

Cultural/Aesthetic Indicators

	WET	BLH	CT/NH	HES	H-M	L-G	WEM	ONT	SA*	MD	WA	ME	NY	NC
Education/research use/proximity	•	•			•		•			•				•
Special habitats:														
endangered, threatened, rare species	•	•			•	•	•			•	•	•	•	•
plant community regionally rare	•	•				•				•	•	•		•
Natural Heritage Site	•	•									•	•		
colonial waterbird rookery	•	•						•						
significant spawning area		•						•				•		
other nationally/regionally significant species/habitat	•	•			•	•	•			•		•	•	•
Difficult-to-replace wetland type (ecological age, etc.)								•			•			
Unusual geologic features						•		•			•			
Dedicated use = conservation	•					•				•				
Prior public investment	•									•				
Buffers adjoining sensitive site														•
Corridor to other undeveloped														•
Historic/archaeological site	•	•				•				•				•
Regional wetland loss rate	•								•					
Recent human population trends									•					
Dominant vegetation form			•		•	•				•	•	•	•	•
Vegetation form richness			•		•	•	•			•				
Open water (% vegetated cover)			•		•		•					•		
Open water interspersion (open water edge complexity)						•	•							
Upland land use type			•			•	•	•						
Upland land cover richness						•								
Wetland contrast with upland			•			•	•	•						
Wetland position (focal point)						•	•							
Wetland acreage	•				•	•							•	•
Distance to another wetland (local wetland density)						•								•
Presence of inlet, outlet (surface water connection)											•	•	•	•
Noise, odors, pollution	•						•							
Unaltered/pristine wetland	•										•			•
Undesirable plant species											•			
Autumn colors/flowering plants			•											
Legal access	•					•	•			•				
Easy physical access to open water						•	•							

* Not yet finalized.

	WET	BLH	CT/NH	HES	H-M	L-G	WEM	ONT	SA*	MD	WA	ME	NY	NC
Open Water Recreation Indicators														
Evidence of recreational use	•		•					•						
Apparent water quality			•											
Open water width			•											
Open water acreage					•		•	•						
Open water % (% vegetated cover)					•									
Depth			•											
Physical access to open water			•		•		•							
Legal access to open water					•		•							
Public parking near wetland			•											
Presence of inlet, outlet (surface water connection)					•									
Proximity to community					•		•							
Dominant vegetation form			•		•									
Wildlife score			•		•									
Aesthetic/cultural score			•											
Groundwater Exchange Indicators														
Tidal or nontidal	•				•					•				
Wetland size					•									
Surrounding topographic relief			•		•									
Surficial geologic type			•		•									
Sediment organic content					•									
Aquifer transmissivity					•									
Precipitation-evaporation ratio			•											
Wetland-watershed acre ratio (position in watershed)			•		•									
Presence of inlet, outlet (surface water connection)			•		•					•				
Wetland not channelized			•							•				
Flood recurrence interval (annual hydroperiod)			•							•				
Flow stability			•											
Natural chemical anomalies			•											
Natural thermal anomalies			•											
Dominant vegetation type = moss			•											
Upslope soil type			•							•				
Upslope soil permeability			•							•				
Impounded upstream or down			•											
Social significance: sole source/sensitive aquifer			•											

* Not yet finalized.

Flood Storage Indicators

	WET	BLH	CT/NH	HES	H-M	L-G	WEM	ONT	SA*	MD	WA	ME	NY	NC
Geomorphic type = not fringe/tidal	•						•	•		•				
Surficial geologic type of watershed					•									
Wetland-watershed acre ratio (position in watershed)	•		•		•		•	•						
Wetland acreage	•				•									
Wetlands as cumulative % of watershed	•								•					
Presence of inlet/outlet	•				•		•			•				
Outlet constriction/type	•		•		•		•			•				
Channelization	•									•				
Dominant vegetation type	•				•		•			•				
Open water % (% vegetated cover)	•				•									
Pattern of input (diffuse/concentrated)					•					•				
Pattern of throughput (diffuse/concentrated)	•				•					•				
Landscape input:														
upstream land cover	•						•		•	•				
upstream soils	•									•				
upstream storage (in lakes, wetlands)	•							•						
channel slope	•								•					
cumulative channel length									•					
annual precipitation									•					
precipitation-evaporation ratio	•													
Social significance:														
downstream hazard areas	•						•			•				
downstream storage	•						•							

* Not yet finalized.

Sediment Retention Indicators

Indicator	WET	BLH	CT/NH	HES	H-M	L-G	WEM	ONT	SA*	MD	WA	ME	NY	NC
Wetland acreage			•		•									
Wetlands as cumulative % of watershed									•					
Presence of outlet (surface water connection)	•		•		•		•			•				
Outlet constriction/type	•		•		•		•			•				
Wetland not channelized										•				
Gradient within wetland (velocity, turbulence)	•				•		•							
Pattern of input (diffuse/concentrated)	•				•					•				
Seasonally flooded duration										•				
Dominant vegetation form			•		•					•				
Vegetation % cover/density	•				•									
Vegetated zone width	•													
Accretion evidence/delta	•													
Wetland-watershed acre ratio (position in watershed)	•		•		•		•							
Landscape inputs:														
presence of inlet	•				•									
slope of drainage area	•		•				•							
land use upslope	•		•		•		•			•				
waves, water level flux	•													
rainfall intensity	•													
upslope soil permeability										•				
upslope soil erosiveness	•						•							
position in watershed	•				•									
known quality of input	•								•					
Social significance:														
downslope sensitive water	•		•											

Nutrient Retention Indicators

Indicator	WET	BLH	CT/NH	HES	H-M	L-G	WEM	ONT	SA*	MD	WA	ME	NY	NC
Wetland acreage			•		•									
Wetlands as cumulative % of watershed									•					
Presence of inlet, outlet (surface water connection)	•		•		•		•			•				
Outlet constriction/type	•		•		•		•			•				
Dominant vegetation form	•		•		•					•				
Vegetation % cover/density	•				•									
Permanently flooded (% of wetland area)	•		•											
Wetland-watershed acre ratio (position in watershed)	•		•		•		•							

* Not yet finalized.

Assessment Method

	WET	BLH	CT/NH	HES	H-M	L-G	WEM	ONT	SA*	MD	WA	ME	NY	NC
Nutrient Retention Indicators *(cont'd.)*														
Gradient within wetland (velocity, turbulence)	•					•	•							
Accretion evidence/delta	•							•						
Sediment type (mineral/organic)	•						•	•						
Wetland not channelized	•									•				
Wetland soil disturbed	•													
Pattern of input (diffuse/concentrated)	•					•				•				
Landscape inputs:														
slope of drainage area	•		•				•							
land use upslope	•		•	•			•			•				
position in watershed (stream order)	•									•				
soil erosiveness upslope	•						•							
channelization upstream	•						•							
known quality of input	•								•					•
Social significance:														
downslope sensitive water	•		•							•				•
Erosion Control Indicators														
Vegetated ground cover %	•		•	•			•			•				
Vegetated zone width	•		•				•							
Depth				•										
Wetland not channelized	•									•				
Dominant vegetation type	•					•	•	•		•				
Vegetation species							•							
Accretion evidence/delta	•													
Plant-water interspersion, instream	•													
Opportunity for erosion:														
open water edge contrast			•											
fetch or % open water	•					•		•						
position relative to waves/flow	•													
waves, water level flux	•													
rainfall intensity	•						•							
surficial or soil type	•					•								
presence of inlet, outlet (lacustrine/riverine)						•		•	•					
channel slope or velocity	•													
impoundment upstream	•													

* Not yet finalized.

Aquatic Habitat Indicators

	WET	BLH	CT/NH	HES	H-M	L-G	WEM	ONT	SA*	MD	WA	ME	NY	NC
Fish access	•		•	•			•							
Lotic/lentic	•		•	•			•							
Presence of inlets/outlets	•									•				
Water chemistry/quality	•		•	•			•			•				
Salinity	•													
Temperature	•						•							
Channel width or stream order			•							•				
Mean depth	•			•										
Maximum depth								•						
Cover % (wood, banks, etc.)	•		•											
Dominant vegetation form	•													
Submerged aquatic vegetation %	•		•							•				
Shade %	•		•											
Meandering/channelized %	•		•	•										
Wetland acreage	•		•											
Daily water level flux	•													
Open water % (% vegetated cover)	•						•	•		•				
Open water interspersion (open water edge complexity)	•			•						•				
Seasonally flooded %	•			•										
Seasonally flooded duration	•			•			•							
Flood recurrence interval (annual hydroperiod)	•			•			•							
Duration of freezing	•													
Streambottom not sand	•													
Upslope land use (nearby)	•			•						•				
Aquatic invertebrate density	•													
Known presence of fish	•		•				•							
Known lack of fish kills			•											
Known spawning area								•						
Presence of undesirable fish	•			•										
Fish standing crop (biomass)				•										
Endangered, threatened, rare species	•		•	•					•					

* Not yet finalized.

Wildlife Habitat Indicators

Wildlife Habitat Indicators	WET	BLH	CT/NH	HES	H-M	L-G	WEM	ONT	SA*	MD	WA	ME	NY	NC
Wetland size	•	•	•		•	•	•	•		•	•			
Dominant vegetation form	•		•		•	•	•	•			•			
Vegetation form richness	•		•		•	•	•			•	•			
Vegetation form interspersion	•		•		•	•	•				•			
Vegetation overstory %		•		•										
Vegetation ground cover %		•		•										
Vegetation understory %		•		•										
Seasonally flooded %	•			•										
Seasonally flooded duration	•			•										
Flood recurrence interval (annual hydroperiod)	•				•									
Daily water level flux	•													
Diversity of hydroperiods (distance to topographic change)		•												
Open water % (% vegetated cover)	•				•	•		•			•			
Open water: permanent, shallow				•	•					•				
Open water interspersion (open water edge complexity)	•		•		•	•	•	•						
Islands & upland inclusions	•		•											
Duration of freezing	•													
Distance to another wetland (local wetland density)	•	•			•	•	•	•			•			
Corridor to other undeveloped	•	•	•							•	•			
Human visitation disturbance	•	•	•	•										
Upland land cover (nearby)	•	•	•		•	•	•			•	•			
Upland land cover richness					•			•						
Local wetland type richness (complex diversity)	•						•	•						
Preferred wildlife foods	•	•			•	•								
Distance to preferred foods				•										
pH or acidity	•						•	•						
Expected contamination	•	•	•											
Presence of inlet/outlet (surface water connection)	•		•					•			•			
Groundwater connection						•								
Very large trees	•	•		•							•			
Dead trees (snags)	•	•		•							•			
Tidally influenced	•										•			
Regional position	•										•			
Endangered, threatened, rare species	•				•	•	•			•				

* Not yet finalized.

Note: Indicators are not listed for HEP, the most commonly used method for assessments of wetlands wildlife habitat assessment, because they are species specific and too numerous to list.

(continued from p. 211)

Adamus, P.R., et al. 1987a. *Wetland Evaluation Technique (WET)*, Volume II. Technical Report Y-87. U.S. Army Corps of Engineers, Waterways Experiment Station, Vicksburg, Miss.

———. 1987b. *Wetland Evaluation Technique for Bottomland Hardwood Functions*. U.S. EPA, Office of Wetlands Protection, Washington, D.C.

Anderson, J.R., et al. 1976. "A Land Use and Land Cover Classification System for Use with Remote Sensor Data." Professional Paper No. 964. U.S. Geological Survey, Denver, Colo.

Bain, M.B., et al. 1985. *Cumulative Impact Assessment: Evaluating the Environmental Effects of Multiple Human Developments*. ANL/EES-TM-309. Argonne National Laboratory, Argonne, Ill.

Bleecker, M., J.L. Hutson, and S.W. Waltman. 1990. "Mapping Groundwater Contamination Potential Using Integrated Simulation Modeling and GIS." In *Proceedings, Application of Geographic Information Systems, Simulation Models, and Knowledge-Based Systems for Landuse Management*, pp. 319–328. Department of Agricultural Engineering, Virginia Polytechnic and State University, Blacksburg, Va.

Bliss, N.B., and W.U. Reybold. 1989. "Small-Scale Digital Soil Maps for Interpreting Natural Resources." *Journal of Soil and Water Conservation* 44:30–34.

Brinson, M.M. 1989. "Strategies for Assessing the Cumulative Effects of Wetland Alteration on Water Quality." *Environmental Management* 12:655–662.

———. 1991. Testimony at a hearing before the Subcommittee on Environmental Protection of the Committee on Environment and Public Works, U.S. Senate, April 9, 1991.

Brinson, M.M., and L.C. Lee. 1989. "In-Kind Mitigation for Wetland Loss: Statement of Ecological Issues and Evaluation of Examples." In R.R. Sharitz and J.W. Gibbons (eds.), *Freshwater Wetlands and Wildlife: Proceedings of a Symposium*, CONF-8603101 (NTIS No. DE9005384), pp. 1069–085.

U.S. Department of Energy, Office of Scientific and Technical Information, Oak Ridge, Tenn.

Brody, M., and E. Pendelton. 1987. *FORFLO: A Model to Predict Changes in Bottomland Hardwood Forests*. National Wetlands Research Center, U.S. Fish and Wildlife Service, Slidell, La.

Brooks, R.P., et. al. 1991. "A methodology for biological monitoring of cumulative impacts on wetland, stream, and riparian components of watersheds." In J.A. Kusler and S. Daly (eds.), *Proceedings of an International Symposium: Wetlands and River Corridor Management*, pp. 387–398. Association of Wetland Managers, Inc., Berne, NY.

Brown, M., and J.J. Dinsmore. 1986. "Implications of Marsh Size and Isolation for Marsh Bird Management." *Journal of Wildlife Management* 50(3):392–397.

Brown, M.T., J. Schaefer, and K. Brandt. 1989. *Buffer Zones for Water, Wetlands, and Wildlife in the East Central Florida Region*. Center for Wetlands, University of Florida, Gainesville, Fla.

Brunner, G.W. 1988. *Comparison of Modeling Techniques for Wetland Areas*. Project Report 88-4. Hydrologic Engineering Center, U.S. Army Corps of Engineers, Davis, Calif.

Burdick, D.M., et al. 1989. "Faunal Changes and Bottomland Hardwood Forest Loss in the Tensas Watershed, Louisiana." *Conservation Biology* 3:282–291.

Cable, T.T., V. Brack, Jr., and V.R. Holmes. 1989. "Simplified Method for Wetland Habitat Assessment." *Environmental Management* 13:207–213.

Chescheir, G.M., et al. 1988. "Hydrology of Wetland Buffer Areas for Pumped Agricultural Drainage Water." In D.D. Hook et al. (eds.), *The Ecology and Management of Wetlands*, pp. 260–274. Croom Helm, Portland, Ore.

Childers, D.L., and J.G. Gosselink. 1990. "Assessment of Cumulative Impacts to Water Quality in a Forested Wetland Landscape." *Journal of Environmental Quality* 19:455–464.

Costanza, R., and F.H. Sklar. 1985. "Articulation, Accuracy and Effectiveness of Mathematical Models: A Review of Freshwater Wetland Applications." *Ecological Modelling* 27:45–68.

Cowardin, L.M., et al. 1979. *Classification of Wetlands and Deepwater Habitats of the United States*. FWS/OBS-79/31. U.S. Fish and Wildlife Service, Washington, D.C.

——. 1988. *Applications of a Simulation Model to Decisions in Mallard Management*. Fish and Wildlife Technical Report 17, U.S. Fish and Wildlife Service, Washington, D.C.

Crumpacker, D.W., et al. 1988. "A Preliminary Assessment of the Status of Major Terrestrial and Wetland Ecosystems on Federal and Indian Lands in the United States." *Conservation Biology* 2:103–115.

Curran, R.P., D.J. Bogucki, and G.K. Gruendling. 1989. "Adirondack wetland inventory for regulatory and ecological purposes using modified NWI techniques." In R.R. Sharitz and J.W. Gibbons (eds.), *Freshwater Wetlands and Wildlife: Proceedings of a Symposium*, CONF-8603101 (NTIS No. DE9005384), pp. 801–809. U.S. Department of Energy, Office of Scientific and Technical Information, Oak Ridge, Tenn.

Dahl, T.E. 1990. *Wetlands Losses in the United States, 1780s to 1980s*. U.S. Fish and Wildlife Service, Washington, D.C.

DeVries, J.J. 1980. *Effects of Floodplain Encroachments on Peak Flow*. Water Resources Support Center, U.S. Army Corps of Engineers, Davis, Calif.

Dreher, D.W., G.C. Schaefer, and D.L. Hey. 1989. *Evaluation of Stormwater Detention Effectiveness in Northeastern Illinois*. Northeastern Illinois Planning Commission, Chicago, Ill.

Faulkner, S.P., W.H. Patrick, Jr., and R.P. Gambrell. 1989. "Field Techniques for Measuring Wetland Soil Parameters." *Soil Science Society of America Journal* 53:883–890.

Field, D.W., et al. 1991. *Coastal Wetlands of the United States: An Accounting of a Valuable National Resource*. Strategic Assessment Branch, National Ocean and Atmospheric Administration, Washington, D.C.

Frayer, W.E., D.D. Peters, and H.R. Pywell. 1989. *Wetlands of the California Central Valley: Status and Trends*. U.S. Department of the Interior, U.S. Fish and Wildlife Service, Portland, Ore.

Frederick, R.B. 1983. "Developing an Energetics Model for Waterfowl Refuge Management." In W.K. Lauenroth, G.V. Skogerboe, and M. Flug (eds.), *Analysis of Ecological Systems: State-of-the-Art in Ecological Modeling*, pp. 253–257. Elsevier, N.Y.

George, T.A., and J. Choate. 1989. "A First Look at the 1987 National Resources Inventory." *Journal of Soil and Water Conservation* 44:555–556.

Gosselink, J.G., et al. 1990. "Landscape Conservation in a Forested Wetland Watershed: Can We Manage Cumulative Impacts?" *BioScience* 40:588–600.

Gosselink, J.G., and R.E. Turner. 1978. "The Role of Hydrology in Freshwater Ecosystems." In R.E. Good, D.F. Whigham, and R.L. Simpson (eds.), *Freshwater Wetlands*, pp. 63–78. Academic Press, N.Y.

Granger, Teri, 1989. *A Guide to Conducting Wetlands Inventories*. Washington State Department of Ecology.

Guertin, D.P., P.K. Barten, and K.N. Brooks. 1987. "The Peatland Hydrologic Impact Model: Development and Testing." *Nordic Hydrology* 18:79–100.

Gunderson, L. 1989. "Historical Hydropatterns in Wetland Communities of Everglades National Park." In R.R. Sharitz and J.W. Gibbons (eds.), *Freshwater Wetlands and Wildlife: Proceedings of a Symposium*, CONF-8603101 (NTIS No. DE90005384), pp. 1099–112. U.S. Department of Energy, Office of Scientific and Technical Information, Oak Ridge, Tenn.

Hammer, D.E., and R.H. Kadlec. 1986. "A Model of Wetland Surface Water Dynamics." *Water Resources Research* 22(13):1951–958.

Heliotis, F.D., and C.B. DeWitt. 1987. "Rapid Water Table Responses to Rainfall in a Northern Peatland Ecosystem." *Water Resources Bulletin* 23:1011-016.

Holland, C.C., and M.E. Kentula. 1991. *The Permit Tracking System (PTS): A Users Manual.* EPA/600/8-91/054. U.S. Environmental Protection Agency, Environmental Research Laboratory, Corvallis, Oregon.

Hollands, G.G. 1987. "Hydrogeologic Classification of Wetlands in Glaciated Regions." In J. Kusler (ed.), *Wetland Hydrology: Proceedings from a National Wetland Symposium*, pp. 26–30. Association of Wetland Managers, Berne, N.Y.

Hughes, R.M., E.P. Larsen, and J.M. Omerik. 1986. "Regional Reference Sites." A method for assessing stream potentials. *Environment Management* 10(5):629–635.

Johnston, C.A., et al. 1988. "Geographic Information Systems for Cumulative Impact Assessment." *Photogrammetric Engineering and Remote Sensing* 54:1609–615.

———. 1990a. "The Cumulative Effect of Wetlands on Stream Water Quality and Quantity: A Landscape Perspective." *Biogeochemistry* 10:105–141.

———. 1990b. "Sediment and Nutrient Retention by Freshwater Wetlands: Effects on Surface Water Quality." Contribution 77, *CRC Reviews in Environmental Control.* Center for Water and the Environment, Natural Resources Research Institute, University of Minnesota, Duluth, Minn.

Jones, J.R., B.R. Borofka, and R.W. Bachmann. 1976. "Factors Affecting Nutrient Loads in Some Iowa Streams." *Water Research* 10:117–122.

Kadlec, J.A. 1984. "Hydrology." In E.J. Murkin and H.R. Murkin (eds.), *Marsh Ecology Research Program: Long-Term Monitoring Procedures Manual*, Technical Bulletin 2, pp. 8–11. Delta Waterfowl Research Station, Portage la Prairie, Manitoba, Canada.

Kadlec, R.H. 1988. "Monitoring Wetland Responses." In J. Zelazny and J.S. Feierabend (eds.), *Increasing Our Wetland Resources*, pp. 114–120. National Wildlife Federation, Washington, D.C.

Kadlec, R.H., and D.E. Hammer. 1988. "Modeling Nutrient Behavior in Wetlands." *Ecological Modelling* 40:37–66.

Kiraly, S.J., F.A. Cross, and J.D. Buffington (eds.). 1990. "Federal Coastal Wetland Mapping Programs." *Biological Report* 90(18). U.S. Fish and Wildlife Service, Washington, D.C.

Kundell, J.E., and S.W. Woolf. 1986. *Georgia Wetlands: Trends and Policy Options.* University of Georgia Press, Athens, Ga.

Kusler, J.A., and P. Riexinger (eds.). 1986. *Proceedings of the National Wetland Assessment Symposium.* Association of State Wetland Managers, Albany, N.Y.

LaBaugh, J.W. 1986. "Wetland Ecosystem Studies from a Hydrologic Perspective." *Water Resources Bulletin* 22(1):1–10.

Lettenmaier, D.P., et al. 1991. "Trends in Stream Quality in the Continental United States, 1978–1987." *Water Resources Research* 27:327–339.

Lonard, R.I., et al. 1981. *Analysis of Methodologies for Assessing Wetlands Values.* U.S. Water Resources Council, Washington, D.C., and Corps of Engineers, Vicksburg, Miss.

Lugo, A.E., M.M. Brinson, and S. Brown (eds.). 1990. *Forested Wetlands.* Elsevier, N.Y.

Marble, A.D. 1990. *A Guide to Wetland Functional Design.* FHWA-IP-90-010. Federal Highway Administration, U.S. Department of Transportation, Washington, D.C.

McWilliams, W.H., and J.F. Rosson, Jr. 1990. "Composition and Vulnerability of Bottomland Hardwood Forests of the Coastal Plain Province in the South Central United States." *Forest Ecology Management* 33/34:485–501.

Missouri Department of Conservation and USDA Soil Conservation Service. 1991. *Wildlife Habitat Appraisal Guide (WHAG)*. Missouri Department of Conservation, Jefferson City, Mo.

Mitsch, W.J., and J.G. Gosselink. 1986. *Wetlands*. Van Nostrand Reinhold, N.Y.

Mitsch, W.J., M. Straskraba, and S.E. Jorgensen. 1988. *Wetland Modelling*. Elsevier, N.Y.

Novitzki, R.P. 1979. "The Hydrologic Characteristics of Wisconsin Wetlands and Their Influence on Floods, Streamflow, and Sediment." In P.E. Greeson, J.R. Clark, and J.E. Clark (eds.), *Wetland Functions and Values: The State of Our Understanding*, pp. 377–388. American Water Resources Association, Minneapolis, Minn.

O'Brien, A.L., and W.S. Motts. 1980. "Hydrogeologic Evaluation of Wetland Basins for Land Use Planning." *Water Resources Bulletin* 16:785–789.

Ogawa, H., and J.W. Male. 1983. *The Flood Mitigation Potential of Inland Wetlands*. Water Resources Research Center, University of Massachusetts, Amherst, Mass.

O'Neil, L.J., T.M. Pullen, Jr., and R.L. Schroeder. 1991. "A Wildlife Community Habitat Evaluation Model for Bottomland Hardwood Forests in the Southeastern United States." U.S. Army Corps of Engineers Waterways Experiment Station, Vicksburg, Miss.

Pavelis, G.A. (ed.). 1987. *Farm Drainage in the United States: History, Status, and Prospects*. Miscellaneous Publication No. 1455. USDA Economic Research Service, Washington, D.C.

Rosenberry, D.O. 1990. "Inexpensive Groundwater Monitoring Methods for Determining Hydrologic Budgets of Lakes and Wetlands." In *Proceedings of a Conference on Enhacing the State's Lake and Wetland Management Programs*, pp. 123–131. Northeast Illinois Planning Commission, Chicago, Ill.

Rosgen, D.L. 1985. "A Stream Classification System." In R.R. Johnson et al., *Riparian Ecosystems and Their Management: Reconciling Conflicting Uses*, General Technical Report RM-120, pp. 91–95. USDA Forest Service, Fort Collins, Colo.

Scott, J.M. et al. 1987. "Species Richness: A Geographic Approach to Protecting Future Biological Diversity." *BioScience* 37:782–788.

———. 1990. *Gap Analysis: Protecting Biodiversity Using Geographic Information Systems*. Idaho Cooperative Fisheries and Wildlife Research Unit, University of Idaho, Moscow, Idaho.

Shaw, S.P., and C.G. Fredine. 1956. "Wetlands of the United States." Circular 39. U.S. Fish and Wildlife Service, Washington, D.C.

Simenstad, C.A., C.D. Tanner, and R.M. Thom. 1989. *Estuarine Wetland Restoration Monitoring Protocol*. Fisheries Research Institute, University of Washington, Seattle, Wash.

Smith, P.G.R., and J.B. Theberge. 1987. "Evaluating Natural Areas Using Multiple Criteria: Theory and Practice." *Environmental Management* 11:447–460.

Southerland, M., A. Hirsch, and A. King. 1991. *Compilation of Natural Resources Priority Listings*. Office of Policy, Planning, and Evaluation, U.S. Environmental Protection Agency, Washington, D.C.

Tiedje, J.M. 1982. "Denitrification." *Methods of Soil Analysis*. Part 2: *Chemical and Microbiological Properties*, pp. 1011–026. Agronomy Monograph No. 9 (2nd ed.). ASA-SSSA, Madison, Wis.

Tiedje, J.M., J. Sorensen, and Y.-Y.L. Chang. 1981. "Assimilatory and Dissimilatory Nitrate Reduction: Perspectives and Methodology for Simultaneous Measurement of Several Nitrogen Cycle Processes." *Ecological Bulletin* 33:331–342.

Tiner, R.W., Jr. 1984. *Wetlands of the United States: Current Status and Recent Trends*. U.S. Fish and Wildlife Service, National Wetlands Inventory, Washington, D.C.

———. 1985. *Wetlands of New Jersey.* National Wetlands Inventory, U.S. Fish and Wildlife Service, Newton Corner, Mass.

Tiner, R.W., Jr., and J.T. Finn. 1986. *Status and Recent Trends of Wetlands in Five Mid-Atlantic States.* U.S. Fish and Wildlife Service and U.S. Environmental Protection Agency, Newton Corner, Mass., and Philadelphia, Pa.

Usher, M.B. (ed.). 1986. *Wildlife Conservation Evaluation.* Chapman and Hall, London.

U.S. Army Corps of Engineers, Lower Mississippi Valley Division. 1980. *Habitat Evaluation System (HES).* U.S. Army Corps of Engineers, Vicksburg, Miss.

USDA Soil Conservation Service. 1991. *Hydric Soils of the United States.* Soil Conservation Service, U.S. Department of Agriculture, Washington, D.C.

U.S. Environmental Protection Agency (EPA). 1983. *The Effects of Wastewater Treatment Facilities on Wetlands in the Midwest.* Appendix A: *Technical Support Document.* EPA-905/3-83-002. U.S. EPA Region 5, Chicago, Ill.

———. 1985. *Freshwater Wetlands for Wastewater Management Handbook.* Chapter 9: *Assessment Techniques and Data Sources.* EPA 904/9-85-135. U.S. EPA Region 4, Atlanta, Ga.

———. 1990a. *Biological Criteria: National Program Guidance for Surface Waters.* EPA 440/5-90-004. Office of Water Regulations and Standards, U.S. EPA, Washington, D.C.

———. 1990b. *Water Quality Standards for Wetlands: National Guidance.* EPA 440/S-90-011. Office of Water Regulations and Standards, U.S. EPA, Washington, D.C.

U.S. Fish and Wildlife Service. 1980. *Habitat Evaluation Procedures (HEP) Manual* (102ESM). U.S. Fish and Wildlife Service, Washington, D.C.

Welcomme, R.L. 1979. *Fisheries Ecology of Floodplain Rivers.* Longman, N.Y.

Williams, R.D., and E.D. Lavey. 1986. *Selected Buffer Strip References.* USDA Water Quality and Watershed Research Laboratory, Durant, Okla.

Winter, T.C. 1977. "Classification of the Hydrologic Settings of Lakes in the North Central United States." *Water Resources Research* 13:753–767.

———. 1981. "Uncertainties in Estimating the Water Balance of Lakes." *Water Resources Bulletin* 17(1):82–115.

Zimmerman, J.H. 1988. "A Multi-Purpose Wetland Characterization Procedure, Featuring the Hydroperiod." In *Proceedings of the National Wetland Symposium: Wetland Hydrology,* ASWM Technical Report 6, pp. 31–49. Association of Wetland Managers, Berne, N.Y.

Appendixes

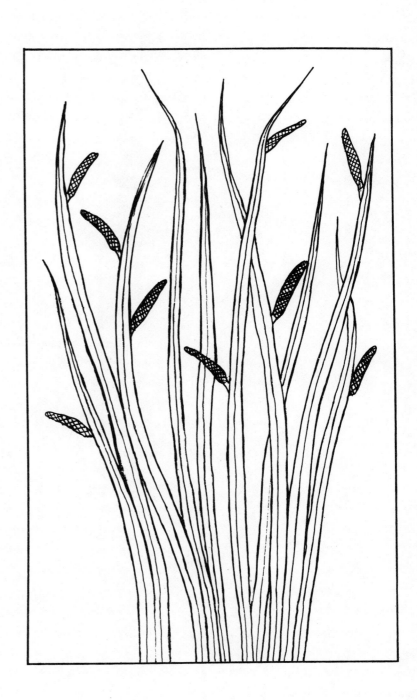

Existing No Net Loss Goals

STATE GOALS

Illinois

Citation:

Interagency Wetlands Policy Act of 1989
Ill. Rev. Stat. ch. 95.5, para. 97 (1989)

Excerpt:

Section 1-4, State Goal: It shall be the goal of the State that there be **no overall net loss*** of the State's existing wetland acres or their functional value due to State supported activities. Further, State agencies shall preserve, enhance and create wetlands where necessary in order to increase the quality and quantity of the State's wetland resource base.

Comments:

The no net loss goal of the Interagency Wetlands Policy Act applies to all state and state-supported activities.

*Bold face emphasis has been added to excerpts throughout this appendix.

Contact:

Illinois Department of Conservation
524 South Second Street
Lincoln Tower Plaza
Springfield, IL 62706
(217) 782-3715

Louisiana

Citation:

Coastal Wetlands Conservation and Restoration
  Plan
House and Senate Committees on Natural
  Resources
Fiscal Year 1990–91

Excerpt:

Coastal Wetlands Conservation and Restoration Policy: The following policy statements are not rules or regulations, but rather are intended to generally guide the state's future coastal wetland conservation and restoration efforts, including structural, management, and institutional programs.

Section 2: It is the policy of the state to aggressively identify and implement projects and programs to offset coastal vegetated wetland losses that have resulted from past human activities and ongoing natural processes. It would be inappropriate, then, to allow future permitted developments that adversely impact coastal vegetated wetlands to go unmitigated. Accordingly, this state shall initiate the development of rules (via the Administrative Procedure Act process) and/or legislation, that would define and establish procedures needed to achieve, at a minimum, compensation for coastal wetland functional values lost due to future permitted activities.

Comments:

Louisiana's policy is designed to prevent future coastal wetland losses and to offset current losses. The state has enacted legislation to promote regulations that provide, at a minimum, for the replacement of lost functional coastal wetland values resulting from permitted activities in the coastal zone and to ensure that federal activities are consistent with the federally approved Louisiana Coastal Resources Program.

Contact:

Coastal Restoration Division
Louisiana Department of Natural Resources
P.O. Box 94396
Baton Rouge, LA 70804
(504) 342-7285

Maine

Citation:

Natural Resources Protection Act
Me. Rev. Stat. Ann. tit. 38, §480A–U (1990)
Chapter 310, Wetland Protection Rules (adopted 6/13/90)

Excerpt:

A. *Preamble*: In recognition of the important roles of wetlands in our natural environment, the Board of Environmental Protection supports the nationwide goal of **no net loss** of wetland functions and values. In some cases, however, the level of mitigation necessary to achieve no net loss of wetlands will not be practicable, or will have an insignificant effect in protecting the State's wetlands resources. In other cases, the preservation of unprotected wetlands or adjacent uplands may achieve a greater level of protection to the environment than would be achieved by strict application of a no net loss standard through creation of replacement wetlands.

Therefore, the Board recognizes that a loss in wetland functions and values may not be avoided in every instance.

Comments:

Maine's wetlands rules endorse the national goal of no net loss, but the state does not require adherence to this goal within its own regulatory program.

Contact:

Department of Environmental Protection
Bureau of Land Quality Control
State House Station 17
Augusta, ME 04333
(207) 289-2111

Massachusetts

Citation:

Water Resources Commission
No Net Loss of Wetlands Policy (adopted 4/9/90)

Excerpt:

Goals: In the short-term, there shall be **no net loss** of wetlands in Massachusetts. In the long-term, there shall be an increase in the quantity and quality of the Commonwealth's wetlands resource base.

Policy: To achieve these goals, it is the Commonwealth's policy to:
- identify, assess, and preserve existing wetlands resources and to restore degraded wetlands resources. . .
- when proposed activities would degrade the quality or quantity of wetlands, the maximum protection possible shall be afforded in accordance with the following hierarchical paradigm of avoidance; minimization; and mitigation. . . .

Comments:

The no net loss policy of the Water Resources Commission is not a mandatory goal but an advisory one that applies to all state activities, agencies, and programs.

Contact:

Executive Office of Environmental Affairs
100 Cambridge Street
Boston, MA 02202
(617) 727-9800

Maryland

Citation:
Natural Resources Article
Md. Nat. Res. Code Ann. §8-1201 et seq. (1989)

Excerpt:
(b) Statewide program for protection, etc.: goals:
It is the intent of the General Assembly to protect
the waters of the State through a comprehensive,
statewide nontidal wetland program in cooperation with federal agencies, other states, and local
government. The goal of the program shall be to
attain **no net overall loss** in nontidal wetland
acreage and function and to strive for a net resource
gain in nontidal wetlands over present conditions.

Comments:
The Nontidal Wetlands Protection Act requires no
net loss of nontidal wetlands in the state regulatory
program. In implementing the no net loss goal, the
act provides the Department of Natural Resources
with the authority to enforce strict permitting and
mitigation requirements. It also allows for comprehensive watershed planning and a Nontidal
Wetlands Compensation Fund dedicated to the
creation, restoration, and enhancement of nontidal
wetlands.

Contact:
Maryland Department of Natural Resources
Nontidal Wetlands Division
Tawes State Office Building
Annapolis, MD 21401
(410) 974-3841

Minnesota

Citation:
Executive Order 91-3
Directing State Departments and Agencies to
Follow a "No Net Loss" Policy in Regard to
Wetlands (issued 1/17/91)

Excerpt:
A. All responsible departments and agencies of
the State of Minnesota shall protect, enhance, and
restore Minnesota's wetlands to the fullest extent
of their authority;

B. All responsible departments and agencies of
the State of Minnesota shall operate to the fullest

extent of their authority under the strict concept
of **"NO-NET LOSS"** of wetlands of the state in
regard to projects under their jurisdiction. . . .

Comments:
This executive order applies the no net loss goal
to all state activities affecting wetlands.

Contact:
Minnesota Department of Natural Resources
Section of Wildlife
Box 7
500 Lafayette Road
Saint Paul, MN 55155
(612) 296-3344

New Jersey

Citation:
Freshwater Wetlands Protection Act
N.J. Stat. Ann. §13:1b–1 et seq. (West 1987)

Excerpt:
Section 13(a): The department [Department of
Environmental Protection] shall require as a condition of a freshwater permit that all appropriate
measures have been carried out to mitigate adverse
environmental impacts, restore vegetation, habitats,
and land and water features, prevent sedimentation and erosion, minimize the area of freshwater
wetland disturbance and insure compliance with
the Federal Act and implementing regulations.

Section 13(b): The department may require the
creation or restoration of an area of freshwater
wetlands of **equal ecological value** to those which
will be lost, and shall determine whether the creation or restoration of freshwater wetlands is conducted onsite or offsite. The department shall
accept and evaluate a proposal to create or restore
an area of freshwater wetlands only after the department has evaluated the permit application for which
the proposal is made, and shall evaluate the proposal to create or restore an area of freshwater
wetlands independently of the permit application.

Comments:
The Freshwater Wetlands Protection Act's approach
to the goal of no net loss depends on the type of
activity imposed on the wetlands. Minor encroachments on the wetlands are allowed without mitigation, but any activity causing adverse impacts must

be mitigated. DEP prefers on-site mitigation, but it may permit off-site mitigation or contributions to the Wetlands Mitigation Bank when on-site mitigation is not feasible. However, permit applications are evaluated independently of mitigation measures, preventing the trading of mitigation for permits. The purpose of the mitigation guidelines within the act is to protect the values and functions of wetlands.

Contact:
Bureau of Regulation
Division of Coastal Resources
Department of Environmental Protection
CN 401
Trenton, NJ 08625
(609) 292-0060

North Dakota

Citation:
North Dakota Wetlands Protection Law
N.D. Cent. Code §61-32-01 et seq. (1987)

Excerpt:
Section 4: The state engineer and the commissioner must jointly find that the wetland acres proposed to be drained will be replaced by an equal acreage of replacement wetlands, or through debits to the wetland bank as provided in section 6 of this Act, before any permit for drainage can be approved by the state engineer or water resource board.

Comments:
The North Dakota Wetlands Protection Law requires acre-for-acre replacement of drained wetlands (located in watersheds of 80 acres or more) or an equivalent deduction from a wetlands bank that records credits and debits for restoration and drainage of wetlands.

Contact:
Office of the State Engineer
900 East Boulevard
Bismarck, ND 58505
(701) 224-2752

Oregon

Citation:
Senate Bill 3
Or. Rev. Stat. §196.668–196.692 (1989)

Excerpt:
Section 3: It is the policy of the state of Oregon to: (1) Promote the protection, conservation and best use of wetland resources, their functions and values through the integration and close coordination of statewide planning goals, local comprehensive plans and state and federal regulatory programs. . . . (4) Maintain a stable resource base through the mitigation of losses of wetland resources and the adoption of the procedural mitigation standard currently used by federal agencies. (5) Establish the opportunity to increase wetland resources by encouraging wetland restoration and creation where appropriate.

Comments:
Oregon's no net loss policy applies to all fill and removal activities that are regulated by the Division of State Lands. The policy is implemented through permit conditioning, mitigation monitoring, and actively prohibiting unauthorized activities.

Contact:
Oregon Division of State Lands
775 Summer Street, NE
Salem, OR 97310
(503) 378-3805

Vermont

Citation:
Vermont Wetland Rules
[As authorized in the Vermont Wetlands Act, Vt. Stat. Ann. tit. 10, §905:7, 8, 9 (1986)] (adopted 2/7/90)

Excerpt:
Section 1-1, Purpose and Authority:
It is the policy of the State of Vermont to identify and protect significant wetlands and the values and functions which they serve in such a manner that the **goal of no net loss** of such wetlands and their functions is achieved.

Comments:
The Vermont Wetlands Rules specifically protect the functions and values of wetlands. The rules divide wetlands into three categories, defining Classes One and Two as significant and Class Three as not significant or not yet mapped by the National Wetlands Inventory. The significance of a wetland

is based on whether it fulfills one or more of the 10 functions outlined within the rules (Class Three wetlands are not under the jurisdiction of the rules because they do not fulfill any of these functions or have not yet been evaluated). For Class One and Two wetlands, compensation plans must yield a no net loss of the wetlands functions or acreage.

Contact:
Vermont Wetlands Office
Division of Water Quality
103 South Main Street
Waterbury, VT 05671
(802) 244-6951

Washington

Citation:
Exec. Order 89-10
Protection of Wetlands (issued 12/11/89)

Excerpt:
Section 1: It is the interim goal of my administration to achieve **no overall net loss** in acreage and function of Washington's remaining wetlands base. It is further the long-term goal to increase the quantity and quality of Washington's wetlands resource base.

Section 2: In the interest of preserving and protecting valuable resources, the Department of Ecology shall provide guidance and each affected state agency shall provide to the Governor an action plan, where appropriate, to lessen the destruction, loss, or degradation of wetlands and to preserve and enhance the natural and beneficial values of wetlands.

Comments:
The executive order directs state agencies to identify impacts on wetlands resulting from their activities and to seek opportunities for wetlands protection in working toward the no net loss goal.

Contact:
Shoreland & Coastal Zone Management Program
Department of Ecology
Baran Hall, Room 101
Mail Stop PV-11
Olympia, WA 98504
(206) 459-6790

Citation:
Coastal Wetlands Planning, Protection and
    Restoration Act, 1990
P.L. 101-646, 16 U.S.C.A. 3951

Excerpt:
Section 303(b)(2): The purpose of the restoration plan is to develop a comprehensive approach to restore and prevent the loss of coastal wetlands in Louisiana. Such plan shall coordinate and integrate coastal wetlands restoration projects in a manner that will ensure the long-term conservation of the coastal wetlands of Louisiana.

Section 304(b), Conservation Plan Goal: If a conservation plan is developed pursuant to this section, it shall have a goal of achieving **no net loss** of wetlands in the coastal areas of Louisiana as a result of development activities initiated subsequent to approval of the plan, exclusive of any wetlands gains achieved through implementation of the preceding section of this title.

Comments:
The no net loss goal in Louisiana's Conservation Plan applies only to regulated activities within coastal areas of Louisiana. Section 303(b)(2) is designed to establish a comprehensive plan for restoration and management of wetlands, while Section 304(b) delineates a no net loss program to prevent future wetlands degradation. A state task force, established under Louisiana's Public Law 101-646, is currently identifying and assigning priority to restoration projects for the state legislature to approve.

Contact:
Coastal Restoration Division
Louisiana Department of Natural Resources
P.O. Box 94396
Baton Rouge, LA 70804
(504) 342-7285

Citation:
Water Resources Development Act of 1990
P.L. 101-640, 33 U.S.C.A. 2317

Excerpt:

Section 307(a)(1), Goals: There is established, as part of the Corps of Engineers water resources development program, an interim goal of **no overall net loss** of the Nation's remaining wetlands base, as defined by acreage and function, and a long-term goal to increase the quality and quantity of the Nation's wetlands, as defined by acreage and function.

Contact:

U.S. Army Corps of Engineers
20 Massachusetts Avenue, NW
CECW-OR
Washington, DC 20314-1000
(202) 272-1780

Citation:

Wetlands Action Plan, 1989
U.S. Environmental Protection Agency

Excerpt:

Goal to Protect the Nation's Wetlands: U.S. EPA has adopted the goal of the National Wetlands Policy Forum to achieve **no overall net loss** of the nation's remaining wetland base, as defined by acreage and function; and to restore and create wetlands, where feasible, to increase the quality and quantity of the nation's wetlands resource base. Consistent with this goal, EPA will review and, when necessary, revise its programs to protect the chemical, physical, and biological integrity of wetlands.

Comments:

To promote the goal of no net loss, the Wetlands Action Plan outlines activities for EPA to execute. This includes technical support to state and local governments developing protection plans for wetlands.

Contact:

EPA Wetlands Division A-104F
401 M Street, SW
Washington, DC 20460
(202) 260-9043

Examining Existing Programs

DECIDING WHICH PROGRAMS TO EXAMINE

A thorough overview of existing programs should include the private sector as well as regulatory and nonregulatory government programs that affect wetlands. Part III of this guidebook includes descriptions of federal, state, local, and private programs that may be included in an overview.

An examination of existing programs need not be detailed, but it should gather information that will provide a clear picture of the existing situation. If more specific information is required at a later date, it can be obtained through the existing network. Because a thorough examination requires time, personnel, and budgetary resources, it should be as streamlined as possible.

SUGGESTED INFORMATION TO COLLECT

Program-specific information in the categories presented below should generate a useful set of overviews of available opportunities for improving wetlands protection efforts—and should also highlight any impediments. It is a good idea to date the information as it is gathered in order to ensure that each program's overview is current and accurate.

Program Name
Authority
The statutory or administrative authority guiding the program.

Administering Agency or Group
The entity that administers each program, along with other groups that have partial jurisdiction or assist in official or voluntary roles.

Contact
A contact person at each agency or group, including title, responsibility, and brief summary of the person's interest and potential involvement in the wetlands strategy.

Constituency
The constituency or "client" to whom the program is directed.

Program Type
The positive/negative and direct/indirect effects on wetlands (represented by $+/-$, D/I) of each program, including:
- *programs directed at wetlands protection (+, D) that have been developed specifically for wetlands or have become wetlands-protection programs (for example, the Clean Water Act, state wetlands acts);*
- *programs with indirect wetlands benefits*

Program	Description	Agency or Group and Contact
1. Land Acquisition Programs	Administered by the Game Div.; primarily includes duck stamp revenues ($1.5 million) to acquire waterfowl habitat—also $800,000 from hunting licenses for general land acquisition. Has $18,000,000 in one-time funding; wetlands given high priority.	LA Wildlife and Fisheries Dept. Tommy Prickett (504) 765-2811
2. Natural Heritage Program	Primary mission is the identifying, indexing of unique natural habitats in Louisiana (including some wetlands).	LA Wildlife and Fisheries Dept. Tommy Prickett (504) 765-2811
3. Refuge Division	Includes approximately 180,000 acres of coastal wetland in four separate refuges. Primary purpose is to provide for wintering waterfowl.	LA Wildlife and Fisheries Dept. Tommy Prickett (504) 765-2811
4. LA Natural and Scenic Rivers	Provides a system to designate rivers, streams and for protection from certain forms of destruction.	LA Wildlife and Fisheries Dept. Blue Watson (504) 765-2369
5. LA Coastal Wetlands Conservation and Restoration Program	An action program that establishes specific coastal restoration, conservation projects through an annual updated plan to be approved by the legislature. Established by Act 6-1989.	Coastal Activities Office, Office of the Governor David Chambers (504) 342-6493
6. Endangered Species Act Program	Protects habitat and the endangered species from encroachment by development and other activities. Example: turtle exclusion devices.	FWS Gerry Bodin (318) 264-6630
7. Coastal Barriers Resources Act (COBRA)	Prevents federal support (flood insurance) of development of coastal areas.	FWS Gerry Bodin (318) 264-6630
8. "404" Program	Through the Fish and Wildlife Coordination Act, COE is required to obtain FWS review of all 404 permits.	FWS Gerry Bodin (318) 264-6630

... (Etc.)

Programs (Sample)

Positive or Negative Program	Program Type	Type of Loss	Resources	Limitation or Problems	Geographical Coverage
+	1	Human activity	Approximately $20 million for land acquisition	Budgetary limitations	Statewide
+	1	Human activity	Five-person staff $400,000 budget	Budgetary limitations	Statewide
+	1	Human activity	42-person staff $2,400,000 budget	Permitting problems	Statewide
+	1	Human activity	Two-person staff $50,000	Staff limitations Equipment & budgetary limitations	Statewide
+	1	All natural and prior human activity	Wetlands Trust Fund $28 million Wetlands Task Force Coastal Wetlands Conservation & Restoration Plan high profile, popular program		Coastal basins
+	1	Human activity	Three-person staff		Statewide
+	1	Development activities	One-person staff		Coastal zone
+	1	Development activities	Three-person staff	Permit system needs improvement & streamlining	Statewide

... (Etc.)

Program Type

1 Programs that are directed at wetlands protection
2 Programs that have indirect wetlands applications

Arizona's Riparian Area Survey

Spurred by a decline in riparian resources resulting from the cumulative effects of water diversion and development, Arizona Governor Rose Mofford issued an executive order in 1989 to form an interagency Riparian Habitat Task Force. The group's mission was to "identify and make recommendations for the development of management tools for protection, conservation, enhancement and, when appropriate, restoration of Arizona's riparian resources."

The task force's efforts focused in part on current and proposed activities of federal, state, and local agencies and Native American tribes whose programs affect riparian areas or manage lands associated with these areas. By surveying a representative group of agencies and tribes, the task force identified how the policies, actions, requirements, and funding of these groups affected riparian resources.

The Survey

The Riparian Habitat Task Force surveyed a representative group of county, state, and federal agencies and Native American tribes, as shown below:

Federal
- Soil Conversation Service
- Forest Service
- National Park Service
- Geological Survey
- Bureau of Reclamation
- Agricultural Stabilization Conservation Service
- Bureau of Land Management
- Army Corps of Engineers
- Cooperative Extension Services
- Fish and Wildlife Service
- Environmental Protection Agency

State
- State Parks
- Office of Tourism
- Game and Fish Department
- State Land Department
- Department of Water Resources
- Department of Environmental Quality
- Department of Commerce
- Department of Transportation
- Geological Survey
- Department of Agriculture

Tribes
- Several Arizona Native American Tribes

Local
- Pima County Transportation and Flood Control District
- Flood Control District of Maricopa County

(+, I) that may not have been intended for wetlands protection but whose activities can be used to protect wetlands (for example, floodplain programs, stormwater and watershed management programs);

- *programs that directly hinder wetlands protection (−, D)* (currently, few programs fall into this category, but in the past many government programs encouraged the drainage and development of wetlands); and
- *programs that indirectly hinder wetlands protection (−, I)* by causing unintentional or inadvertent negative effects (many public works projects fall into this category).

Type of Wetlands Loss Addressed

Activities causing wetlands loss: physical (e.g., filling), chemical (e.g., discharging pollutants), or biological (e.g., introducing exotic species). Existing regulatory and nonregulatory programs do not cover many of these activities. This information should help identify gaps in coverage and highlight areas in need of further attention. Comparing this information with the state's assessment of greatest threats to the wetlands resource can also help determine where to focus efforts.

Resources

Resources that might help (or hinder) a strategy's development and implementation, including human resources, in-kind services, money, political clout, and public profile.

Coordination

Existing mechanisms for coordination, if any, with other programs or agencies.

To obtain the relevant information about riparian ecosystem management, the task force distributed questionnaires to each group. The answers enabled the task force to develop summaries of agency and tribal activities and programs as well as the problems associated with riparian area management in Arizona. Examples of questions from the questionnaire follow:

— Please list and describe (1) laws and legal responsibilities, (2) regulations, (3) plans, (4) programs, (5) policies, and (6) other mechanisms of your agency that directly or indirectly relate to the protection and maintenance of riparian areas.

— Are there any *overlaps* between your agency's and other agencies' authorities, activities, plans, programs, etc., which affect aspects of riparian resources? What are they?

— What authorities, activities, plans, programs, etc., related to riparian resources do you have that *conflict* with other agencies?

Survey Responses

- None of the groups surveyed has specific statutory mandates to protect riparian ecosystems.
- The Arizona State Land Department has developed a strategic plan to minimize conflicts between development and ecosystem protection on state trust lands.
- Conflicts exist between federal and local agencies with overlapping jurisdiction. For example, the federal Bureau of Reclamation is not subject to local ordinances. This has often resulted in construction of structures that may increase flooding and erosion.
- Native American tribes have authority over riparian areas and wetlands on their reservations and are not subject to the jurisdiction of the Department of Water Quality.
- The groups surveyed view urban development; intensive recreation; grazing; lack of state statutes; lack of public awareness; and discharges from agriculture, industry, and municipalities as major threats to the riparian ecosystem.

The results of the survey have helped the state focus on the problems with current riparian protection and management and have suggested potential solutions. The survey has also assisted in identifying various groups that should participate in any riparian area protection and management strategy.

Specific Techniques

Techniques for accomplishing the program's mission (e.g., permits, zoning, tax incentives, etc.).

Important Features

Innovative ways to preserve wetlands, particularly good or bad features.

COMPILING INFORMATION

A matrix can be used to compile collected information, facilitating comparison of existing programs, identification of areas for possible coordination, identification of gaps in programs, and so on. (See "Matrix of Louisiana Programs [sample]".)

Computer data bases offer more sophisticated approaches to compiling program information. Based on a matrix-type format, data bases can call up fields of information to facilitate analysis. For example, all programs addressing wetlands drainage can be readily identified. Computer data bases are particularly helpful in storing and processing large amounts of information.

Developing a Monitoring and Evaluation Plan

This appendix presents steps for designing plans to monitor and evaluate wetlands strategies. The methodologies can be applied to specific strategy components as well as overall goals and objectives. These are general guidelines, not hard-and-fast blueprints; wetlands managers can tailor them for state-specific circumstances.

DEVELOPING A MONITORING PLAN

A monitoring plan allows wetlands managers to track measurable program results on a continuous basis. Monitoring provides rapid feedback (weekly or monthly) on program activities. Various aspects of a program can be monitored, ranging from costs to outcomes. The results can be used to identify problems, fine-tune implementation methods, and measure progress toward goals and objectives.

Designing a monitoring plan involves the following six steps.

Step 1

Identify Components to Monitor

The first step in developing a monitoring plan is to identify which program results or outcomes to measure in order to keep a "finger on the pulse" of the program. Measurement techniques are generally quantitative; thus, it must be possible to quantify or repeatedly measure outcomes over short periods of time. In addition to quantitative variables, however, monitoring may also cover issues related to quality control, drawing on the subjective perceptions of program participants.

Typical aspects of a program that can be monitored include:

- program costs,
- time involved at various stages in program implementation and overall,
- program penetration (i.e., number of participants relative to the eligible population), and
- outcomes (e.g., number of projects reviewed, acres preserved or altered, etc.).

Step 2

Develop a Reporting or Tracking Mechanism

Effective monitoring requires the ability to obtain and review program information quickly. This information can come from permits and authorizations; records from local, state, and federal agencies; site visits; and resource assessment studies that may cover areas larger than those covered by single programs.

A tracking system and an easily accessible data base facilitate monitoring progress and changes in programs. A tracking system provides access to information on current programs, while a data base compiles information that allows comparisons with previous programs or program results as well as the creation of cumulative status reports. The data base should be designed for easy updating, access, and selection with key variables used to sort data. The data will probably come from a variety of different sources (i.e., agencies or consultants) and will need to be standardized. Also, as in any data base design, the system should allow more variables to be added if new situations develop (such as changes in regulations) that require different information than originally anticipated.

Step 3
Specify Measurement Techniques

Perhaps the most difficult aspect of program monitoring, apart from defining what needs to be measured, is deciding how to measure progress or outcomes over time. Typically, monitoring objectives and techniques are closely tied to program objectives. Thus, if a program is designed to provide technical assistance to local government planners through training and site review assistance, a monitoring plan would track the number of training sessions and number of attendees along with the number and types of site reviews. In addition, local governments requesting the most assistance might also be tracked.

Generally, it makes sense to develop a monitoring plan first and then to specify measurement techniques and data needs. These techniques can range from simple review of written records to site visits and possibly site analysis. The level of complexity depends on the nature of the data required; more complex approaches often deal with larger amounts of information. (For these, it's best to develop data collection and recording protocols to ensure that data are collected in a consistent manner.)

Monitoring makes some people uneasy; it can appear to be a performance appraisal, which it isn't. Program managers can help set the stage for successful monitoring by informing staff about the monitoring effort and when it will occur. If outside consultants are used, program managers must ensure open access to program files and full cooperation from program staff.

Step 4
Specify Time Lines

Specific review periods for monitoring should be established. Ongoing tracking can be summarized in weekly, monthly, or quarterly reports. Monitoring visits or data reviews can occur either monthly or quarterly.

Monitoring time lines should be coordinated with evaluation activities to avoid duplication and to ensure that data collection efforts provide adequate information for both purposes. Other factors may influence the timing of monitoring, including political schedules, climate conditions (i.e., seasonal access), and so forth. In any case, the monitoring schedule should be set in advance so that it isn't overlooked during day-to-day program implementation.

Step 5
Select the Monitor

Monitoring can be conducted either in-house or by outside consultants. Using an outside consultant or neutral party is usually unnecessary, however, since monitoring provides only descriptive progress reports rather than more politically sensitive assessments of program effectiveness. In addition, the swift pace of monitoring activities and reporting is usually best handled by those involved with day-to-day activities of a program, and the audience for the monitoring results is usually internal program staff and managers. In cases where staff resources are limited, however, using an outside consultant can be helpful.

Step 6
Report Results

Reporting of monitoring results is a periodic summary of findings. The issuance of reports should be closely linked to the monitoring schedule and the needs of management. For internal staff needs, reports can be simple status reports or data-tracking summaries. Management reports can be more formal, with written discussions and suggested courses of action where appropriate.

It is important to note that monitoring activities may uncover violations of federal, state, or local regulations. Monitoring is not intended as an enforcement tool, however, and policy decisions should be made about how to treat such cases.

DEVELOPING AN EVALUATION PLAN

The following seven-step procedure for conducting evaluations (a comprehensive overview of program implementation and impacts) applies to both impact evaluations (quantitative evaluations that measure program outcomes) and process evaluations (qualitative evaluations that examine the context in which a program operates). As discussed below, in some cases the two types of evaluation occur concurrently; in other cases, they are staged for best results.

Step 1

Identify Key Aspects to Evaluate

As with monitoring, deciding what needs to be evaluated is crucial. For example, evaluations can assess the development and implementation of an entire wetlands strategy or simply specific policies or procedures. In light of budget limitations, it is helpful to rank those aspects of the program (or strategy) to be evaluated.

The following are possible areas to examine in a process evaluation:

- clarity of goals,
- adequacy of staffing,
- efficacy of implementation procedures (i.e., strengths and weaknesses of program design),
- adequacy of public involvement effort,
- effectiveness of efforts to build political support, and
- interaction and cooperation of federal, state, and local agencies.

The following are possible areas to examine in an impact evaluation:

- progress toward no net loss/net gain goal,
- the number of people who became aware of a particular program as a result of promotional material,
- the costs associated with a particular program, and
- number of permits filed, fines levied, or enforcement actions taken.

Step 2

Define Evaluation Standards

After the key aspects to be evaluated are selected, evaluators must develop the standards against which these elements will be judged. Often these standards directly relate to program goals and objectives—particularly where a performance measure is desired. Evaluators, however, should not rely only on quantifiable results as adequate measures of program effectiveness. Qualitative information is equally important in determining why goals and objectives have or haven't been met. Thus, both qualitative and quantitative evaluations should be undertaken. (The different methodological approaches for these two types of evaluation are described further in step 4.)

Clearly specifying goals and objectives to serve as evaluation standards is perhaps the most important preevaluation activity. Doing so establishes the evaluation's direction and general methodology. In many cases program goals are themselves unclear, and this process helps refine them.

Step 3

Determine the Degree of Accuracy Needed

Before establishing the evaluation methodology, it is necessary to identify the target audience for the evaluation results. This audience influences the level of accuracy needed and thus the level of effort required.

If the evaluation is prepared for internal use in an agency or even within a program, it may be sufficient to conduct a procedural review and spot-check a few sites or, in the case of permit applications, to investigate a few cases. Most of this work can be performed by internal staff since it doesn't involve a high level of precision or statistical accuracy.

On the other hand, if the audience is a regulatory or legislative body or some other official review committee, a higher degree of precision and verifiable results will probably be needed. This may require the development of statistically representative samples and tests of significance to measure actual impacts. Costs typically increase with the level of accuracy desired.

Step 4

Specify an Evaluation Methodology

The first decision to make in developing the evaluation methodology is what kind of evaluation to conduct and, if both process and impact evaluations are to be conducted, whether they should be done separately or combined into a comprehensive evaluation. Several factors influence this decision, including available funding, the time frame of the program and the stage of its implementation, and the need for quantified measurements.

It is unwise to conduct only an impact evaluation, as this won't generate sufficient information to explain why expected impacts have or have not occurred. Ideally, the two evaluations should begin at the same time so the impact evaluation can benefit from the data collection for the process evaluation. The timing of the evaluations, however, is often staggered. A process evaluation is sometimes begun during the early stages of program implementation and continues for the duration of the program, whereas impact evaluations must often be delayed to ensure that impacts have occurred and data are available.

Step 5
Develop a Work Plan and Time Lines

Once the evaluation methodology is determined, evaluators must establish the process for conducting the evaluation. Generally, a work plan is developed describing each task and defining the required data. Also, interviewees or survey samples are identified and data sources specified. The party responsible for each task can be specified at this time if multiple staff or contractors are involved. Once all the tasks are identified, a specific time line is developed. It contains due dates for key activities (or milestones) and deliverables such as summaries, data, or reports.

Step 6
Identify Who Will Conduct the Evaluation

As with monitoring, evaluations can be conducted in-house, by outside consultants, or with a combination of the two. Once again, the audience for the results and the political climate must be considered when deciding who should conduct the evaluation. It is generally preferable to use outside evaluators. They are viewed as independent; they can obtain unbiased and candid responses from all parties; they have experience and facilities (e.g., survey services); and they possess appropriate credentials. The one disadvantage of using outside contractors is that they often cost more than in-house staff.

Step 7
Make Use of Findings

The value of an evaluation depends on the use of the results. Most evaluations occur during the tenure of a program, thus providing the opportunity to enhance program implementation and correct design flaws. A procedure must be established, however, to ensure incorporation of evaluation recommendations in program planning and the development of new programs. Evaluation reports can be used by project planners, management, advisory committees, the state legislature, and the executive branch.

Measuring No Net Loss

Part I.2 includes an overview of the types of information needed to measure progress toward no net loss. This appendix presents a conceptual framework for compiling this information to track gains and losses of wetlands acreage and function. This framework can best be described as a hierarchical classification scheme; it is deliberately simplistic and nonscientific in nature. In effect, it serves as a "shell" that wetlands managers and others responsible for meeting the goal of no net loss can modify to fit state-specific needs. The framework was developed to track vegetated wetlands losses/gains as identified by reported data sources discussed in Part I.2.

The categories and terms used in this framework are suggestive in nature and intended merely as a starting point. Users should provide suitable definitions and refinements compatible with existing policies or regulatory requirements.

Recording Area/Function Losses

Table 1 includes categories useful in tracking losses of area and function within, for example, a specific geographic area, watershed, or political subdivision. The categories in the left and right columns provide a readily discernible "balance sheet" of total acreage and associated functions affected by "loss" or "gain" actions.

The following describes how the framework is used:

- *Losses* are divided into two categories, *permanent* and *reversible.* Permanent losses have been distinguished from reversible ones to better characterize the severity of the loss as well as prospects for future "recapture" through regulatory controls or restoration efforts. A loss occurs when an area no longer meets the definition of a vegetated wetland or when the natural vegetation is constrained, altered, or removed, thus preventing a return to natural conditions. This would include areas that may still meet the definition of a wetland, such as lawns, cropped wetlands, or other areas manipulated for aesthetic or horticultural purposes; it would not include timber harvesting or other temporary impacts. Any loss of wetlands area is also assumed to be a total loss of wetlands function. Although some limited functions may remain in areas that still meet the wetlands definition (e.g., cropped wetlands), most functions have been eliminated; thus, a loss is deemed to have occurred.

- *Gains* are classified as either *created* (i.e., wetlands construction on nonwetlands sites) or *restored* (i.e., wetlands construction on former wetlands sites).

- Each major loss or gain type could be further characterized by its landscape position relative to its water source (e.g., tidal waters or nontidal streams, lakes, ponds or groundwater sources, etc.). This information should be entered as "recorded data" (see below) to avoid overcomplicating the interpretation of the "balance sheet." *Hydrologically connected* wetlands are wetlands receiving or discharging surface water or groundwater from or to another surface water body, water course, or wetland. *Isolated* wetlands are wetlands that are not hydrologically connected through surface or subsurface water flow to surface water bodies, water courses, or wetlands.
- Additional data can be recorded (preferably using a data base management system) for each category (see table 1, note 2):
  — For each loss or gain, basic information about wetlands type, acreage, location, and function should be identified. Wetlands types can be recorded using the U.S. Fish and Wildlife Service's (FWS) classification system (or a state equivalent). A federal or state drainage basin location/code should also be listed to better characterize cumulative and landscape-level impacts. Although the functions of a given wetland may be difficult to record, some attempt to classify the wetland's most prominent functional attributes (e.g., habitat, water quality, hydrological) would be useful. This can draw upon best professional judgment or the use of more formalized functional assessment methods (see Part IV.2).
  — For created wetlands, gains can be further characterized by their source of hydrology—surface or ground water. If desired, three subcategories of surface water sources could be used to distinguish the wetlands hydrology source— "contiguous waters," "water impoundment," and "water diversion." These subcategories could be combined to describe a variety of wetlands hydrological sources. Groundwater sources are classified as "excavated" (topsoil or overburden material has been removed to sustain wetlands) or "well" type.
  — For restored wetlands, gains can be classified into three principal project types: (1) hydrological restorations (e.g., removal of drain tiles or ditching), (2) natural regeneration (e.g., an area considered nonwetlands is allowed to revert to natural conditions), and (3) combination projects (e.g., various actions including fill removal, grading, or vegetative management techniques are used to restore wetlands conditions).

Table 2
Tracking Other Functional Shifts

Table 2 displays a classification matrix that can be used to track shifts in wetlands function that are *not accounted for* in table 1. The categories on the left and right columns again provide a "balance sheet" of the total acreage affected by functional shifts. The table depicts the balance between functions that are changing for the better (enhancements) or the worse (impairments) or that are changing in a manner that yields a new set of functions forming a trade-off between old and new (i.e., wetlands *type* changes). Several aspects of the framework are discussed below.

- *Impairments* are actions that reduce wetlands functions. Degradation means the loss of one or more wetlands functions from either direct impacts (i.e., occurring within wetlands, such as sediment accretion) or indirect impacts (i.e., occurring outside wetlands, such as waterborne pollutants entering wetlands from surrounding land uses). A special type of functional impairment, fragmentation, occurs when a wetlands complex is partially destroyed by encroachments that form barriers to wildlife or water flow (e.g., road crossings). Fragmentation may result in a functional shift over a much larger area than the direct area of loss. This category is used to record estimations of the extent and nature of indirect functional impacts beyond those accounted for under the area/function loss category in table 1.
- *Enhancements* are actions that increase or improve wetlands functions. Functional shifts can occur as a result of direct rehabilitation (e.g., control of exotic vegetation) or indirect actions (e.g., upstream channel restoration or establishment of protective buffers). As the counterpoint to fragmen-

tation, restoration of former wetlands contiguous to existing wetlands can produce far-reaching functional shifts. Again, this category can be used to record estimates of the extent and nature of the shift beyond those identified in the gain/restoration category in table 1.

- *Type changes* include actions taken to convert one wetlands type to another. Substantial changes in hydrological and plant-community characteristics will force a corresponding shift in wetlands functions. Changes in wetlands type should be closely tracked for cumulative and landscape-level effects that can alter the ecological base of an entire watershed.

Table 1
Recording Losses/Gains of Wetlands Area and Function

LOSSES	GAINS
Permanent	**Created**
• Hydrologically connected	• Hydrologically connected
• Isolated	• Isolated
Reversible	**Restored**
• Hydrologically connected	• Hydrologically connected
• Isolated	• Isolated

Notes:

1. This conceptual framework is intended to assist in tracking wetlands losses/gains from reported data sources (e.g., permits, restoration projects). A separate resource assessment should be performed to supplement information derived from reported data sources (see Part I.2).

2. Data recorded for each category could include the following information:
   A. For permanent/reversible wetlands losses:
      - Type (FWS/state classification);
      - Area (acreage, hectares, etc.);
      - Location (drainage basin and political jurisdiction); and
      - Function. Any loss of area is also considered to be a total loss of function. Best professional judgment or a functional assessment should be used to identify the most prominent functional losses. At a minimum the evaluator could indicate that changes have principally affected water quality, habitat, hydrological functions, or a combination of one or more of these functions.
   B. For created wetlands:
      - Surface water source type (e.g., contiguous waters, water impoundment, water diversion).
      - Groundwater source type (e.g., excavation or well).
   C. For restored wetlands:
      - Restoration project type (e.g., hydrological restoration, natural regeneration, or combination project).

3. Permanent losses could include fills, structures, major drainage, deep excavation, deep inundation, and other similar activities.

4. Reversible losses could include discharges, minor drainage, shallow excavation, shallow inundation, land clearing and vegetative modifications, and other similar activities.

Table 2
Recording Shifts in Wetlands Function

FUNCTIONAL SHIFTS

Impairments

- Degradation
  - Direct
  - Indirect
- Fragmentation

Enhancements

- Rehabilitation
  - Direct
  - Indirect
- Contiguous restoration

Type Changes

- Emergent to forested
- Emergent to shrub
- Shrub to forested

Type Changes

- Forested to emergent
- Shrub to emergent
- Forested to shrub

Notes:

1. This framework is intended to assist in tracking shifts in wetlands functions, relying on reported data sources (e.g., permits, enhancement projects). A separate resource assessment should be performed to supplement information derived from these data sources (see Part I.2).

2. Data recorded for any wetlands functional shift category should include:
   - Type (FWS/state classification);
   - Area (acreage, hectares, etc.);
   - Location (drainage basin and political jurisdiction); and
   - Function. Best professional judgement or a functional assessment methodology should be used to identify prominent functions affected by the shift(s). At a minimum the evaluator could indicate that changes have principally affected either water quality, habitat, hydrological functions, or a combination of one or more of these functions.

Tracking Gains/Losses

Again, it is important to note that tables 1 and 2 represent only one possible method of no net loss accounting—principally from the perspective of a wetlands manager. The classification categories may not be suitable for all states. Specific definitions of terms used may be inappropriate or require substantial alteration. In addition, important information addressing the specifics of each loss/gain or functional-shift "action" must be incorporated into the system by state managers. Each manager must identify unique informational needs, such as permit numbers, project managers' names, precise locations, or important dates.

To maximize the immediate and long-term benefits of an accounting system, wetlands managers should work with experienced data-management specialists to establish their system. In particular, managers must be careful to ensure that the desired kinds of analyses can in fact be accomplished by the chosen data-management system. Managers should be able to evaluate losses/gains and functional shifts at different levels (e.g., by wetlands vegetative or hydrologic type, geographic area, political jurisdiction). Once established, a no net loss accounting system will serve as an invaluable tool for identifying specific needs and opportunities to improve the overall management of a state's wetlands resources.

Wetlands Contacts

State Agencies

ALABAMA

Tim Forester
Department of Environmental Management
1751 Congressman W.L. Dickinson Drive
Montgomery, AL 36131
(205) 271-7786

ALASKA

Doug Redburn
Department of Environmental Conservation
3220 Hospital Drive
Juneau, AK 99811
(907) 465-2653

ARIZONA

Sue Monroe
Department of Environmental Quality
Point Source and Monitoring Unit
2655 E. Magnolia, Suite 2
Phoenix, AZ 85003
(602) 392-4032

ARKANSAS

Steve Brown
Department of Pollution Control and Ecology
8001 National Drive
Little Rock, AR 72219-8913
(501) 562-7444

CALIFORNIA

Edward Anton
State Water Resources Control Board
Paul R. Bonderson Building
901 P Street
P.O. Box 100
Sacramento, CA 95812-0100
(916) 445-9552

Peter Grenell
California Coastal Conservancy
1330 Broadway, Suite 1100
Oakland, CA 94612
(510) 658-5254

COLORADO

John Scherschligt
Water Quality Control Division
4210 East 11th Avenue
Denver, CO 80220
(303) 331-4756

CONNECTICUT

Douglas Cooper
Department of Environmental Protection
State Office Building, Room 207
165 Capital Avenue
Hartford, CT   06106
(203) 566-7280

DELAWARE

David Saveikis
Department of Natural Resources and Environmental Control
89 Kings Highway, Box 1401
Dover, DE   19903
(302) 739-4691

FLORIDA

Mark Latch
Department of Environmental Regulations
2600 Blairstone Road
Tallahassee, FL   32301
(904) 488-0130

GEORGIA

Stuart Stevens
Department of Natural Resources
1200 Glynn Avenue
Brunswick, GA   31523
(912) 264-7218

HAWAII

Brian Choy
Department of Health
645 Halekauwila Street
Honolulu, HI   96813
(808) 586-4400

IDAHO

Steve Bauer
Department of Health & Welfare
Division of Environmental Quality
1410 N. Hilton
Boise, ID   83720-9000
(208) 334-5845

ILLINOIS

Marvin Hubbell
Department of Environmental Conservation
524 S. 2nd Street, Lincoln Tower Plaza
Springfield, IL   62706
(217) 782-3715

INDIANA

Marty Maupin
Indiana Department of Environmental Management
105 South Meridian
P.O. Box 6015
Indianapolis, IN   46206-6015
(317) 232-8603

IOWA

Darrell McAllister
Department of Natural Resources
Wallace State Office Building
Des Moines, IA 50319
(515) 281-5145

KANSAS

Eric Schenck
Environmental Services
Department of Wildlife & Parks
Box 54A, Rt. 2
Pratte, KS   67124-9599
(316) 672-5911

KENTUCKY

Bob Logan
Division of Water
18 Reilly Road
Frankfort, KY   40601
(502) 564-3410

LOUISIANA

David Chambers
Office of the Governor
P.O. Box 94004
Baton Rouge, LA   70804-9004
(504) 342-6493

MAINE

Don Witherall
Department of Environmental Protection
State House Station 17
Augusta, ME 04333
(207) 289-2111

MARYLAND

David Burke
Department of Natural Resources
Tawes State Office Bldg.
Annapolis, MD 21401
(410) 974-3841

MASSACHUSETTS

Christy Foote-Smith
Department of Environmental Quality
1 Winter Street
Boston, MA 02108
(617) 292-5692

MICHIGAN

Peg Bostwick
Department of Natural Resources
Land & Water Management Division
Box 30028
Lansing, MI 48909
(517) 335-2694

MINNESOTA

Tom Landwehr
Department of Natural Resources
Box 7
500 Lafayette Road
St. Paul, MN 55155
(612) 296-3344

MISSISSIPPI

James Morris
Department of Environmental Quality
Office of Pollution Control
P.O. Box 10385
Jackson, MS 39289
(602) 961-5171

MISSOURI

Sarah Steelman
Department of Natural Resources
Division of Geology and Land Survey
111 Fairground Road
P.O. Box 250
Rolla, MO 65401
(314) 364-1752

MONTANA

Jack Thomas
Water Quality Bureau
A-206 Cogswell Building
Helena, MT 59620
(406) 444-2406

NEBRASKA

John Bender
Department of Environmental Control
301 Centennial Mall South
Lincoln, NE 68509
(402) 471-2186

NEVADA

Wendall McCurry
Division of Environmental Protection
201 S. Fall Street
Carson City, NV 89710
(702) 885-4670

NEW HAMPSHIRE

Ken Kettenring
New Hampshire Wetlands Bureau
P.O. Box 2008
Concord, NH 03301
(603) 271-2147

NEW JERSEY

Robert Tudor
Department of Environmental Protection
501 East State Street, CN 401
Trenton, NJ 08625
(609) 292-0062

NEW MEXICO

David Tague
Environmental Improvement Division
Surface Water Quality Bureau
1190 St. Francis Drive
Santa Fe, NM   87503
(505) 827-2800

NEW YORK

Pat Riexinger
Department of Environmental Conservation
50 Wolf Road
Albany, NY   12233
(518) 457-9713

NORTH CAROLINA

John Dorney
Department of Environmental, Health and Natural
  Resources
Division of Environmental Management
P.O. Box 27687
Raleigh, NC   27611
(919) 733-5083

NORTH DAKOTA

David Sprynczynatyk
Office of the State Engineer
900 East Boulevard
Bismarck, ND   58505
(701) 224-4940

OHIO

Gail Hess
Ohio Environmental Protection Administration
1800 Water Mark Drive
P.O. Box 1049
Columbus, OH   43666
(614) 644-3076

OKLAHOMA

Sylvia Ritzky
Department of Pollution Control
P.O. Box 53504
Oklahoma City, OK   73152
(405) 271-4468

OREGON

Ken Bierly
Division of State Lands
775 Summer Street NE
Salem, OR   97310
(503) 378-3805

PENNSYLVANIA

Roger Fickes
Department of Environmental Resources
P.O. Box 1467
Harrisburg, PA   17120
(717) 541-7803

RHODE ISLAND

Dean Albro
Department of Environmental Management
291 Promenade Street
Providence, RI   02908
(401) 277-6820

SOUTH CAROLINA

Sally Knowles
Department of Health and Environmental Control
2600 Bull Street
Columbia, SC   29201
(803) 277-6867

SOUTH DAKOTA

Clark Haberman
Department of Enviorment Natural Resources
Joe Foss Building
523 E. Capital
Pierre, SD   57501-3181
(605) 773-6038

TENNESSEE

Tom Talley
University of Tennessee
Water Resources Research Institute
Knoxville, TN   37996
(615) 974-2151

TEXAS

Don Cook
Texas General Land Office
Stephen F. Austin Building
1700 N. Congress Avenue, Room 730
Austin, TX   78701-1495
(512) 463-5193

UTAH

Mike Reichert
Water Quality Management and Groundwater
     Section
Bureau of Water Pollution Control
Salt Lake City, UT   84114-4870
(801) 538-6146

VERMONT

Catherine O'Brien
Water Quality Division
Department of Environmental Conservation
Waterbury, VT   05671-4008
(802) 244-6951

VIRGINIA

Joseph Hassell
State Water Control Board
P.O. Box 11143
Richmond, VA   23227
(804) 527-5072

WASHINGTON

Mary Burg
Department of Ecology
Mail Stop PV-11
Olympia, WA   98504
(206) 459-6790

WEST VIRGINIA

Jan Taylor
Water Resources Board
1260 Greenbrier Street
Charleston, WV   25311
(304) 348-4002

WISCONSIN

Scott Hausmann
Department of Natural Resources
Water Regulation Section
P.O. Box 7921
Madison, WI   53707
(608) 266-7360

WYOMING

Bill DiRienzo
Department of Environmental Quality
Water Quality Division
Herschler Building 4W
Cheyenne, WY   82002
(307) 777-7081

U.S. Environmental Protection Agency (EPA)

U.S. ENVIRONMENTAL
PROTECTION AGENCY
WETLANDS DIVISION
OFFICE OF WETLANDS, OCEANS,
AND WATERSHEDS
WASHINGTON, DC

Division Director

Responsible for general program management and administrative support.

John Meagher, Director
U.S. EPA
OWOW (A-104F)
401 M Street, SW
Washington, DC 20460
tel: (202) 260-1917
fax: (202) 260-8000

Suzanne Schwartz, Deputy Director
tel: (202) 260-8447
fax: (202) 260-7546

Wetlands and Aquatic Resources Regulatory Branch (WARRB)

Responsible for all Section 404 regulatory activities except for state programs.

Greg Peck, Acting Chief
tel: (202) 260-8794
fax: (202) 260-7546

Enforcement and Regulatory Policy Section Responsible for the development of policy, regulations, and guidance; also responsible for general Section 404 program development, management, and regional assistance.

Cliff Rader, Acting Chief
tel: (202) 260-6587
fax: (202) 260-7546

Elevated Cases Section Responsible for handling of elevated cases under Section 404(c) or 404(q) and for developing related guidance and providing case-related assistance to the regions.

Will Garvey, Acting Chief
tel: (202) 260-9900
fax: (202) 260-7546

Wetlands Strategies and State Programs Branch (WSSPB)

Responsible for state program activities and all other non-Section 404 activities.

Glenn Eugster, Acting Chief
tel: (202) 260-9043
fax: (202) 260-8000

Outreach and State Programs Section
Responsible for working with state, tribal, and local governments and other federal agencies; public information and education activities; international activities; and wetlands grants.

Glenn Eugster, Chief
tel: (202) 260-6045
fax: (202) 260-8000

Lorraine Williams, State Grants and
  Program Financing
tel: (202) 260-5084
fax: (202) 260-8000

Wetlands Strategies and Initiatives Section
Responsible for development of and support for initiatives in such areas as comprehensive planning and water quality certification and for ecosystem or state special initiatives (i.e., nonpoint sources, stormwater, water quality standards, and coastal Louisiana).

Dianne Fish, Chief
tel: (202) 260-1699
fax: (202) 260-8000

Research and Science Liaison Responsible for the development of technical methods and information; liaison with the research community.

Doreen Robb, Research and Science Liaison
tel: (202) 260-1906
fax: (202) 260-8000

U.S. ENVIRONMENTAL PROTECTION AGENCY REGIONAL WETLANDS CONTACTS

Region I: CT, MA, ME, NH, RI, VT

Douglas Thompson, Chief
U.S. EPA—Region I
Wetlands Protection Section (WWP-1900)
John F. Kennedy Federal Building
Boston, MA 02203-1911
(617) 565-4430

Region II: NJ, NY

Dan Montella, Chief
U.S. EPA—Region II
Wetlands Section (2WM-MWP)
26 Federal Plaza, Room 837
New York, NY 10278
(212) 264-5170

Region III: DE, MD, PA, VA, WV

Barbara D'Angelo, Chief
U.S. EPA—Region III
Wetlands and Marine Policy Section (3ES42)
841 Chestnut Street
Philadelphia, PA 19107
(215) 597-9301

Region IV: AL, FL, GA, KY, MS, NC, SC, TN

Gail Vanderhoogt, Chief
U.S. EPA—Region IV
Wetlands Planning Unit (4WM-MWB)
345 Courtland Street, NE
Atlanta, GA 30365
(404) 347-2126

Region V: IL, IN, MI, MN, OH, WI

Doug Ehorn, Deputy Chief
U.S. EPA—Region V
Water Management Division
Wetlands Protection Section
230 South Dearborn Street
Chicago, IL 60604
(312) 353-2079

Region VI: AR, LA, NM, OK, TX

Norman Thomas, Chief
U.S. EPA—Region VI
Technical Assistance Section (6E-FT)
1445 Ross Avenue
Dallas, TX 75202
(214) 655-2260

Region VII: IA, KS, MO, NE

Dianne Hershberger, Chief
U.S. EPA—Region VII
Wetlands Protection Section (ENRV-404)
726 Minnesota Avenue
Kansas City, KS 66101
(913) 551-7573

Region VIII: CO, MT, ND, SD, UT, WY

Gene Reetz, Chief
U.S. EPA—Region VIII
Water Quality Requirement Section (8WM-SP)
999 18th Street
500 Denver Place
Denver, CO 80202-2405
(303) 293-1575

Region IX: AZ, CA, HI, NV

Phil Oshida, Chief
U.S. EPA—Region IX
Wetlands Section (W-7-2)
1235 Mission Street
San Francisco, CA   94103
(415) 744-2180

Region X: AK, ID, OR, WA

Bill Reilly, Chief
U.S. EPA—Region X
Water Resources Assessment Section (WD-138)
1200 Sixth Avenue
Seattle, WA   98101
(206) 442-1412

U.S. ENVIRONMENTAL PROTECTION AGENCY REGIONAL WATER QUALITY STANDARDS COORDINATORS

Region I: CT, MA, ME, NH, RI, VT

Eric Hall, Water Quality Standards Coordinator
U.S. EPA—Region I
Water Management Division
John F. Kennedy Federal Building
Boston, MA   02203
(617) 565-3533

Region II: NJ, NY

Rick Balla, Water Quality Standards Coordinator
U.S. EPA—Region II
Water Management Division
26 Federal Plaza
New York, NY   10278
(212) 264-1559

Region III: DE, MD, PA, VA, WV

Edward Ambragio, Water Quality Standards
   Coordinator
U.S. EPA—Region III
Water Management Division
841 Chestnut Street
Philadelphia, PA   19107
(215) 597-4491

Region IV: AL, FL, GA, KY, MS, NC, SC, TN

Fritz Wagener, Water Quality Standards Coordinator
U.S. EPA—Region IV
Water Management Division

345 Courtland Street, NE
Atlanta, GA   30365
(404) 347-2126

Region V: IL, IN, MI, MN, OH, WI

Dave Allen, Water Quality Standards Coordinator
U.S. EPA—Region V
Water Management Division
230 South Dearborn Street
Chicago, IL   60604
(312) 886-6696

Region VI: AR, LA, NM, OK, TX

Cheryl Overstreet, Water Quality Standards
   Coordinator
U.S. EPA—Region VI
Water Management Division
1445 Ross Avenue
First Interstate Bank Tower
Dallas, TX   75202
(214) 655-7145

Region VII: IA, KS, MO, NE

John Houlihan, Water Quality Standards
   Coordinator
U.S. EPA—Region VII
Water Compliance Branch
726 Minnesota Avenue
Kansas City, KS   66101
(913) 551-7432

Region VIII: CO, MT, ND, SD, UT, WY

Jim Luey, Acting Water Quality Standards
   Coordinator
U.S. EPA—Region VIII (8WM-SP)
Water Management Division
999 18th Street
Denver, CO   80202-2405
(303) 293-1577

Region IX: AZ, CA, HI, NV

Phil Woods, Water Quality Standards Coordinator
U.S. EPA—Region IX
Water Management Division (W-3-1)
75 Hawthorne Street
San Francisco, CA   94105
(415) 744-1994

Region X: AK, ID, OR, WA

Sally Marquis, Water Quality Standards Coordinator
U.S. EPA—Region X
Water Management Division (WD-139)
1200 Sixth Avenue
Seattle, WA   98101
(206) 442-2116

Department of the Army
U.S. Army Corps of Engineers (Civil Works)

HEADQUARTERS, DIRECTORATE OF CIVIL WORKS

John F. Studt, Chief
U.S. Army Corps of Engineers
Regulatory Branch (CECW-OR)
20 Massachusetts Avenue, NW
Washington, DC 20314-1000
tel: (202) 272-0199
fax: (202) 504-5069

LOWER MISSISSIPPI VALLEY DIVISION

Leo Max Reed, Chief
U.S. Army Corps of Engineers
Lower Mississippi Valley Division (CELMV-CO-R)
P.O. Box 80
Vicksburg, MS 39180-0080
(601) 634-5818 or (601) 634-5821

Memphis District

Larry D. Watson, Chief
U.S. Army Corps of Engineers
Memphis District (CELMM-CO-R)

B-202 Clifford Davis Federal Building
Memphis, TN 38103-1894
(901) 544-3471

New Orleans District

Ronald J. Ventola, Chief
U.S. Army Corps of Engineers
New Orleans District (CELMN-OD-R)
P.O. Box 60267
New Orleans, LA 70160-0267
(504) 862-2270 or (504) 862-2255

St. Louis District

Susan Harrison, Acting Chief
U.S. Army Corps of Engineers
St. Louis District (CELMS-OD-R)
1222 Spruce Street
St. Louis, MO 63103-2833
(314) 331-8575

Vicksburg District

E. Galen McGregor, Chief
U.S. Army Corps of Engineers
Vicksburg District (CELMK-OD-F)
3515 I-20 Frontage Road

Vicksburg, MS 39180-5191
(601) 631-5276 or (601) 631-5289

MISSOURI RIVER DIVISION

Mores V. Bergman, Chief
U.S. Army Corps of Engineers
Missouri River Division (CEMRD-CO-R)
P.O. Box 103, Downtown Station
Omaha, NE 68101-0103
(402) 221-7290

Kansas City District

Mel Jewett, Chief
U.S. Army Corps of Engineers
Kansas City District (CEMRK-OD-R)
700 Federal Building
Kansas City, MO 64106-2896
(816) 426-3645

Omaha District

John Morton, Chief
U.S. Army Corps of Engineers
Omaha District (CEMRO-OP-N)
215 North 17th Street
Omaha, NE 68102-4978
(402) 221-4133

NEW ENGLAND DIVISION

William F. Lawless, Chief
U.S. Army Corps of Engineers
New England Division (CNEED-OD-P)
424 Trapelo Road
Waltham, MA 02254-9149
(617) 647-8057

NORTH ATLANTIC DIVISION

Lenny Kotkiewicz, Chief
U.S. Army Corps of Engineers
North Atlantic Division (CENAD-CO-OP)
90 Church Street
New York, NY 10007-9998
(212) 264-7535

Baltimore District

Donald W. Roeseke, Chief
U.S. Army Corps of Engineers
Baltimore District (CENAB-OP-PN)
P.O. Box 1715
Baltimore, MD 31203-1715
(301) 962-3670

New York District

Joseph Seebode, Chief
U.S. Army Corps of Engineers
New York District (CENAN-PL-E)
26 Federal Plaza
New York, NY 10278-0090
(212) 264-3996

Norfolk District

William H. Poore, Jr., Chief
U.S. Army Corps of Engineers
Norfolk District (CENAO-OP-N)
803 Front Street
Norfolk, VA 23510-1096
(804) 441-7068

Philadelphia District

Frank Cianfrani, Chief
U.S. Army Corps of Engineers
Philadelphia District (CENAP-OP-N)
U.S. Custom House
2nd & Chestnut Streets
Philadelphia, PA 19106-2991
(215) 597-2812

NORTH CENTRAL DIVISION

Mitchell A. Isoe, Chief
U.S. Army Corps of Engineers
North Central Division (CENCD-CO-MO)
536 S. Clark Street
Chicago, IL 60605-1592
(312) 353-6379

Buffalo District

Paul G. Leuchner, Chief
U.S. Army Corps of Engineers

Buffalo District
1776 Niagara Street
Buffalo, NY 14207-3199
(716) 879-4313

Chicago District

John Rogner, Chief
U.S. Army Corps of Engineers
Chicago District (CENCC-CO)
219 S. Dearborn Street
Chicago, IL 60604-1797
(312) 353-6428

Detroit District

Gary R. Mannesto, Chief
U.S. Army Corps of Engineers
Detroit District (CENCE-CO-OR)
P.O. Box 1027
Detroit, MI 48231-1027
(313) 226-2432

Rock Island District

Steven J. Vander Horn, Chief
U.S. Army Corps of Engineers
Rock Island District (CENCR-OD-R)
P.O. Box 2004
Clock Tower Building
Rock Island, IL 61204-2004
(309) 788-6361

St. Paul District

Ben Wopat, Chief
U.S. Army Corps of Engineers
St. Paul District (CENCS-CO-PO)
1421 USPO & Custom House
180 East Kellog Boulevard
St. Paul, MN 55101-1479
(612) 220-0375

NORTH PACIFIC DIVISION

John Zammit, Chief
U.S. Army Corps of Engineers
North Pacific Division (CENPD-CO-R)
P.O. Box 2870
Portland, OR 97208-2870
(503) 326-3780

Alaska District

Robert K. Oja, Chief
U.S. Army Corps of Engineers
Alaska District (CENPA-CO-NF)
P.O. Box 898
Anchorage, AK 99506-0898
(907) 753-2712

Portland District

Burt Paynter, Chief
U.S. Army Corps of Engineers
Portland District (CENPP-OP-PN)
P.O. Box 2946
Portland, OR 97208-2946
(503) 326-6995

Seattle District

Warren Baxter, Chief
U.S. Army Corps of Engineers
Seattle District (CENPS-OP-PO)
P.O. Box C-3755
Seattle, WA 98124-2255
(206) 764-3495

Walla Walla District

Dean Hilliard, Chief
U.S. Army Corps of Engineers
Walla Walla District (CENPW-OP-RM)
City-County Airport
Walla Walla, WA 99362-9265
(509) 522-6720 or (509) 522-6724

OHIO RIVER DIVISION

Roger D. Graham, Chief
U.S. Army Corps of Engineers
Ohio River Division (CEORD-CO-OR)
P.O. Box 1159
Cincinnati, OH 45201-1159
(513) 684-3972

Huntington District

Mike Gheen, Chief
U.S. Army Corps of Engineers

Huntington District (CEORH-OR-R)
502 8th Street
Huntington, WV 25701-2070
(304) 529-5487

Louisville District

Don Purvis, Chief
U.S. Army Corps of Engineers
Louisville District (CEORH-OR-R)
P.O. Box 59
Louisville, KY 40201-0059
(502) 582-6461

Nashville District

Joseph R. Castleman, Chief
U.S. Army Corps of Engineers
Nashville District (CEORN-OR-R)
P.O. Box 1070
Nashville, TN 37202-1070
(615) 736-5181

Pittsburgh District

Eugene J. Homyak, Chief
U.S. Army Corps of Engineers
Pittsburgh District (CEORP-OR-R)
1000 Liberty Avenue
Pittsburgh, PA 15222-4186
(412) 644-6872

PACIFIC OCEAN DIVISION

Stanley T. Arakaki, Chief
U.S. Army Corps of Engineers
Pacific Ocean Division (CEPOD-CO-O)
Building 230
Fort Shafter, HI 96858-5440
(808) 438-9258

SOUTH ATLANTIC DIVISION

James M. Kelly, Chief
U.S. Army Corps of Engineers
South Atlantic Division (CESAD-CO-R)
Room 313
77 Forsythe Street SW
Atlanta, GA 30335-6801
(404) 331-2778

Charleston District

Clarence H. Ham, Chief
U.S. Army Corps of Engineers
Charleston District (CESAC-CO-M)
P.O. Box 919
Charleston, SC 29402-0919
(803) 724-4330

Jacksonville District

John Hall, Chief
U.S. Army Corps of Engineers
Jacksonville District (CESAJ-CO-OR)
P.O. Box 4970
400 West Bay Street
Jacksonville, FL 32232-0019
(904) 791-1666

Mobile District

Ron Krizman, Chief
U.S. Army Corps of Engineers
Mobile District (CESAM-OP-R)
109 St. Joseph Street
P.O. Box 2288
Mobile, AL 36628-0001
(205) 690-2658

Savannah District

Steven Osvald, Chief
U.S. Army Corps of Engineers
Savannah District (CESAS-OP-R)
P.O. Box 889
Savannah, GA 31402-0889
(912) 944-5347

Wilmington District

G. Wayne Wright, Chief
U.S. Army Corps of Engineers
Wilmington District (CESAW-CO-R)
P.O. Box 1890
Wilmington, NC 28402-1890
(919) 251-4629

SOUTH PACIFIC DIVISION

Theodore E. Durst, Chief
U.S. Army Corps of Engineers

South Pacific Division (CESPD-CO-O)
630 Sansome Street, Room 1216
San Francisco, CA 94111-2206
(415) 705-1443

Los Angeles District

Charles M. Holt, Chief
U.S. Army Corps of Engineers
Los Angeles District (CESPL-CO-O)
P.O. Box 2711
Los Angeles, CA 90053-2325
(213) 894-5606

Sacramento District

Art Champ, Chief
U.S. Army Corps of Engineers
Sacramento District (CESPK-CO-O)
650 Capitol Mall
Sacramento, CA 95814-4794
(916) 551-2275

San Francisco District

Calvin C. Fong, Chief
U.S. Army Corps of Engineers
San Francisco District (CESPN-CO-O)
211 Main Street
San Francisco, CA 94105-1905
(415) 744-3036

SOUTHWESTERN DIVISION

Ken Waldie, Chief
U.S. Army Corps of Engineers
Southwestern Division (CESWD-CO-R)
1114 Commerce Street
Dallas, TX 75242-0216
(214) 767-2432 or (214) 767-2436

Albuquerque District

Andrew J. Rosenau, Chief
U.S. Army Corps of Engineers
Albuquerque District (CESWA-CO-O)
P.O. Box 1580
Albuquerque, NM 87103-1580
(505) 766-2776

Fort Worth District

Wayne A. Lea, Chief
U.S. Army Corps of Engineers
Fort Worth District (CESWF-OD-M)
P.O. Box 17300
Fort Worth, TX 76102-0300
(817) 334-2681

Galveston District

Marcos DeLaRosa, Chief
U.S. Army Corps of Engineers
Galveston District (CESWG-CO-MO)
P.O. Box 1229
Galveston, TX 77553-1229
(409) 766-3930

Little Rock District

Louie C. Cockmon, Jr., Chief
U.S. Army Corps of Engineers
Little Rock District (CESWL-CO-L)
P.O. Box 867
Little Rock, AR 72203-0867
(501) 324-5296

Tulsa District

Don Ringeisen, Chief
U.S. Army Corps of Engineers
Tulsa District (CESWT-OD-R)
P.O. Box 61
Tulsa, OK 74121-0061
(918) 581-7261

WATERWAYS EXPERIMENT STATION

Russell F. Theriot, Manager
Wetlands Research Program
U.S. Army Corps of Engineers
Waterways Experiment Station
Environmental Laboratory (CEWES-EL-W)
3909 Halls Ferry Road
Vicksburg, MS 39180-6199
tel: (601) 634-2733
fax: (601) 634-3528

U.S. Fish and Wildlife Service

REGION I:
CA, HI, ID, NV, OR, WA

Dennis Peters   (503) 231-6154
    Wetlands Coordinator
Jana Grote   (503) 231-6156
    Private Lands Coordinator
    Farm Bill Coordinator

U.S. Fish and Wildlife Service
1002 Northeast Holladay Street
Portland, OR   97232-4181

REGION II:
AZ, NM, OK, TX

John Peterson   (505) 766-2914
    Private Lands Coordinator
Warren Hagenbuck   (505) 766-2914
    Wetlands Coordinator
    Farm Bill Coordinator

U.S. Fish and Wildlife Service
P.O. Box 1306
Albuquerque, NM   87103

REGION III:
IL, IN, IA, MI, MN, MO, OH, WI

Ron Erickson   (612) 725-3417
    Wetlands Coordinator
Rick Schultz   (612) 725-3570
    Private Lands Coordinator
    Farm Bill Coordinator

U.S. Fish and Wildlife Service
Federal Building, Fort Snelling
Twin Cities, MN   55111

REGION IV:
AL, AR, FL, GA, KY, LA, MS, NC, SC, TN, PR, VI

John Hefner   (404) 331-6343
    Wetlands Coordinator
Ronnie Haynes   (404) 331-6343
    Private Lands Coordinator
    Farm Bill Coordinator

U.S. Fish and Wildlife Service
75 Spring Street, SW
Atlanta, GA   30303

REGION V:
CT, DE, ME, MA, MD, NH, NJ, NY, PA, RI, VT, VA, WV

Ralph Tiner (617) 965-5100x379
 Wetlands Coordinator
Elizabeth Herland (617) 965-5100x380
 Private Lands Coordinator
 Farm Bill Coordinator

U.S. Fish and Wildlife Service
One Gateway Center, Suite 700
Newton Corner, MA   02158

REGION VI:
CO, KS, MT, NE, ND, SD, UT, WY

Chuck Elliot (303) 236-2985
 Wetlands Coordinator
Rick Dornfeld (303) 236-8152
 Private Lands Coordinator
 Farm Bill Coordinator

U.S. Fish and Wildlife Service
Box 25486, Denver Federal Center
Denver, CO   80225

REGION VII:
AK

Jon Hall (907) 786-3471
 Wetlands Coordinator

Robin West (907) 786-3443
 Private Lands Coordinator
Marcus Horton (907) 786-3431
 Farm Bill Coordinator

U.S. Fish and Wildlife Service
1011 East Tudor Road
Anchorage, AK   99503

REGION VIII:
WASHINGTON, DC
(NATIONAL OFFICE)

Gary Hickman (703) 358-1710
 Wetlands Coordinator
Gene Whitaker (703) 358-2161
 Private Lands Coordinator
 Farm Bill Coordinator
Tim Taylor (703) 358-2161
 Private Lands Coordinator
 Farm Bill Coordinator
Bob Misso (703) 358-2161
 Private Lands Coordinator
 Farm Bill Coordinator

U.S. Fish and Wildlife Service
Interior Building
1849 C Street NW
Mail Stop 725, Arlington Square
Washington, DC   20240

U.S. Department of Agriculture Soil Conservation Service State Conservationists

Note: The following list is organized alphabetically by state.

Ernest V. Todd
665 Opelika Road
P.O. Box 311
Auburn, AL   36830
(205) 821-8070

Burton L. Clifford
201 East 9th
Suite 300
Anchorage, AK   99501-3687
(907) 271-2424

Donald W. Gohmert
Suite 200
201 E. Indianola Avenue
Phoenix, AZ   85012
(602) 640-2247

Ronnie D. Murphy
Room 5204
Federal Office Building
700 West Capitol Avenue
Little Rock, AR   72201
(501) 378-5445

Pearlie S. Reed
2121 C Second Street
Davis, CA   95616
(916) 449-2848

Duane L. Johnson
655 Parfet Street
Room E200C
Lakewood, CO   80215-5517
(303) 236-2886

Judith K. Johnson
16 Professional Park Road
Storrs, CT   06268-1299
(203) 487-4011

Elsa K. Cottrell
Treadway Towers
Suite 207
9 East Loockerman Street
Dover, DE   19901-7377
(302) 678-4160

Niles T. Glasgow
Federal Building, Room 248
401 SE First Avenue
Gainesville, FL   32601
(904) 377-0946

Hershel R. Read
Federal Building, Box 13
355 East Hancock Avenue
Athens, GA   30601
(404) 546-2272

Joan Perry
Director, Pacific Basin Office
Suite 602, GCIC Building
414 W. Soledad Avenue
Agana, Guam 96910
(671) 472-7490

Warren M. Lee
300 Ala Moana Boulevard
Room 4316
P.O. Box 50004
Honolulu, HI   96850
(808) 541-2601

Paul H. Calverley
3244 Elder Street
Room 124
Boise, ID   83705
(208) 334-1601

John J. Eckes
Springer Federal Building
301 N. Randolph Street
Champaign, IL   61820
(217) 398-5267

Robert L. Eddleman
6013 Lakeside Boulevard
Indianapolis, IN   46278
(317) 290-3200

J. Michael Nethery
693 Federal Building
210 Walnut Street
Des Moines, IA   50309
(515) 284-4261

James N. Habiger
760 South Broadway
Salina, KS   67401
(913) 823-4565

Billy W. Milliken
333 Waller Avenue
Room 305
Lexington, KY   40504
(606) 233-2749

Horace J. Austin
3737 Government Street
Alexandria, LA   71302
(318) 473-7751

Charles Whitmore
USDA Building
University of Maine
Orono, ME   04473
(207) 581-3446

Jerome J. Hammond, Acting
John Hanson Business Center
339 Revell Highway
Suite 301
Annapolis, MD   21401
(301) 757-0861

Richard D. Swenson, Acting
451 West Street
Amherst, MA   01002
(413) 256-0441

Homer R. Hilner
Room 101
1405 S. Harrison Road
East Lansing, MI   48823-5202
(517) 337-6702

Gary R. Nordstrom
Farm Credit Services Building
375 Jackson Street
Room 600
St. Paul, MN   55101-1854
(612) 290-3675

Louie P. Heard
Federal Building, Suite 1321
100 West Capitol Street
Jackson, MS   39269
(601) 965-5205

Russell C. Mills
555 Vandiver Drive
Columbia, MO   65202
(314) 875-5214

Richard J. Gooby
Federal Building, Room 443
10 East Babcock Street
Bozeman, MT   59715
(406) 587-6813

Ron E. Moreland
Federal Building, Room 345
100 Centennial Mall, N.
Lincoln, NB 68508-3866
(402) 437-5300

William D. Goddard
1201 Terminal Way
Room 219
Reno, NV 89502
(702) 784-5863

David L. Mussulman
Federal Building
Durham, NH 03824
(603) 868-7581

Barbara T. Osgood
1370 Hamilton Street
Somerset, NJ 08873
(201) 246-1662

Ray T. Margo, Jr.
517 Gold Avenue, SW
Room 3301
Albuquerque, NM 87102
(505) 766-2173

Paul A. Dodd
James M. Hanley Federal Building
Room 771
100 S. Clinton Street
Syracuse, NY 13260
(315) 423-5521

Bobbye Jack Jones
4405 Bland Road
Suite 205
Raleigh, NC 27609
(919) 790-2888

Ronnie L. Clark
Federal Building
Rosser Avenue & Third Street
P.O. Box 1458
Bismarck, ND 58502
(701) 250-4421

Joseph C. Branco
200 North High Street, Room 522
Columbus, OH 43215
(614) 469-6962

C. Budd Fountain
USDA Agricultural Center Building
Stillwater, OK 74074
(405) 624-4360

Jack P. Kanalz
Federal Building, Room 1640
1220 SW Third Avenue
Portland, OR 97204
(503) 326-2751

Richard N. Duncan
One Credit Union Place
Suite 340
Harrisburg, PA 17110
(717) 782-2202

Humberto Hernandez
Director, Caribbean Area
Federal Building, Room 639
Chardon Avenue
Hato Rey, Puerto Rico 00918
Mailing Address: USDA-SCS
GPO Box 4868
San Juan, Puerto Rico 00936
(809) 753-4206

Robert J. Klumpe
46 Quaker Lane
West Warwick, RI 02893
(401) 828-1300

Billy R. Abercrombie
1835 Assembly Street, Room 950
Strom Thurmond Federal Building
Columbia, SC 29201
(803) 765-5681

Ronald E. Hendricks
Federal Building
200 Fourth Street, SW
Huron, SD 57350
(605) 353-1783

Jerry S. Lee
675 Estes Kefauver, FB-USCH
801 Broadway
Nashville, TN 37203
(615) 736-5471

Harry W. Oneth
W.R. Poage Federal Building
101 S. Main Street
Temple, TX 76501-7682
(817) 774-1214

Francis T. Holt
Wallace F. Bennett
Federal Building, Room 4402
125 South State Street
Salt Lake City, UT   84138
Mailing Address:
P.O. Box 11350
Salt Lake City, UT   84147-0350
(801) 524-5050

John C. Titchner
69 Union Street
Winooski, VT   05404
(802) 951-6795

George C. Norris
Federal Building, Room 9201
400 North Eighth Street
Richmond, VA   23240
(804) 771-2455

Lynn A. Brown
West 920 Riverside Avenue
Room 360
Spokane, WA   99201
(509) 353-2335

Rollin N. Swank
75 High Street, Room 301
Morgantown, WV   26505
(304) 291-4151

Duane L. Johnson
6515 Watts Road, Suite 200
Madison, WI   53719-2726
(608) 264-5577

Frank S. Dickson, Jr.
Federal Office Building
100 East B Street, Room 3124
Casper, WY   82601
(307) 261-5201